Brilliant
Microsoft®
Word® 2013

Steve Johnson

Perspection, Inc.

PEARSON

Harlow, England • London • New York • Boston • San Francisco • Toronto • Sydney • Auckland • Singapore • Hong Kong
Tokyo • Seoul • Taipei • New Delhi • Cape Town • São Paulo • Mexico City • Madrid • Amsterdam • Munich • Paris • Milan

Pearson Education Limited
Edinburgh Gate
Harlow
Essex CM20 2JE
England

and Associated Companies throughout the world

Visit us on the World Wide Web at:
www.pearson.com/uk

Original edition, entitled WORD 2013 ON DEMAND, 1st edition, 9780789750501 by JOHNSON, STEVE; PERSPECTION, INC., published by Pearson Education, Inc., publishing as Que, Copyright © 2013 Perspection, Inc.

ISBN: 978-1-292-00121-0

British Library Cataloguing-in-Publication Data
A catalogue record for this book is available from the British Library

10 9 8 7 6 5 4 3 2 1
17 16 15 14 13

Printed and bound in the United States of America

Brilliant Guides

What you need to know and how to do it

When you're working on your computer and come up against a problem that you're unsure how to solve, or want to accomplish something in an application that you aren't sure how to do, where do you look?? Manuals and traditional training guides are usually too big and unwieldy and are intended to be used as an end-to-end training resource, making it hard to get to the info you need right away without having to wade through pages of background information that you just don't need at that moment – and helplines are rarely that helpful!

Brilliant guides have been developed to allow you to find the info you need easily and without fuss and guide you through the task using a highly visual, step-by-step approach – providing exactly what you need to know when you need it!!

Brilliant guides provide the quick easy-to-access information that you need, using a detailed index and troubleshooting guide to help you find exactly what you need to know, and then presenting each task on one or two pages. Numbered steps then guide you through each task or problem, using numerous screenshots to illustrate each step. Added features include "See Also…" boxes that point you to related tasks and information in the book, whilst "Did you know?…" sections alert you to relevant expert tips, tricks and advice to further expand your skills and knowledge.

In addition to covering all major office applications, and related computing subjects, the *Brilliant* series also contains titles that will help you in every aspect of your working life, such as writing the perfect CV, answering the toughest interview questions and moving on in your career.

Brilliant guides are the light at the end of the tunnel when you are faced with any minor or major task!

Acknowledgments

Perspection, Inc.

Brilliant Microsoft Word 2013 has been created by the professional trainers and writers at Perspection, Inc. to the standards you've come to expect from Que publishing. Together, we are pleased to present this training book.

Perspection, Inc. is a software training company committed to providing information and training to help people use software more effectively in order to communicate, make decisions, and solve problems. Perspection writes and produces software training books, and develops multimedia and web-based training. Since 1991, we have written more than 130 computer books, with several bestsellers to our credit, and sold over 5 million books.

This book incorporates Perspection's training expertise to ensure that you'll receive the maximum return on your time. You'll focus on the tasks and skills that increase productivity while working at your own pace and convenience.

We invite you to visit the Perspection web site at:

www.perspection.com

Acknowledgments

The task of creating any book requires the talents of many hard-working people pulling together to meet impossible deadlines and untold stresses. We'd like to thank the outstanding team responsible for making this book possible: the writer, Steve Johnson; the production editor, James Teyler; the editor and proofreader, Beth Teyler; and the indexer, Katherine Stimson.

At Que publishing, we'd like to thank Greg Wiegand and Loretta Yates for the opportunity to undertake this project, Cindy Teeters for administrative support, and Lori Lyons for your production expertise and support.

Perspection

About the Author

Steve Johnson has written more than 80 books on a variety of computer software, including Adobe Edge Animate, Adobe Photoshop CS6, Adobe Dreamweaver CS6, Adobe InDesign CS6, Adobe Illustrator CS6, Adobe Flash Professional CS5, Microsoft Windows 8, Microsoft Office 2013 and 2010, Microsoft Office 2008 for the Macintosh, and Apple OS X Mountain Lion. In 1991, after working for Apple Computer and Microsoft, Steve founded Perspection, Inc., which writes and produces software training. When he is not staying up late writing, he enjoys coaching baseball, playing golf, gardening, and spending time with his wife, Holly, and three children, JP, Brett, and Hannah. Steve and his family live in Northern California, but can also be found visiting family all over the western United States.

Contents

C

Introduction

Welcome to *Brilliant Microsoft® Word® 2013*, a visual quick reference book that shows you how to work efficiently with Microsoft Word. This book provides complete coverage of basic to advanced Word skills.

How This Book Works

You don't have to read this book in any particular order. We've designed the book so that you can jump in, get the information you need, and jump out. However, the book does follow a logical progression from simple tasks to more complex ones. Each task is presented on no more than two facing pages, which lets you focus on a single task without having to turn the page. To find the information that you need, just look up the task in the table of contents or index, and turn to the page listed. Read the task introduction, follow the step-by-step instructions in the left column along with screen illustrations in the right column, and you're done.

What's New

If you're searching for what's new in Word 2013, just look for the icon: **New!**. The new icon appears in the table of contents and throughout this book so you can quickly and easily identify a new or improved feature in Word 2013. A complete description of each new feature appears in the New Features guide in the back of this book.

Keyboard Shortcuts

Most menu commands have a keyboard equivalent, such as Ctrl+P, as a quicker alternative to using the mouse. A complete list of keyboard shortcuts is available on the web at *www.perspection.com*.

How You'll Learn

How This Book Works

What's New

Keyboard Shortcuts

Step-by-Step Instructions

Real World Examples

Workshops

Microsoft Office Specialist

Get More on the Web

Step-by-Step Instructions

This book provides concise step-by-step instructions that show you "how" to accomplish a task. Each set of instructions includes illustrations that directly correspond to the easy-to-read steps. Also included in the text are time-savers, tables, and sidebars to help you work more efficiently or to teach you more in-depth information. A "Did You Know?" provides tips and techniques to help you work smarter, while a "See Also" leads you to other parts of the book containing related information about the task.

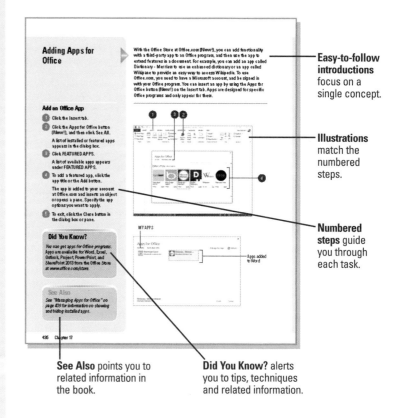

Easy-to-follow introductions focus on a single concept.

Illustrations match the numbered steps.

Numbered steps guide you through each task.

See Also points you to related information in the book.

Did You Know? alerts you to tips, techniques and related information.

Real World Examples

This book uses real world examples files to give you a context in which to use the task. By using the example files, you won't waste time looking for or creating sample files. You get a start file and a result file, so you can compare your work. Not every topic needs an example file, such as changing options, so we provide a complete list of the example files used through out the book. The example files that you need for project tasks along with a complete file list are available on the web at *www.perspection.com*.

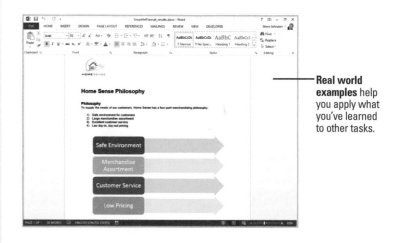

Real world examples help you apply what you've learned to other tasks.

Workshops

This book shows you how to put together the individual step-by-step tasks into in-depth projects with the Workshops. You start each project with a sample file, work through the steps, and then compare your results with a project results file at the end. The Workshop projects and associated files are available on the web at *www.perspection.com*.

The **Workshops** walks you through in-depth projects to help you put Microsoft Word to work.

Microsoft Office Specialist

This book prepares you for the Microsoft Office Specialist (MOS) exam for Microsoft Word 2013. Each MOS certification exam has a set of objectives, which are organized into broader skill sets. To prepare for the MOS certification exam, you should review and perform each task identified with a MOS objective to confirm that you can meet the requirements for the exam. Information about the MOS program is available in the back of this book. The MOS objectives and the specific pages that cover them are available on the web at *www.perspection.com*.

Get More on the Web

In addition to the information in this book, you can also get more information on the web to help you get up to speed faster with Word 2013. Some of the information includes:

Transition Helpers

◆ **Only New Features.** Download and print the new feature tasks as a quick and easy guide.

Productivity Tools

◆ **Keyboard Shortcuts.** Download a list of keyboard shortcuts to learn faster ways to get the job done.

More Content

◆ **Photographs.** Download photographs and other graphics to use in your Office documents.

◆ **More Content.** Download new content developed after publication. For example, you can download a chapter on SharePoint server and Office 365.

You can access these additional resources on the web at *www.perspection.com.*

Keyboard Shortcuts

k

Microsoft Word 2013

If a command on the ribbon or a menu includes a keyboard reference, known as a **keyboard shortcut**, in a ScreenTip or next to the command name, you can perform the action by pressing and holding the first key, and then pressing the second key to perform the command quickly. In some cases, a keyboard shortcut uses three keys. Simply press and hold the first two keys, and then press the third key. For keyboard shortcuts in which you press one key immediately followed by another key, the keys to press are separated by a comma (,). Keyboard shortcuts provide an alternative to using the mouse and make it easy to perform repetitive commands.

Finding a Keyboard Shortcut

To help you find the keyboard shortcut you're looking for, the shortcuts are organized in categories and listed with page numbers.

Alignment, 5	References, Footnotes, and Endnotes, 9
Copy/Cut and Paste, 7	Review and Comment, 9
Fields, 9	Ribbon, 2
File and Dialog Boxes, 2	Print and Preview, 3
Find and Replace, 5	Text and Text in an Outline, 4
Font and Format, 6	SmartArt Graphics, 8
Full Screen Reading View, 3	Special Characters, 7
Help, 2	Styles, 6
Line Spacing, 5	Undo and Redo, 7
Mail Merge, 8	Views, 3
Move Around, 3	Web Pages, 7

Function Keys

Alt+Function, 10	Alt+Shift+Function, 11
Function, 9	Shift+Function, 9
Ctrl+Function, 10	Ctrl+Shift+Function, 10
Ctrl+Alt+Function, 11	

If you're searching for new keyboard shortcuts in Microsoft Word 2013, just look for the letter: N. The N appears in the Keyboard Shortcuts table so you can quickly and easily identify new or changed shortcuts.

1

Additional content is available on the web. You can download keyboard shortcuts.

Getting Started with Word

1

Introduction

Microsoft Word 2013 is a powerful word-processing program that enables you to easily compose and edit documents for print or online use. Word contains new tools specifically designed to improve the way you interact with the program, and the way you collaborate with one another in preparing documents.

This chapter introduces you to the terminology and the basic Word skills you use in the program. In Word, files are called **documents**. Each new document is similar to a blank page. As you type and add additional text and other objects, your document gets longer. Unlike looking at a piece of paper, Word provides many views, such as the Read Mode view, that helps you see the document in the best possible way for the task at hand.

With the results-oriented visual interface, you navigate through various tasks with a click of the mouse, or by using shortcut keys on your keyboard. Word is set up with a tab-based Ribbon and dialog boxes that provide you with the tools you need when you need them to get the job done. The customizable Quick Access Toolbar gives you easy access to commonly-used commands, such as Save and Undo.

When you finish the design of your document, you can save it in the default XML-based format or another format; a web page for example, to use in another office program. You can save a document to your computer, SkyDrive cloud-based online storage system, or SharePoint server, such as Office 365. Microsoft also offers the Office.com Online web site, a resource to check for information on Word.

What You'll Do

Start Word

View the Word Window

Use the Ribbon and Choose Commands

Work with the Ribbon and Toolbars

Choose Dialog Box Options

Use the Status Bar

Use Task and Window Panes

Open an Existing Document

Open Files of Different Types

Convert an Existing Document

Change Document Views

Read a Document

Get Help While You Work

Save a Document

Save a Document with Different Formats

Save a Document to Online Services

Work with Accounts

Check Compatibility and Accessibility

Document Properties

Zoom the View In and Out

Recover a Document

Close a Document and Exit Word

1

Starting Word

The two quickest ways to start Microsoft Word are to select it on the Start screen (Win 8) (**New!**) or on the Start menu (Win 7). Word lets you work the way you like and start programs with a click of a button. When you start Word, a program window opens, displaying the Start screen (**New!**) where you can create or open a document in order to quickly get started.

Start Word

1 Start Windows, if necessary, and then use the method for your Windows version.

- ◆ **Windows 8.** Display the Start screen; click or tap the **Start** button on the Charm bar.

- ◆ **Windows 7.** Click **Start** on the taskbar, point to **All Programs** (which changes to Back), and then point to **Microsoft Office**.

2 Click **Word 2013**.

If Office asks you to activate the program, follow the instructions enter an account or product key. to complete the process.

TIMESAVER *To change the accounts, click the File tab, click Account, and then click the Switch Account link.*

Start screen   User name (account)

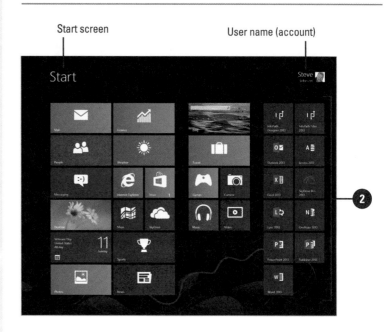

Did You Know?

You can create a program shortcut from the Start menu to the desktop.
Right-click the Microsoft Word 2013 program on the Start menu or screen. For Win 8, click the Pin To Taskbar button on the App bar. For Win 7, point to Send To, and then click Desktop (Create Shortcut).

You can start Word and open a document from an Explorer window.
Double-clicking any Word file icon in an Explorer window opens that file and Word.

Word 2013 System Requirements

Hardware/Software	Minimum (Recommended)
Computer Processor	1 gigahertz (Ghz) or faster x86 (32 bit) or x64 (64 bit) processor with SSE2
Operating System	Windows 7, Windows 8, Windows Server 2008 R2, or Windows Server 2012
Available RAM	1 GB (32 bit), 2 GB (64 bit)
Hard Drive	3 GB of available space
Monitor Resolution	1024 x 576
Video Card	Graphics hardware acceleration requires a DirectX10 graphics card
Browser	Microsoft IE 8, 9, or 10; Firefox 10.x or later; Apple Safari 5; or Google Chrome 17.x
.NET version	3.5, 4.0, or 4.5

Viewing the Word Window

File tab
Click to access Word file commands.

Quick Access Toolbar
Click to access commands on this customizable toolbar.

Tabs
Click to access tools and commands.

Dialog Box Launcher
Click to open dialog boxes or task panes.

Document window
Enter text and graphics here.

Ribbon
Commands and tools grouped by category onto different tabs.

Lists and Galleries
Click the down arrows to access lists and galleries.

Status bar
Displays information about the active document.

View buttons
Use to switch between views.

Zoom controls
Use to zoom in or out using the slide, or the buttons.

Using the Ribbon

The **Ribbon** is a results oriented way of working in Word 2013. The Ribbon is located at the top of the document window and is comprised of **tabs** that are organized by task or objects. The controls on each tab are organized into **groups**, or subtasks. The controls, or **command buttons**, in each group execute a command, or display a menu of commands or a drop-down gallery. Controls in each group provide a visual way to quickly make document changes. The File tab displays Backstage view, where you can access file-related commands.

If you prefer using the keyboard instead of the mouse to access commands on the Ribbon, Word provides easy to use shortcuts. Simply press and release the [Alt] or [F10] key to display **KeyTips** over each feature in the current view, and then continue to press the letter shown in the KeyTip until you press the one that you want to use. To cancel an action and hide the KeyTips, press and release the [Alt] or [F10] key again. If you prefer using the keyboard shortcuts found in previous versions of Word, such as Ctrl+P (for Print), all the keyboard shortcuts and keyboard accelerators work exactly the same in Word 2013.

Tabs

Word provides three types of tabs on the Ribbon. The first type is called a **standard** tab—such as File, Home, Insert, Design, Page Layout, References, Mailings, Review, and View—that you see whenever you start Word. The second type is called a **contextual** tab—such as Picture Tools, Drawing, or Table—that appears only when they are needed based on the type of task you are doing. Word recognizes what you're doing and provides the right set of tabs and tools to use when you need them. The third type is called a **program** tab that replaces the standard set of tabs when you switch to certain views or modes.

Live Preview

When you point to a gallery option, such as WordArt, on the Ribbon, Word displays a **live preview** of the option change so that you can see what your change will look like before selecting it. The Paste Options button also displays a live preview for pasted content.

Display Options

If you want more display screen, you can collapse and expand the Ribbon as you need it. Click the Ribbon Display Options button (**New!**) to select an option: Auto-hide Ribbon, Show Tabs, or Show Tabs and Commands. Auto-hide Ribbon collapses the Ribbon until you click the top of the program. Show Tabs displays only tabs until you click a tab to show it. Show Tabs and Commands displays the Ribbon all the time.

> **TIMESAVER** *To collapse the Ribbon, click the Collapse the Ribbon button (Ctrl+F1) or double-click the current tab. Click a tab to auto display it (Ribbon remains collapsed). To expand the Ribbon, press Ctrl+F1 or double-click a tab.*

Key Tip   Standard tabs   Contextual tab   Ribbon Display Options

Collapse the Ribbon

Choosing Commands

Word commands are organized in groups on the Ribbon, Quick Access Toolbar, and Mini-Toolbar. Commands are available as buttons or options on the Ribbon, or as menus on button or option arrows or the File tab. The Quick Access Toolbar and Mini-Toolbar (**New!**) display frequently used buttons that you may be already familiar with from previous versions of Word, while the File tab on the Ribbon displays file related menu commands; to exit the File tab, click the Back button (**New!**). In addition to the File tab, you can also open a **shortcut menu** with a group of related commands by right-clicking a program element.

Choose a Menu Command Using the File Tab

1. Click the **File** tab on the Ribbon.

2. Click the command you want.

    TIMESAVER *You can use a shortcut key to choose a command. Press and hold down the first key and then press the second key. For example, press and hold the Ctrl key and then press S (or Ctrl+S) to select the Save command.*

3. To return to the program window, click the **Back** button (**New!**).

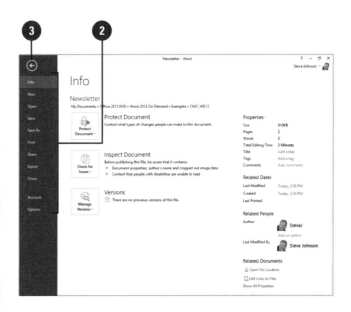

Choose a Command from a Shortcut Menu

1. Right-click an object (text or graphic element).

    TIMESAVER *Press Shift+F10 to display the shortcut menu for a selected command.*

2. Click a command on the shortcut menu or the Mini-Toolbar (**New!**). If the command is followed by an arrow, point to the command to see a list of related options, and then click the option you want.

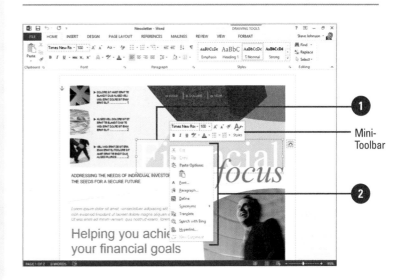

Mini-Toolbar

Working with the Ribbon and Toolbars

Word includes its most common commands, such as Save and Undo, on the **Quick Access Toolbar**. Click a toolbar button to choose a command. If you are not sure what a toolbar button does, point to it to display a ScreenTip. When Word starts, the Quick Access Toolbar appears at the top of the window, unless you've changed your settings. You can customize the Quick Access Toolbar or Ribbon by adding command buttons or groups to it. You can also move the toolbar below or above the Ribbon so it's right where you need it. In addition to the Quick Access Toolbar, Word also displays the Mini-Toolbar when you point to selected text. The **Mini-Toolbar** appears above the selected text and provides quick access to formatting tools.

Choose a Command Using a Toolbar or Ribbon

◆ **Get command help**. If you're not sure what a button does, point to it to display a ScreenTip. If the ScreenTip includes *Press F1 for more help*, press F1.

◆ **Choose a command**. Click the button, or button arrow, and then click a command or option.

Dialog Box Launcher   ScreenTip

Add or Remove Items from the Quick Access Toolbar

◆ **Add or remove a common button**. Click the **Customize Quick Access Toolbar list arrow**, and then click a button name (checked item appears on the toolbar).

◆ **Add a Ribbon button or group**. Right-click the button or group name on the Ribbon, and then click **Add to Quick Access Toolbar**.

◆ **Remove a button or group**. Right-click the button or group name on the Quick Access Toolbar, and then click **Remove from Quick Access Toolbar**.

Customize Quick Access   Click to add or remove
Toolbar list arrow   frequently used buttons

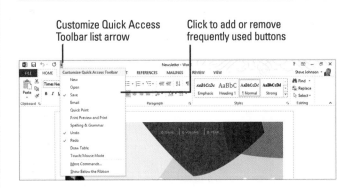

Right-click to add a button or group

Customize the Ribbon or Quick Access Toolbar

1 Click the **File** tab, and then click **Options**.

2 Click the **Customize Ribbon** or **Quick Access Toolbar**.

3 Click the **Choose commands from** list arrow, and then click **All Commands** or a specific Ribbon.

4 Click the list arrow (right column), and then select the tabs or toolbar you want to change.

5 For the Ribbon, click **New Tab** to create a new tab, or click **New Group** to create a new group on the selected tab (right column), or click **Rename** to change the name.

6 To import or export a customized Ribbon or Quick Access Toolbar, click the **Import/Export** list arrow, select a command, and then select an import file or create an export file.

7 Click the command you want to add (left column) or remove (right column), and then click **Add** or **Remove**.

◆ To insert a separator line between buttons in the Quick Access Toolbar, click **<Separator>**, and then click **Add**.

8 Click the **Move Up** and **Move Down** arrow buttons to arrange the order.

9 To reset the Ribbon or Quick Access Toolbar, click the **Reset** list arrow, and then select a reset option.

10 Click **OK**.

Customize keyboard shortcuts

For Your Information

Moving Toolbars and the Ribbon

You can move the Quick Access Toolbar to another location. Click the Customize Quick Access Toolbar list arrow, and then click Show Below The Ribbon or Show Above The Ribbon. You can minimize the Ribbon. Click the Minimize The Ribbon (Ctrl+F1) button on the right side of the Ribbon (to the left of the Help button). Click the Expand The Ribbon button to maximize it. When the Ribbon is minimized, you can click a tab to auto maximize it. When you click an option or in the document, the Ribbon minimizes again. Just like an auto-hide option.

Customize Keyboard Shortcuts

You can assign your own keyboard shortcuts to commands in Word. Click the File tab, click Options, click Customize Ribbon, click Customize, select a category, select a command, click in the Press new shortcut key box, press the keyboard shortcut keys you want, and then click Assign. To remove a keyboard shortcut, select it in Current keys, and then click Remove. To reset all the keyboard shortcuts back to the defaults set by Word, click Reset All, and then click Yes. When you're done, click Close, and then click OK.

Choosing Dialog Box Options

A **dialog box** is a window that opens when you click a Dialog Box Launcher. **Dialog Box Launchers** are small icons that appear at the bottom corner of some groups. When you point to a Dialog Box Launcher, a ScreenTip with a thumbnail of the dialog box appears to show you which dialog box opens. A dialog box allows you to supply more information before the program carries out the command you selected. After you enter information or make selections in a dialog box, click the OK button to complete the command. Click the Cancel button to close the dialog box without issuing the command. In many dialog boxes, you can also click an Apply button to apply your changes without closing the dialog box. Rather than clicking to move around a dialog box, you can press the Tab key to move from one box or button to the next. You can also use Shift+Tab to move backward, or Ctrl+Tab and Ctrl+Shift+Tab to move between dialog box tabs.

Choose Dialog Box Options

All dialog boxes contain the same types of options, including the following:

◆ **Tabs**. Each tab groups a related set of options. Click a tab to display its options.

◆ **Option buttons**. Click an option button to select it. You can usually only select one.

◆ **Up and down arrows**. Click the up or down arrow to increase or decrease the number, or type a number in the box.

◆ **Check box**. Click the box to turn on or off the option. A checked box means the option is selected; a cleared box means it's not.

◆ **List box**. Click the list arrow to display a list of options, and then click the option you want.

◆ **Text box**. Click in the box and type the requested information.

◆ **Button**. Click a button to perform a specific action or command. A button name followed by an ellipsis (...) opens a dialog box.

◆ **Preview box**. Many dialog boxes show an image that reflects the options you select.

Tabs List box Up and down arrows Check box Preview box Buttons

Option buttons Slider

Using the Status Bar

The **Status bar** appears across the bottom of your screen and displays document information—such as word count, page numbers, language, and current display zoom percentage—and some Word program controls, such as view shortcut buttons, zoom slider, and Fit To Window button. With the click of the mouse, you can quickly customize exactly what you see on the Status bar. In addition to displaying information, the Status bar also allows you to check the on/off status of certain features, such as Signatures, Permissions, Selection Mode, Page Number, Caps Lock, Num Lock, Macro Recording and Playback, and much more.

Add or Remove Items from the Status Bar

◆ **Add Item**. Right-click the Status bar, and then click an unchecked item.

◆ **Remove Item**. Right-click the Status bar, and then click a checked item.

Right-click the Status bar   Status information

Using Task and Window Panes

Task panes are separate windows that appear when you need them, such as Navigation or Format Picture pane, or when you click a Dialog Box Launcher icon, such as Clipboard. A task pane displays various options that relate to the current task. Many task panes are organized into categories and groups of options (**New!**), which you can display by clicking a tab (if available), clicking a category icon button (like a tab) at the top, and expanding a group below. Task panes function differently depending on the type. **Window panes** are sections of a window, such as a split window. If you need a larger work area, you can use the Close button in the upper-right corner of the pane to close a task or window pane, or move a border edge (for task panes) or **splitter** (for window panes) to resize it.

Work with Task and Window Panes

◆ **Open a Task Pane.** It appears when you need it or when you click a **Dialog Box Launcher** icon.

◆ **Close a Task or Window Pane.** Click the **Close** button in upper-right corner of the pane.

◆ **Resize a Task Pane.** Point to the Task Pane border edge until the pointer changes to double arrows, then drag the edge to resize it.

◆ **Resize a Window Pane.** Point to the window pane border bar until the pointer changes to a double bar with arrows, then drag the edge to resize it.

◆ **Display Options in a Pane.** Click a tab (if available), click a category icon button (like a tab) at the top of the pane (**New!**), click to expand a category, and then select the options you want.

Did You Know?

You can insert window panes. Click the View tab, click the Split button in the Window group.

Click to open task pane

Task pane options

Close

Format Picture pane

Click icons to display options; some panes also have tabs

Available options

Click to expand/collapse options

Move Task Panes

1. Open the task pane you want to move.

2. Point to the title bar.

   The cursor changes to a 4-headed arrow.

3. Drag the task pane to a new location.

   The task pane becomes undocked.

4. To redock a task pane, drag the task pane to the left or right side of the program window. Keep dragging until the task pane snaps into place.

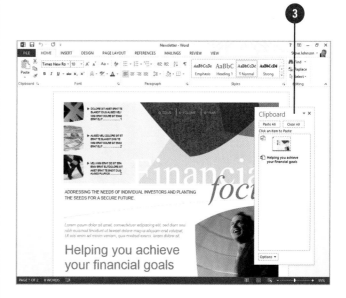

Opening an Existing Document

You can open an existing document from the Start screen (**New!**) when the Word program starts or Open screen by using the File tab. On the Open screen, you can choose a recently used document, locate and select the document on your SkyDrive, SharePoint, or computer. SkyDrive (**New!**) is a cloud-based online personal storage system, which requires a Microsoft account to access, while SharePoint server (**New!**) is a cloud-based online organizational storage and management system. When you open a document from Word 97-2003 or Word 2007-Word 2010 goes into compatibility mode—indicated on the title bar—where it disables new features that cannot be displayed or converted well by previous versions. The document stays in compatibility mode until you convert it to the Word 2013 file format. The Open screen allows you to pin recently used documents or folders (**New!**) that you want to remain accessible regardless of recent use. The Pin icon to the right of the file name on the File tab makes it easy to pin or unpin as needed.

Open a Document from the Program Window

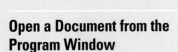

1. Click the **File** tab, and then click **Open**.

2. Click **Computer**.

3. Click **Browse** or a recent folder.

4. If you want to open a specific file type, click the **Files of type** list arrow, and then click a file type.

    - **Strict Open XML Document.** You can also open documents in the Strict Open XML format (**New!**) to resolve leap year issues with 1900.

5. Navigate to the location where you want to open the file, and then select the file.

6. Click **Open**, or click the **Open** button arrow, and then click one of the following options:

    - **Open Read-Only.**
    - **Open as Copy.**
    - **Open in Browser.**
    - **Open in Transform.**
    - **Open in Protected View.**
    - **Open and Repair.**

Access SharePoint   Access SkyDrive   Recent folder locations

Open a Recently Opened Document or Folder

1. Click the **File** tab, and then click **Open**.

   TIMESAVER *In the Start screen (New!), click a recent document.*

2. Click **Recent Documents** or **Computer (New!)**.

3. To pin or unpin a document or folder, point to a document or folder (displays the pin):

   - **Pin a document or folder.** Click the **Pin** icon on the Recent Documents or Recent Folders list.

   - **Unpin a document or folder.** Click the **Unpin** icon to display a pin on the Recent Documents or Recent Folders list.

4. Click the document or folder you want to open.

Pinned item

Access local files

Unpinned item

Did You Know?

You can add recently used documents to the File tab. Click the File tab, click Options, click Advanced, select the Quickly Access This Number Of Recent Documents check box, specify the number of documents you want to display, and then click OK.

You can change the number of recently opened files that appear on the File tab. Click the File tab, click Options, click Advanced, change the Show This Number Of Recent Documents list, and then click OK.

You can change the default file location of the Open dialog box. Click the File tab, click Options, click Save, enter a new location in the Default File Location box, and then click OK.

Open recent documents on the Start screen

Click to open a document from the Open dialog box

Opening Files of Different Types

Word recognizes and can open files created in a wide variety of other programs including, but not limited to: OpenDocument, WordPerfect, PDF (Portable Document Format), Microsoft Works, Text Files, Rich Text Format, XML, and web pages. You can also select a format option to help you Recover Text from any File. When you open a document that was created in an older version of Word, Word opens it automatically into the current version. When you open a PDF document, Word asks you to convert it to an editable document. The resulting document is optimized using PDF Reflow (**New!**) to allow you to edit the text.

Open a File in a Non-Word Format

1. Click the **File** tab, and then click **Open**.

2. Click **Computer**.

3. Click **Browse** or a recent folder.

4. Click the **Files of type** list arrow, and then select the type of file that you want to open.

5. Click the **Look in** list arrow, and then navigate to the file.

6. Select the document file you want to open.

7. Click **Open**.

8. If prompted, click **OK** to convert the PDF to an editable Word document.

9. If the document opens in Read Mode view for security purposes, view the document or click **Enable Editing** to edit it in Print Layout view.

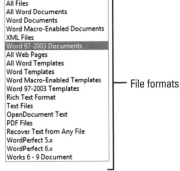

File formats

Converting an Existing Document

When you open a document from Word 97-2003 or Word 2007-2010 (**New!**), Word 2013 goes into compatibility mode—indicated on the title bar—where it disables new features that cannot be displayed or converted well by previous versions. When you save a document, Word 2013 saves Word 97-2003 or 2007-2010 files in their older format using compatibility mode. The document stays in compatibility mode until you convert it to the Word 2013 file format. Word 2007-2010 and Word 2013 use the same file extensions, however there may be feature differences between the versions.

Convert a Word 97-2003 or 2007-2010 Document to Word 2013

1. Open the Word document 97-2003 or 2007-2010 you want to convert to the Word 2013 file format.

   The Word document opens in compatibility mode.

2. Click the **File** tab, and then click **Info**.

3. Click **Convert**.

4. Click **OK** to convert the file to the Word 2013 format.

   Word exits compatibility mode, which is only turned on when a previous version is in use.

Compatibility mode

Did You Know?

You can maintain compatibility when you save as in the Save dialog box. In the Save As dialog box, select the Maintain Compatibility With Previous Versions Of Word check box (**New!**), specify a name and location, and then click Save.

You can display extensions in the Save and Open dialog boxes and Recent Documents list. Changing the Windows option also changes Word. In the Folder Options dialog box on the View tab, clear the Hide Extensions For Known File Types check box, and then click OK.

Changing Document Views

Word displays the contents of a document in different ways to help you work efficiently with your content. The available views include Read Mode (**New!**), Print Layout, Web Layout, Outline, and Draft. You can change the view from the View tab, or you can click a view button—Read Mode, Print Layout, or Web Layout—at the bottom right corner of the window.

Read Mode view (**New!**) displays the full screen and removes distracting screen elements to provide a more comfortable view to read your documents. You can also display the Navigation pane to quickly jump to different parts of your document or search for information in the document or on the web.

Print Layout view displays a gray gap between each page to clearly delineate where each actual page break occurs. Word displays each new document in Print Layout view by default. This view is best for previewing your work before printing, and it works well with the Zoom feature on the View tab to increase

and decrease the page view size and display multiple pages of the same document simultaneously onscreen.

Web Layout view displays the document as it will appear on the Web. You can save documents as HTML code to make Web content creation easy.

Outline view displays the document as an outline with headings and subheadings. When you shift to Outline view, each heading has a clickable plus or minus sign next to it to expand or collapse the content under the heading. You can drag a plus, or minus sign to move the heading and all of its associated text.

Draft view displays the document as a single, long piece of "paper," divided into pages by perforation marks. This view is fine for composition but inadequate for editing or previewing your work prior to printing or other publication.

Print Layout view

Read Mode view

Web Layout view

Outline view

Draft view

Reading a Document

Read Mode view is designed with a display and tools optimized for reading a document. Word changes the screen size and removes distracting elements to provide a comfortable view for reading. You can customize the view by changing the column width, page color, and layout, or showing comments. If you want to hide tools, you can use the Auto-hide Reading Toolbar button. You can use the Navigation pane to quickly jump to different parts of your document or search for information within it or on the web using Bing. If a table, chart, or picture is hard to see, you can zoom in and out to view it (**New!**). When you reopen a document, Word remembers where you were, even if you reopen an online document from a different computer, and displays a resume callout (**New!**).

Read and Review a Document

1 Click the **Read Mode View** button.

◆ The **Read Mode View** button is also available on the View tab.

2 To navigate pages, click the **Previous** or **Next** buttons or swipe on tablets or touch screens.

3 To show or hide the Reading Toolbar, click the **Auto-hide Reading Toolbar** button.

4 To work with text, select and right-click the text, and then do any of the following:

◆ **Copy.** Copies to the Clipboard.

◆ **Define.** Displays a pop-up with a definition of the text.

◆ **Translate.** Translates the text using the Research pane.

◆ **Search with Bing.** Creates a search in your web browser.

◆ **New Comment.** Creates a comment in a pop-up.

◆ **Highlight.** Highlights the text with a selected color.

5 To zoom (**New!**) in a table, chart, or picture, double-click it, and then click to zoom in and out. To exit zoom, click outside the object.

6 To exit Read Mode view, click another view button, or click the **View** tab, and then click **Edit Document**.

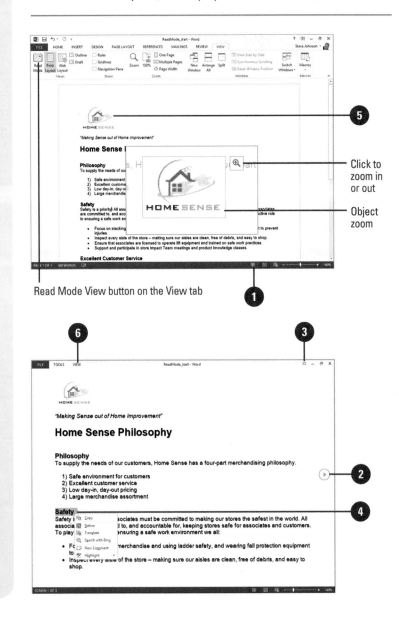

Read Mode View button on the View tab

Click to zoom in or out

Object zoom

Display Headings, Pages, or Search Results

① Click the **Read Mode View** button.

② Click the **View** tab, and then click **Navigation Pane**.

③ To search for text, enter search criteria. The results are highlighted on the page. Click the **Next** or **Previous** button to view each one.

④ Click the **Headings**, **Pages**, or **Results** tab.

⑤ Click a heading name or thumbnail of a page to display it.

⑥ To close the Navigation pane, click the **Close** button on the pane.

⑦ To exit Read Mode view, click another view button.

Highlighted search items

Change Read Mode View Options

① Click the **Read Mode View** button.

② Click the **View** tab.

③ Click the view you want to display.

◆ **Edit Document.** Switches to Print Layout view.

◆ **Navigation Pane.** Displays the Navigation pane.

◆ **Show Comments.** Displays the Comments pane.

◆ **Column Width.** Changes the column width to narrow, default or wide.

◆ **Page Color.** Changes the page color to none, sepia, or inverse.

◆ **Layout.** Changes the layout to column or page.

④ To exit Read Mode view, click another view button.

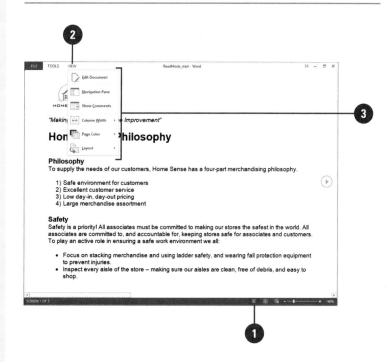

Getting Help While You Work

At some time, everyone has a question or two about the program they are using. The Office Help Viewer provides the answers and resources you need, including feature help, articles, tips, templates, training, and downloads. By connecting to Office.com on the Microsoft web site, you not only have access to standard product help information, but you also have access to updated information over the web without leaving the Help Viewer. The web browser-like Help Viewer allows you to browse a catalog of topics to locate information (**New!**), use popular searches (**New!**), or enter your own phrases to search for information. When you use any of these help options, a list of possible answers is shown to you with the most likely answer or most frequently-used at the top of the list.

Use the Help Viewer to Get Answers

1. Click the **Help** button on the Ribbon.

   TIMESAVER *Press F1.*

2. Locate the Help topic you want.

   ◆ **Popular searches.** Click a popular search (**New!**).

   ◆ **Help topic.** Click a topic tile on the home page (**New!**).

3. Read the topic, and then click any links to get Help information.

4. Click the **Back**, **Forward**, and **Home** buttons on the toolbar to move around in the Help Viewer.

5. If you want to print the topic, click the **Print** button on the toolbar.

6. To keep the Help Viewer window (not maximized) on top or behind, click to toggle the **Keep Help On Top** button (pin pushed in) and **Don't Keep Help On Top** button (pin not pushed in) on the toolbar.

   TIMESAVER *Press Ctrl+T to toggle Help On Top (**New!**).*

7. When you're done, click the **Close** button.

Click to change the topic font size

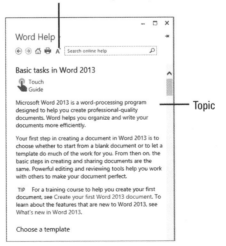
Topic

Search for Help

1 Click the **Help** button on the Ribbon.

2 To use a popular search, click one of the popular searches (**New!**).

3 Type one or more keywords in the Search For box, and then click the **Search** button to display results.

◆ **Prev or Next.** Scroll to the bottom, and then click **Prev** or **Next** to view more results.

4 Click a topic.

5 Read the topic, and then click any links to get information on related topics or definitions.

6 When you're done, click the **Close** button.

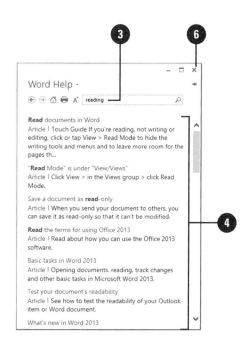

Use Local or Online Help

1 Click the **Help** button on the Ribbon.

2 Click the **Help** list arrow at the top of the Help Viewer.

3 Click the option where you want to get help information:

◆ **Help from Office.com** to get product help from this computer and the internet (online).

◆ **Help from your computer** to get product help from this computer only (offline).

4 When you're done, click the **Close** button.

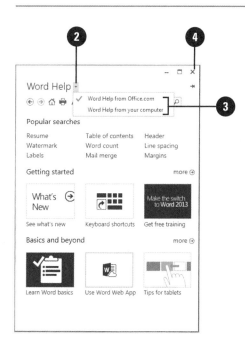

Saving a Document

After you create a Word document, you can save it to your computer, SkyDrive (**New!**) cloud-based online storage system, or Office 365 SharePoint service (**New!**). When you save a document for the first time or if you want to save a copy of a file, use the Save As command. When you want to save an open document, use the Save button on the Quick Access Toolbar. When you save a document, Word 2013 saves 97-2003 files in an older format using compatibility mode and 2007-2013 files in an XML (Extensible Markup Language) based file format. The XML format significantly reduces file sizes, provides enhanced file recovery, and allows for increased compatibility, sharing, reuse, and transportability. If you have issues with leap year dates for 1900, you can use the Strict Open XML Document format (**New!**) with ISO8601. A Word 97-2003 or 2007-2010 document stays in compatibility mode—indicated on the title bar—until you convert it to the 2013 file format. Compatibility mode disables new features that cannot be displayed or converted well by previous versions.

Save a Document for Word 2013

1. Click the **File** tab, and then click **Save As**.

2. Click **Computer**.

3. Click **Browse** or a recent folder.

4. Click the **Save in** list arrow, and then select the location where you want to save the file.

5. Type a document file name.

6. Click the **Save as type** list arrow, and then click **Word Document**.

7. To enter Document properties, click the **Authors** or **Tags** box, and then enter the text you want.

8. To maintain file format compatibility, select the **Maintain compatibility with previous versions of Word** check box (**New!**), if available.

9. Click **Save**.

10. If prompted to upgrade, click **OK**.

Save a Word 97-2003, 2007-2010 Document in Compatibility Mode

1. Open the Word 97-2003, 2007-2010 document you want to continue to save in the original format.

   The Word document opens in compatibility mode.

2. Click the **Save** button on the Quick Access Toolbar, or click the **File** tab, and then click **Save**.

   Word stays in compatibility mode.

Set Save Options

1. Click the **File** tab, and then click **Options**.

2. In the left pane, click **Save**.

3. Set the save options you want:

   ◆ **Default Save Format.** Click the **Save files in this format** list arrow, and then click the default format you want.

   ◆ **Don't show the Backstage when opening or saving files.** Select to enable (**New!**).

   ◆ **Show additional places for saving, even if sign-in may be required.** Select to enable (**New!**).

   ◆ **Save to Computer by default.** Select to enable (**New!**).

   ◆ **Default local file location.** Specify the complete path to the folder location where you want to save your documents.

4. Click **OK**.

Saving a Document with Different Formats

Word is a versatile suite of programs that allow you to save your documents in a variety of different formats—see the table on the following page for a complete list and description. For example, you might want to save your document as a web page that you can view in a web browser or save your document in the OpenDocument format for use in the OpenOffice program. Or you can save a document in an earlier 97-2003 version in case the people you work with have not upgraded to Word 2013. If you save a document to 97-2003, some new features and formatting are converted to uneditable pictures or not retained. The format is compatible with versions before 2003 with a software patch. However, for best results, if you're creating a document for someone with Word 97 to Word 2003, it's better to save it with the .doc file format. If you have issues with leap year dates for 1900, you can use the Strict Open XML Document format (**New!**) with ISO8601.

Save a Document with Another Format

1. Click the **File** tab, and then click **Export**.

2. Click **Change File Type**.

3. Click the file type you want.

4. Click the **Save As** button.

   The Save As dialog box opens with the selected file type.

   ◆ You can also click the **File** tab, click **Save As**, and then select a file format.

5. Navigate to the location where you want to save the file.

6. Type a document file name.

7. Click **Save**.

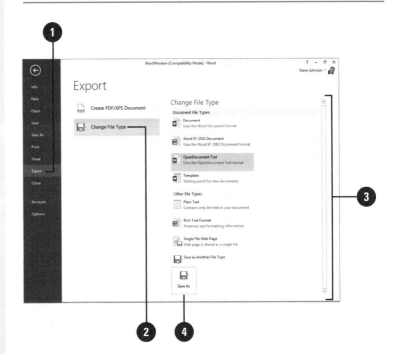

Did You Know?

You can access options from the Save dialog box. In the Save dialog box, click Tools, and then click the option you want, either General Options, Web Options, or Compress Pictures.

Word 2013 Save File Formats

Save As file type	Extension	Used to save
Word Document	.docx	Word 2007-2013 document
Word Macro-Enabled Document	.docm	Word 2007-2013 document that contains Visual Basic for Applications (VBA) code
Word 97-2003 Document	.doc	Word 97 to Word 2003 document
Word Template	.dotx	Word 2007-2013 Template
Word Macro-Enabled Template	.dotm	Word 2007-2013 template that includes preapproved macros
Word 97-2003 Templates	.dot	Word 97-2003 template
PDF	.pdf	Fixed-layout electronic file format that preserves document formatting developed by Adobe
XPS Document Format	.xps	Fixed-layout electronic file format that preserves document formatting developed by Microsoft
Single File Web Page	.mht; .mhtml	Web page as a single file with an .htm file
Web Page	.htm; .html	Web page as a folder with an .htm file
Web Page, Filtered	.htm; .html	Web page as a folder with an .htm file with a reduced file size
Rich Text Format	.rtf	Text files with formatting
Plain Text	.txt	Plain text files; no formatting
Word XML Document	.xml	XML document
Word 2003 XML Document	.xml	Word 2003 XML document
Strict Open XML Document (**New!**)	.docx	Word 2013 document format to resolve leap year issues with 1900
OpenDocument Text	.odt	OpenDocument text document; a document created from the OpenOffice program
Works 6 - 9 Document	.wps	Works 6.0-9.0 files

Saving a Document to Online Services

Word 2013 is integrated to work with online services (**New!**) to make it easier to save and open documents on other devices and share them with others. With a Microsoft or SharePoint account, you can save documents directly to a SkyDrive (**New!**), a personal cloud-based online storage system, or Office 365 SharePoint (**New!**), a customized Microsoft web site with SharePoint services. With your documents on a SkyDrive or SharePoint site, you can do a lot of things. You can sync the files from the SkyDrive or SharePoint site to other desktops or devices, such as a tablet or mobile phone for easy access from anywhere. You can view or edit documents online from the desktop Word program or browser-based Word Web App. You can share a document with other people using e-mail or social networks (**New!**) and even work on the same document at the same time with more than one person (**New!**).

Save a Document to Online Storage

1 Click the **File** tab, and then click **Save As**.

2 To add a shortcut place for easy access later, click **Add a Place**, click **Office 365 SharePoint** or **SkyDrive**, and then follow the on-screen connection instructions.

3 Click the SkyDrive or SharePoint name.

4 Click **Browse** or a recent folder.

5 Navigate to the location where you want to save the file.

6 Type a document file name.

7 Click the **Save as type** list arrow, and then click **Word Document**.

8 Click **Save**.

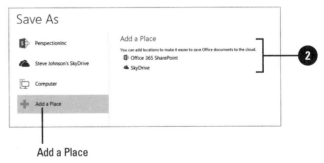

Add a Place

Working with Accounts

When you set up Word 2013 or Office 2013, it requests a Microsoft account to work with online services, such as SkyDrive or SharePoint. You can add, switch, or modify accounts or sign out entirely. You can also use to other online services (**New!**), such as Flickr and YouTube for images and video, and Facebook, Linkedin, and Twitter for sharing. Before you can use the services, you need to add them to Word, which requires an established account with a user name and password.

Work with Online Accounts

1. Click the **File** tab, and then click **Account (New!)**.

    TIMESAVER *Click the User Account list arrow, and then click an account option.*

2. Click any of the following links:

    ◆ **Change photo.** Click to open your account profile.

    ◆ **About me.** Click to open your account profile.

    ◆ **Sign out.** Click to sign out of your account.

    ◆ **Switch Account.** Click to switch or add accounts.

3. Click the **Back** button to exit the File tab.

User Account list arrow

Switch accounts

Add an account

Add Online Services

1. Click the **File** tab, and then click **Account (New!)**.

2. Click **Add a service (New!)**, point to a service type (options vary):

    ◆ **Images & Videos**, and then click **Flickr** or **YouTube**.

    ◆ **Storage**, and then click **Office 365 SharePoint** or **SkyDrive**.

    ◆ **Sharing**, and then click **Facebook**, **LinkedIn**, or **Twitter**.

3. Follow the on-screen instructions to add the service.

4. Click the **Back** button to exit the File tab.

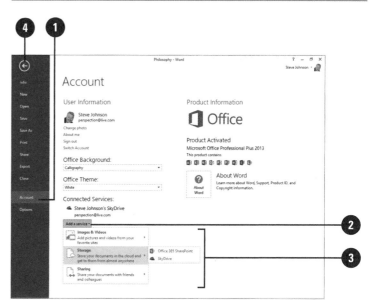

Checking Compatibility

The Compatibility Checker identifies the potential loss of functionality between a Word 2013 document and a Word 97-2003, 2007-2010 document. The Compatibility Checker generates a report that provides a summary of the potential losses and the number of occurrences in the document. You can also specify what versions to show compatibility issues. Use the report information to determine what caused each message and for suggestions on how to change it. If the loss is due to a newer feature in Word 2013—such as custom layouts or Quick Styles applied to shapes, pictures, and WordArt—you might be able to simply remove the effect or feature. In other cases, you might not be able to do anything about it. To maintain a visual appearance, SmartArt graphics and other objects with new effects are converted to bitmaps to preserve their overall look and cannot be edited. In Word 2013, the Format tab under Text Box Tools has been integrated with the Format tab under Drawing Tools. However, if you're working with a document in compatibility mode, the Format tab under Text Box Tools is still available.

Check Compatibility

1. Click the **File** tab, and then click **Info**.

2. Click the **Check For Issues** button, and then click **Check Compatibility**.

   Word checks compatibility of the document for non supported features in earlier versions of the Word program.

3. Click the **Select versions to show** list arrow, and then select one or more versions to check.

4. View the compatibility summary information, so you can make changes, as necessary.

5. To have the compatibility checker review the Office document when the Office program saves the file, select the **Check compatibility when saving documents** check box.

6. Click **OK**.

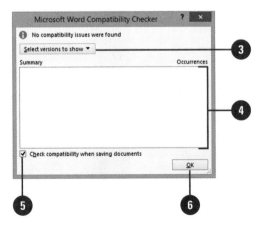

Checking Accessibility

The Accessibility Checker identifies potential difficulties that people with disabilities might have reading or interactive with an Office document. The Accessibility Checker generates a list of errors and warning and possible fixes in the Accessibility Checker panel. Use the information to determine what caused each issue and for suggestions on how to fix it. In addition to the Accessibility Checker, you can also add alternative text (also known as alt text) to objects and other items to provide information for people with visual impairments who may be unable to easily or fully see it. Alternative text also helps people with screen readers understand the content in a document. You can create alternative text for shapes, pictures, charts, tables, SmartArt graphics, or other objects. When you point to an object with alternative text in a screen reader or DAISY (Digital Accessible Information System) or in most browsers, the alternative text appears.

Check Accessibility and Add Alternative Text

1. Click the **File** tab, and then click **Info**.

2. Click the **Check For Issues** button, and then click **Check Accessibility**.

   Office checks compatibility that people with disabilities might find difficult to read.

3. View the compatibility summary information of errors and warnings in the Accessibility Checker panel.

4. Select an issue under Inspection Results to find out how to fix it under Additional Information.

5. To add alternative text, right-click the object or item, point to a command (varies depending on the object or item), such as **<item>**, and then click an Alt command, or click **Format <item>**. In the Format pane, click the **Layout & Properties** button (**New!**), expand Alt Text, enter a title and description.

6. When you're done with the Accessibility Checker or Format panel, click the **Close** button on the panel.

Documenting Properties

Word automatically documents properties while you work—such as file size, save dates, and various statistics—and allows you to document other properties, such as title, author, subject, keywords, category, and status. You can view or edit standard document properties or create advanced custom properties by using the **Document Information Panel**, which is an XML-based Microsoft InfoPath form hosted in the Office program. You can use document properties—also known as **metadata**—to help you manage and track files; search tools can use the metadata to find a document based on your search criteria. If you associate a document property to an item in the document, the document property updates when you change the item.

View and Edit Document Properties

1. Click the **File** tab, and then click **Info**.

2. To display other properties, click the **Properties** button, and then select an option:

   ◆ **Show Document Panel.** Shows Document panel in the document.

   ◆ **Advanced Properties.** Displays the Properties dialog box.

3. Enter the standard properties, such as author, title, subject, keywords, category, status, and comments.

   ◆ **Show All Properties.** Click the link to displays more options.

Document Panel

Zooming the View In and Out

Working with the Zoom tools gives you one more way to control exactly what you see in a Word document. The Zoom tools are located in the bottom-right corner of the window. Large documents are difficult to work with and difficult to view. Many documents, when viewed at 100%, are larger than the maximized size of the window. When this happens, viewing the entire document requires reducing the zoom.

Change the View

1 Use any of the following zoom options available on the Status bar:

◆ **Zoom Out**. Click to zoom out (percentage gets smaller).

◆ **Zoom In**. Click to zoom in (percentage gets larger).

◆ **Slider**. Drag to zoom out or in to the percentage you want.

◆ **Zoom Level**. Click to display the Zoom dialog box, where you can select the magnification you want.

2 For additional zoom options, click the **View** tab, and then use any of the following options:

TIMESAVER *Double-click the zoom percentage on the Status bar to open the Zoom dialog box.*

◆ **Zoom**. Click to display the Zoom dialog box, where you can select the magnification you want.

This is the same as Zoom Level above.

◆ **100%**. Click to display the view at 100%.

◆ **One Page**. Click to display one page at a time.

◆ **Two Pages**. Click to display two pages at at time.

◆ **Page Width**. Click to display the page to the current window width.

Zoom dialog box

Recovering a Document

If Word encounters a problem and stops responding, the program automatically tries to recover the file. The recovered files are stored and managed by Word. You can use the Manage Versions button on the Info screen under the File tab to open any available recovered unsaved files. If you have a lot of recovered files, you can also delete all file versions to save disk space. To use the AutoRecover option, you need to enable it in the Save category of the Options dialog box. You can set AutoRecover options to periodically save a temporary copy of your current file, which ensures proper recovery of the file and allows you to revert to an earlier version of a file. In addition, if you didn't save your changes when you closed a document, you can select an AutoRecover option to save your work as a safe guard.

Recover or Revert a Document

1. Click the **File** tab, and then click **Info**.

2. To open a recovered or previous version, click a file from the available list.

3. Click the **Manage Versions** button, and then click **Recover Unsaved Documents**.

   TIMESAVER *Click the File tab, click Recent, and then click Recover Unsaved Documents folder icon.*

4. Select the file version you want to recover.

5. Click **Open**.

Did You Know?

You can delete all draft versions of unsaved files. Click the File tab, click Info, click the Manage Versions button, click Delete All Unsaved Documents, and then click Yes to confirm the deletions.

Use AutoRecover

1. Click the **File** tab, and then click **Options**.

2. In the left pane, click **Save**.

3. Select the **Save AutoRecover information every x minutes** check box.

4. Enter the number of minutes, or click the **Up** and **Down** arrows to adjust the minutes.

5. Select the **Keep the last autosaved version if I close without saving** check box as a safe guard to save your work if you don't save it.

6. Specify the complete path to the folder location where you want to save your AutoRecover file.

7. Click **OK**.

Closing a Document and Exiting Word

After you finish working on a document, you can close it. Closing a document frees up more computer memory for other activities. Closing a document is different from exiting, or quitting, Word; after you close a document, Word is still running. You close a document by using the Close command on the File tab (**New!**), which keeps the Word program window open. Since each document opens in its own program window (**New!**), you don't need an Exit command, so you exit Word by using the Close button on the program window. To protect your files, always save your documents and exit before turning off the computer.

Close a Document

1 Click the **File** tab, and then click **Close**.

TIMESAVER *Press Ctrl+W.*

2 If you have made changes to any open files since last saving them, a dialog box opens, asking if you want to save changes. Click **Save** to save any changes, or click **Don't Save** to ignore your changes.

Exit Word

1 Click the **Close** button on the Word program window.

◆ **Close All.** Right-click the Word icon on the taskbar, and then click **Close all windows**.

TIMESAVER *To create an Exit button, add the Exit command to the Quick Access Toolbar.*

2 If you have made changes to any open files since last saving them, a dialog box opens asking if you want to save changes. Click **Save** to save any changes, or click **Don't Save** to ignore your changes.

Working with Simple Documents

2

Introduction

Whether you're typing a carefully worded letter, creating a professional resume, or producing a can't-miss promotional newsletter for your business or neighborhood group, Microsoft Word is the program for you. Word contains all the tools and features you need to produce interesting documents that say exactly what you mean and that have the look to match.

Word is designed especially for working with text, so it's a snap to create and edit letters, reports, mailing lists, tables, or any other word-based communication. What makes Word perfect for your documents is its editing capabilities combined with its variety of views. For example, you can jot down your ideas in Outline view. Then switch to Normal view to expand your thoughts into complete sentences and revise them without retyping the entire page. When you're done revising the document, switch to Read Mode view to read and proof your work. Finally, in Print Layout view you can quickly add formatting elements, such as bold type and special fonts, to make your documents look professional.

In addition, Word offers a Find and Replace feature that allows you to look for text and make changes as necessary. The Actions feature works with other Microsoft Office programs to enhance your documents. Contact information can be pulled from your address book in Outlook, to your Word document.

If you accidentally make a change, you can use the Undo feature to remove, or "undo," your last change. Word remembers your recent changes, and gives you the opportunity to undo them. If you decide to Redo the Undo, you can erase the previous change.

Creating a Blank Document

When you start Word, the program opens by default with the Start screen (**New!**) on the Backstage, where you can open a new document so that you can begin working in it. If you're already working in Word, you can use the New command (**New!**) on the File tab to create a new document. Each new document displays a default name—such as "Document1," "Document2" and so on—numbered according to how many new documents you have started during the work session until you save it with a more meaningful name. The document name appears on the title bar and taskbar buttons.

Start a Blank Document

1. Start a blank Word document from either of the following:

   ◆ **Start Screen.** Start Word 2013 from Windows (**New!**).

   ◆ **New Screen.** Click the **File** tab, and then click **New** (**New!**).

   TIMESAVER *To create a blank Word document without the New screen, press Ctrl+N.*

2. Click **Blank Document**.

   A new blank document appears in the Word program window.

Did You Know?

You can start Word and not show the Start screen. Click the File tab, click Options, clear the Show The Start Screen When This Application Starts check box (**New!**), and then click OK.

See Also

See "Saving a Document" on page 22 or "Saving a Document to Online Services" on page 26 for information on saving a document.

Back button   ② New screen

Use to open documents   ② Start screen

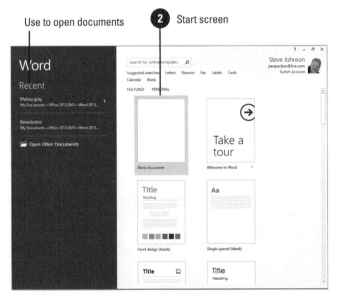

Creating a Document Using a Template

Word provides a collection of professionally designed templates that you can use to help you create documents. Start with a template when you have a good idea of your content but want to take advantage of a template's professional look. A **template** is a Word document file that provides you with an unified design, which includes themes, so you only need to add text and graphics. In the Start or New screen (**New!**), you can choose a template from those already installed with Word or from the library on the Microsoft Office Online web site. If you frequently use a template, you can pin it (**New!**) to the Start or New screen.

Start a Document with a Template

1. Start a Word document from either of the following:

   - **Start Screen.** Start Word 2013 from Windows (**New!**).
   - **New Screen.** Click the **File** tab, and then click **New** (**New!**).

2. Use one of the following (**New!**):

   - **Featured or Personal.** Click a template.
   - **Suggested searches.** Click a search option, click a category, and then click a template.
   - **Search for online templates.** Type criteria in the Search box, click the **Search** button or press Enter, click a category, and then click a template.

3. To pin a template to the New screen, point to a template, and then click the **Pin to List** button (**New!**). To unpin a template, click the **Pin from List** (**New!**).

4. To navigate, click the **Home** button.

5. Click **Create**.

Did You Know?

You can download templates on the web. Go to *www.microsoft.com*, click the Office link, and then search for Office Templates.

New on the File tab

Creating a New Document From an Existing One

Instead of creating a document from scratch, you can also create a document from an existing document you already have. If you have a document that is close to what you want to create, you can select it from the Start or New screen to create an untitled document with the contents of an existing document. When you place a document or template in the default personal templates location (**New!**) specified in the Word Options dialog box under Save, you can select the document or template from the Personal tab in the Start or New screen to create a new document from an existing one.

Create a New Document From an Existing Document

1. Start a Word document from either of the following:

    ◆ **Start Screen.** Start Word 2013 from Windows (**New!**).

    ◆ **New Screen.** Click the **File** tab, and then click **New** (**New!**).

2. Click **Personal** (**New!**).

    TROUBLE? *If Personal is not available, you need to specify a default personal templates location in Word options.*

3. Select the document or template file you want to open.

    A new document appears in the Word window.

See Also

See "Setting Up for Personal Templates" on page 111 for information on setting up the default personal templates location.

Normal document   Template document

Default personal templates location

Templates and documents

Creating a Letter or Memo

You can create a letter in Word as quickly as you can grab a pen and paper and start writing. With all of the text, formatting, spelling, and graphic features that Word has to offer, writing a letter is a very easy way to communicate with clients, friends, and family. Memos are another commonly used document whose creation has been simplified via the use of Word templates. You can create and customize a memo form all your own. Add your company logo, change font attributes, adjust line spacing, and other important parts of your document and you have a customized memo.

Create a Letter or Memo

1. Start a Word document from either of the following:

   ◆ **Start Screen.** Start Word 2013 from Windows (**New!**).

   ◆ **New Screen.** Click the **File** tab, and then click **New** (**New!**).

2. Click **Letters** next to Suggested searches.

3. Click a category to display the templates you want to use.

4. To navigate back to the main screen, click the **Home** button.

5. Click the template you want to use.

6. To navigate to other templates, click the **Next** or **Previous** button. To close the option, click the **Close** button.

7. Click **Create**.

   A new document appears in the Word window.

8. Edit the text in the place holders to make it your own document.

Opening and Editing PDF Documents

If you have a PDF document, you can open it in Word (**New!**). When you open a PDF document, Word asks you to convert it to an editable document. The resulting document is optimized using PDF Reflow (**New!**) to allow you to edit the text. The original graphics might not look exactly like the original PDF. PDF Reflow also works when you copy content from a PDF document and then paste it into a Word document. PDF Reflow gets the best results when the PDF was originally created in a Word document or another word-processing program. If PDF Reflow cannot detect an element, Word converts a text element to plain text or a text box, or a chart or diagram to points on a grid or a bitmap image. PDF documents appear in Read Mode view for viewing or in Print Layout view for editing.

Open a PDF Document

1. Click the **File** tab, and then click **Open**.

2. Click **Computer**.

3. Click **Browse** or a recent folder.

4. Click the **Files of type** list arrow, and then click **PDF Files** or **All Word Documents**.

5. Navigate to and select the PDF file you want.

6. Click **Open**.

7. If prompted, click **OK** to convert the PDF to an editable Word document.

8. If the document opens in Read Mode view for security purposes, view the document or click **Enable Editing** to edit it in Print Layout view.

Edit a PDF Document

1. Open the PDF file you want to edit in Word.

2. If prompted, click **OK** to convert the PDF to an editable Word document.

3. If the document opens in Read Mode view for security purposes, view the document or click **Enable Editing** to edit it in Print Layout view.

4. Edit the document in Print Layout view using the tools on the Ribbon.

Did You Know?

You can disable open uneditable files or e-mail attachments in Read Mode view. Click the File tab, click Options, click General, clear the Open E-mail Attachments And Other Uneditable Files In Reading View check box, and then click OK.

PDF document in
Read Mode view

PDF document in
Print Layout view

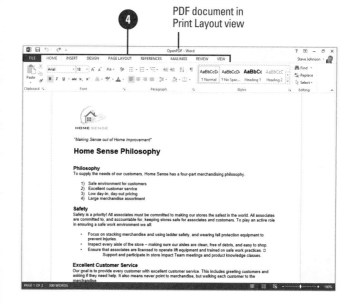

Setting Up the Page

Every document you produce and print might need a different page setup. You can achieve the look you want by printing on a standard paper size (such as letter, legal, or envelope), international standard paper sizes, or any custom size that your printer accepts. The default setting is 8.5 x 11 inches, the most common letter and copy size. You can also print several pages on one sheet. You can also select the page orientation (portrait or landscape) that best fits the entire document or any section. **Portrait** orients the page vertically (taller than it is wide) and **landscape** orients the page horizontally (wider than it is tall).

Set the Page Orientation and Size Quickly

1. Click the **Page Layout** tab.

2. To quickly change the page orientation, click the **Orientation** button, and then click **Landscape** or **Portrait**.

3. To quickly change the page size, click the **Size** button, and then click the size you want.

Set Custom Page Size Options

1. Click the **Page Layout** tab.

2. Click the **Page Size** Dialog Box Launcher, or click the **Size** button, and then click **More Paper Sizes.**

3. Click the **Paper** tab.

4. Click the **Paper Size** list arrow, and then select the paper size you want, or specify a custom size.

5. Select the paper source for the first page and other pages.

6. Click the **Apply To** list arrow, and then click **This Section, This Point Forward**, or **Whole Document**.

7. Verify your selections in the Preview box.

8. To make your changes the default settings for all new documents, click **Set As Default**, and then click **Yes**.

9. Click **OK**.

Moving and Resizing Document Windows

Every Office program and document opens inside a **window**, which contains a title bar, Ribbon, and work area to create and edit your data. Most often, you'll probably fill the entire screen with one window. But when you want to move or copy information between programs or documents or use two monitors, it's easier to display several windows at once, where one document appears in one window (**New!**). You can arrange two or more windows on the screen at the same time. However, you must make the window active to work in it. You can also click the document buttons on the taskbar to switch between open documents.

Resize and Move a Window

◆ **Maximize button**. Click to make a window fill the entire screen.

◆ **Restore Down button**. Click to reduce a maximized window to a reduced size.

◆ **Minimize button**. Click to shrink a window to a taskbar button. To restore the window to its previous size, click the taskbar button.

◆ **Close button**. Click to shut a window.

Restore Down button

Minimize button

Close button

Maximize button

Resize and Move a Window Using a Mouse

① If the window is maximized, click the **Restore Down** button.

② Use the following methods:

◆ **Move**. Move the mouse over the title bar.

◆ **Resize**. Move the mouse over one of the borders of the window until the mouse pointer changes into a two-headed arrow. The directions of the arrowheads show you the directions in which you can resize the window.

③ Drag to move or resize the window.

Arrange or Switch Between Windows

1. Open the documents you want to arrange or switch between.

2. Click the **View** tab.

3. In the Window group, perform any of the following:

   ◆ Click **Switch Windows**, and then click the document name you want.

   ◆ Click **Arrange All**, click an arrange window option (Tiled, Horizontal, Vertical, or Cascade), and then click OK.

   ◆ Click **New Window** to open a new window containing a view of the current document.

Working with Multiple Documents

If you're working on two similar documents and want to do a quick compare to see if they are the same, you can use the View Side By Side command on the View tab. When you view two documents side by side, you can enable synchronous scrolling to scroll both documents together at the same time. When you're done, you can reset the window position of the documents being compared side by side so they share the screen equally. If you want to work on two different parts of a document, you can use the Split button to create two separate scrolling sections for the same document.

Compare Windows Side By Side

1. Open the documents you want to compare side by side.

2. Click the **View** tab.

3. In the Window group, perform any of the following:

   - Click the **View Side By Side** button to compare two documents vertically.

     - To compare the documents horizontally, click the **Arrange All** button.

   - Click the **Synchronous Scrolling** button to synchronize the scrolling of two documents so that they scroll together. To enable this feature turn on View Side By Side.

   - Click the **Reset Window Position** button to reset the window position of the documents being compared side-by-side so that they share the screen equally. To enable this feature turn on View Side By Side.

4. When you're done, click the **View Side By Side** button to return to the full screen.

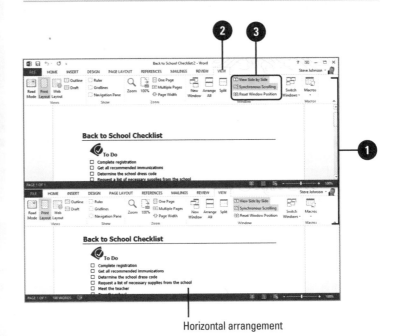

Horizontal arrangement

Split Windows

1. Open the documents you want to split.

2. Click the **View** tab.

3. Click the **Split** button.

4. Click to split the document where you want.

5. Scroll each part of the window separately.

6. To remove the split, click the **Remove Split** button or double-click the divider line.

Did You Know?

You can resize a split window. Drag the divider line to the new location you want.

6 Toggles to Split button

Navigating a Document

If you have a long document with headings or you're searching for key-words, you can use the Navigation pane to find your way around it. In the Navigation pane, you can view thumbnails for all pages, search for key phrases, quickly move between headings, promote or demote headings, insert new headings, browse headings from a co-author, rearrange heading content, and collapse/ expand heading levels of an outline. You can perform any of these tasks in the Navigation panel by using the following tabs: Headings, Pages, and Results.

Navigate a Document

1. Click the **View** tab.

2. Click the **Navigation Pane** check box.

   ◆ You can also click the **Page** button on the Status bar to open/close the Navigation pane.

3. To work with headings, click the **Headings** tab, and then do any of the following:

   ◆ **Display a Heading.** Click the heading name, or click the **Previous Heading** or **Next Heading** button.

   ◆ **Collapse/Expand a Heading.** Click the arrow next to the heading name.

   ◆ **Move a Heading.** Drag the heading name in the pane. The heading and its content move.

   ◆ **Create a Heading.** Right-click a heading name, and then click **New Heading Before** or **New Heading After**.

   ◆ **Promote or Demote a Heading.** Right-click a heading name, and then click **Promote** or **Demote**.

4. To view page thumbnails, click the **Pages** tab.

   ◆ **Display a Page.** Click the page thumbnail.

5. To exit, click the **Close** button on the pane.

Page button on the Status bar

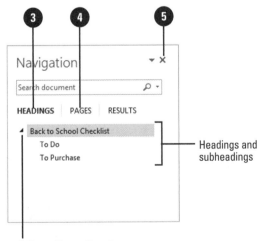

Collapse/Expand headings

Headings and subheadings

Search a Document

1. Click the **View** tab.

2. Click the **Navigation Pane** check box.

   ◆ You can also click the **Page** button on the Status bar to open/close the Navigation pane.

3. To set search options, click the Search Options button arrow, and then select an option.

   ◆ **Options.** Opens the Find Options dialog box.

   ◆ **Advanced Find.** Opens the Find and Replace dialog box with the Find tab.

   ◆ **Replace.** Opens the Find and Replace dialog box with the Replace tab.

   ◆ **Go To.** Opens the Find and Replace dialog box with the Go To tab.

   ◆ **Find.** Click Graphics, Tables, Equations, Footnotes/Endnotes, or Comments to find them.

4. Click in the Search document box, and then type keywords.

   The search criteria that matches the content appears highlighted in the document.

5. Click the **Results** tab.

6. To navigate to a search element, click the item in the pane.

   ◆ **Next or Previous.** Click the **Next** or **Previous** button arrow to go between the search results.

7. To exit, click the **Close** button on the pane.

Page button on the Status bar

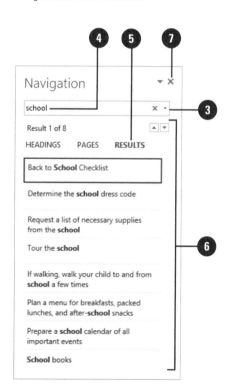

Selecting Text

The first step in working with text is to highlight, or **select**, the text you want. Once you've selected it, you can copy, move, format, and delete words, sentences, and paragraphs. When you finish with or decide not to use a selection, you can click anywhere in the document to **deselect** the text. If you need to select all or similar text or objects in a document, you can use the Select button on the Home tab.

Select Text

1. Position the pointer in the word, paragraph, line, or part of the document you want to select.

2. Choose the method that accomplishes the selection you want to complete in the easiest way.

   Refer to the table for methods to select text.

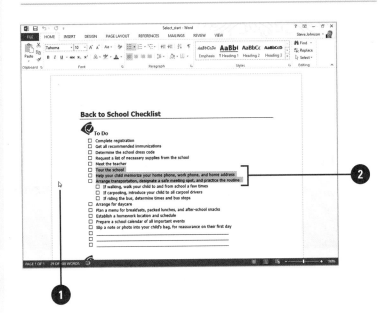

Did You Know?

AutoComplete finishes your words.
As you enter common text, such as your name, months, today's date, and common salutations and closings, Word provides the rest of the text in a ScreenTip. Press Enter to have Word complete your words.

Selecting Text

To select	Do this
A single word	Double-click the word.
A single paragraph	Triple-click a word within the paragraph.
A single line	Click in the left margin next to the line.
Any part of a document	Click at the beginning of the text you want to highlight, and then drag to the end of the section you want to highlight.
A large selection	Click at the beginning of the text you want to highlight, and then press and hold Shift while you click at the end of the text that you want to highlight.
The entire document	Triple-click in the left margin.
An outline heading or subheading in Outline view	Click the bullet, plus sign, or minus sign.

Select Text and Other Items

1. Click the **Home** tab.

2. Click the **Select** button.

3. Select any of the following commands:

   ◆ **Select All.** Click to select everything in a document.

   ◆ **Select Objects.** Click to turn off object selection in a document. Click to select objects in the document. When you're done, click Select Objects again on the menu to turn it off.

   ◆ **Select All Text With Similar Formatting (No Data).** Click to select all text with similar formatting to the current selection or insertion point.

   ◆ **Selection Pane.** Click to open the Selection pane, where you can select, reorder, show, or hide objects in a document. Click Selection Pane again on the menu or the Close button to close the pane.

Selection pane

Editing Text

Before you can edit text, you need to highlight, or select, the text you want to modify. Then you can delete, replace, move (cut), or copy text within one document or between documents even if they're from different programs. In either case, the steps are the same. Text you cut or copy is temporarily stored in the Office Clipboard. When you paste the text, the Paste Options button appears below it. When you click the button, a menu appears with options to specify how Office pastes the information in the document. To copy or move data without using the Clipboard, you can use a technique called **drag-and-drop**. Drag-and-drop makes it easy to copy or move text short distances.

Select and Edit Text

① Move the I-beam pointer to the left or right of the text you want to select.

② Drag the pointer to highlight the text, or click in the document to place the insertion point where you want to make a change.

> **TIMESAVER** *Double-click a word to select it; triple-click a paragraph to select it.*

③ Perform one of the following editing commands:

◆ To replace text, type your text.

◆ To delete text, press the Backspace key or the Delete key.

Correct Typing Errors Using the Keyboard

To Delete	Press
One character at a time to the left of the insertion point	Backspace
One word at a time to the left of the insertion point	Ctrl+Backspace
One character at a time to the right of the insertion point	Delete
One word at a time to the right of the insertion point	Ctrl+Delete
Selected text	Backspace or Delete

Insert and Delete Text

1. Click in the document to place the insertion point where you want to make the change.

   ◆ To insert text, type your text.

   ◆ To delete text, press the Backspace key or the Delete key.

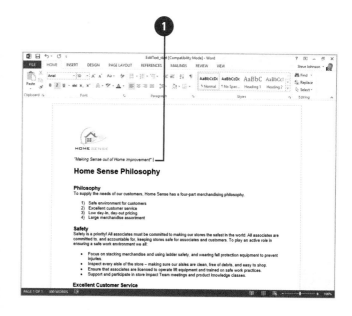

Copy or Move Text Using Drag-and-Drop

1. If you want to drag text between programs or documents, display both windows.

2. Select the text you want to move or copy.

   TIMESAVER *You can also select objects and other elements.*

3. Point to the selected text, and then click and hold the mouse button.

   If you want to copy the text, also press and hold Ctrl. A plus sign (+) appears in the pointer box, indicating that you are dragging a copy of the selected text.

4. Drag the selection to the new location, and then release the mouse button and keyboard.

5. Click anywhere in the document to deselect the text.

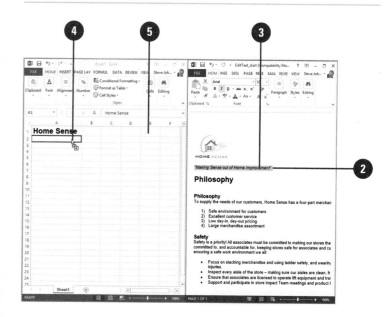

Copying and Moving Text

You can **copy** and **move** text or data from one location to another on any Office document. When you copy data, a duplicate of the selected information is placed on the Clipboard. When you move text, the selected information is removed and placed on the Clipboard. To complete the copy or move, you **paste** the data stored on the Clipboard in another location. The live preview on the Paste Options menu allows you to view your paste results before you actually paste it. You can use the Office Clipboard to store multiple pieces of information from several different sources in one storage area shared by all Office programs. You can paste these pieces of information into any Office program, either individually or all at once. With Paste Special, you can gain additional control over what you want to paste.

Copy or Move Using the Clipboard

1. Select the element you want to copy.

2. Click the **Home** tab.

3. Click the **Copy** or **Cut** button.

4. Click the location where you want to paste the data.

5. Click the **Paste** button or click the **Paste** button arrow, point to an option to display a live preview of the paste, and then click to paste the item.

   When you point to a paste option for the live preview, use the ScreenTip to determine the option.

   The data remains on the Clipboard, available for further pasting, until you replace it with another selection.

   If you don't want to paste this selection anywhere else, press Esc to remove the marquee.

6. If you want to change the way the data pastes into the document, click the **Paste Options** button, point to an option for the live preview, and then select the option you want.

Copy and Paste Information to the Clipboard Task Pane

1. Click the **Home** tab.

2. Click the **Clipboard** Dialog Box Launcher.

3. Select the data you want to copy.

4. Click the **Copy** button.

   The text or data is copied on the Clipboard task pane.

5. Click the location where you want to paste data.

6. Click the Clipboard item you want to paste, or point to the item, click the list arrow, and then click **Paste**.

   ◆ To change Office Clipboard options, click the **Options** button on the pane.

7. Click the **Close** button in the task pane.

Paste Information with Special Results

1. Select the text or data that you want to copy.

2. Click the **Home** tab.

3. Click the **Copy** button.

4. Click the location where you want to paste the text or data.

5. Click the **Paste** button, and then click **Paste Special**.

6. Click the option buttons with the paste results you want.

7. Click **OK**.

Finding and Replacing Text

The Find and Replace commands make it easy to locate or replace specific text in a document. For example, you might want to find each figure reference in a long report to verify that the proper graphic appears. When you use the Find command, Word highlights the word or phrases that it finds in the document using the Navigation pane, which you can click to display them. You can use the Advanced Find to set more options in the Find and Replace dialog box. For example, you can use the More button to select find options, such as Match case, Format, or Special, or use the Reading Highlight button to specify whether to highlight the current find or all the items found in the document.

Find Text

1. Click at the beginning of the document.

2. Click the **Home** tab.

3. To use the Navigation pane, click the **Find** button. Click an item in the Navigation pane to highlight and go to the item.

4. To use the Find and Replace dialog box, click the **Find** button arrow, and then click **Advanced Find**.

5. Type the text you want to find.

6. To highlight all items found, click the **Reading Highlight** button, and then click **Highlight All**.

7. To specify where you want to find, click the **Find in** button, and then click **Current Selection** or **Main Document**.

8. Click **Find Next** until the text you want to locate is highlighted.

   You can click **Find Next** repeatedly to locate each instance of the content.

9. To find all places with the contents you want, click **Find All**.

10. If a message box opens when you reach the end of the document, click **OK**.

11. Click **Close** or **Cancel**.

Results tab in the Navigation pane

Highlighted search results

Click to display more options

Replace Text

1. Click at the beginning of the Office document.

2. Click the **Home** tab.

3. Click the **Replace** button.

4. Type the text you want to search for.

5. Type the text you want to substitute.

6. Click **Find Next** to begin the search, and then select the next instance of the search text.

7. Click **Replace** to substitute the replacement text, or click **Replace All** to substitute text throughout the entire document.

   You can click **Find Next** to locate the next instance of the content without making a replacement.

8. If a message box appears when you reach the end of the document, click **OK**.

9. Click **Close** or **Cancel**.

Did You Know?

You can go to different locations in Word. Click the Home tab, click the Find button arrow, click Go To, select the Go To What option you want, specify a location, and then click Next or Previous. When you're done, click Close.

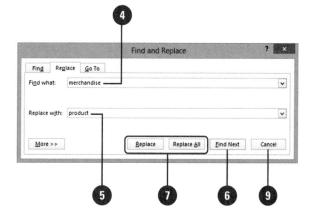

Inserting Hyphens

If a word doesn't fit at the end of a line, you can set hyphenation options to hyphenate the word to display partly on one line and partly on the next line, or move the word to the beginning of the next line. You can set options to automatically or manually hyphenate words in a document, and to specify the maximum amount of space allowed between a word and the right margin without hyphenating the word. When you manually hyphenate a document, Word searches the text for words to hyphenate and asks if you want to insert a hyphen in the text. You can also manually insert an optional or nonbreaking hyphen. An **optional hyphen** is a hyphen that you specify where you want a word to break if it falls at the end of a line. A **nonbreaking hyphen** prevents a hyphenated word from breaking if it falls at the end of a line.

Set Hyphenation Options

1. Click the **Page Layout** tab.

2. To manually hyphenate part of a document, select the text you want to hyphenate first.

3. Click the **Hyphenation** button, and then click a hyphenation option:

   ◆ **None.** Removes automatic hyphens and moves words that break on a line to the next line.

   ◆ **Automatic.** Inserts a hyphen in a word as needed.

   ◆ **Manual.** Word searches for text to hyphenate and asks if you want to insert a hyphen.

Did You Know?

You can insert an optional or non-breaking hyphen. Click where you want to insert the hyphen. For an optional hyphen, press Ctrl+Hyphen. For an nonbreaking hyphen, press Ctrl+Shift+Hyphen.

Customize Hyphenation

① Click the **Page Layout** tab.

② Click the **Hyphenation** button, and then click **Hyphenation Options**.

③ In the Hyphenation zone box, specify the maximum amount of space between the word and the right margin you want.

④ Specify the limit for hyphens on consecutive lines you want.

⑤ Select or clear any of the following check boxes:

◆ **Automatically hyphenate document.** Automatically hyphenates the document.

◆ **Hyphenate words with CAPS.** Hyphenates words in a document with capitals.

⑥ Click **OK**.

Did You Know?

You can remove manual hyphens. Click the Home tab, click Replace, click More if necessary, click Special, and then click Optional Hyphen to remove manual hyphens or Nonbreaking Hyphen to remove nonbreaking hyphens. Leave the Replace With box empty, and then click Replace All.

Inserting Information the Smart Way

Actions, a replacement for smart tags, help you integrate actions typically performed in other programs directly in Word. For example, you can insert a financial symbol to get a stock quote, add a person's name and address in a document to the contacts list in Microsoft Outlook, or copy and paste information with added control. Word analyzes what you type and recognizes certain types that it marks with actions. The types of actions you can take depend on the type of data with the action. To use an action, you right-click an item to view any custom actions associated with it.

Change Options for Actions

1. Click the **File** tab, and then click **Options**.

2. In the left pane, click **Proofing**, and then click **AutoCorrect Options**.

3. Click the **Actions** tab.

4. Select the **Enable additional actions in the right-click menu** check box.

5. Select the check boxes with the actions you want.

6. To get properties about an action, select the action, and then click **Properties**.

7. To add more actions, click **More Actions**, and then follow the online instructions.

8. Click **OK**.

9. Click **OK** again.

Online resources for Actions

Insert Information Using an Action

1. Click an item, such as text, where you want to insert an action.

2. Type the information needed for the action, such as the date, a recognized financial symbol in capital letters, or a person's name from you contacts list, and then press Spacebar.

3. Right-click the item, and then point to **Additional Actions** (name varies depending on item).

4. Click the action option you want; options vary depending on the action. For example, click Send mail or Schedule a Meeting.

Did You Know?

You can remove an action from text or item. Select text or item, and then press Delete to remove it.

Outlook email meeting invitation

Correcting Text Automatically

Office's **AutoCorrect** feature automatically corrects common capitalization and spelling errors as you type. AutoCorrect comes with hundreds of text and symbol entries you can edit or remove. You can add words and phrases to the AutoCorrect dictionary that you misspell, or add often-typed words and save time by just typing their initials. You can use AutoCorrect to quickly insert symbols. For example, you can type (c) to insert ©. Use the AutoCorrect Exceptions dialog box to control how Word handles capital letters. If you use math symbols in your work, you can use Math AutoCorrect to make it easier to insert them. It works just like AutoCorrect. When you point to a word that AutoCorrect changed, a small blue box appears under the first letter. When you point to the small blue box, the AutoCorrect Options button appears, which gives you control over whether you want the text to be corrected, or change AutoCorrect settings.

Set AutoCorrect Options

1. Click the **File** tab, and then click **Options**.

2. Click **Proofing**, and then click **AutoCorrect Options**.

3. Click the **AutoCorrect** tab.

4. Select the **Show AutoCorrect Options buttons** check box to display the button to change AutoCorrect options.

5. Select the **Replace text as you type** check box.

6. Select the capitalization and correction check boxes you want.

7. To change AutoCorrect exceptions, click **Exceptions**, click the **First Letter** or **INitial CAps** tab, make the changes you want, and then click **OK**.

8. To add an AutoCorrect entry, type incorrect text, type the replace with text, and then click **Add**.

9. To use Math AutoCorrect, click the **Math AutoCorrect** tab, and then select the **Use Math AutoCorrect rules outside of math regions** check box.

10. Click **OK**, and then click **OK** again.

Add or Edit an AutoCorrect Entry

① Click the **File** tab, and then click **Options**.

② Click **Proofing**, and then click **AutoCorrect Options**.

③ Click the **AutoCorrect** tab.

④ Do one of the following:

◆ **Add.** Type a misspelled word or an abbreviation.

◆ **Edit.** Select the one you want to change.

⑤ Type the replacement entry.

⑥ Click **Add** or **Replace**. If necessary, click **Yes** to redefine entry.

⑦ Click **OK**, and then click **OK** again.

Replace Text as You Type

◆ To correct capitalization or spelling errors automatically, continue typing until AutoCorrect makes the required correction.

Point to the small blue box under the corrected text, and then click the AutoCorrect Options button list arrow to view your options. Click an option, or click a blank area of the document to deselect the AutoCorrect Options menu.

◆ To create a bulleted or numbered list, type 1. or * (for a bullet), press Tab or Spacebar, type any text, and then press Enter. AutoCorrect inserts the next number or bullet. To end the list, press Backspace to erase the extra number or bullet.

Examples of AutoCorrect Changes

Type of Correction	If You Type	AutoCorrect Inserts
Capitalization	cAP LOCK	Cap Lock
Capitalization	TWo INitial CAps	Two Initial Caps
Capitalization	thursday	Thursday
Common typos	can;t	can't
Common typos	windoes	windows
Superscript ordinals	2nd	2nd
Stacked fractions	1/2	½
Smart quotes	" "	" "
Em dashes	Madison--a small city in Wisconsin--is a nice place to live.	Madison—a small city in Wisconsin— is a nice place to live.
Symbols	(c)	©
Symbols	(r)	®

Undoing and Redoing an Action

You may realize you've made a mistake shortly after completing an action. The Undo feature lets you "take back" one or more previous actions, including text you typed, edits you made, or commands you selected. For example, if you were to enter a title, and then decide you don't like it, you can undo it instead of selecting the text and deleting it. If you decide the text you deleted was alright, you can use the Redo feature to restore it or the Repeat feature to repeat the last action

Undo an Action

1. Click the **Undo** button on the Quick Access Toolbar to undo the last action you completed.

2. Click the **Undo** button arrow on the Quick Access Toolbar to see recent actions that can be undone.

3. Click an action. Word reverses the selected action and all actions above it.

Undo button

Redo or Repeat an Action

1. Click the **Redo** button on the Quick Access Toolbar to restore your last undone action or click the **Repeat** button on the Quick Access Toolbar to repeat the last action.

   TROUBLE? *If the Redo button is not available on the Quick Access Toolbar, click the Customize Quick Access Toolbar list arrow, and then click Redo.*

Redo button   Repeat button

Formatting Documents

Introduction

Once you type a document and get the content how you want it, the finishing touches can sometimes be the most important. An eye catching document will draw the reader in, while a boring font without a lot of extra details will draw the reader away from all your hard work. To create that interest, Microsoft Word can help you change your document for a fresh look. One of the first elements you can change is your font attributes. Applying bold, underline, or italics when appropriate, can emphasize text. You might find that having different font sizes in your document to denote various topics will also enhance your document.

You can change the **kerning**—the amount of space between each individual character, for a special effect on a title or other parts of text. You can also apply a dropped capital letter to introduce a body of text, add a shading or border onto your document.

Word has various tools to help you format your document. You can search and replace formatting effects, display rulers, change a paragraph alignment, set paragraph tabs and indents, and change your line spacing. There are times when typing a paragraph will not do your text justice. Creating a bulleted or numbered list might better show your information. To further enhance the appearance of the text in a paragraph, you can quickly add a border and shading to selected text. If you have confidential information in a document or text that you don't want others to see, you can use a formatting option to hide the text.

What You'll Do

Format Text

Format Text for Emphasis

Select Text with Similar Formatting

Set Formatting Options

Find and Replace Formatting

Find and Replace Custom Formatting

Change Paragraph Alignment

Change Line Spacing

Change Character Spacing

Display Rulers

Set Paragraph Tabs

Set Paragraph Indents

Create Bulleted and Numbered Lists

Apply Borders and Shading

Hide Text

Formatting Text

A **font** is a collection of alphanumeric characters that share the same typeface, or design, and have similar characteristics. You can format text and numbers with font attributes—such as bolding, italics, or underlining—to enhance data to catch the reader's attention. The main formats you apply to text are available on the Home tab in the Font group or in the Font dialog box. Some of the formats available include strikethrough, subscript, superscript, and underline style and color. When you point to selected text, Office displays the Mini-Toolbar above it. The **Mini-Toolbar** provides easy access to common formatting toolbar buttons, such as font, font size, increase and decrease font size, bold, italic, font color, increase and decrease list level, and styles (**New!**). If you don't want to display the Mini-Toolbar, you can use Word Options to turn it off.

Format Text Quickly

1. Select the text you want to format.

2. Click the **Home** tab.

3. To change fonts, click the **Font** list arrow on the Ribbon or Mini-Toolbar, and then point for a live preview, or click the font you want, either a theme font or any available fonts.

   The font name appears in the font style.

   To change the font size, click one or more of the font size buttons on the Ribbon or Mini-Toolbar:

   ◆ Click the **Font Size** list arrow, and then click the font size you want.

   ◆ Click the **Increase Font Size** button or **Decrease Font Size** button.

   To apply other formatting, click one or more of the formatting buttons on the Ribbon or Mini-Toolbar: **Bold**, **Italic**, **Underline**, **Shadow**, **Strikethrough**, or **Font Color**.

   ◆ To select an underline style, click the **Underline** button arrow, and then select a style or color.

Mini-Toolbar

Format Text Using the Font Dialog Box

1. Select the text you want to format.

2. Click the **Home** tab.

3. Click the **Font** Dialog Box Launcher.

   The Font dialog box opens, displaying the Font tab.

4. Select the font, font style, and font size you want.

5. If you want, click the **Font Color** list arrow, and then click a color.

6. If you want, click the **Underline** list arrow, click a style, click **Underline Color** list arrow, and then click a color.

7. Click **OK**.

Did You Know?

You can tell the difference between a TrueType and printer font. A TrueType (outline) font is a font that uses special software capabilities to print exactly what is seen on the screen. A printer (screen) font is a font that comes only in specified sizes. If you are creating a document for publication, you need to use printer fonts.

What is a point? The size of each font character is measured in points (a point is approximately 1/72 of an inch).

Each computer has different fonts installed. Users with whom you share files may not have all the fonts you've used in a document installed on their computers.

Preview box

Formatting Text for Emphasis

If you want to add emphasis or style to text in a document, you can apply text formatting. In addition to the standard formatting options — **Bold**, *Italic*, <u>Underline</u>, etc. — Word provides additional text formatting, including Color, Gradient, Strikethrough, Superscript, Subscript, and Highlight, as well as enhanced text effects, including presets, Outline, Shadow, Reflection, Glow, Number Styles (**New!**), Ligatures (**New!**) (letter spacing), and Stylistic Sets (**New!**). In the Font dialog box, you can apply even more effects, including 3-D formatting. To help you format sentences and change capitalization, you can change text case.

Apply Formatting Text Effects

1. Select the text you want to format.

2. Click the **Home** tab.

3. Click the formatting (**Font, Font Style, Size, Bold, Italic, Underline** (select a style and color), **Strikethrough, Superscript, Subscript,** or **Font Color** (select a color or a Gradient) you want.

4. To add a visual effect to text, click the **Text Effect** button, and then click a preset effect or an option:

   - Outline
   - Shadow
   - Reflection
   - Glow
   - Number Styles (**New!**)
   - Ligatures (**New!**)
   - Stylistic Sets (**New!**)

5. To change text case, click the **Case** button, and then click the option you want:

   - Sentence case.
   - lowercase
   - UPPERCASE
   - Capitalize Each Word
   - tOGGLEcASE

6. To highlight text, click the **Highlight** button arrow, and then click the color you want.

   - Add highlight. Click a color.
   - Remove highlight. Click **No Color**.

Applied style

All caps and highlighted text

Apply Other Formatting Effects to Text

① Select the text you want to format.

② Click the **Home** tab.

③ Click the **Font Dialog Box Launcher**.

④ Click the formatting (**Font, Font style, Size, Font color, Underline style,** and **Underline color**) you want.

⑤ Click to select the effects (**Strikethrough, Double strikethrough, Superscript, Subscript, Small caps, All caps,** and **Hidden**) you want.

⑥ To custom text effects, such as a text fill or outline with a solid or gradient, shadow, reflection, glow and soft edges, or 3-D format, click **Text Effects**, click the **Text Fill & Outline (New!)** or **Text Effects (New!)** button, expand options as needed, specify the options you want, and then click **OK**.

⑦ Check the results in the Preview box.

⑧ To make the new formatting options the default for all new Word documents, click **Set As Default**, and then click **Yes**.

⑨ Click **OK**.

Did You Know?

You can quickly clear formatting. Select the text to which you want to clear formatting, click the Home tab, and then click the Clear Formatting button.

Text effects

Text effect   Strikethrough text   All caps and highlighted text

Selecting Text with Similar Formatting

A quick way to select text with similar formatting is to use the Select Text with Similar Formatting command. After you select the text with the formatting you want to find, click the Select button on the Home tab, and then choose the Select Text with Similar Formatting command. Word highlights all the text with similar formatting in the document. With the text selected, you can change the text formatting.

Select Similar Text Formatting

1. Select the text you want to find.

2. Click the **Home** tab.

3. Click the **Select** button, and then click **Select Text with Similar Formatting**.

Did You Know?

You can quickly clear formatting. Select the text to which you want to clear formatting, click the Home tab, and then click the Clear Formatting button.

See Also

See "Revealing Formatting Styles" on page 96 for more information on using the Select Text With Similar Formatting command.

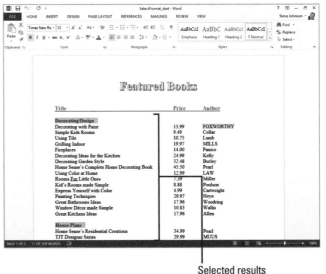

Selected results

Setting Formatting Options

When you work within a document, you can set options to customize the way formatting appears in Word. In Word Options on the Display pane, you can set options to show or hide formatting marks. Formatting marks help you see characters that are not visible, such as tabs, spaces, paragraph marks, and hidden text. On the Advanced pane, you can set options to keep track of formatting (in the Style Inspector and direct formatting) and mark formatting inconsistencies, so you can create consistently formatted documents. When you cut, copy, and paste text and objects within the same document, between documents, or other programs, you can set options to keep source formatting or merge formatting with the current selection.

Change Formatting Options

1. Click the **File** tab, and then click **Options**.

2. In the left pane, click **Display**.

3. Select or clear any of the check boxes to display or hide the formatting marks you want.

   ◆ **Tab characters**, **Spaces**, **Paragraph marks**, **Hidden text**, **Optional hyphens**, or **Object anchors**. (Default off).

   ◆ **Show all formatting marks.** (Default off).

4. In the left pane, click **Advanced**.

5. Select or clear any of the check boxes.

   ◆ **Keep track of formatting.** (Default off).

   ◆ **Mark formatting inconsistencies.** (Default off).

6. Select formatting options for when you cut, copy, and paste text and objects within the same document, between documents, or other programs.

   ◆ **Keep Source Formatting (Default).**

   ◆ **Merge Formatting.**

7. Click **OK**.

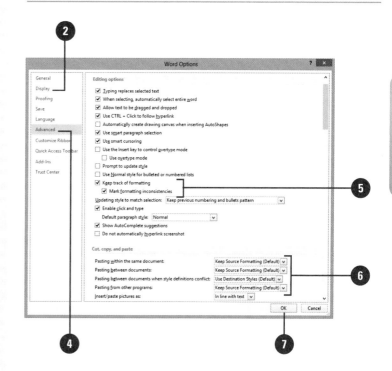

Finding and Replacing Formatting

Suddenly you realize all the bold text in your report would be easier to read in italics. Do you spend time making these changes one by one? No. The Find and Replace feature locates the formatting and instantly substitutes new formatting. If your search for a formatting change is an easy one, click Less in the Find and Replace dialog box to decrease the size of the dialog box. If your search is a more complex one, click More to display additional options. With the Match Case option, you can specify exact capitalization. The Reading Highlight button highlights items found to make them easier to read. The Go To tab quickly moves you to a place or item in your document. You can search for an item, such as bookmark or comment, or location, such as a page or section.

Find Formatting

1. Click the **Home** tab.

2. Click the **Find** button arrow, click **Advanced Find**, and then click **More** to expand the dialog box.

3. To clear any previous settings, click **No Formatting**.

4. If you want to locate formatted text, type the word or words.

5. Click **Format**, and then click the formatting you want to find.

6. To highlight located items, click **Reading Highlight**, and then click **Highlight All**.

7. Click **Find Next** to select the next instance of the formatted text.

8. Click **OK** to confirm Word finished the search.

9. Click **Close** or **Cancel**.

Current find settings

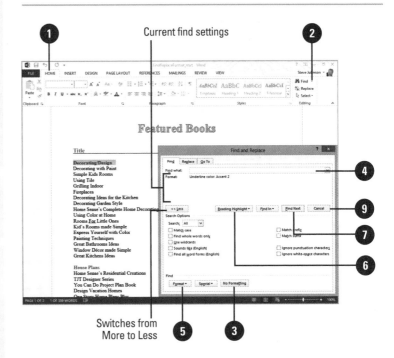

Switches from More to Less

Did You Know?

You can find an item or location.
Click the Home tab, click the Find button arrow, click Go To, click an item to find, enter an item number or name, click Next, Previous, or Go To to locate the item, and then click Close.

Replace Formatting

① Click the **Home** tab.

② Click the **Replace** button, and then click **More** to expand the dialog box.

③ If you want to locate formatted text, type the word or words.

④ Click **Format**, and then click the formatting you want to find. When you're done, click **OK**.

⑤ Press Tab, and then type any text you want to substitute.

⑥ Click **Format**, and then click the formatting you want to substitute. When you're done, click **OK**.

⑦ To substitute every instance of the formatting, click **Replace All**.

To substitute the formatting one instance at a time, click **Find Next**, and then click **Replace**.

If you want to cancel the replace, click **Cancel**.

⑧ If necessary, click **Yes** to search from the beginning of the document.

⑨ Click **OK** to confirm Word finished searching.

⑩ Click **Close** or **Cancel**.

Did You Know?

You can find and replace special characters and document elements.
In Word, you can search for and replace special characters (for example, an em dash) and document elements (for example, a tab character). Click More in the Find And Replace dialog box, click Special, and then click the item you want from the menu.

Finding and Replacing Custom Formatting

If your search for formatting involves a complex search for a specific type of formatted text, click More in the Find and Replace dialog box to increase the size of the dialog box and display additional options. The expanded Find and Replace dialog box provides options to find exact capitalization, find whole words only, use wildcards, and locate words that sound like English or different forms of English words. With the Special button, you can find and replace special characters and elements, such as graphics, tabs, fields, white space, and page breaks.

Find or Replace Special Formatting

1. Click the **Home** tab.

2. Click the **Find** button arrow, and then click **Advanced Find** or click the **Replace** button.

3. To clear any previous settings, click **No Formatting**.

4. If you want to locate formatted text, type the word or words you want to find and/or replace.

5. Click **More** to expand the dialog box.

6. Click **Special**, and then click the specialized formatting item you want to find.

7. Click **Find Next** to select the next instance of the formatted text.

8. To substitute every instance of the formatting, click **Replace All**.

   To substitute the formatting one instance at a time, click **Find Next**, and then click **Replace**.

9. Click **OK** to confirm Word finished the search.

10. Click **Close** or **Cancel**.

Switches from More to Less

Use Find and Replace Options

1. Click the **Home** tab.

2. Click the **Find** button arrow, and then click **Advanced Find** or click the **Replace** button.

3. To clear any previous formatting and settings, click **No Formatting**.

4. If you want to locate formatted text, type the word or words you want to find and/or replace.

5. Click **More**, and then select or clear the options you want:

   ◆ **Search.** Select a search direction: All, Down, or Up.

   ◆ **Match Case.** Select to find exact capitalization.

   ◆ **Find whole words only.** Select to find words with space on either side.

   ◆ **Use wildcards.** Select to use wildcards, such as asterisk (*) or question mark (?).

   ◆ **Sounds like (English).** Select to find English sounding words.

   ◆ **Find all word forms (English).** Select to find all English forms of a word.

   ◆ **Match prefix** or **Match suffix.** Select to find text at the beginning or end of a word.

   ◆ **Ignore punctuation characters** or **Ignore white-space characters.** Select to ignore punctuation (periods, commas, etc.) or white space characters.

6. Click **Find Next** to select the next instance of the formatted text, or click **Replace**

7. Click **OK** to confirm Word finished the search.

8. Click **Close** or **Cancel**.

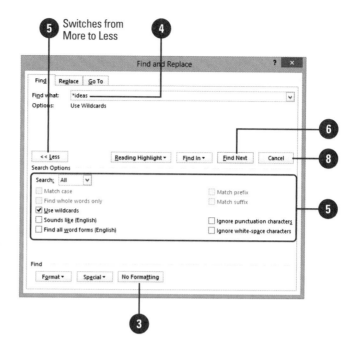

Switches from More to Less

For Your Information

Using Wildcards

A wildcard allows you to search for variable text. For example, you can use the asterisk (*) wildcard to search for a string of characters ("s*d" finds "sad" and "started"), or use the question mark (?) wildcard to search for any single character (s?t finds "sat" and "set"). To search for a character that's defined as a wildcard, type a backslash (\) before the character. For example, type \? to find a question mark.

Changing Paragraph Alignment

Text starts out positioned evenly along the left margin, and uneven, or **ragged**, at the right margin. **Left-aligned text** works well for body paragraphs in most cases, but other alignments vary the look of a document and help lead the reader through the text. **Right-aligned text**, which is even along the right margin and ragged at the left margin, is good for adding a date to a letter. **Justified text** spreads text evenly between the margins, creating a clean, professional look, often used in newspapers and magazines. **Centered text** is best for titles and headings. You can use Click-And-Type to quickly center titles or set different text alignment on the same line, or you can use the alignment buttons on the Home tab to set alignment on one or more lines.

Align New Text with Click-And-Type

◆ Position the I-beam at the left, right, or center of the line where you want to insert new text.

When the I-beam shows the appropriate alignment, double-click to place the insertion point, and then type your text.

Click-And-Type Text Pointers

Pointer	Purpose
I≡	Left-aligns text
≡I	Right-aligns text
I	Centers text
I⁺≡	Creates a new line in the same paragraph
■I	Creates a text around a picture

Align Existing Text

1 Position the I-beam, or select at least one line in each paragraph to align.

2 Click the appropriate button on the Home tab.

◆ **Align Left** button

◆ **Center** button

◆ **Align Right** button

◆ **Justify** button

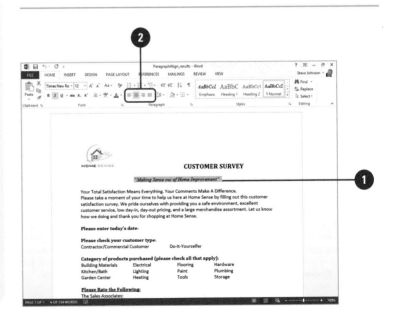

Changing Line Spacing

The lines in all Word documents are single-spaced by default, which is appropriate for letters and most documents. But you can easily change your document line spacing to double or 1.5 lines to allow extra space between every line. This is useful when you want to make notes on a printed document. Sometimes, you'll want to add space above and below certain paragraphs, for headlines, or indented quotations to help set off the text.

Change Line Spacing

1. Select the text you want to change.

2. Click the **Home** tab.

3. Click the **Line Spacing** button arrow, and then click a spacing option.

   ◆ To apply a new setting, click the number you want.

   ◆ To apply the setting you last used, click the **Line Spacing** button.

   ◆ To enter precise parameters, click **Line Spacing Options**, specify the line or paragraph settings you want, and then click **OK**.

   ◆ To apply the setting you last used, click **Add Space Before Paragraph** or **Add Space After Paragraph**.

   TIMESAVER *Press Ctrl+1 for single-spacing, Ctrl+5 for 1.5 spacing, or Ctrl+2 for double-spacing.*

Line Spacing Options

Changing Character Spacing

Kerning is the amount of space between each individual character that you type. Sometimes the space between two characters is larger than others, which makes the word look uneven. You can use the Font dialog box to change the kerning setting for selected characters. Kerning works only with OpenType/TrueType or Adobe Type Manager fonts. You can expand or condense character spacing to create a special effect for a title, or re-align the position of characters to the bottom edge of the text—this is helpful for positioning the copyright or trademark symbols. In addition, you can set text formatting for OpenType/TrueType fonts that include a range of ligature settings (where two or three letters combine into a single character), number spacing and forms, and stylistic sets (added font sets in a given font). Many of these options are based on specifications from font designers.

Change Character Spacing

1. Select the text you want to format.

2. Click the **Home** tab.

3. Click the **Font Dialog Box Launcher**.

4. Click the **Advanced** tab.

5. Click the **Spacing** list arrow, click an option, and then specify a point size to expand or condense spacing by the amount specified.

6. Click the **Position** list arrow, click an option, and then specify a point size to raise or lower the text in relation to the baseline (bottom of the text).

7. Select the **Kerning for fonts** check box, and then specify a point size.

8. To make the new formatting options the default for all new Word documents, click **Set As Default**, and then click **Yes**.

9. Click **OK**.

Change OpenType Features

1 Select the text you want to format.

2 Click the **Home** tab.

3 To set quick OpenType options, click the **Text Effects** button, point to **Number Styles (New!)**, **Ligatures (New!)**, or **Stylistic Sets (New!)**, and then select an option.

4 To set advanced options, click the **Font Dialog Box Launcher**.

5 Click the **Advanced** tab.

6 Click any of the follow list arrows, and then select an option:

◆ **Ligatures.** Select **Standard Only** (current standard), **Standard and Contextual** (current standard plus font specific additions), **Historical and Discretionary** (old standard), or **All**.

◆ **Number Spacing.** Select **Default** (specified by font designer), **Proportional** (varying width spacing), or **Tabular** (same width spacing).

◆ **Number Forms.** Select **Default** (specified by font designer), **Lining** (same height, not below base-line), or **Old-Style** (flow above or below the line of text).

◆ **Stylistic Sets.** Select **Default** (specified by font designer) or a specific set number.

7 Select the **Use Contextual Alternates** check box to provide fine-tuning of letters or letter combinations based on the surrounding characters.

8 To make the new formatting options the default for all new Word documents, click **Set As Default**, and then click **Yes**.

9 Click **OK**.

Preview

Displaying Rulers

Word rulers do more than measure. The **horizontal ruler** above the document shows the length of the typing line and lets you quickly adjust left and right margins and indents, set tabs, and change column widths. The **vertical ruler** along the left edge of the document lets you adjust top and bottom margins and change table row heights. You can hide the rulers to get more room for your document. As you work with long documents, use the document map to jump to any heading in your document. Headings are in the left pane and documents in the right.

Show and Hide the Rulers

1 Click the **View** tab.

2 Select or clear the **Ruler** check box.

◆ To view the horizontal ruler, click the **Web Layout View** or **Draft View** button.

◆ To view the horizontal and vertical rulers, click the **Print Layout View** button.

Did You Know?

You can change the ruler measurements. Change the ruler to show inches, centimeters, millimeters, points, or picas. Click the File tab, click Options, click Advanced, click the Show Measurement In Units list arrow, select the measurement you want, and then click OK.

You can set your text to be hyphenated. Hyphenation prevents ugly gaps and short lines in text. Click the Page Layout tab, click the Hyphenation button, and then click None, Automatic, or Manual, or Hyphenation Options. Click Hyphenation Options to set the hyphenation zone and limit the number of consecutive hyphens (usually two), and then click OK.

Setting Paragraph Tabs

In your document, **tabs** set how text or numerical data aligns in relation to the document margins. A **tab stop** is a predefined stopping point along the document's typing line. Default tab stops are set every half-inch, but you can set multiple tabs per paragraph at any location. Choose from four text tab stops: left, right, center, and decimal (for numerical data). The bar tab inserts a vertical bar at the tab stop. You can use the Tab button on the horizontal ruler to switch between the available tabs.

Create and Clear a Tab Stop

1. Select one or more paragraphs in which you want to set a tab stop.

2. Click the **Tab** button on the horizontal ruler until it shows the type of tab stop you want.

3. Click the ruler where you want to set the tab stop.

4. If necessary, drag the tab stop to position it where you want.

    To display a numerical measurement in the ruler where the tab is placed, press and hold Alt as you drag.

5. To clear a tab stop, drag it off the ruler.

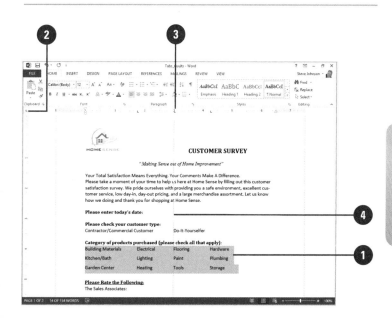

Did You Know?

You can view formatting marks. Sometimes it's hard to see the number of spaces or tabs between words. You can change the view to display formatting marks, a period for space and an arrow for tabs. Click the Home tab, and then click Show/Hide ¶ button to toggle on and off. Click the File tab, click Options, click Display, select the formatting mark check boxes you want to view, and then click OK.

Tab Stops

Tab Stop	Purpose
⌞	Aligns text to the left of the tab stop
⌟	Aligns text to the right of the tab stop
⊥	Centers text on the tab stop
⊥ᵔ	Aligns numbers on the decimal point
I	Inserts a vertical bar at the tab stop

Setting Paragraph Indents

Quickly indent lines of text to precise locations from the left or right margin with the horizontal ruler. Indent the first line of a paragraph (called a **first-line indent**) as books do to distinguish paragraphs. Indent the second and subsequent lines of a paragraph from the left margin (called a **hanging indent**) to create a properly formatted bibliography. Indent the entire paragraph any amount from the left and right margins (called **left indents** and **right indents**) to separate quoted passages.

Indent Paragraph Lines Precisely

1 Click the **View** tab, and then select the **Ruler** check box to display the Ruler.

2 Click the paragraph or select multiple paragraphs to indent:

- ◆ To change the left indent of the first line, drag the First-line Indent marker.

- ◆ To change the indent of the second and subsequent lines, drag the Hanging Indent marker.

- ◆ To change the left indent for all lines, drag the Left Indent marker.

- ◆ To change the right indent for all lines, drag the Right Indent marker.

  As you drag a marker, the dotted guideline helps you accurately position the indent. You can also press and hold Alt to see a measurement in the ruler.

Did You Know?

You can indent using the Tab key. You can indent the first line of a paragraph by clicking at the beginning of the paragraph, and then pressing Tab. You can indent the entire paragraph by selecting it, and then pressing Tab.

Hanging Indent marker

First-line Indent marker

Left Indent marker

Right Indent marker

Hanging indent

First-line indent

Current indent settings are for this paragraph

Indent a Paragraph

1 Click the paragraph, or select multiple paragraphs to indent.

2 Click the **Home** tab.

3 Click the **Increase Indent** button or **Decrease Indent** button to move the paragraph right or left one-half inch.

Did You Know?

You can add line numbers to a document or page. Click the Page Layout tab, click the Line Numbers button, and then click Continuous, Restart Each Page, Restart Each Section, Suppress for Current Paragraph, or Line Numbering Options.

Set Indentation Using the Tab Key

1 Click the **File** tab, and then click **Options**.

2 In the left pane, click **Proofing**, and then click **AutoCorrect Options**.

3 Click the **AutoFormat As You Type** tab.

4 Select the **Set left- and first-indent with tabs and backspaces** check box.

5 Click **OK**.

Creating Bulleted and Numbered Lists

The best way to draw attention to a list is to format the items with bullets or numbers. You can even create multi-level lists. For different emphasis, change any bullet or number style to one of Word's many predefined formats. For example, switch round bullets to check boxes or Roman numerals to lowercase letters. You can also insert a picture as a bullet or customize the numbering list style—including fixed-digits, such as 001, 002, etc. If you move, insert, or delete items in a numbered list, Word sequentially renumbers the list for you.

Create a Bulleted List

1. Click where you want to create a bulleted list.

2. Click the **Home** tab.

3. Click the **Bullets** button arrow, and then select a bullet style.

4. Type the first item in your list, and then press Enter.

5. Type the next item in your list, and then press Enter.

6. Click the **Bullets** button, or press Enter again to end the list.

Create a Numbered List

1. Click where you want to create a numbered list.

2. Click the **Home** tab.

3. Click the **Numbering** button arrow, and then select a numbering style.

4. Type the first item in your list, and then press Enter.

5. Type the next item in your list, and then press Enter.

6. Click the **Numbering** button, or press Enter again to end the list.

Change Bullet or Number Styles

1. Select the list, and then click the Home tab.

2. Click the **Bullets** or **Numbering** button arrow.

3. Click a predefined format, or click **Define New Bullet** or **Define New Number Format**.

4. Select the appropriate options:

   ◆ **Bullet.** Click **Symbol**, **Picture**, or **Font**, and then select the picture you want.

   ◆ **Number.** Select a numbering style, font, and format.

5. Specify the alignment and any other formatting you want.

6. Click **OK**.

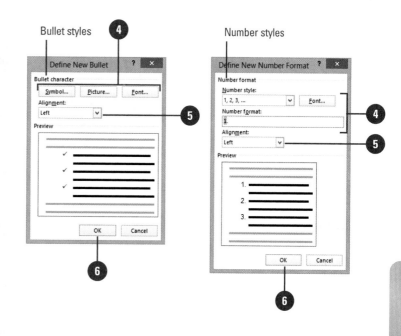

Bullet styles   Number styles

Create a Multi-Level Bulleted or Numbered List

1. Start the list as usual.

2. Press Tab to indent a line to the next level bullet or number, type the item, and then press Enter to insert the next bullet or number.

3. Press Shift+Tab to return to the previous level bullet or number.

4. To format the multi-level list, select the list, click the **Multi-Level List** button on the Home tab, and then select a format.

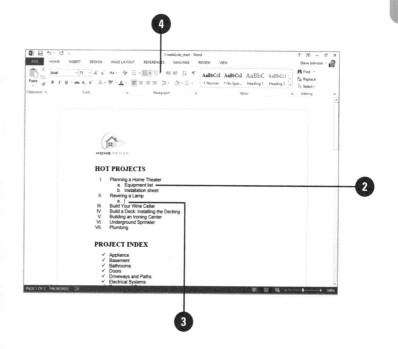

Did You Know?

You can quickly create a numbered list. Click to place the insertion point at the beginning of a line, type 1., press the Spacebar, type the first item, and then press Enter. Press Enter or Backspace to end the list.

Applying Borders and Shading

To enhance the appearance of the text in a paragraph, you can quickly add a border and shading to selected text. When you add a border, you can specify what sides you want to include or exclude. For example, you can add a border on just the top and the bottom and leave the sides open. Shading colors the background behind the selected text or paragraph. If you want to customize borders and shading by changing line style, color, and width preferences, you can make changes in the Borders and Shading dialog box.

Apply a Border

1. Select the paragraph text you want to format.

2. Click the **Home** tab.

3. Click the **Borders and Shading** button arrow, and then click to select the border commands to add or remove a border.

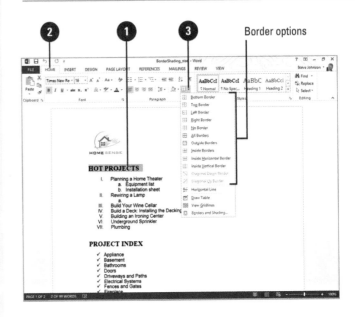

Border options

Apply Paragraph Shading

1. Select the paragraph text you want to format.

2. Click the **Home** tab.

3. Click the **Shading** button arrow, and then click to select the shading color you want to apply to the selected text.

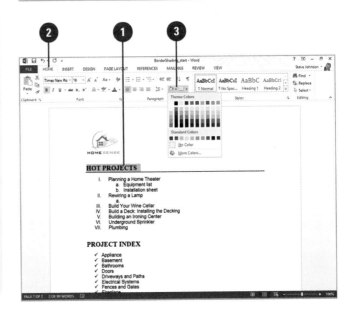

Apply Paragraph Shading and Borders

1. Select the paragraph text you want to format.

2. Click the **Home** tab.

3. Click the **Borders and Shading** button arrow, and then click **Borders and Shading**.

4. Click the **Borders** tab.

5. Click to select the type of Setting you want for your border.

6. Click to select the type of Style.

7. Apply any other options you want.

8. Look in the preview box to see the new border.

9. Click the **Shading** tab.

10. Click to select the shading fill color you want to apply to your table.

11. Apply any other options you want.

12. Look in the preview box to see the new shading color.

13. Click **OK**.

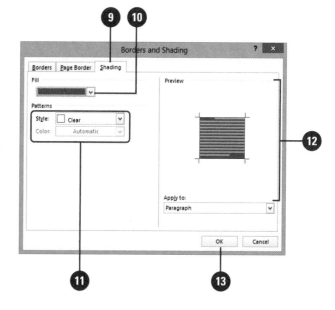

Hiding Text

If you have confidential information in a document or text that you don't want others to see, you can hide the text. When you hide text, you can't view or print the text unless you select the Hidden Text option in the Options dialog box. When you display or print hidden text, the characters appear with a dotted lined underneath. Hiding text does not protect your text from being seen, but it does conceal it from others.

Hide or Unhide Text

1. Select the text you want to hide or the hidden text.

2. Click the **Home** tab, and then click the **Font Dialog Box Launcher**.

3. Click the **Font** tab.

4. Select or clear the **Hidden** check box.

5. Click **OK**.

Display or Print Hidden Text

1. Click the **File** tab, and then click **Options**.

2. In the left pane, click **Display**.

3. Select the **Hidden text** check box.

4. Select the **Print hidden text** check box.

5. Click **OK**.

Using Styles, Themes, and Templates

Introduction

Microsoft Word documents are based on templates, which are predesigned and preformatted files that serve as the foundation of the documents. Each template is made up of styles that have common design elements, such as coordinated fonts, sizes, and colors, as well as, page layout designs. Start with a Word template for memos, reports, fax cover pages, web pages, and so on. Apply the existing styles for headings, titles, body text, and so forth. Then modify the template's styles, or create your own to better suit your needs. Make sure you get the look you want by adding emphasis using italics, boldface, and underline, changing text alignment, adjusting line and paragraph spacing, setting tabs and indents, or creating bulleted and numbered lists. When you're done, your document is sure to demand attention and convey your message in its appearance.

Not everyone has an eye for color, and pulling it all together can be daunting, so Word provides you with professionally designed themes, which you can apply to any document. A **theme** is a set of unified design elements that provides a consistent look for a document by using color themes, fonts, and effects, such as shadows, shading, and animations. By using templates, styles, and themes, you can create professional looking documents in no time.

What You'll Do

Apply a Quick Style

Create and Modify Styles

Manage Styles

Reveal Formatting Styles

Apply or Create a Style Set

Use the Format Painter

Add Custom Colors

Understand Themes

View and Apply a Theme

Create Theme Colors

Choose Theme Fonts

Choose Theme Effects

Create a Custom Theme

Choose a Custom Theme

Set Up for Personal Templates

Create a Personal Template

Open a Template

Change a Template

Applying a Quick Style

A **style** is a collection of formatting settings saved with a name in a document or template that you can apply to text at any time. Word provides different style sets to make it easy to format text. Each style set consists of a variety of different formatting style combinations, which you can view using the Quick Style Set gallery. To quickly see if you like a Quick Style Set, point to a thumbnail in the gallery to display a live preview of it in the selected text. If you like it, click the thumbnail to apply it. You can also access styles from the Mini-Toolbar (**New!**) when you select text. If you prefer, you can also use the Styles or Apply Styles pane.

Apply a Style

1. Select the text to which you want to apply a style.

   ◆ **Mini-Toolbar.** You can also click the **Styles** button (**New!**) on the Mini-Toolbar to select a style.

2. Click the **Home** tab.

3. Click the scroll up or down arrow, or click the **More** list arrow in the Styles group to see additional styles.

4. Click the style you want to apply from the gallery.

Did You Know?

You can clear style formatting. Select the text you want to clear, click the Home tab, and then click the Clear Formatting button.

You can reset the style back to the default style set. Click the Design tab, click the More list arrow, and then click Reset To The Default Style Set (**New!**).

Styles button on Mini-Toolbar

Applied style

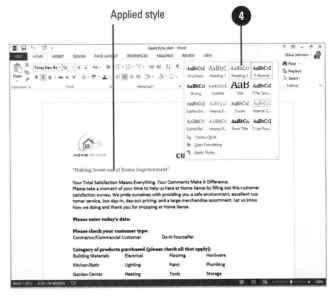

Apply a Style Using the Styles Pane

1. Select the text to which you want to apply a style.

2. Click the **Home** tab.

3. Click the **Styles Dialog Box Launcher**.

   The Styles pane appears.

4. To show a preview of the styles in the pane, select the **Show Preview** check box.

5. To apply a style, click the style you want to apply in the pane.

6. When you're done, click the **Close** button on the pane.

Apply or Reapply a Style Using the Apply Styles Pane

1. Select the text to which you want to apply a style.

   ◆ **Mini-Toolbar.** You can also click the **Styles** button (**New!**) on the Mini-Toolbar, and then click **Apply Styles**.

2. Click the **Home** tab.

3. Click the **More** list arrow in the Styles group, and then click **Apply Styles**.

   The Apply Styles pane appears.

4. Click the **Style Name** list arrow, and then select the style you want to apply from the list.

5. To reapply the current style, click **Reapply**.

6. When you're done, click the **Close** button on the pane.

Creating and Modifying Styles

Word provides a variety of styles to choose from. But sometimes you need to create a new style or modify an existing one to get the exact look you want. When you create a new style, specify if it applies to paragraphs or characters, and give the style a short, descriptive name that describes its purpose so you and others recall when to use that style. A **paragraph style** is a group of format settings that can be applied only to all of the text within a paragraph (even if it is a one-line paragraph), while a **character style** is a group of format settings that is applied to any block of text at the user's discretion. To modify a style, adjust the formatting settings of an existing style.

Create a New Style

1 Select the text whose formatting you want to save as a style.

2 Click the **Home** tab.

3 Click the scroll up or down arrow, or click the **More** list arrow in the Styles group, and then click **Create a Style**.

4 Type a short, descriptive name.

5 Click **Modify**.

6 Click the **Style type** list arrow, and then click **Paragraph** to include the selected text's line spacing and margins in the style, or click **Character** to include only formatting, such as font, size, and bold, in the style.

7 Click the **Style for following paragraph** list arrow, and then click the name of style you want to be applied after a paragraph with the new style.

8 Select the formatting options you want.

9 To add the style to the Quick style gallery, select the **Add to Quick Style list** check box.

10 Click **OK**.

11 Click **OK**.

Modify a Style

1. Click the **Home** tab.

2. Click the scroll up or down arrow, or click the **More** list arrow in the Styles group.

3. Right-click the style you want to modify, and then click **Modify**.

4. Specify any style changes (Style based on or Style for following paragraph) you want.

5. Click **Format**, and then click the type of formatting you want to modify:

   ◆ To change character formatting, such as font type and boldface, click **Font**.

   ◆ To change line spacing and indents, click **Paragraph**.

6. Select the formatting options you want.

7. Check the Preview box, and review the style description. Make any formatting changes as needed.

8. To add the style to the Quick style gallery, select the **Add to the Styles gallery** check box.

9. Click **OK**.

Did You Know?

You can view the list of styles. Click the Home tab, click the More list arrow in the Styles group, click Apply Style, and then click the Styles button to display the Styles list. From the Styles list pane, you can create a new style, inspect styles, manage styles, and change style options.

Managing Styles

The Styles pane give you another way to work with styles. You can view a master list of individual styles, preview styles as shown in the document, disable linked styles, and manage styles. The Styles pane allows you to work with the main document styles, such as body and heading text. You can modify or delete a style, select all instances of a style, or add a style to the Quick Styles gallery. If you want to work with the more indepth styles that Word uses to create lists, comment text, footer, header, index, tables, table of contents, and other stylized elements, you can use the Manage Styles dialog box.

Change Styles Pane Options

1. Click the **Home** tab.

2. Click the **Styles Dialog Box Launcher**.

3. Click **Options**.

4. Click the list arrows, and then select the styles you want to show and how the list is sorted.

5. Select the check boxes to show the types of formatting (paragraph, font, or bullet and numbering) you want to show in the Styles pane.

6. Select or clear the check boxes to show or hide built-in styles in the Styles pane.

7. Click the **Only in this document** or **New document based on this template** option.

8. Click **OK**.

9. When you're done, click the **Close** button on the pane.

Manage Styles

1 Click the **Home** tab.

2 Click the **Styles Dialog Box Launcher**.

3 To preview styles, select the **Show Preview** check box.

4 Use the Styles pane to make the any of the following changes:

◆ **Modify.** Point to the style, click the list arrow, and then click **Modify Style**.

◆ **Delete.** Point to the style, click the list arrow, click **Delete**, and then click **Yes**.

◆ **Select All.** Point to the style, click the list arrow, and then click **Select All x Instance(s)**.

◆ **Add to Quick Style Gallery.** Point to the style, click the list arrow, and then click **Add to Quick Style Gallery**.

5 Click **Manage Styles**.

6 Click the tab with the operation you want to perform: **Edit**, **Recommend**, **Restrict**, or **Set Defaults**.

7 Click the **Sort order** list arrow, and then select the way you want to display the styles.

8 Select the style you want, and then use the options and commands to make the changes you want.

9 When you're done, click **OK**.

10 Make any additional changes, and then click the **Close** button on the pane.

Revealing Formatting Styles

Word uses wavy blue underlines to indicate possible instances of inconsistent formatting. If you see a wavy blue underline while formatting a document, you can open the Reveal Formatting pane to display the format of selected text, such as its font and font effects. The Reveal Formatting pane allows you to display, change, or clear formatting for the selected text. You can also select text based on formatting so that you can compare the formatting used in the selected text with formatting used in other parts of the documents. To open the Reveal Formatting pane, you use the Style Inspector on the Styles pane.

Select or Clear Text Formatting

1. Select the text whose formatting you want to select or clear away.

2. Click the **Styles Dialog Box Launcher**.

3. Click the **Style Inspector** button.

4. Click the **Reveal Formatting** button.

   ◆ To provide more screen space to work, you can close the Style Inspector and Styles pane.

5. Select the text you want to reveal.

6. Point to the Selected Text box, click the list arrow, and then click either **Select All Text With Similar Formatting** or **Clear Formatting**.

   ◆ To apply the formatting to your surrounding text, click **Apply Formatting of Surrounding Text**.

7. When you're done, click the **Close** button on the pane.

See Also

See "Selecting Text with Similar Formatting" on page 70 for information on using the Select Text With Similar Formatting command available on the Home tab.

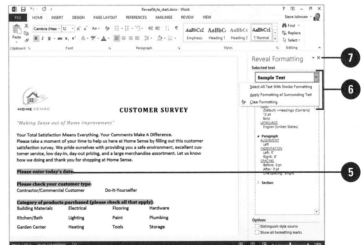

Compare Text Formatting

1. Select the first instance of formatting you want to compare.

2. Click the **Styles Dialog Box Launcher**.

3. Click the **Style Inspector** button.

4. Click the **Reveal Formatting** button.

   ◆ To provide more screen space to work, you can close the Style Inspector and Styles pane.

5. Select the first instance of formatting you want.

6. Select the **Compare to another selection** check box.

7. Select the second instance of formatting to compare.

8. When you're done, click the **Close** button on the pane.

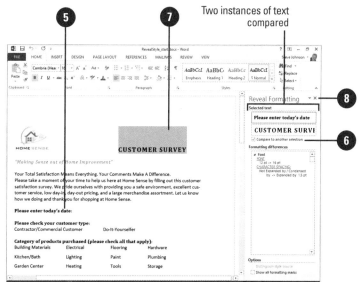

Two instances of text compared

Applying or Creating a Style Set

Not sure where to begin to create a fancy invitation or flyer? You can use style sets in Word to quickly format a document with a distinct style. Word provides predefined document style sets—such as Elegant, Simple, Stylish, Black & White, Centered, Casual, Lines, Distinctive, and Classics from the past—to make it easy to format an entire document. Each style set consists of a variety of different formatting style combinations, which you can view using the Document Formatting gallery (**New!**) on the Design tab. You can also apply a theme, theme colors, theme fonts, theme effects, and paragraph spacing that you can use along with individual styles to create a custom style set (**New!**).

Apply a Document Style Set

1. Click the **Design** tab (**New!**).

2. Click the scroll up or down arrow, or click the **More** list arrow in the Document Formatting group (**New!**) to see additional styles.

3. Click the style set you want..

Applied style

Current document style set

Built-in document Style sets

Create a Document Style Set

① Format a document with the individual styles that you want to save as a document style set.

② Click the **Design** tab (**New!**).

③ Click the scroll up or down arrow, or click the **More** list arrow in the Document Formatting group (**New!**) to see additional styles.

④ Click **Save as a New Style Set**.

The Save Quick Style Set dialog box opens, displaying the Quick Styles folder.

⑤ Type a file name.

⑥ If necessary, click the **Save as type** list arrow, and then click **Word Templates**.

⑦ Click **Save**.

Did You Know?

You can set the default style set. Click the Design tab, click the style set you want to use as the default when you create a new document,click the Set As Default button on the tab, and then click Yes.

You can reset the document back to the default style set. Click the Design tab, click the More list arrow in the Document Formatting group, and then click Reset To The Default Style Set.

Using the Format Painter

After formatting text in a document, you might want to apply those same formatting changes to other areas in the document. For example, redoing the same formatting, you can **paint** (that is, copy) the formatting from one area to others. The Format Painter lets you "pick up" the style of one section and apply, or "paint," it to another. To apply a format style to more than one item, double-click the Format Painter button on the Home tab instead of a single-click. The double-click keeps the Format Painter active until you want to press Esc to disable it, so you can apply formatting styles to any text or object you want in your document.

Apply a Format Style Using the Format Painter

1. Select the text containing the formatting you want to copy.

2. Click the **Home** tab.

3. Click the **Format Painter** button.

   If you want to apply the format to more than one item, double-click the Format Painter button.

4. Drag to select the text or click the object to which you want to apply the format.

5. If you double-clicked the Format Painter button, drag to select the text or click the object to which you want to apply the format, and then press Esc when you're done.

Did You Know?

You can use the Esc key to cancel format painting. If you change your mind about painting a format, cancel the marquee by pressing Esc.

Adding Custom Colors

In addition to the standard and theme colors, Word allows you to add more colors to your document. These additional colors are available on each color button palette on the Ribbon or in a dialog box, such as the Fill Color or Font Color button. These colors are useful when you want to use a specific color, but the document color theme does not have that color. Colors that you add to a document appear in all color palettes and remain in the palette even if the color theme changes.

Add a Color to the Menus

1. Click the **Font Color** button on the Home tab, and then click **More Colors**.

   This is one method. You can also use other color menus to access the Colors dialog box.

2. Click the **Custom** tab.

3. Click the **Color Model** list arrow, and then click **RGB** or **HSL**.

4. Select a custom color using one of the following methods:

   ◆ If you know the color values, enter them, either Hue, Sat, Lum, or Red, Green, and Blue.

   ◆ Drag across the palette until the pointer is over the color you want. Drag the black arrow to adjust the amount of black and white in the color.

   The new color appears above the current color at the bottom right.

5. Click **OK**.

   The current selection is changed to the new color, plus the new color is added to the Recent Colors section of all document color menus.

Added custom color

Understanding Themes

A theme helps you create professional-looking documents that use an appropriate balance of color for your document content. You can use a default color theme or create a custom one.

Themes in Office are made up of a palette of twelve colors. These colors appear on color palettes when you click a color-related button, such as Fill Color or Font Color button on the Home tab or in a dialog box. These twelve colors correspond to the following elements in a document:

Four Text and Background. The two background colors (light and dark combinations) are the canvas, or drawing area, color of the document. The two text colors (light and dark combinations) are for typing text and drawing lines, and contrast with the background colors.

Six Accent. These colors are designed to work as a complementary color palette for objects, such as shadows and fills. These colors contrast with both the background and text colors.

One hyperlink. This color is designed to work as a complementary color for objects and hyperlinks.

One followed hyperlink. This color is designed to work as a complementary color for objects and visited hyperlinks.

The first four colors in the Theme Colors list represent the document text and background colors (light and dark for each). The remaining colors represent the six accent and two hyperlink colors for the theme. When you apply another theme or change any of these colors to create a new theme, the colors shown in the Theme Colors dialog box and color palettes change to match the current colors.

Accent 3   Accent 2
Accent 1   Accent 5   Accent 4

Text/Background -   Text/Background -   Accent 6
Light 1   Light 2

Twelve theme colors

Sample color themes: Dark and Light

Viewing and Applying a Theme

A document theme consists of theme colors, fonts, and effects. You can quickly format an entire document with a professional look by applying a theme. Office comes with more themes and styles. To quickly see if you like a theme, point to one on the themes gallery to display a ScreenTip with name and information about it, and a live preview of it on the current document. If you like the theme, you can apply it. When you apply a theme, the background, text, graphics, charts, and tables all change to reflect the theme. You can choose from one or more standard themes. When you add new content, the document elements change to match the theme ensuring all of your material will look consistent. You can even use the same theme in other Microsoft Office programs, such as Excel and PowerPoint, so all your work matches. Can't find a theme you like? Search Office.com online.

View and Apply a Theme

1. Open the document you want to apply a theme.

2. Click the **Design** tab.

3. Click the **Themes** button to display the themes gallery.

4. Point to a theme.

    A live preview of the theme appears in the document, along with a ScreenTip.

5. Click the theme you want to apply to the active document.

Did You Know?

You can apply themes from Office.com. Click the Design tab, click the Themes button, scroll down the list, and then select an available Office.com theme. Go to *www.office.com* to download and use other online themes.

You can search for themes at Microsoft Office Online. Open your browser, go to *www.office.com*, click in the Search Office Online box, type themes, and then press Enter. Review the results list to find the theme you want. Follow the site instructions to download and use online themes.

Creating Theme Colors

You may like a certain color theme except for one or two colors. You can change an existing color theme and apply your changes to the entire document. You can add other custom colors to your theme by using RGB (Red, Green, and Blue) or HSL (Hues, Saturation, and Luminosity) color modes. The RGB color mode is probably the most widely used of all the color modes. You can accomplish this by using sliders, dragging on a color-space, or entering a numeric value that corresponds to a specific color. Once you create this new color theme, you can add it to your collection of color themes so that you can make it available to any document.

Apply or Create Theme Colors

1. Open the document you want to apply a color theme.

2. Click the **Design** tab.

3. To apply theme colors to a document, click the **Theme Colors** button, and then click a color theme.

   ◆ To apply individual theme colors, select the element, click a color button, such as Font Color on the Home tab, and then click a theme color.

4. To create theme colors, click the **Theme Colors** button, and then click **Create New Theme Colors**.

5. Click the **Theme Colors** button arrows (Text/Background, Accent, or Hyperlink, etc.) for the colors you want to change.

6. Click a new color, or click **More Colors** to select a color from the **Standard** or **Custom** tab, and then click **OK**.

7. If you don't like your color choices, click the **Reset** button to return all color changes to their original colors.

8. Type a new name for the color theme.

9. Click **Save**.

Select Custom Colors

1 Select the text you want to apply a custom color.

2 Click the **Font Color** button on the Home tab, and then click **More Colors**.

This is one method. You can also use other color menus to access the Colors dialog box.

3 Click the **Custom** tab.

4 Click the **Color Model** list arrow, and then click **RGB** or **HSL**.

5 Select a custom color using one of the following methods:

◆ If you know the color values, enter them, either Hue, Sat, Lum, or Red, Green, and Blue.

◆ Drag across the palette until the pointer is over the color you want. Drag the black arrow to adjust the amount of black and white in the color.

The new color appears above the current color at the bottom right.

6 Click **OK**.

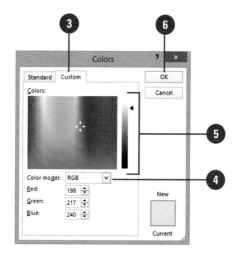

Did You Know?

You can edit a custom color theme. On the Design tab, click the Theme Colors button, right-click the theme color you want to edit, click Edit, make changes, and then click Save.

You can delete a custom color theme. On the Design tab, click the Theme Colors button, right-click the theme color you want to edit, click Edit, click Delete, and then click Yes.

The Properties of Color

Characteristic	Description
Hue	The color itself; every color is identified by a number, determined by the number of colors available on your monitor.
Saturation	The intensity of the color. The higher the number, the more vivid the color.
Luminosity	The brightness of the color, or how close the color is to black or white. The larger the number, the lighter the color.
Red, Green, Blue	Primary colors of the visible light spectrum. RGB generates color using three 8-bit channels: 1 red, 1 green, and 1 blue. RGB is an additive color system, which means that color is added to a black background. The additive process mixes various amounts of red, green and blue light to produce other colors.

Choosing Theme Fonts

A document theme consists of theme colors, fonts, and effects. Theme fonts include heading and body text fonts. Each document uses a set of theme fonts. When you click the Theme Fonts button on the Design tab, the name of the current heading and body text font appear highlighted in the gallery menu. To quickly see if you like a theme font, point to one on the menu, and a live preview of it appears on the current document. If you want to apply the theme, click it on the menu. You can apply a set of theme fonts to another theme or create your own set of theme fonts.

Apply and Choose Theme Fonts

1. Open the document you want to apply theme fonts.

2. Click the **Home** tab.

3. Select the text you want to change.

   TIMESAVER *To select the entire document, press Ctrl+A.*

4. Click the **Font** list arrow, and then click the theme font you want.

5. Click the **Design** tab.

6. Click the **Theme Fonts** button.

   The current theme fonts appear highlighted in the menu.

   TIMESAVER *Point to the Fonts button to display a ScreenTip with the current theme fonts.*

7. Click the theme fonts you want from the gallery menu.

Create Theme Fonts

1. Click the **Design** tab.

2. Click the **Theme Fonts** button, and then click **Create New Theme Fonts**.

3. Click the **Heading font** list arrow, and then select a font.

4. Click the **Body font** list arrow, and then select a font.

5. Type a name for the custom theme fonts.

6. Click **Save**.

Did You Know?

The Font Color button on the Ribbon displays the last font color you used. To apply this color to another selection, simply click the button, not the list arrow.

Choosing Theme Effects

Theme effects are sets of lines, fills, and special effects styles for shapes, graphics, charts, SmartArt, and other design elements. By combining the lines, fills, and special effects styles with different formatting levels (subtle, moderate, and intense), Word provides a variety of visual theme effects. Each document uses a set of theme effects. Some are more basic while others are more elaborate. When you click the Theme Effects button on the Design tab, the name of the current theme effects appears highlighted in the gallery menu. While you can apply a set of theme effects to another theme, you cannot create your own set of theme effects at this time.

View and Apply Theme Effects

1. Open the document you want to apply a theme effect.

2. Click the **Design** tab.

3. Click the **Theme Effects** button.

   The current theme effects appear highlighted in the menu.

   TIMESAVER *Point to the Effects button to display a ScreenTip with the current theme effects name.*

4. Click the theme effects you want from the menu.

Did You Know?

You can delete a custom theme effects or fonts. On the Design tab, click the Theme Effects or Theme Fonts button, right-click the theme you want to edit, click Edit, click Delete, and then click Yes.

See Also

See "Viewing and Applying a Theme" on page 103 for information on applying a theme from the Themes gallery.

Creating a Custom Theme

If you have special needs for specific colors, fonts, and effects, such as a company sales or marketing document, you can create your own theme by customizing theme colors, theme fonts, and theme effects, and saving them as a theme file (.thmx), which you can reuse. You can apply the saved theme to other documents. When you save a custom theme, the file is automatically saved in the Document Themes folder and added to the list of custom themes used by Word and other Office programs. When you no longer need a custom theme, you can delete it.

Create a Custom Theme

1. Click the **Design** tab, and then create a theme by customizing theme colors, theme fonts, and theme effects.

2. Click the **Themes** button, and then click **Save Current Theme**.

   Office themes are typically stored in the following location:

   Windows 8 or 7. C:/Users /*your name*/AppData/Roaming /Microsoft/Templates/Document Themes

3. Type a name for the theme file.

4. Click **Save**.

Default Document Themes folder

Did You Know?

You can remove a custom theme from the gallery menu. Simply move or delete the theme file from the Document Themes folder into another folder.

Choosing a Custom Theme

When you create your own theme by customizing theme colors, theme fonts, and theme effects, and saving them as a theme file (.thmx), you can apply the saved theme to other documents. When you save a custom theme file in the Document Themes folder, you can choose the custom theme from the Themes gallery. If you save a custom theme file in another folder location, you can use the Browse for Themes command to locate and select the custom theme file you want to reuse.

Choose and Apply a Custom Theme

1. Click the **Design** tab.

2. Click the **Themes** button to see additional themes.

3. Point to the gallery you want to display the theme name, and then click the one you want.

4. To select and apply a custom theme from a file, click the **Themes** button, and then click **Browse for Themes**.

5. If you want to open a specific file type, click the **Files of type** list arrow, and then select an Office Theme file type:

   - **Office Themes and Themed Documents.**

   - **Office Themes.**

6. If the file is located in another folder, click the **Look in** list arrow, and then navigate to the file.

   Office themes are typically stored in the following location:

   Windows 8 or 7. C:/Users /*your name*/AppData/Roaming /Microsoft/Templates/Document Themes

7. Click the theme file you want.

8. Click **Open**.

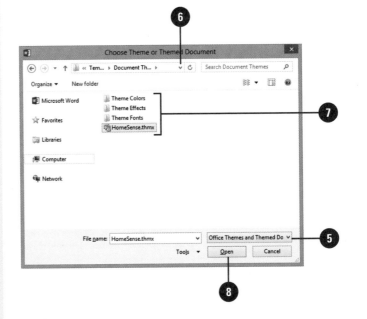

Setting Up for Personal Templates

If you want to create your own custom personal templates and access them from the Start or New screen, you should create a My Templates folder (**New!**)—such as C:\Users*user name*\My Templates—and then specify the folder as the default for your personal templates (**New!**). If you don't create a folder, Microsoft creates one named Custom Office Templates in the C:\Users*user name*\Documents folder. You can specify your default personal templates folder in the Options dialog box under Save. After you set up your personal templates folder, you can access them from the Start or New screen under Personal (**New!**).

Set Up for Personal Templates

1. In Windows Explorer, navigate to the location where you want to store your personal templates, and then create a folder named My Templates.

   ◆ **Personal Templates Folder.** C:\Users*user name*\My Templates; typical location, yours can differ.

2. Click the **File** tab, and then click **Options**.

3. In the left pane, click **Save**.

4. In the Default personal templates location box, enter the path to a personal templates folder.

   My Templates Folder. C:\Users*user name*\My Templates; typical location, yours can differ.

   Custom Office Templates Folder. C:\Users*user name*\Documents\ Custom Office Templates.

5. Click **OK**.

See Also

See "Creating a Personal Template" on page 112 for more information on creating a custom template for use in the My Templates folder.

Creating a Personal Template

You can create your own personal template as easily as you create a document. Like those that come with Word, custom templates can save you time. Perhaps each month you create an inventory document in which you enter repetitive information; all that changes is the actual data. By creating your own template, you can have a custom form that is ready for completion each time you take inventory. A template file (.dotx) saves all the customization you made to reuse in other documents. You can store your template anywhere you want; however, you may find it handy to store it in a My Templates folder (**New!**), or the default Custom Office Templates folder (**New!**). When you set up the default personal templates folder in the Options dialog box under Save, your personal templates appear under Personal in the Start or New screen.

Create a Personal Template

1. Enter all the necessary information in a new document—including text, graphics, and formatting.

2. Click the **File** tab, and then click **Save As**.

3. Click **Computer**, and then click **Browse**.

4. Click the **Save as type** list arrow, and then select a template format.

   ◆ **Word Template**. Creates a template for Word 2007-2013.

   ◆ **Word Macro-Enabled Template**. Creates a template for Word 2007-2013 with macros.

   ◆ **Word 97-2003 Template**. Creates a template for Word 97-2003.

5. Navigate to your personal templates folder.

   My Templates. C:\Users\ *user name*\My Templates; your location might differ.

   Custom Office Templates. C:\Users*user name*\Documents\ Custom Office Templates.

6. Type a name for your template.

7. Click **Save**.

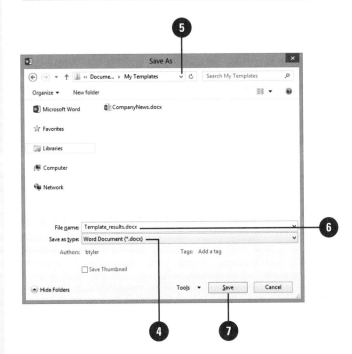

Opening a Template

You may not realize it, but every document you create is based on a template. When you start a new document without specifying a template, Word creates a new document based on the default template file. When you specify a particular template in the Start or New screen (**New!**), whether it's one supplied by Word or one you created yourself, Word starts a new document that contains the text, graphics, and formatting contained in that template. The template itself does not change when you enter data in the new document, because you are working on a new file, not with the template file.

Open a Template

1. Click the **File** tab, and then click **Open**.

2. Click **Computer**, and then click **Browse**.

3. Click the **Files of type** list arrow, and then click **Templates**.

4. Click the **Look in** list arrow, and then select the folder that contain the template you want to open.

   Personal Templates. C:\Users\ *user name*\My Templates; your location might differ, or C:\Users\ *user name*\Documents\Custom Office Templates (default).

   Office Templates. C:\Program Files\Microsoft Office\ Templates\1033

5. Click the file name of the template you want to open.

6. Click **Open**.

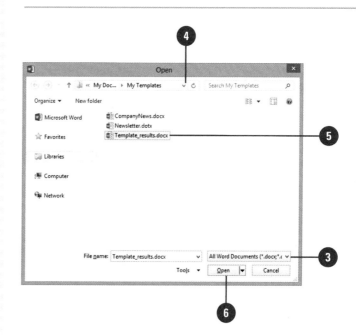

See Also

See "Setting Up for Personal Templates" on page 111 for more information on creating a My Templates folder and setting the default personal templates folder.

Changing a Template

Office has a selection of premade Word templates designed for you to use. These templates are available in the Start or New screen under Featured (**New!**). If you like one of these templates, you can use it as the basis of your own template. To customize one, open the template, make the changes you want, and then save it. If you save the original template back in the same location with the same name as the original, you create a new default template. The original one is replaced by the newly saved template. If you don't want to change the original, save the template in your My Templates or Custom Office Templates folder.

Change a Word Template

1. Click the **File** tab, and then click **New**.

2. Open the template you want to change using the following:

   ◆ **Featured Templates.** Click **Featured**, and then click the template you want, and then click **Create**.

   ◆ **Personal Templates.** Click **Personal**, and then click the custom template you want.

3. Make the changes you want to the template.

4. Click the **File** tab, and then click **Save As**.

5. Click **Computer**, and then click **Browse**.

6. Click the **Save as type** list arrow, and then click **Word Template**.

7. Navigate to a templates folder.

   Office Templates. C:\Program Files\Microsoft Office\Templates\1033

   Personal Templates. C:\Users\ *user name*/My Templates; your location might differ, or C:\Users\ *user name*\Documents\Custom Office Templates (default).

8. Type a new file name or the same as the existing name to replace it.

9. Click **Save**, and then click **Yes**, if necessary, to replace the file.

You might need admin permission to save Office templates

Adding Graphics and Multimedia to Documents

5

Introduction

Although well-illustrated documents can't make up for a lack of content, you can capture the attention of your audience if your documents are vibrant and visually interesting. Microsoft Office comes with a vast array of clip art, and there are endless amounts available through other software packages or on the web. When going online to look at clips, you can categorize them so that it's easier to find the best choice for your document. You can use the Microsoft Office.com web site to search for and download clip art images or use Bing image search on the web.

You can easily enhance a document by adding a picture—one of your own or one of the hundreds that come with Microsoft Office. If you need to modify your pictures, you can resize them, compress them for storage, change their brightness or contrast, recolor them, or crop them.

WordArt is another feature that adds detail to your document. Available in other Office programs, WordArt can bring together your documents—you can change its color, shape, shadow, or size. Because WordArt comes with so many style choices, time spent customizing your documents is minimal.

In Office programs, you can insert SmartArt graphics to create diagrams that convey processes or relationships. Office provides a wide-variety of built-in SmartArt graphic types from which to choose, including graphical lists, process, cycle, hierarchy, relationship, matrix, and pyramid. Using built-in SmartArt graphics makes it easy to create and modify charts without having to create them from scratch.

Locating and Inserting Online Pictures

If you need a picture to insert into a document and don't have one, you can search for and insert clip art from Office.com (**New!**) or a picture from the web using Bing Image Search (**New!**). Office.com is a clip gallery that Microsoft maintains on its web site. Clip art includes photos and illustrations, such as vector images, which are mathematically defined to make them easy to resize and manipulate. To add an online picture to a document, you click the Online Pictures button on the Insert tab, and then locate, select, and insert the picture you want.

Locate and Insert Online Clip Art from Office.com

1. Click the **Insert** tab.

2. Click the **Online Pictures** button.

3. In the Search Office.com box, enter search criteria to locate the online picture you want.

    ◆ To cancel the search, click the **Close** button in the Search box.

4. Click the **Search** button or press Enter.

5. Select the picture(s) you want.

    ◆ To preview a larger picture, point to a picture, and then click the **View Larger** button.

6. Click **Insert**.

7. Select the picture, and then move and resize it, as desired.

View Larger button

Locate and Insert Online Pictures from Bing Image Search

1. Click the **Insert** tab.

2. Click the **Online Pictures** button.

3. In the Search Office.com box, enter search criteria to locate the online picture you want.

   ◆ To cancel the search, click the Close button in the Search box.

4. Click the **Search** button or press Enter.

5. If prompted, click **Show all web results**. If a message bar appears, read it, then click the **Close** button to dismiss it.

6. Select the picture(s) you want.

   ◆ To preview a larger picture, point to a picture, and then click the **View Larger** button.

7. Click **Insert**.

8. Select the picture, and then move and resize it, as desired.

Did You Know?

You can select multiple pictures from within a search. To select multiple pictures in consecutive order, press Shift, click first image, and then click the last image. To select multiple pictures in non-consecutive order, press Ctrl, and then click images.

View Larger button

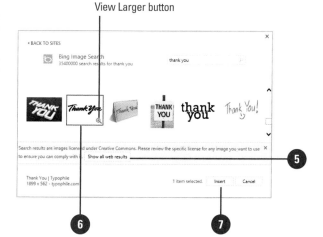

Inserting Pictures from an Online Service

If you have an account for an online service (**New!**) for images and video, such as Flickr or YouTube, you can insert pictures into a document directly from the service. Before you can use an online service, you need to add them (establishing a connection to your Microsoft account) to Word, which requires an established account with a user name and password. In addition to the image and video online services, you can also establish connections to access pictures stored on other online services, such as a SkyDrive (**New!**) or Office 365 SharePoint (**New!**). To add an online picture from an online service to a document, you click the Online Pictures button on the Insert tab, click the service icon, and then locate, select, and insert the picture you want.

Add Online Services

1. Click the **File** tab, and then click **Account** (**New!**).

2. Click **Add a service** (**New!**), point to a service type (options vary):

   ◆ **Images & Videos**, and then click **Flickr** or **YouTube**.

   ◆ **Storage**, and then click **Office 365 SharePoint** or **SkyDrive**.

3. Follow the on-screen instructions to sign-in and connect to the service.

   After the service is connected to your Microsoft account, it appears in the list of connected services.

4. To manage or remove a connected service, click the **Manage** or **Remove** link; options vary depending on the service.

   When you manage a connected service, your web browser opens, displaying options for the account.

5. Click the **Back** button to exit the File tab.

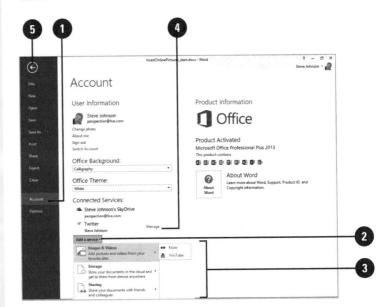

Insert Pictures from an Image Online Service

1 Click the **Insert** tab.

2 Click the **Online Pictures** button.

3 If the online service isn't connected, click the online service icon, such as Flickr, click **Connect**, and then enter your user name and password to establish a connection to the online service.

The online service appears in the Insert Pictures window.

4 To manage the account, click the **Manage** link, make any option changes, click **Save**, and then close your web browser.

5 Click the **See more** link for more pictures.

◆ To quickly insert a recent picture, click one from the Recently Used list in the Insert Pictures window.

6 Select the picture(s) you want.

◆ To preview a larger picture, point to a picture, and then click the **View Larger** button.

7 Click **Insert**.

8 Select the picture, and then move and resize it, as desired.

3 Flickr

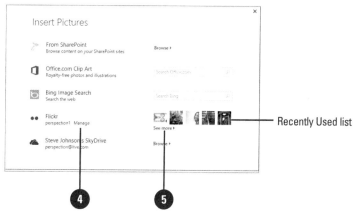

Recently Used list

4　　**5**

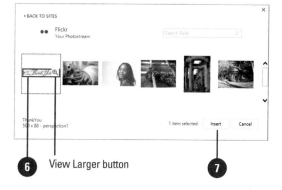

6 View Larger button　　**7**

Inserting a Picture from a SkyDrive or SharePoint

If you have pictures stored on a SkyDrive (**New!**) or Office 365 SharePoint (**New!**), you can access them from Online Pictures on the Insert tab. Before you can use an online service, you need to add them (establishing a connection to your Microsoft account) to Word, which requires an established account with a user name and password. After you establish a connection, you can browse for pictures directly on the SkyDrive or Office 365 SharePoint sites.

Insert a Picture from SkyDrive or SharePoint

1. Click the **Insert** tab.

2. Click the **Online Pictures** button.

3. Click **Browse** for SharePoint or SkyDrive.

   The main folder for your SkyDrive or SharePoint site appears.

4. Navigate to the folder that contains the picture files you want to insert.

5. Click the file you want to insert.

6. Click **Insert**.

See Also

See "Inserting Pictures from an Online Service" on page 118 for information on adding an online service to connect to a SkyDrive or Office 365 SharePoint site.

SkyDrive

SkyDrive

SharePoint

SharePoint

Inserting a Picture from a File

Word makes it possible for you to insert pictures, graphics, scanned photographs, art, photos, or artwork from a collection of stock images or other program into a document. When you use the Pictures button on the Insert tab, you specify the source of the picture. When you insert pictures from files on your hard disk drive, scanner, digital camera, or web camera, Word allows you to select multiple pictures, view thumbnails of them, and insert them all at once, which speeds up the process.

Insert a Picture from a File

1. Click the **Insert** tab.

2. Click the **Pictures** button.

3. Navigate to the folder that contains the picture files you want to insert.

4. Click the file you want to insert.

5. Click **Insert**.

   ◆ To link a picture file, click the **Insert** button arrow, and then click **Link to File**.

   ◆ To insert and link a picture file, click the **Insert** button arrow, and then click **Insert and Link**.

   TROUBLE? *If you see a red "x" instead of a picture or motion clip in your document, then you don't have a graphics filter installed on your computer for that clip.*

Did You Know?

You can change a picture. Select the picture, click the Change Picture button on the Format tab, select a picture, and then click Insert.

You can add graphic formats. If the graphic format you want to insert is not in the list, you can use Office Setup's Add or Remove Features option to install additional graphic formats.

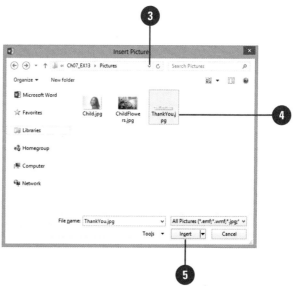

Inserting a Picture Screen Shot

If you're working on a training manual, presentation, or document that requires a picture of your computer screen, then the Screenshot button on the Insert tab just made your life a lot easier. You use the Screen Clipping tool to drag a selection around the screen area that you want to capture, and then select the picture from the Screenshot gallery. The Screenshot gallery holds multiple screen shots, so you can capture several screens before you insert them into your document. After you insert the screen shot into a document, you can use the tools on the Picture Tools tab to edit and improve it.

Insert a Picture Screen Shot

1 Click the **Insert** tab.

2 Click the **Screenshot** button.

3 Click **Screen Clipping**.

4 Display the screen you want to capture, and then drag the large plus cursor to select the screen area to capture.

5 Click the **Screenshot** button, and then click the thumbnail of the screen shot you want to insert.

6 Use the tools on the Picture Tools tab to edit and improve the screen shot.

Inserted screen shot

Did You Know?

You can copy the window or screen contents. To make a copy of the active window, press Alt+Print Scrn. To copy the entire screen as it appears on your monitor, press Print Scrn.

Adding an Artistic Style to a Picture

With the Artistic Quick Style gallery, you can transform a picture into a piece of artwork. The Artistic Quick Style gallery makes it easy to change the look of a picture to a sketch, drawing, or painting. The Picture Quick Style gallery provides a variety of different formatting options—such as Pencil Sketch, Line Drawing, Watercolor Sponge, Mosaic Bubble, Glass, Pastels Smooth, Plastic Wrap, Photocopy, and Paint Strokes—to create a professional look. To quickly see if you like an Artistic Quick Style, point to a thumbnail in the gallery to display a live preview of it in the selected shape. If you like it, you can apply it.

Add an Artistic Style to a Picture

1. Click the picture you want to change.

2. Click the **Format** tab under Picture Tools.

3. Click the **Artistic Effects** button.

   The current style appears highlighted in the gallery.

4. Point to a style.

   A live preview of the style appears in the picture.

5. Click the style you want from the gallery to apply it to the selected picture.

Did You Know?

You can quickly return a picture back to its original form. Select the picture, click the Format tab, and then click the Reset Picture button.

See Also

See "Applying Picture Effects" on page 127 for information on adding more effects to a picture.

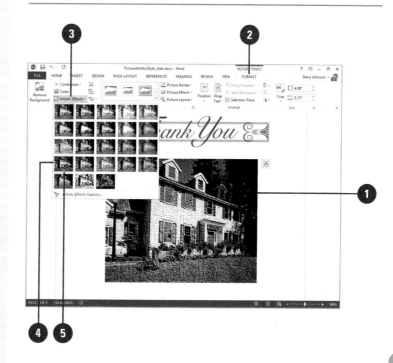

Adding a Quick Style to a Picture

Instead of changing individual attributes of a picture—such as shape, border, and effects—you can quickly add them all at once with the Picture Quick Style gallery. The Picture Quick Style gallery provides a variety of different formatting combinations. To quickly see if you like a Picture Quick Style, point to a thumbnail in the gallery to display a live preview of it in the selected shape. If you like it, you can select the one you want to apply it.

Add a Quick Style to a Picture

1. Click the picture you want to change.

2. Click the **Format** tab under Picture Tools.

3. Click the scroll up or down arrow, or click the **More** list arrow in the Picture Styles group to see additional styles.

   The current style appears highlighted in the gallery.

4. Point to a style.

   A live preview of the style appears in the current shape.

5. Click the style you want from the gallery to apply it to the selected picture.

Applying a Shape to a Picture

After you insert a picture into your document, you can select it and apply one of Office's shapes to it. The picture appears in the shape just like it has been cropped. The Crop to Shape gallery makes it easy to choose the shape you want to use. Live preview is not available with the Crop to Shape gallery. You can try different shapes to find the one you want. If you don't find the one you want, you can use the Reset Picture button to return the picture back to its original state.

Apply a Shape to a Picture

1. Click the picture you want to change.

2. Click the **Format** tab under Picture Tools.

3. Click the **Crop** button arrow, and then point to **Crop to Shape**.

4. Select the shape you want to apply to the selected picture.

Did You Know?

You can save a shape as a picture in the PNG format. Right-click the shape, click Save As Picture, type a name, and then click Save.

You can copy the window or screen contents. To make a copy of the active window, press Alt+Print Scrn. To copy the entire screen as it appears on your monitor, press Print Scrn.

Applying a Border to a Picture

After you insert a picture, you can add and modify the picture border by changing individual outline formatting using the Picture Border button on the Format tab under Picture Tools. The Picture Border button works just like the Shape Outline button and provides similar options to add a border, select a border color, and change border width and style. You can try different border combinations to find the one you want. If you don't find one that works for you, you can use the No Outline command on the Picture Border gallery to remove it.

Apply a Border to a Picture

1. Click the picture you want to change.

2. Click the **Format** tab under Picture Tools.

3. Click the **Picture Border** button.

4. Click a color, or point to **Weight**, or **Dashes**, and then select a style, or click **More Lines** to select multiple options.

5. Drag a sizing handle to change the size or angle of the line or arrow.

Did You Know?

You can remove a border. Select the picture, click the Format tab, click the Picture Border button, and then click No Outline.

Applying Picture Effects

You can change the look of a picture by applying effects, such as shadows, reflections, glow, soft edges, and 3-D rotations. You can also apply effects to a shape by using the Picture Effects gallery for quick results, or by using the Format Shape pane (**New!**) for custom results. From the Picture Effects gallery, you can apply a built-in combination of 3-D effects or individual effects to a picture. To quickly see if you like a picture effect, point to a thumbnail in the Picture Effects gallery to display a live preview of it. If you like it, you can apply it. If you no longer want to apply a picture effect to an object, you can remove it. Simply select the picture, point to the effect type on the Picture Effects gallery, and then select the No effect type option.

Add an Effect to a Picture

1. Click the picture you want to change.

2. Click the **Format** tab under Picture Tools.

3. Click the **Picture Effects** button, and then point to one of the following:

   - **Preset** to select No 3-D, one of the preset types, or 3-D Options.

   - **Shadow** to select No Shadow, one of the shadow types, or Shadows Options.

   - **Reflection** to select No Reflection, one of the Reflection Variations, or Reflection Options.

   - **Glow** to select No Glow, one of the Glow Variations, More Glow Colors, or Glow Options.

   - **Soft Edges** to select No Soft Edges or a point size to determine the soft edge amount, or Soft Edges Options.

   - **3-D Rotation** to select No Rotation, one of the rotation types, or 3-D Options.

   When you point to an effect, a live preview of the style appears in the current shape.

4. Click the effect you want from the gallery to apply it.

Modifying Picture Size

Once you have inserted a picture or other objects into your document, you can resize them to meet your needs. You can use the sizing handles to quickly resize a picture. When you resize or move objects, a live layout preview (**New!**) with your changes appear on the page. To resize a picture more precisely, you can use height and width options in the Size group on the Format tab. If you want to set unique or multiple options at the same time, you can use the Layout dialog box (**New!**). These options allow you to make sure your pictures keep the same relative proportions as the original and lock size proportions.

Resize a Picture

1. Click the object you want to resize.

2. Drag one of the sizing handles to increase or decrease the object's size.

   ◆ Drag a middle handle to resize the object up, down, left, or right.

   ◆ Drag a corner handle to resize the object proportionally.

   A live layout preview (**New!**) appears for the objects.

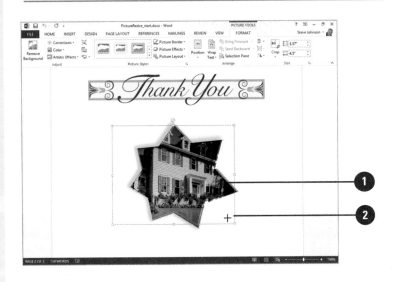

Resize a Picture Precisely

1. Click the object you want to resize.

2. Click the **Format** tab under Picture Tools.

3. Click the up and down arrows or enter a number (in inches) in the Height and Width boxes on the Ribbon and press Enter.

   If the **Lock aspect ratio** check box is selected in the Format Picture dialog box (under Size), height or width automatically changes when you change one of them. Click the **Size Dialog Box Launcher** to change the option.

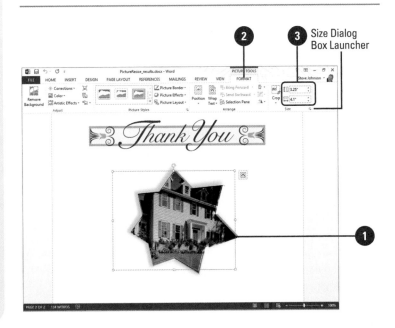

Size Dialog Box Launcher

Precisely Scale a Picture

1. Click the object you want to resize.

2. Click the **Format** tab under Picture Tools.

3. Click the **Size Dialog Box Launcher**.

4. Click the up and down arrows or enter a number in the Height and Width boxes in the following:

   ◆ **Height and Width.** Select the **Absolute** option (fixed position), or select the **Relative** option (**New!**), and then select a relative to option. Enter a height and width size in inches.

   ◆ **Scale.** Enter a percentage size.

   If the Lock aspect ratio check box is selected, height or width automatically changes when you change one of them.

5. To keep the picture proportional, select the **Lock aspect ratio** check box.

6. To keep the picture the same relative size, select the **Relative to original picture size** check box.

7. If you want to remove your changes, click **Reset**.

8. Click **Close**.

Did You Know?

Resizing bitmaps can cause distortion. Bitmap images are made up of dots, and do not lend themselves as easily to resizing because the dots can't expand and contract, which can lead to distortion. To avoid distortion, resize bitmaps proportionally and try to resize smaller instead of larger.

Compressing a Picture

Office allows you to compress pictures in order to minimize the file size of the image. In doing so, however, you may lose some visual quality, depending on the compression setting. You can pick the resolution that you want for the pictures in a document based on where or how they'll be viewed (for example, on the web or printed). You can also set other options, such as Delete cropped areas of picture, to get the best balance between picture quality and file size or automatically compress pictures when you save your document.

Compress a Picture

1 Click to select the pictures you want to compress.

2 Click the **Format** tab under Picture Tools.

3 Click the **Compress Pictures** button.

4 Select the **Apply only to this picture** check box to apply compression setting to only the selected picture. Otherwise, clear the check box to compress all pictures in your document.

5 Select or clear the **Delete cropped areas of pictures** check box to reduce file.

6 Click the **Print**, **Screen**, **E-mail**, or **Document** option to specify a target output.

7 Click **OK**.

Correcting a Picture

Once you have inserted a picture, you can control the image's colors, brightness, and contrast using Picture tools. The brightness and contrast controls let you make simple adjustments to the tonal range of a picture. The brightness and contrast controls change a picture by an overall lightening or darkening of the image pixels. In addition, you can sharpen and soften pictures by a specified percentage. If you want to set unique or multiple options, you can use the Format Picture pane (**New!**). You can experiment with the settings to get the look you want. If you don't like the look, you can use the Reset Picture button to return the picture back to its original starting point.

Change Brightness and Contrast or Sharpen and Soften

1. Click the picture you want to change.

2. Click the **Format** tab under Picture Tools.

3. Click the **Corrections** button, and then do one of the following:

   - **Brightness and Contrast.** Click a brightness and contrast option.

     A positive brightness lightens the object colors by adding more white, while a negative brightness darkens the object colors by adding more black. A positive contrast increases intensity, resulting in less gray, while a negative contrast to decrease intensity, resulting in more gray.

   - **Sharpen and Soften.** Click a sharpen and soften option.

4. To set custom correction percentages, click the **Corrections** button, click **Picture Corrections Options**, specify the options you want in the Format Picture pane (**New!**), and then click the **Close** button in the pane.

Recoloring a Picture

You can recolor clip art and other objects to match the color scheme of your document. For example, if you use a flower clip art as your business logo, you can change shades of pink in the spring to shades of orange in the autumn. The Color Picture Quick Style gallery provides a variety of different recolor formatting combinations. To quickly see if you like a Color Picture Quick Style, point to a thumbnail in the gallery to display a live preview of it in the selected shape. If you like it, you can apply it. You can also use a transparent background in your picture to avoid conflict between its background color and your document's background. With a transparent background, the picture takes on the same background as your document.

Recolor a Picture

1. Click the picture whose color you want to change.

2. Click the **Format** tab under Picture Tools.

3. Click the **Color** button.

4. Click one of the Color options.

   ◆ **Recolor.** Click an option to apply a color type:

   No Recolor. Click this option to remove a previous recolor.

   Grayscale. Converts colors into whites, blacks and shades of gray between black and white.

   Sepia. Converts colors into very light gold and yellow colors like a picture from the old west.

   Washout. Converts colors into whites and very light colors.

   Black and White. Converts colors into only white and black.

   ◆ **Color Saturation** or **Color Tone.** Click an option to apply a color saturation or tone based on the recolor selection.

   ◆ **More Variations.** Point to this option to select a specific color.

   ◆ **Picture Color Options.** Click this option to set custom recolor options by percentage.

No Recolor

Set a Transparent Background

1. Click the picture you want to change.

2. Click the **Format** tab under Picture Tools.

3. Click the **Color** button, and then click **Set Transparent Color**.

4. Move the pointer over the object until the pointer changes shape.

5. Click the color you want to set as transparent.

6. Move the pointer over the picture where you want to apply the transparent color, and then click to apply it.

7. When you're done, click outside the image.

Did You Know?

Why is the Set Transparent Color command dimmed? Setting a color as transparent works only with bitmaps. If you are working with an object that is not a bitmap, you will not be able to use this feature.

You can't modify some pictures in Office. If the picture is a bitmap (.BMP, .JPG, .GIF, or .PNG), you need to edit its colors in an image editing program, such as Adobe Photoshop, Microsoft Paint, or Paint Shop Pro.

You can reset a picture back to its original state. Click the picture you want to reset, click the Format tab under Picture Tools, and then click the Reset Picture button.

Cropping and Rotating a Picture

You can crop clip art to isolate just one portion of the picture. Because clip art uses vector image technology, you can crop even the smallest part of it and then enlarge it, and the clip art will still be recognizable. You can also crop bitmapped pictures, but if you enlarge the area you cropped, you lose picture detail. Use the Crop button to crop an image by hand. In addition, you can crop a picture while maintaining a selected resize aspect ratio or crop a picture based on a fill or fit. You can also rotate a picture by increments or freehand.

Crop a Picture Quickly

1. Click the picture you want to crop.

2. Click the **Format** tab under Picture Tools.

3. Click the **Crop** button.

4. Drag the sizing handles until the borders surround the area you want to crop.

5. Click outside the image when you are finished.

Crop a Picture with an Aspect Ratio

1. Click the picture you want to crop.

2. Click the **Format** tab under Picture Tools.

3. Click the **Crop** button arrow, point to **Aspect Ratio**, and then select an aspect ratio.

4. Drag the sizing handles until the borders surround the area you want to crop.

5. Click outside the image when you are finished.

Ratio options

Crop a Picture with a Fill or Fit

1 Click the picture you want to crop.

2 Click the **Format** tab under Picture Tools.

3 Click the **Crop** button arrow, and then select an option:

◆ **Fill.** Resizes the picture so the entire picture area is filled while maintaining the aspect ratio. Any area outside of the picture area is cropped.

◆ **Fit.** Resizes the picture so the entire picture displays inside the picture area while maintaining the aspect ratio.

4 Drag the sizing handles until the borders surround the area you want to crop.

5 Click outside the image when you are finished.

Rotate a Picture

1 Click the object you want to rotate.

2 Position the pointer (which changes to the Free Rotate pointer) over the green rotate lever at the top of the object, and then drag to rotate the object.

3 Click outside the object to set the rotation.

Did You Know?

You can rotate or flip a picture. Select the picture, click the Format tab, click the Rotate button, and then click Rotate Right 90, Rotate Left 90, Flip Vertical, Flip Horizontal, or click More Rotation Options.

Free Rotate pointer

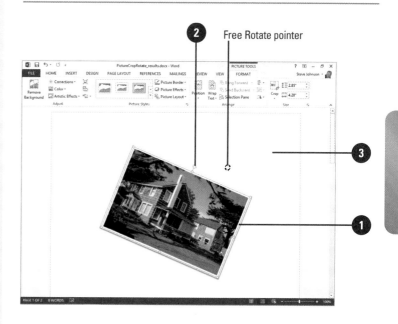

Removing a Picture Background

Sometimes you want to use an element from a picture instead of the entire picture. With the Remove Background command, you can specify the element you want in a picture, and then remove the background. You can use automatic background removal or you can manually draw lines to specify which parts of the picture background you want to keep and which to remove.

Remove a Picture Background

1. Click the picture you want to change.

2. Click the **Format** tab under Picture Tools.

3. Click the **Remove Background** button.

4. Drag the handles on the marquee lines to specify the part of the picture you want to keep. The area outside the marquee gets removed.

5. To manually specify which areas to keep and which areas to remove, do the following:

   ◆ **Mark Areas to Keep.** Click the button, and then draw lines to specify which parts of the picture you do not want automatically removed.

   ◆ **Mark Areas to Remove.** Click the button, and then draw lines to specify which parts of the picture you do want removed in addition to those automatically marked.

   ◆ **Delete Mark.** Click the button, and then click marked lines to remove them.

6. Click the **Keep Changes** button to close and keep the removal or click the **Discard All Changes** button to close and cancel the automatic removal.

Background removed

Creating WordArt Text

The WordArt feature lets you create stylized text to draw attention to your most important words. Most users apply WordArt to a word or a short phrase, such as *Home For Sale*. You should apply WordArt to a document sparingly. Its visual appeal and unique look requires uncluttered space. When you use WordArt, you can choose from a variety of text styles that come with the WordArt Quick Style gallery, or you can create your own using tools in the WordArt Styles group. To quickly see if you like a WordArt Quick Style, point to a thumbnail in the gallery to display a live preview of it in the selected text. If you like it, you can apply it. You can also use the free angle handle (pink diamond) inside the selected text box to adjust your WordArt text angle.

Insert WordArt Text

1. Click the **Insert** tab.

2. Click the **WordArt** button, and then click one of the WordArt styles.

   A WordArt text box appears on the document with selected placeholder text.

3. Type the text you want WordArt to use.

   ◆ Drag a resize handle as needed to increase or decrease the size of the WordArt text box.

4. If applicable, use the Font and Paragraph options on the Home tab to modify the text you entered.

5. To edit WordArt text, click to place the insertion point where you want to edit, and then edit the text.

Did You Know?

You can convert text in a text box to WordArt. Select the text box, click the Format tab under Drawing Tools, and then click the WordArt text style you want from the Ribbon.

You can remove WordArt text. Select the WordArt text you want to remove, click the Format tab, click the Quick Styles button, and then click Clear WordArt.

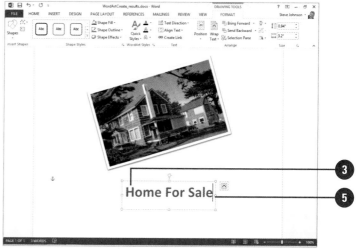

Formatting WordArt Text

In addition to applying one of the preformatted WordArt styles, you can also create your own style by shaping your text into a variety of shapes, curves, styles, and color patterns. The WordArt Styles group gives you tools for changing the fill and outline of your WordArt text. To quickly see if you like a WordArt Style, point to a thumbnail in the gallery to display a live preview of it in the selected text. If you like it, you can apply it.

Apply a Different WordArt Style to Existing WordArt Text

1. Click the WordArt object whose style you want to change.

2. Click the **Format** tab under Drawing Tools.

3. Click the **Quick Styles** button in the WordArt Styles group to see available preset styles.

    The current style appears highlighted in the gallery.

4. Point to a style.

    A live preview of the style appears in the current shape text.

5. Click the style you want from the gallery to apply it to the selected shape.

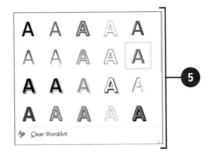

Did You Know?

You can add more formatting to WordArt text. Select the WordArt object, click the Home tab, and then use the formatting button in the Font and Paragraph groups.

You can change the WordArt fill color to match the background. Click the WordArt object, right-click the object, click Format Shape, click the Background option, and then click Close.

Apply a Fill to WordArt Text

① Click the WordArt object you want to change.

② Click the **Format** tab under Drawing Tools.

③ Click the **Text Fill** or **Shape Fill** button arrow, and then click or point to one of the following:

◆ **Color** to select a theme or standard color.

◆ **No Fill** to remove a fill color.

◆ **Picture** to select a picture file.

◆ **Gradient** to select No Gradient, one of the shadow types, or More Gradients.

◆ **Texture** to select one of the texture types, or More Textures.

Shape Fill button

Apply an Outline to WordArt Text

① Click the WordArt object you want to change.

② Click the **Format** tab under Drawing Tools.

③ Click the **Text Outline** or **Shape Outline** button.

④ Click a color, or point to **Weight** or **Dashes**, and then select a style.

Shape Outline button

Did You Know?

You can change the shape of WordArt text. Select the WordArt object, click the Format tab under Drawing Tools, click the Change WordArt Shape button, and then select a shape.

Applying WordArt Text Effects

You can change the look of WordArt text by applying effects, such as shadows, reflections, glow, soft edges, 3-D rotations, and transformations. You can apply effects to a shape by using the Text Effects gallery for quick results. From the Text Effects gallery you can apply a built-in combination of 3-D effects or individual effects to WordArt text. To quickly see if you like the effect, point to a thumbnail in the Text Effects gallery to display a live preview of it. If you like it, you can apply it. If you no longer want to apply the effect, you can remove it. Simply, select the WordArt text, point to the effect type on the Text Effects gallery, and then select the No effect type option.

Apply an Effect to WordArt Text

1. Click the WordArt object you want to change.

2. Click the **Format** tab under Drawing Tools.

3. Click the **Text Effects** button.

4. Point to one of the following:

   ◆ **Shadow** to select No Shadow, one of the shadow types, or Shadows Options.

   ◆ **Reflection** to select No Reflection, one of the Reflection Variations, or Reflection Options.

   ◆ **Glow** to select No Glow, one of the Glow Variations, More Glow Colors, or Glow Options.

   ◆ **Bevel** to select No Bevel, one of the bevel variations, or 3-D Options.

   ◆ **3-D Rotation** to select No Rotation, one of the rotation types, or 3-D Rotation Options.

   ◆ **Transform** to select No Transform, or one of the transform types (Follow Path or Warp).

5. Click the effect you want to apply to the selected shape.

WordArt text effect

Modifying WordArt Text Position

You can apply a number of text effects to your WordArt objects that determine alignment and direction. The effects of some of the adjustments you make are more pronounced for certain WordArt styles than others. Some of these effects make the text unreadable for certain styles, so apply these effects carefully. You can apply effects to a shape by using the Format Shape pane (**New!**) for custom results. You can also use the free rotate handle (circle arrow) at the top of the selected text box to rotate your WordArt text.

Change WordArt Text Direction

1. Right-click the WordArt object you want to change, and then click **Format Shape** or **Format Object**.

2. Click **Text Options** in the Format Shape pane (**New!**).

3. Click **Layout & Properties (New!)**.

4. Click the **Vertical alignment** or **Horizontal alignment** list arrow, and then select an option: **Top**, **Middle**, **Bottom**, **Top Center**, **Middle Center**, or **Bottom Center**.

5. Click the **Text Direction** list arrow, and then select an option: **Horizontal**, **Rotate all text 90°**, **Rotate all text 270°**, or **Stacked**.

6. Click the **Close** button in the pane.

Rotate WordArt Text

1. Click the WordArt object you want to change.

2. Position the pointer (which changes to the Free Rotate pointer) over the circle arrow rotate lever at the top of the object, and then drag to rotate it.

3. When you're done, release the mouse button.

4. Click outside the object to deselect it.

Creating SmartArt Graphics

SmartArt graphics allow you to create diagrams that convey processes or relationships. Office provides a wide variety of built-in SmartArt graphic types, including graphical lists, process, cycle, hierarchy, relationship, matrix, pyramid, picture, and Office.com. Using built-in SmartArt graphics makes it easy to create and modify charts without having to create them from scratch. To quickly see if you like a SmartArt graphic layout, point to a thumbnail in the gallery to display a live preview of it in the selected shape. If you like it, you can apply it.

Create a SmartArt Graphic

1 Click the **Insert** tab.

2 Click the **SmartArt** button.

3 In the left pane, click a category, such as All, List, Process, Cycle, Hierarchy, Relationship, Matrix, Pyramid, Picture, or Office.com.

4 In the middle pane, click a SmartArt graphic style type.

5 Click **OK**.

The SmartArt graphic appears in the document.

Did You Know?

You can change a SmartArt diagram type. Select the SmartArt graphic, click the Design tab under SmartArt Tools, click the More list arrow for Layouts, click More Layout, select a diagram type, and then click OK.

SmartArt Graphic Purposes

Type	Purpose
List	Show non-sequential information
Process	Show steps in a process or timeline
Cycle	Show a continual process
Hierarchy	Show a decision tree or create an organization chart
Relationship	Illustrate connections
Matrix	Show how parts relate to a whole
Pyramid	Show proportional relationships up and down
Picture	Convert a picture to a SmartArt graphic
Office.com	Show SmartArt graphics from Office.com

6 Click the **Text Pane** button, or click the control with two arrows along the left side of the selection to show the Text pane.

7 Label the shapes by doing one of the following:

◆ Type text in the [Text] box.

You can use the arrow keys to move around the Text pane, or use the Promote or Demote buttons to indent.

◆ At the end of a line, press Enter to insert a line (shape), or select line text, and then press Delete to remove a line (shape).

◆ Click a shape, and then type text directly into the shape.

8 When you're done, click outside of the SmartArt graphic.

Did You Know?

You cannot drag text into the Text pane. Although you can't drag text into the Text pane, you can copy and paste text.

You can create a blank SmartArt graphic. In the Text pane, press Ctrl+A to select all the placeholder text, and then press Delete.

Text Pane button

Using the Text Pane with SmartArt Graphics

After you create a layout for a SmartArt graphic, a Text pane appears next to your selected SmartArt graphic. The bottom of the Text pane displays a description of the SmartArt graphic. The Text pane and SmartArt graphic contain placeholder text. You can change the placeholder text in the Text pane or directly in the SmartArt graphic. The Text pane works like an outline or a bulleted list and the text corresponds directly with the shape text in the SmartArt graphic. As you add and edit content, the SmartArt graphic automatically updates, adding or removing shapes as needed while maintaining the design. If you see a red "x" in the Text pane, it means that the SmartArt graphic contains a fixed number of shapes, such as Counterbalance Arrows (only two).

Show or Hide the Text Pane

1. Click the SmartArt graphic you want to modify.

2. Click the **Design** tab under SmartArt Tools.

3. Do any of the following:

   ◆ **Show**. Click the **Text Pane** button, or click the control with two arrows along the left side of the SmartArt graphic selection to show the Text pane.

   ◆ **Hide**. Click the **Text Pane** button, click the **Close** button on the Text pane, deselect the SmartArt graphic.

   The Text Pane button toggles to show or hide the Text pane.

Text pane

Work with Text in the Text Pane

1. Click the SmartArt graphic you want to modify.

2. Click the **Design** tab under SmartArt Tools.

3. If necessary, click the **Text Pane** button to show the Text pane.

4. Do any of the following tasks:

   ◆ **New line.** At the end of a line, press Enter.

   ◆ **Indent line right.** Press Tab, or click the **Promote** button.

   ◆ **Indent line left.** Press Shift+Tab, or click the **Demote** button.

   ◆ **Delete line.** Select the line text, and then press Delete.

Did You Know?

You can format text in the Text pane.
When you apply formatting to text in the Text pane, it doesn't display in the Text pane, but it does display in the SmartArt graphic.

You can remove a shape from a SmartArt graphic. Select the SmartArt graphic, click the shape you want to remove, and then press Delete.

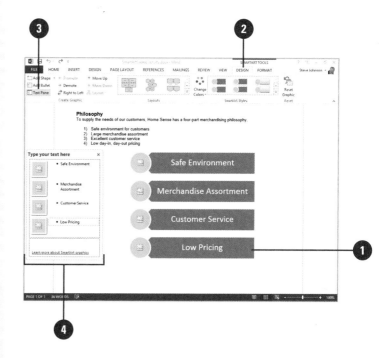

Formatting a SmartArt Graphic

If your current SmartArt graphics don't quite convey the message or look you want, use live preview to quickly preview layouts in the Quick Styles and Layout Styles groups and select the one you want. If you only want to change the color, you can choose different color schemes using theme colors by using the Change Color button. If the flow of a SmartArt graphic is not the direction you want, you can change the orientation.

Apply a Quick Style to a SmartArt Graphic

1. Click the SmartArt graphic you want to modify.

2. Click the **Design** tab under SmartArt Tools.

3. Click the scroll up or down arrow, or click the **More** list arrow in the SmartArt Styles group to see additional styles.

4. Point to a style.

   A live preview of the style appears in the current shape.

5. Click the layout for the SmartArt graphic you want from the gallery.

Change a Smart Graphic Orientation

1. Click the SmartArt graphic you want to modify.

2. Click the **Design** tab under SmartArt Tools.

3. Click the **Right to Left** button.

   The button toggles, so you can click it again to switch back.

Change a SmartArt Graphic Layout

1. Click the SmartArt graphic you want to modify.

2. Click the **Design** tab under SmartArt Tools.

3. Click the scroll up or down arrow, or click the **More** list arrow in the Layouts group to see additional styles.

   The gallery displays layouts designed for bulleted lists.

4. To view the entire list of diagram layouts, click **More Layouts**.

5. Point to a layout.

   A live preview of the style appears in the current shape.

6. Click the layout for the SmartArt graphic you want from the gallery.

7. If you opened the entire list of layouts, click **OK**.

Change a SmartArt Graphic Colors

1. Click the SmartArt graphic you want to modify.

2. Click the **Design** tab under SmartArt Tools.

3. Click the **Change Colors** button.

   The gallery displays the current layout with different theme colors.

4. Point to a style.

   A live preview of the style appears in the current shape.

5. Click the layout for the SmartArt graphic you want from the gallery.

Modifying a SmartArt Graphic Shape

After you create a SmartArt graphic, you can add, remove, change, or rearrange shapes to create a custom look. For shapes within a SmartArt graphic, you can change the shape from the Shape gallery or use familiar commands—such as Bring to Front, Send to Back, Align, Group, and Rotate—to create your own custom SmartArt graphic. If you no longer want a shape you've added, simply select it, and then press Delete to remove it.

Add a Shape to a SmartArt Graphic

1. Select the shape in the SmartArt graphic you want to modify.

2. Click the **Design** tab under SmartArt Tools.

3. Click the **Add Shape** button to insert a shape at the end, or click the **Add Shape** button arrow, and then select the position (Add Shape After, Before, Above, Below, or Assistant) where you want to insert a shape.

Added shape

Change Shapes in a SmartArt Graphic

1. Select the shapes in the SmartArt graphic you want to modify.

2. Click the **Format** tab under SmartArt Tools.

3. Click the **Change Shape** button, and then click a shape.

4. To change the size of the selected shape, click the **Larger** or **Smaller** button.

Format Shapes in a SmartArt Graphic

1. Select the shapes in the SmartArt graphic you want to modify.

2. Click the **Format** tab under SmartArt Tools.

3. In the Shape Styles section, use any of the following:

   ◆ Shape Style. Click the **More** list arrow, and then select a style.

   ◆ Shape Fill. Click the **Shape Fill** button, and then select a fill, such as a color, picture, gradient, or texture.

   ◆ Shape Outline. Click the **Shape Outline** button, and then select an outline, such as color, weight, dashes, or arrow.

   ◆ Shape Effects. Click the **Shape Effects** button, and then select an effect, such as Shadow, Reflection, Glow, Soft Edges, Bevel, or 3-D Rotation.

Did You Know?

You can reset a SmartArt graphic back to its original state. Select the SmartArt graphic, click the Design tab under SmartArt Tools, and then click the Reset Graphic button.

Shape Styles gallery

Resizing a SmartArt Graphic

You can change the size of individual shapes within a SmartArt graphic or of an entire SmartArt graphic. If the size of an individual shape within a SmartArt graphic changes, the other shapes in the graphic may also change based on the type of layout. When you resize a shape with text or increase or decrease text size, the text may automatically resize to fit the shape depending on the space available in the SmartArt graphic. When you resize an entire SmartArt graphic, shapes within it scale proportionally or adjust to create the best look. When shapes resize or move, a live layout preview (**New!**) with your changes appear on the page.

Resize a SmartArt Graphic

1. Select the shapes in the SmartArt graphic or the entire SmartArt graphic you want to modify.

2. Click the **Format** tab under SmartArt Tools.

3. Use one of the following methods:

   ◆ Drag a middle handle to resize the object up, down, left, or right.

   ◆ Drag a corner handle to resize the object proportionally.

   ◆ Click the **Size** button, and then specify the size you want.

   ◆ Click the **Larger** or **Smaller** button to increase or decrease selected shapes in standard increments.

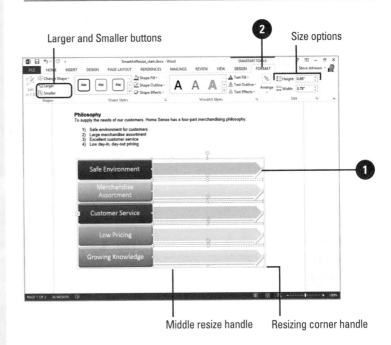

Larger and Smaller buttons

Size options

Middle resize handle

Resizing corner handle

Did You Know?

You can arrange shapes in a SmartArt graphic. Select the shape in the SmartArt graphic, click the Format tab under SmartArt Tools, click the Arrange button, and then select an arrange button option: Bring To Front, Send To Back, Align, Group, or Rotate.

You can edit a SmartArt graphic shape in 2-D. Select the SmartArt graphic with the 3-D style, click the Format tab under SmartArt Tools, and then click the Edit In 2-D button.

Adding Pictures to a SmartArt Graphic

With SmartArt graphic layouts, you can insert pictures in the SmartArt shapes. In addition to the pictures, you can also add descriptive text using the Text pane or shape itself. The process is very simple. Insert a SmartArt picture layout, insert pictures, and then add descriptive text. If you already have pictures in your document, you can convert them to a SmartArt graphic.

Add a SmartArt Graphic to a Picture

1 Use either of the following to add pictures to a SmartArt graphic:

- **Create New.** Click the **Insert** tab, click the **SmartArt** button, click **Picture**, click a layout, and then click **OK**.

- **Convert Picture.** Select a picture, click the **Format** tab under Picture Tools, click the **Picture Layout** button, and then select a layout.

2 To add a shape, click the **Design** tab under SmartArt Tools, click the **Add Shape** button arrow, and then select the type of shape you want to add.

3 To add a picture, double-click a graphic placeholder, select a picture file, and then click **Insert**.

4 Label the shapes by doing one of the following:

- Type text in the [Text] box.

- Click a shape, and then type text directly into the shape.

Did You Know?

Convert a SmartArt graphic to shapes. Select the SmartArt graphic, click the Design tab under SmartArt Tools, and then click the Convert To Shapes button.

Convert picture

Creating an Organization Chart

An organization chart shows the reporting relationships between individuals in an organization. For example, you can show the relationship between a manager and employees within a company. You can create an organization chart using a SmartArt graphic or using Microsoft Organization Chart. A SmartArt graphic organization chart makes it easy to add shapes using the graphic portion or the Text pane.

Create an Organization Chart Using a SmartArt Graphic

1 Click the **Insert** tab.

2 Click the **SmartArt** button.

3 In the left pane, click **Hierarchy**.

4 In the middle pane, click a SmartArt organization chart type.

5 Click **OK**.

The SmartArt graphic appears with a Text pane to insert text.

6 Label the shapes by doing one of the following:

♦ Type text in the [Text] box.

You can use the arrow keys to move around the Text pane.

♦ Click a shape, and then type text directly into the shape.

7 To add shapes from the Text pane, place the insertion point at the beginning of the text where you want to add a shape, type the text you want, press Enter, and then to indent the new shape, press Tab or to promote, press Shift+Tab.

You can also click the **Add Shape** button arrow on the **Design** tab under SmartArt Tools, and then select the type of shape you want to add.

8 When you're done, click outside of the SmartArt graphic.

Modifying an Organization Chart

Like any SmartArt graphic, you can add special effects—such as soft edges, glows, or 3-D effects, and animation—to an organization chart. If your organization chart doesn't quite look the way you want, live preview can help you preview layouts in the Quick Styles and Layout Styles groups and select the one you want. If you only want to change the color, you can choose different color schemes using theme colors by using the Change Color button.

Change the Layout or Apply a Quick Style to an Organization Chart

1 Click the SmartArt graphic you want to modify.

2 Click the **Design** tab under SmartArt Tools.

3 Click the scroll up or down arrow, or click the **More** list arrow in the Layouts group or Quick Styles group to see additional styles.

The gallery displays different layouts or the current layout with different theme colors.

4 Point to a style.

A live preview of the style appears in the current shape.

5 Click the layout or style for the SmartArt graphic you want from the gallery.

Did You Know?

You can change organization chart lines to dotted lines. Right-click the line you want to modify, click Format Object, click Line Style, click Dash type, click a style, and then click Close.

You can change the colors of an organization chart. Click the SmartArt graphic you want to modify, click the Design tab under SmartArt Tools, click the Change Colors button, and then click the color theme you want.

Inserting or Embedding Online Video

If you want to include a video in a Word document and don't have one, you can search for and insert an online video from the web using Bing Video Search (**New!**) or a connected online service, such as YouTube (**New!**), or you can paste a copied video embed code from other online sources (**New!**), such as Vimeo. An embed code is HTML code that specifies the location of the video on the web. The embed code links the video to the document that is stored on the web; the actual video is not part of your document, which is good; it prevents a large document size. To add an online video to a document, you click the Online Video button on the Insert tab, and then locate, select, and insert the video you want or paste the video embed code.

Insert and Embed Online Video

1. Click the **Insert** tab.

2. Click the **Online Video** button.

3. Use any of the following to locate an online picture:

   - **Bing Video Search.** Enter a keyword for the search, and then click the **Search** button.

   - **Online Services.** Click a service icon, such as YouTube. Connect to the service as needed. Enter a keyword for the search, and then click the **Search** button.

   - **From a Video Embed Code.** Copy the paste code from an online video site, such as Vimeo, and then paste it in the Paste embed code here box.

4. Select the video(s) you want.

   - To preview a larger poster image for the video, point to a video, and then click the **View Larger** button.

5. Click **Insert**.

6. Select the video object, and then move and resize it, as desired.

7. To play the video, click the video object in the document, and then click the **Play** button. Use the Playback controls. Click outside the video object to exit.

View Larger button

Adding Tables and Charts to Documents

Introduction

There are times when typing a paragraph will not do your text justice. Creating a bulleted or numbered list might better show your information. Another way to organize items in a document is with a table. A **table** is an object that is inserted into the Word document that displays text in rows and columns. You can set up your table with existing text, or create the table, even draw it out, and enter in new text. Once created, you can adjust the cells (where the text is contained in the rows and columns). You can also adjust the table to insert or delete rows, columns or individual cells, change the alignment of text, sort the text, or even apply a border or shading to the table.

Instead of adding a table of data, you can also insert a chart. Charts add visual interest and useful information represented by lines, bars, pie slices, or other markers. When you insert and create a chart in a document, the chart is an embedded object from Excel 2013. Word uses Microsoft Excel to embed and display the information in a chart. You can resize or move the embedded chart just as you would any graphic object. Your chart is what your reader sees, so make sure to take advantage of the pre-built chart layouts and styles to make the chart appealing and visually informative. There are a wide variety of chart types, available in 2-D and 3-D formats, from which to choose. For each chart type, you can select a predefined chart layout and style to apply the formatting you want.

After you finish creating a chart, you can save it as a chart template. A chart template file saves all the customization you made to a chart for use in other documents. You can save any chart in a document as a chart template file and use it to form the basis of your next document chart, which is useful for standard company financial reporting.

What You'll Do

Create a Table

Enter Text in a Table

Sort Table Contents or Lists

Modify a Table

Adjust and Align Table Cells

Add a Quick Style to a Table

Format a Table

Change Table Options

Sum Table Rows and Columns

Calculate a Value in a Table

Insert and Create a Chart

Work with Chart Data

Change a Chart Type

Change a Chart Layout and Style

Format a Chart

Change Chart Elements

Change Chart Titles and Labels

Format Line and Bar Charts

Edit and Filter Chart Data

Save a Chart Template

Manage Chart Templates

Creating a Table

A **table** organizes information neatly into rows and columns. The intersection of a row and a column is called a **cell**. You can insert tables by specifying a size, or drawing rows and columns to create a custom table, or you can create a table from existing text separated by paragraphs, tabs, or commas. In addition, you can create **nested tables** (a table created within a table cell), **floating tables** (tables with text wrapped around them), or **side-by-side tables** (separate but adjacent tables). If you decide not to use a table, you can convert it to text.

Create a Table from Existing Text

1. Select the text for the table.

2. Click the **Insert** tab.

3. Click the **Table** button, and then click **Convert Text to Table**.

4. Enter the number of columns.

5. Select an AutoFit column width option.

6. Click a symbol to separate text into cells.

7. Click **OK**.

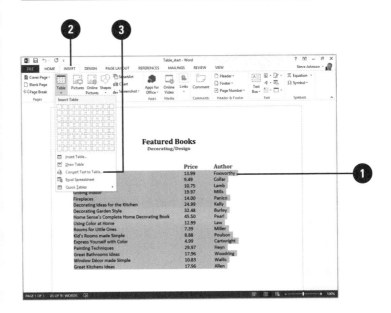

Did You Know?

You can convert a table back to text. Select the table, click the Layout tab under Table Tools, click the Convert To Text button, select the Separate text with option (typically Tabs), and then click OK.

You can insert a Quick Table. If you need a calendar, or a specific table layout, such as double table, matrix, tabular list, you can use the Quick Tables command to select the one you want. The tables come with predefined data or information, which you can delete.

Create a New Table Quickly

1. Click to place the insertion point where you want to insert a table.

2. Click the **Insert** tab.

3. Click the **Table** button, and then drag to select the number of rows and columns you want, or click **Insert Table**, enter the number of columns and rows you want, and then click **OK**.

4. Release the mouse button to insert a blank grid in the document.

5. When you're done, click outside of the table.

Draw a Custom Table

1. Click the **Insert** tab.

2. Click the **Table** button, and then click **Draw Table**.

3. Draw the table.

   ◆ A rectangle creates individual cells or the table boundaries.

   ◆ Horizontal lines create rows.

   ◆ Vertical lines create columns.

   ◆ Diagonal lines split cells.

4. If necessary, press and hold Shift, and then click one or more lines to erase them.

5. When you're done, click outside of the table.

Entering Text in a Table

Once you create your table, you enter text into cells just as you would in a paragraph, except pressing Tab moves you from cell to cell. As you type in a cell, text wraps to the next line, and the height of a row expands as you enter text that extends beyond the column width. The first row in the table is good for column headings, whereas the left-most column is good for row labels. Before you can modify a table, you need to know how to select the rows and columns of a table.

Enter Text and Move Around a Table

1. The insertion point shows where text that you type will appear in a table. After you type text in a cell:

- Press Enter to start a new paragraph within that cell.

- Press Tab to move the insertion point to the next cell to the right (or to the first cell in the next row).

- Press the arrow keys or click in a cell to move the insertion point to a new location.

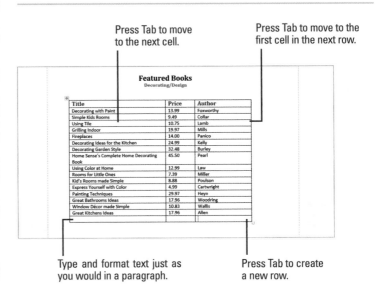

Press Tab to move to the next cell.

Press Tab to move to the first cell in the next row.

Type and format text just as you would in a paragraph.

Press Tab to create a new row.

Select Table Elements

Refer to this table for methods of selecting table elements, including:

- The entire table

- One or more rows and columns

- One or more cells

Did You Know?

You can delete contents within a cell. Select the cells whose contents you want to delete, and then press Backspace or Delete.

Selecting Table Elements

To Select	Do This
The entire table	Click ⊞ next to the table, or click anywhere in the table, click the Layout tab under Table Tools, click the Select button, and then click Select Table.
One or more rows	Click in the left margin next to the first row you want to select, and then drag to select the rows you want.
One or more columns	Click just above the first column you want to select, and then drag with ↓ to select the columns you want, or click the Layout tab under Table Tools, click the Select button and then click Select Column or Select Row.
A single cell	Drag a cell or click the cell with ↗.
More than one cell	Drag with ↗ to select a group of cells.

Sorting Table Contents or Lists

After you enter contents in a table or create a bulleted or numbered list, you can reorganize the information by sorting the information. For example, you might want to sort information in a client list alphabetically by last name or numerically by their last invoice date. **Ascending order** lists information from A to Z, earliest to latest, or lowest to highest. **Descending order** lists information from Z to A, latest to earliest, or highest to lowest. You can sort a table columns based on one or more adjacent columns. A sort, for example, might be the telephone directory numerically by area code and then alphabetically by last name.

Sort Table Contents or Lists

1. Select the table column, adjacent columns, or list you want to sort.

2. Click the **Home** tab or the **Layout** tab under Table Tools.

3. Click the **Sort** button.

4. If necessary, click the **Sort by** list arrow, and then select a column name.

5. Click the **Type** list arrow, and then click table cell content type.

6. Click the **Ascending** or **Descending** option.

7. If necessary, click the second **Sort by** list arrow, select another column name, and then select the related sorting options you want.

8. Click the **Header row** or **No header row** option as it applies to the table.

9. Click **OK**.

Did You Know?

You can show or hide gridlines in a table. Select the table you want to change, click the Layout tab under Table Tools, and then click View Gridlines to toggle it on and off.

Modifying a Table

As you begin to work on a table, you might need to modify its structure by adding more rows, columns, or cells to accommodate new text, graphics, or other tables. You can insert rows or columns by using buttons on the Layout tab under Table Tools or on the Mini-Toolbar (**New!**), or by using an Add button (+) on the table (**New!**). The table realigns as needed to accommodate the new structure. When you insert rows, columns, or cells, the existing rows shift down, the existing columns shift right, and you choose what direction the existing cells shift. Similarly, when you delete unneeded rows, columns, or cells from a table, the table realigns itself.

Insert Additional Rows or Columns

1. Select the row above which you want the new rows to appear, or select the column to the left of which you want the new columns to appear.

2. Drag to select the number of rows or columns you want to insert.

3. Click the **Layout** tab under Table Tools.

   ◆ **Mini-Toolbar**. Click the **Insert** button on the Mini-Toolbar (**New!**), and then select an insert option.

4. Click the Row & Column buttons you want:

   ◆ **Insert Above**.

   ◆ **Insert Below**.

   ◆ **Insert Left**.

   ◆ **Insert Right**.

   TIMESAVER *Point to the left or top edge of the table to display an Add button where you want to insert a row or column, and then click the Add button (+) (**New!**) to create the new rows or columns.*

Add button

Mini-Toolbar

Delete Table, Rows, Columns, or Cells

1. Select the rows, columns, or cells you want to delete.

2. Click the **Layout** tab under Table Tools.

3. Click the **Delete** button on the Layout tab or Mini-Toolbar (**New!**), and then click the delete option you want:

   ◆ **Delete Cells**. Select the direction in which you want the remaining cells to shift to fill the space, and then click OK.

   ◆ **Delete Columns**.

   ◆ **Delete Rows**.

   ◆ **Delete Table**.

Mini-Toolbar

Did You Know?

You can set column widths to fit text. Word can set the column widths to fit the cells' contents or to fill the space between the document's margins. Click in the table, click the Layout tab under Table Tools, click the AutoFit button in the Cell Size group, and then click AutoFit To Contents or AutoFit To Window.

You can evenly distribute columns and rows. Select the columns or rows you want to distribute evenly in a table, click the Layout tab under Table Tools, and then click the Distribute Vertically or Distribute Horizontally button in the Cells Size group.

You can resize a table. Drag a corner or middle resize handle to resize the table manually.

Adjusting Table Cells

Often there is more to modifying a table than adding or deleting rows or columns; you need to make cells just the right size to accommodate the text you are entering in the table. For example, a title in the first row of a table might be longer than the first cell in that row. To spread the title across the top of the table, you can merge (combine) the cells to form one long cell. Sometimes, to indicate a division in a topic, you need to split (or divide) a cell into two. You can also split one table into two at any row. Moreover, you can modify the width of any column and height of any row to better present your data.

Merge and Split Table Cells and Tables

- To merge two or more cells into a single cell, select the cells you want to merge, click the **Layout** tab under Table Tools, and then click the **Merge Cells** button.

- To split a cell into multiple cells, click the cell you want to split, click the **Layout** tab under Table Tools, and then click the **Split Cells** button. Enter the number of rows or columns (or both) you want to split the selected cell into, clear the **Merge cells before split** check box, and then click **OK**.

- To split a table into two tables separated by a paragraph, click in the row that you want as the top row in the second table, click the **Layout** tab under Table Tools, and then click the **Split Table** button.

- To merge two tables into one, delete the paragraph between them.

Did You Know?

You can quickly adjust columns and rows. Position the pointer over the boundary of the column or row you want to adjust until it becomes a resize pointer. Drag the boundary to a new location.

Merge and Split buttons

The three cells in this row will merge into one.

Merged cells

Adjust Column Widths and Row Heights

1. Select the columns or rows you want to change.

2. Select the **Ruler** check box on the View tab to display the ruler.

3. Click the **Layout** tab under Table Tools.

4. Point to the column or width (cursor changes to a double-arrow), and then drag to adjust it or manually change the Height and Width boxes in the Cell Size group:

   ◆ **Height.** To change the row height, enter a height in the Height box and then press Enter, or use the Up and Down arrows.

   ◆ **Width.** To change the column width, enter a width in the Width box and then press Enter, or use the Up and Down arrows.

Change Table Properties

1. Click in the table you want to change.

2. Click the **Layout** tab under Table Tools.

3. Click the **Properties** button.

4. Click an alignment option, and then specify an indent from the left (when you select the Left alignment option).

5. Click a text wrapping option.

6. Click **OK**.

Aligning Table Cells

Tables distinguish text from paragraphs. In turn, formatting, alignment, and text direction distinguish text in table cells. You can customize your table by realigning the cells' contents both horizontally and vertically, changing the direction of text within selected cells, such as the column headings, and resizing the entire table. You can also modify the appearance and size of the cells and the table.

Change Text Direction Within Cells

1. Select the cells you want to change.

2. Click the **Layout** tab under Table Tools.

3. Click the **Text Direction** button until the text is the direction you want.

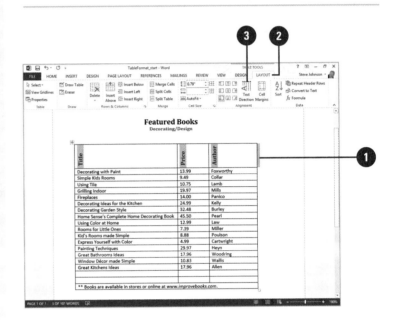

Align Text Within Cells

1. Select the cells, rows, or columns you want to align.

2. Click the **Layout** tab under Table Tools.

3. To align text in a cell, row or column, click one of the alignment buttons in the Alignment group.

4. To evenly distribute the height and width of the selected row and columns, select the row or column, and then click **Distribute Rows** or **Distribute Columns**.

Change Cells Margins

1. Select a cell in the table you want to change.

2. Click the **Layout** tab under Table Tools.

3. Click the **Cell Margins** button.

4. Specify cell margin sizes you want for the table.

5. Click **OK**.

Did You Know?

You can create nested tables. Select the table or cells, click the Home tab, click the Cut or Copy button, right-click the table cell, and then click Paste As Nested Table.

Change Cell Sizes

1. Select the cells in the table you want to change.

2. Click the **Layout** tab under Table Tools.

3. Click the **Up** and **Down** arrows for the **Table Row Height** and **Table Column Width**.

4. To automatically adjust the column width based on the size of the text, click the **AutoFit** button, and then click **AutoFit Contents**, **AutoFit Window**, or **Fixed Column Width**.

Adding a Quick Style to a Table

Instead of changing individual attributes of a table, such as shape, border, and effects, you can quickly add them all at once with the Table Quick Style gallery. The Table Quick Style gallery provides a variety of different formatting combinations. To quickly see if you like a Table Quick Style, point to a thumbnail in the gallery to display a live preview of it in the selected shape. If you like the style, you can apply it. In addition to applying one of the preformatted tables from the Table Quick Style gallery, you can also create your own style by setting individual table attributes.

Add a Quick Style to a Table

1. Click the table you want to change, or select the cells you want to modify.

2. Click the **Design** tab under Table Tools.

3. Click the scroll up or down arrow, or click the **More** list arrow in the Table Styles group to see additional styles.

   The current style appears highlighted in the gallery.

   TIMESAVER *Click the gallery title bar arrow to narrow down the list of styles: All, Document Matching, Light, Medium, or Dark.*

4. Point to a style.

   A live preview of the style appears in the current shape.

5. Click the style you want from the gallery to apply it to the selected table.

Did You Know?

You can clear table formatting. Select the table you want to change, click the Design tab under Table Tools, click the More list arrow in the Table Styles group, and then click Clear.

Create or Modify a Table Style

① Click the table you want to change, or select the cells you want to modify.

② Click the **Design** tab under Table Tools.

③ Click the **More** list arrow in the Table Styles group, and then click **New Table Style** or **Modify Table Style**.

④ Enter or change the table name.

⑤ Specify the following table properties:

◆ **Style type.** Select Table as the type.

◆ **Style based on.** Select Table Normal or a style of your choice as the baseline (initial settings) for the table style.

⑥ Click the **Apply formatting to** list arrow, and then select an option where to apply to style.

⑦ Specify the style options that you want to use as the table style.

◆ **Format.** Click to access dialog boxes with additional options: Table Properties, Borders and Shading, Banding, Font, Paragraph, Tabs, and Text Effects.

The results of the style options appear in the preview.

⑧ Click the **Only in this document** or **New document based on this template** option.

⑨ Click **OK**.

Format button

Formatting a Table

When applying a Table Quick Style to a table makes it easy to format a table, you may need a custom style to match your corporate color scheme or a unique presentation. You can change individual table attributes of a table, such as shading and borders. You can select shading colors to fill in table cells and border styles and attributes to create the custom table you want. You can quickly apply Border Styles (**New!**) just like you apply Table Quick Styles. If you apply a border style or individual set of border attributes to a cell, you can use the Border Painter (**New!**) to copy the format to other cells in your table, just like the Format Painter on the Home tab.

Apply Fill Shading to a Table

1. Click the table you want to change, or select the cells you want to modify.

2. Click the **Design** tab under Table Tools.

3. Click the **Shading** button, and then click or point to one of the following:

   ◆ **Color** to select a theme or standard color.

   ◆ **No Color** to remove a color fill.

   ◆ **More Colors** to select a standard or custom color (using the RGB or HSL model).

Apply a Border to a Table

1. Click the table you want to change, or select the cells you want to modify.

2. Click the **Design** tab under Table Tools.

3. To apply a border style, click the **Border Styles** button (**New!**), and then click a style. You can point to a style to preview it.

4. Use the **Line Width**, **Line Style**, and **Pen Color** buttons to select the border attributes you want.

5. Click the **Border** button.

6. Click a border option, such as No Border, All Borders, Outside Borders, Inside Horizontal Border, Inside Vertical Border, Diagonal Down Border, or Diagonal Up Border.

Border styles

Apply a Border Painter to a Table

1. Click the table and then select the cells with the border formatting you want to apply else where.

2. Click the **Design** tab under Table Tools.

3. Click the **Border Painter** button (**New!**).

4. Drag the painter cursor over the borders you want to apply formatting.

5. When you're done, click the **Border Painter** button again to turn it off.

Changing Table Style Options

When you create a table, you typically include a header row or first column to create horizontal or vertical headings for your table information. You can use Quick Style options, such as a header or total row, first or last column, or banded rows and columns, to show or hide a special row and column formatting. The Total Row option displays a row at the end of the table for column totals. The Banded Row or Banded Column option formats even rows or columns differently from odd rows or columns to make a table easier to view.

Change Table Columns Options

1. Click the table you want to change.

2. Click the **Design** tab under Table Tools.

3. Select any of the following row and column check box options:

   ◆ **First Column** to format the first column of the table as special.

   ◆ **Last Column** to format the last column of the table as special.

   ◆ **Banded Columns** to format even columns differently than odd columns.

Change Table Rows Options

1. Click the table you want to change.

2. Click the **Design** tab under Table Tools.

3. Select any of the following row and column check box options:

   ◆ **Header Row** to format the top row of the table as special.

   ◆ **Total Row** to format the bottom row of the table for column totals.

   ◆ **Banded Rows** to format even rows differently than odd rows.

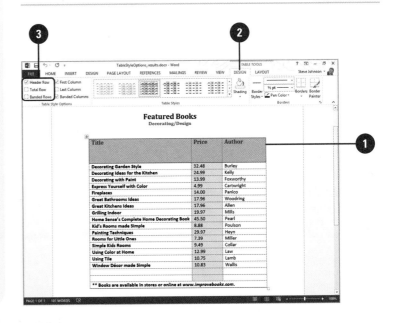

Summing Table Rows and Columns

The fastest way to total the rows or columns of a table is by clicking the Formulas button on the Layout tab under Table Tools. The disadvantage of using this method is that if you subsequently edit the values in the rows and columns of the table, the sums will not automatically update. You would need to remember to click Formula again for each row and column that was updated. To ensure sum totals are automatically calculated anytime the data in a table changes, use the equation functions of Word.

Add the Contents of Rows and Columns

1. Click the cell in which you want the sum to appear.

2. Click the **Layout** tab under Table Tools.

3. Click the **Formula** button. If Word proposes a formula that you do not want to use, delete it from the Formula box.

   ◆ If the cell you selected is at the bottom of a column of numbers, Microsoft Word proposes the formula =SUM(ABOVE).

   ◆ If the cell you selected is at the right end of a row of numbers, Word proposes the formula =SUM(LEFT).

4. Click **OK**.

The sum of the cell rows appears here

Word provides the sum formula

Calculating a Value in a Table

Sometimes the simple equations proposed by Word do not adequately cover what you are trying to calculate in the table. When that is the case, you need to create a custom equation to do the work. The Formula dialog box gives you a choice of 18 paste functions to help you create your formula. Should you need help, you can activate Help to see examples of how to use each paste function, or for more complex formulas, try Microsoft's Online Community to look for advice from other users.

Calculate a Value

1. Click the cell in which you want the result to appear.

2. Click the **Layout** tab under Table Tools.

3. Click the **Formula** button. If Word proposes a formula that you do not want to use, delete it from the Formula box.

4. Click the **Paste Function** list arrow, and then select a function.

5. To reference the contents of a table cell, type the cell references in the parentheses in the formula. For instance, to average the values in cells a1 through a4, the formula would read =Average(a1,a4). If you are doing the average of a row in the last column of the row, simplify this to =Average(left).

6. In the Number format box, enter a format for the numbers. For example, to display the numbers as a decimal percentage, click 0.00%. For now, enter 0 to display the average as the nearest whole number. To display a true average, enter 0.00 in the Number Format box.

7. Click **OK**.

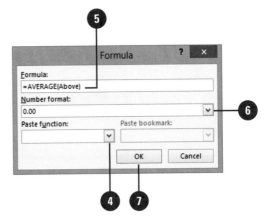

Inserting and Creating a Chart

A **chart** provides a visual, graphical representation of numerical data. Charts add visual interest and useful information represented by lines, bars, pie slices, or other markers. A group of data values from a worksheet row or column of data makes up a **data series**. Each data series has a unique color or pattern on the chart. Titles on the chart, horizontal (x-axis), and vertical (y-axis) identify the data. Gridlines are horizontal and vertical lines to help the reader view data values in a chart. When you insert and create a chart, it's an **embedded object** from Excel 2013 with a worksheet window (**New!**) containing sample data. You can then resize or move the window or chart object just as you would any other.

Insert and Create a Chart

1. Click to place the insertion point where you want to insert a Chart.

2. Click the **Insert** tab.

3. Click the **Insert Chart** button.

4. Click a category in the left pane.

   ◆ **Recent.** Click to display and use recently used templates for easy access (**New!**).

   ◆ **Templates.** Click to display and use custom chart templates.

5. Click the chart type you want.

6. Click **OK**.

   A Microsoft Excel worksheet opens on top of your Word document (**New!**), displaying a sample chart.

   The chart data appears with a blue fill, while the data series appear with a red and purple fill for easy identification (**New!**).

7. To create a chart, change the sample data in the Excel worksheet. You can enter, paste, or import data.

8. To close the worksheet and view the chart, click the **Close** button on the Excel worksheet and return to Word.

Working with Chart Data

You can enter chart data in the Excel worksheet either by typing it or by inserting it from a different source. The worksheet is designed to make data entry easy, so direct typing is best when you're entering brief, simple data. For more complex or longer data, and when you're concerned about accuracy, insert and link your data to the chart. When you first insert a chart, the worksheet contains sample labels and numbers.

Open and View Chart Data

1. Click the chart you want to modify.

   A chart consists of the following elements.

   - **Data markers**. A graphical representation of a data point in a single cell in the datasheet. Typical data markers include bars, dots, or pie slices.

   - **Legend**. A pattern or color that identifies each data series.

   - **X-axis**. A reference line for the horizontal data values.

   - **Y-axis**. A reference line for the vertical data values.

   - **Tick marks**. Marks that identify data increments.

2. Click the **Design** tab under Chart Tools.

3. Click the **Edit Data** button, and then click **Edit Data (New!)** or **Edit Data in Excel 2013**.

   A chart worksheet or Microsoft Excel worksheet opens on top of your Word document.

   The chart data appears with a blue fill, while the data series appear with a red and purple fill for easy identification (**New!**).

4. To close the worksheet and view the chart, click the **Close** button on the Excel worksheet and return to Word.

A data series   Worksheet

Chart

Y-axis   Data marker

Tick mark   Legend   X-axis

Enter Data in the Worksheet

1. Click the chart you want to modify, click the **Edit Data** button on the Design tab under Chart Tools, and then click **Edit Data (New!)** or **Edit Data in Excel 2103**.

2. To delete the sample data, click the upper-left heading button to select all the cells, and then press Delete.

3. Use one of the following to select a cell, row, column, or datasheet.

   ◆ To select a cell, click it.

   ◆ To select an entire row or column, click the row heading or column heading button.

   ◆ To select a range of cells, drag the pointer over the cells you want to select, or click the upper-left cell of the range, press and hold Shift, and then click the lower-right cell. When you select a range of cells, the active cell is white, and all other selected cells are outlined in black.

4. Type the data you want to enter in the cell.

5. Press Enter to move the insertion point down one row or press Tab to move the insertion point right to the next cell.

6. To adjust the chart data range, drag the lower right corner resize handle in blue. To adjust the chart data series, drag the resize handle in red or purple.

7. To close the worksheet and view the chart, click the **Close** button on the Excel worksheet and return to Word.

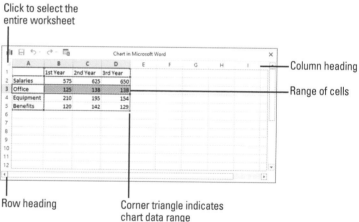

Click to select the entire worksheet

Column heading

Range of cells

Row heading

Corner triangle indicates chart data range

Changing a Chart Type

Your chart is what your reader sees, so make sure to take advantage of the pre-built chart layouts and styles to make the chart appealing and visually informative. Start by choosing the chart type that is best suited for presenting your data. There are a wide variety of chart types, available in 2-D and 3-D formats, from which to choose. For each chart type, you can select a predefined chart layout and style to apply the formatting you want. If you want to format your chart beyond the provided formats, you can customize a chart, and then save it as a template. You can change the chart type for the entire chart, or you can change the chart type for a selected data series to create a combination chart. You can change the chart type for the entire chart, or you can can change it for a selected data series to create a combination chart.

Change a Chart Type for an Entire Chart

1. Select the chart you want to change.

2. Click the **Design** tab under Chart Tools.

3. Click the **Change Chart Type** button.

4. Click a category in the left pane.

   ◆ **Recent.** Click to display and use recently used templates for easy access (**New!**).

   ◆ **Templates.** Click to display and use custom chart templates.

5. Click the chart type you want.

6. Click **OK**.

Did You Know?

You can reset chart formatting. Click the chart you want to reset, click the Format tab under Chart Tools, and then click the Reset To Match Style button.

You can quickly access chart formatting. Double-click a chart element to open the Format pane (**New!**).

You can delete a chart. Click the chart object, and then press Delete.

Changing a Chart Layout and Style

Office's pre-built chart layouts and styles can make your chart more appealing and visually informative. Start by choosing the chart type that is best suited for presenting your data. There are a wide variety of chart types, available in 2-D and 3-D formats, from which to choose. For each chart type, you can select a predefined chart layout and style to apply the formatting you want. If you want to format your chart beyond the provided formats, you can customize a chart. Save your customized settings so that you can apply that chart formatting to any chart you create. To change a chart design, you can use layout, style, and color options on the Design tab under Chart Tools or use the Chart Styles button (**New!**) (one of three) in the upper-right corner of the selected chart.

Change a Chart Layout or Style

1. Select the chart you want to change.

2. Click the **Design** tab under Chart Tools.

3. To change the chart layout, click the **Quick Layout** button, and then click the layout you want.

4. To quickly change the chart style and colors, click the **Chart Styles** button (**New!**) near the chart, click **STYLE** or **COLOR**, and then click a style or color. You can also use options on the Design tab:

   ◆ **Style.** Click the scroll up or down arrow, or click the **More** list arrow in the Chart Styles group, and then click the chart style you want.

   ◆ **Color.** Click the **Change Colors** button, and then click a color.

Did You Know?

You can record macros with chart elements. When you use the macro recorder with charts, it now records formatting changes to charts and other objects.

Styles

Layouts

Formatting Chart Elements

Before you can format a chart element, you need to select it first. You can select a chart element directly on the chart or use the Chart Elements list arrow on the Ribbon. After you select a chart element, you can use the Format Selection button to open the Format pane (**New!**), where you can change formatting options, including number, fill, border color and styles, shadow, 3-D format, and alignment. Formatting options vary depending on the selected chart element. In the same way you can apply shape fills, outlines, and effects to a shape, you can also apply them to elements and shapes in a chart.

Format a Chart Object

1. Select the chart element you want to modify.

2. Click the **Format** tab under Chart Tools.

3. Click the **Format Selection** button.

   ◆ You can also double-click a chart element.

4. In the Format pane (**New!**), click a button (Fill & Line, Effects, or Options), expand a category, and then select the options you want.

   Some common formatting option categories include the following:

   ◆ **Number** to change number formats.

   ◆ **Fill** to remove or change the fill color, either solid, gradient, picture, or texture.

   ◆ **Border** to remove or change the border color and styles, either solid or gradient line.

   ◆ **Shadow** to change shadow options, including color, transparency, size, blur, angle, and distance.

   ◆ **3-D Format** to change 3-D format options, including bevel, depth, contour, and surface.

   ◆ **Alignment** to change text alignment, direction, and angle.

   ◆ **Series Options** to change gap depth and width, and shape.

5. Click the **Close** button in the pane.

Changing Chart Elements

The layout of a chart typically comes with a chart title, X and Y axes, axis titles, and a legend. However, you can also include other elements, such as data labels, a data table, gridlines. A **legend** is a set of labels that helps the reader connect the colors and patterns in a chart with the data they represent. Legend text is derived from the data series plotted within a chart. If the legend chart location doesn't work with the chart type, you can reposition it. **Data labels** show data values in the chart to make it easier for the reader to see, while a **Data table** shows the data values in a table next to the chart. To change elements, you can use the Add Chart Element button on the Design tab under Chart Tools or use the Chart Elements button (**New!**) (one of three) in the upper-right corner of the selected chart. If you want a customized look, you can double-click an element to set options using the Format pane (**New!**).

Change the Chart Elements

1. Select the chart you want to modify.

2. Click the **Design** tab under Chart Tools.

3. To quickly show or hide chart elements, click the **Chart Elements** button near the chart, and then select or clear the element check box (**New!**), or click an arrow, and then a command.

4. Click the **Add Chart Element** button (**New!**), and then point to one of the following options:

   ◆ **Axes** to display the horizontal and vertical axes.

   ◆ **Axis Titles** to display the horizontal and vertical axis titles.

   ◆ **Chart Tile** to display or position the main chart title. Double-click the text box to modify text.

   ◆ **Data Labels** to show or hide data labels.

   ◆ **Data Table** to show or hide a data table along with the chart.

   ◆ **Gridlines** to display different types of gridlines.

   ◆ **Legend** to display or position the chart legend.

Changing Chart Titles

The layout of a chart typically comes with a chart title, axis titles, and a legend. However, you can also include other elements, such as data labels, and a data table. You can show, hide, or change the positions of these elements to achieve the look you want. The chart title typically appears at the top of the chart. However, you can change the title position to appear as an overlap text object on top of the chart. When you position the chart title as an overlay, the chart is resized to the maximum allowable size. In the same way, you can also reposition horizontal and vertical axis titles to achieve the best fit in a chart. If you want a more custom look, you can set individual options using the Format pane (**New!**).

Change Chart Title

1. Select the chart you want to modify.

2. Click the **Design** tab under Chart Tools.

3. Click the **Add Chart Elements** button, point to **Chart Titles**, and then click one of the following:

   - **None** to hide the chart title.

   - **Centered Overlay Title** to insert a title on the chart without resizing it.

   - **Above Chart** to position the chart title at the top of the chart and resize it.

   - **More Title Options** to set custom chart title options.

4. Double-click the text box to place the insertion point, and then modify the text.

Did You Know?

You can link a chart or axis title to a worksheet cell. On the chart, click the chart or axis title you want to link, click in the formula bar, type equal sign (=), select the worksheet cell that contains the data or text you want to display in the chart, and then press Enter.

Changing Chart Labels

A **legend** is a set of text labels that helps the reader connect the colors and patterns in a chart with the data they represent. Legend text is derived from the data series plotted within a chart. You can rename an item within a legend by changing the text in the data series. If the legend chart location doesn't work with the chart type, you can reposition the legend at the right, left, top or bottom of the chart or overlay the legend on top of the chart on the right or left side. **Data labels** show data values in the chart to make it easier for the reader to see, while a Data table shows the data values in an associated table next to the chart. You can have data labels appears as callouts (**New!**) or just about any shape (**New!**), and even add leader lines (**New!**) to them. You can use the Format tab under Chart Tools to change and format data labels. If you want a customized look, you can set individual options using the Format pane (**New!**). In addition, you can change the label display for axes and show or hide major or minor gridlines.

Change the Chart Legend, Data Labels, and Axis Titles

1. Select the chart you want to modify.

2. Click the **Design** tab under Chart Tools.

3. Click the **Add Chart Elements** button, point to one of the following, and then click an available option.

   - **Axes.** Click to show, hide, or position axis labels or tick marks.

   - **Axis Titles.** Click to add or remove an axis title on the chart.

   - **Chart Title.** Click to add, remove, or position a chart title.

   - **Data Labels.** Click to show or hide data labels on the chart for each data series (**New!**).

   - **Data Table.** Click to show or hide a table next to the chart with the chart data.

   - **Gridlines.** Click to show or hide major or minor gridlines.

   - **Legend.** Click to select a legend position on the chart.

Callouts

Formatting Line and Bar Charts

If you're using a line or bar chart, you can add trendlines, series lines, drop lines, high-low lines, up/down bars, or error bars with different options to make the chart easier to read. **Trendlines** are graphical representations of trends in data that you can use to analyze problems of prediction. For example, you can add a trendline to forecast a trend toward rising revenue. **Series lines** connect data series in 2-D stacked bar and column charts. **Drop lines** extend a data point to a category in a line or area chart, which makes it easy to see where data markers begin and end. **High-low lines** display the highest to the lowest value in each category in 2-D charts. Stock charts are examples of high-low lines and up/down bars. **Error bars** show potential error amounts graphically relative to each data marker in a data series. Error bars are usually used in statistical or scientific data. To format these charts, you can use the Add Chart Element button (**New!**) on the Design tab under Chart Tools.

Format Line and Bar Charts

1. Select the line or bar chart you want to modify.

2. Click the **Design** tab under Chart Tools.

3. Click the **Add Chart Element** button (**New!**), and then point to one of the following options:

   - **Trendline** to remove or add different types of trendlines: Linear, Exponential, Linear Forecast, and Two Period Moving Average.

   - **Lines** to hide Drop Lines, High-Low Lines or Series Lines, or show series lines on a 2-D stacked Bar/Column Pie or Pie or Bar of Pie chart.

   - **Up/Down Bars** to hide Up/Down Bars, or show Up/Down Bars on a line chart.

   - **Error Bars** to hide error bars or show error bars with using Standard Error, Percentage, or Standard Deviation.

Editing Chart Data

You can edit chart data in a worksheet one cell at a time, or you can manipulate a range of data. If you're not sure what data to change to get the results you want, use the Edit Data Source dialog box to help you. In previous versions, you were limited to 32,000 data points in a data series for 2-D charts. Now you can have as much as your memory to store. You can work with data ranges by series, either Legend or Horizontal. The Legend series is the data range displayed on the axis with the legend, while the Horizontal series is the data range displayed on the other axis. Use the Collapse Dialog button to temporarily minimize the dialog to select the data range you want. After you select your data, click the Expand Dialog button to return back to the dialog box.

Edit the Data Source

1. Click the chart you want to modify.

2. Click the **Design** tab under Chart Tools.

3. Click the **Select Data** button on the Design tab under Chart Tools.

4. In the Select Data Source dialog box, use any of the following:

   ◆ **Chart data range.** Displays the data range of the plotted chart.

   ◆ **Switch Row/Column.** Click to switch plotting the data series from rows or columns.

   ◆ **Add.** Click to add a new Legend data series to the chart.

   ◆ **Edit.** Click to make changes to a Legend or Horizontal series.

   ◆ **Remove.** Click to remove the selected Legend data series.

   ◆ **Move Up and Move Down.** Click to move a Legend data series up or down in the list.

   ◆ **Hidden and Empty Cells.** Click to plot hidden data and determine what to do with empty cells.

5. Click **OK**.

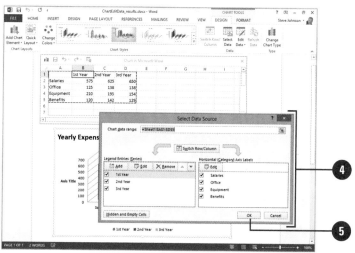

Filtering Chart Data

Instead of using the Select Data Source dialog box to make changes to the data series in a chart, you can quickly filter chart data and category names with the Chart Filters button. With the Chart Filters button (**New!**) (one of three) in the upper-right corner of the selected chart, you can specify what data points and label names you want to appear on the chart. The Chart Filters menu allows you to quickly preview filter changes to data series and categories, apply filter changes, change the data series range, and open the Select Data Source dialog box to make additional data changes.

Filter the Chart Data and Category Names

1. Select the chart you want to modify.

2. Click the **Design** tab under Chart Tools.

3. Click the **Chart Filter** button (**New!**).

4. Click the **Values** tab.

5. To preview a chart filter, point to a data series or category on the menu.

6. To filter on or off chart data series or categories, select or clear the element check box.

7. To edit or change the chart data, do either of the following:

   ◆ Edit a Data Series. Point to a data series, and then click the **Edit Series** button.

   ◆ Select Source Data. Click the **Select Data** link to open the Select Data Source dialog box to further customize the data.

8. To show or hide data series or category label names, click the **Names** tab, and then select an option on the menu.

9. To apply the change, click the **Apply** button (**New!**) on the menu.

Saving a Chart Template

A chart template file (.crtx) saves all the customization you made to a chart for use in other documents. You can save any chart in a document as a chart template file and use it to form the basis of your next document chart, which is useful for standard company financial reporting. Although you can store your template anywhere you want, you may find it handy to store it in the Templates/Charts folder that Microsoft Office uses to store its templates. If you store your design templates in the Templates/Charts folder, those templates appear as options when you insert or change a chart type using My Templates. When you create a new chart or want to change the chart type of an existing chart, you can apply a chart template instead of re-creating it.

Create a Custom Chart Template

1. Click the chart you want to save as a template.

2. Right-click the chart, and then click **Save As Template**.

   ◆ The Save As Template button on the Design tab under Chart Tools is no longer available in Word 2013 (**New!**).

3. Make sure the Charts folder appears in the Save in box.

   Microsoft Office templates are typically stored in the following location:

   Windows 8 or 7. C:/Users/*your name*/AppData/Roaming/Microsoft/Templates/Charts

4. Type a name for the chart template.

5. Click **Save**.

Chart template file format

Managing Chart Templates

If you no longer need a chart template, you can use the Chart Type dialog box to access and manage chart templates files (.crtx). You can click the Manage Templates button to open the Charts folder and move, copy, or delete chart templates. Microsoft Office stores chart template files in the Charts folder, so all Office programs can use them. When you store templates in the Charts folder, those templates appear as options when you insert or change a chart type using My Templates. So, if you no longer need a chart template, you can move it from the Charts template folder for later use or you can permanently delete it from your computer.

Move or Delete a Custom Chart Template

1. Select a chart.

2. Click the **Design** tab under Chart Tools.

3. Click the **Change Chart Type** button.

   TIMESAVER *To open the Chart Types dialog box, you can click the Charts Dialog Box Launcher on the Insert tab.*

4. Click **Templates** in the left pane.

5. Click **Manage Templates**.

   The Charts folder opens.

   Windows 8 or 7. C:/Users/*your name*/AppData/Roaming/Microsoft/Templates/Charts

6. To move a chart template file from the Charts folder, drag it to the folder where you want to store it, or right-click the file and use the Cut and Paste commands.

7. To delete a chart template file, right-click it, and then click **Delete**.

8. When you're done, click the **Close** button.

9. Click **Cancel** in the Change Chart Type dialog box.

Creating Desktop Publishing Documents

Introduction

When you want to add objects to a document, you can use Microsoft Word as a drawing package. Word provides a wide range of predesigned shapes, line options or freeform tools that allow you to draw, size, and format your own shapes and forms.

You can add several types of drawing objects to your documents—shapes, text boxes, lines, and freeforms. **Shapes** are preset objects, such as stars, circles, or ovals. **Text boxes** are objects with text, a shape without a border. **Lines** are simply the straight or curved lines (arcs) that can connect two points or are used as arrows. **Freeforms** are irregular curves or polygons that you can create as a freehand drawing.

Once you create a drawing object, you can move, resize, nudge, copy or delete it on your documents. You can also change its style by adding color, creating a fill pattern, rotating it, and applying a shadow or 3-D effect. Take a simple shape and by the time you are done adding various effects, it could become an attractive piece of graphic art for your document. If you'd like to use it later, you can save it to the Clip Organizer.

Object placement on your documents is a key factor to successfully communicating your message. To save time and effort, multiple objects should be grouped if they are to be considered one larger object. Grouping helps you make changes later on, or copy your objects to another document. Word has the ability to line up your objects with precision— rulers and grids are part of the alignment process to help you. By grouping and aligning, you are assured that your drawing objects will be accurately placed.

What You'll Do

Add Desktop Publishing Effects

Add a Watermark

Add Page Backgrounds

Arrange Text in Columns

Wrap Text Around an Object

Work with Text Boxes

Draw and Resize Shapes

Add Text to a Shape

Create and Edit Freeforms

Add a Quick Style to a Shape

Add Formatting to Shape Text

Apply Colors Fill

Apply Picture, Texture, and Gradient Fills

Apply Shape Effects

Align and Distribute Objects

Align Objects to Grids and Guides

Change Stacking Order

Rotate and Flip Objects

Group and Ungroup Objects

Select Objects Using the Selection Pane

Adding Desktop Publishing Effects

A few simple elements—drop caps, borders, and shading—make your newsletters and brochures look like a professional produced them. A **drop cap** is the enlarged first letter of a paragraph that provides instant style to a document. Instead of using a desktop publishing program to create a drop cap effect, you can quickly achieve the same thing in Word. You can change the drop cap position, font, and height, and then enter the distance between the drop cap and paragraph.

Add a Drop Cap

1. Click the **Print Layout View** button.

2. Click the **Insert** tab.

3. Click the paragraph where you want the drop cap.

4. Click the **Drop Cap** button, and then select the drop cap style you want.

Customize a Drop Cap

1. Click the **Print Layout View** button.

2. Click the **Insert** tab.

3. Click the paragraph with the drop cap.

4. Click the **Drop Cap** button, and then click **Drop Cap Options**.

5. Click a drop cap position.

6. Change the drop cap font and height, and then enter the distance between the drop cap and text.

7. Click **OK**.

Adding a Watermark

A **watermark** is a background effect—some text or a graphic, that prints in a light shade behind your text on your document. You can use a washed out version of your company logo, or you can add text such as SAMPLE, DRAFT, PROPOSAL, or CONFIDENTIAL. If you can't find the watermark you need, check out Office.com. If you decide to change your watermark, it's as easy as typing in some new text.

Add or Remove a Watermark

1. Click the **Print Layout View** button.

2. Click the **Design** tab.

3. Click the **Watermark** button.

4. Do one of the following:

   ◆ **Add.** Click the border you want to add.

   ◆ **Add from Office.com.** Click **More Watermarks from Office.com**.

   ◆ **Remove.** Click **Remove Watermark**.

Customize or Remove a Watermark

1. Click the **Print Layout View** button.

2. Click the **Design** tab.

3. Click the **Watermark** button, and then click **Custom Watermark**.

4. To remove a watermark, click the **No watermark** option.

5. To insert a picture as a watermark, click the **Picture watermark** option, click **Select Picture**, select a picture, and then click **OK**.

6. To customize watermark text, click the **Text watermark** option, and then select the settings you want.

7. Click **OK**.

Adding Page Backgrounds

Borders are lines or graphics that appear around a page, paragraph, selected text, or table cells. With borders, you can change the line style, width, and colors, and you can add shadows and 3D effects. In addition to a page border, you can also change the page color. If you apply a theme color as the page color, it changes if you change the document theme. **Shading** is a color that fills the background of selected text, paragraphs, or table cells. For more attractive pages, add clips or columns.

Add Borders and Shading

1. Select the text you want to have a border.

2. Click the **Design** tab.

3. Click the **Page Borders** button.

4. Click the **Borders** tab.

5. Do one of the following:

   ◆ Click a box setting to modify all border edges.

   ◆ Click the edge in the diagram to modify individual border edges.

6. Click a border style, color, and width.

7. Click the **Shading** tab.

8. Click the **Fill** list arrow, and then click a fill color.

9. Click **OK**.

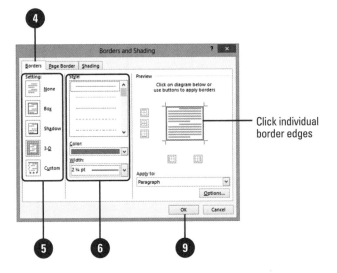

Click individual border edges

Add or Remove a Page Border

1. Click the page you want to have a border.

2. Click the **Design** tab.

3. Click the **Page Borders** button.

4. Click the **Page Border** tab.

5. Click a box setting.

6. Click a line style, or click the Art list arrow, and then select a line or art style.

7. Click the **Width** list arrow, and then select a width.

8. Click the **Apply to** list arrow, and then select the pages you want to have borders.

9. Click **OK**.

Add Page Color

1. Click the page you want to add a page color.

2. Click the **Design** tab.

3. Click the **Page Color** button.

4. Do one of the following:

   ◆ **Add.** Click the color you want to add.

   ◆ **Remove.** Click **No Color**.

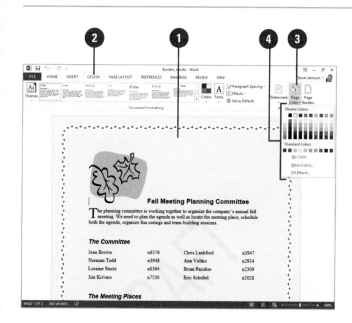

Arranging Text in Columns

Newspaper-style columns can give newsletters and brochures a more polished look. You can format an entire document, selected text, or individual sections into columns. You can create one, two, or three columns of equal size. You can also create two columns and have one column wider than the other. Word fills one column with text before the other, unless you insert a column break. Column breaks are used in two-column layouts to move the text after the insertion point to the top of the following column. You can also display a vertical line between the columns. To view the columns side by side, switch to print layout view.

Create and Customize Columns

1. Click the **Page Layout** tab.

2. Select the text you want to arrange in columns.

3. Click the **Columns** button.

4. Select the number of columns you want.

5. To customize the number of columns, widths and spacing, or add lines between columns, click the **Columns** button, click **More Columns**, specify the options you want, and then click **OK**.

Did You Know?

You can remove columns quickly. Select the columns, click the Columns button on the Page Layout tab, and then click the first column.

You can align text in a column. Click the Align Left, Center, Align Right, or Justify button on the Home tab to align paragraphs in columns.

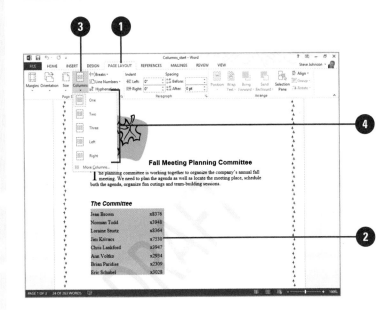

Modify Columns

1. Click the **Page Layout** tab, and then click in the columns you want to modify.

2. Click the **Columns** button, and then click **More Columns**.

3. Click a column preset format.

4. If necessary, enter the number of columns you want.

5. Enter the width and spacing you want for each column.

6. To place a vertical line between columns, select the **Line between** check box.

7. Click **OK**.

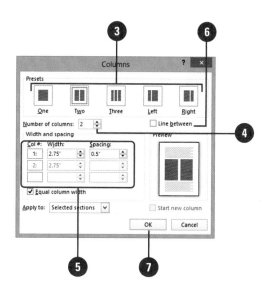

Insert a Column Break

1. Click where you want to insert a column break.

2. Click the **Page Layout** tab.

3. Click the **Break** button, and then click **Column**.

4. To delete a column break, click the column break dotted line in Draft view or select lines above and below the break, and then press the Delete key.

Wrapping Text Around an Object

When integrating pictures, shapes, charts, tables, or other objects with your text, you need to wrap the text around the object regardless of where it is placed on the page. Rather than having to constantly reset margins and make other tedious adjustments, Word simplifies the task with text wrapping. Unless your object or table is large enough to span the entire page, your layout will look better if you wrap your text around it instead of leaving excessive white space. In addition to wrapping text, you can change the position of the object on the page. You access text wrapping options by using the Wrap Text button on the Page Layout tab or the Layout Options button (**New!**) directly on the page.

Wrap Text Around an Object or Picture

1. Select the picture or object.

2. Select a wrap text options using any of the following:

   ◆ **Wrap Text button.** Click the **Page Layout** tab, and then click the **Wrap Text** button.

   ◆ **Layout Options button.** Click the **Layout Options** button (**New!**) on the page.

3. Click the text wrapping option you want.

   ◆ **In Line with Text.** No wrapping around the text.

   ◆ **With Text Wrapping.** Wraps around the text with the specified method.

4. To set the position of the object (**New!**), click **Move with text** or **Fix position on page**.

5. To customize the text wrapping options, click the **Page Layout** tab, click the **Wrap Text** button, click **More Layout Options**, specify the options you want, and then click **OK**.

Layout Options

Text wrapping options

Change the Object or Picture Position for Text to Wrap Around

1. Select the picture or object.

2. Click the **Page Layout** tab.

3. Click the **Position** button, and then click the text wrapping option you want.

4. To customize text position, click the **Position** button, click **More Layout Options**, specify the options you want, and then click **OK**.

Wrap Text Tightly Around an Object or Picture

1. Select the picture or object.

2. Click the **Page Layout** tab.

3. To change text position, click the **Position** button, select a position or click **More Layout Options**, specify the options you want, and then click **OK**.

4. Click the **Wrap Text** button, and then click **Tight**.

5. Click the **Wrap Text** button, and then click **Edit Wrap Points**.

6. Drag edit points around the object or picture to tighten text around it.

7. Click a blank area of the document to deselect the object or picture.

Working with Text Boxes

In addition to normal text on a page, you can also create independent text boxes to hold other types of information—such as titles, heading, pull quotes, and side bars—similar to those found on a desktop publishing page. You can insert a text box with predefined information or you can create a blank text box. If you can't find the predefined text box you need, check out Office.com. You can even link two or more text boxes together to have text flow to different parts of a document. If you no longer need the text boxes to link, you can quickly break the link.

Insert a Text Box Pull Quote or Side Bar

1 Click where you want to insert a text box.

2 Click the **Insert** tab.

3 Click the **Text Box** button.

4 Click the predefined text box you want to insert.

◆ **Add from Office.com.** Click **More Text Boxes from Office.com**.

Create a Text Box from Existing Text

1 Select the text you want to place in a text box.

2 Click the **Insert** tab.

3 Click the **Text Box** button.

4 Click **Draw Text Box**.

Did You Know?

You can change text direction in a text box. Select the text box you want to modify, click the Text Direction button on the Format tab under Drawing Tools.

Create a Text Box

1. Click the **Insert** tab.

2. Click the **Text Box** button.

3. Point to where you want to place the text box, and then drag to create a text box the size you want.

4. If necessary, click the text box to select it.

5. Type the text you want.

6. To resize the text box, drag a size handle.

Link Text Boxes

1. Select the source text box.

2. Click the **Format** tab under Drawing Tools.

3. Click the **Create Link** button.

4. Point to the destination text box (the pointer changes to a pitcher), and then click to link the text boxes.

Did You Know?

You can break a link. Select the text box with the link you want to break, click the Break Link button on the Format tab under Drawing Tools, and then click the destination text box to break the link.

Drawing and Resizing Shapes

Word supplies ready-made shapes, ranging from hearts to lightning bolts to stars. The ready-made shapes are available directly on the Shapes gallery on the Insert and Format tabs. Once you have placed a shape on a document, you can resize it using the sizing handles. Many shapes have an **adjustment handle**, a small yellow diamond located near a resize handle that you can drag to alter the shape. When you resize or move objects, a live layout preview (**New!**) with your changes appear on the page. For precision when resizing, use the Size Dialog Box Launcher to specify the new size of the shape.

Draw a Shape

1 Click the **Insert** tab.

2 Click the **Shapes** button.

3 Click the shape you want to draw.

4 Drag the pointer on the document where you want to place the shape until the drawing object is the shape and size that you want.

The shape you draw uses the line and fill color defined by the document's theme.

TIMESAVER *To draw a proportional shape, hold down Shift as you drag the pointer.*

Did You Know?

You can move a shape. Click the shape to select it, and then drag it to another location. As you drag, a live layout preview (**New!**) appears on the page.

You can quickly delete a shape. Click the shape to select it, and then press Delete.

You can draw a perfect circle or square. To draw a perfect circle or square, click the Oval or Rectangle button on the Shapes gallery, and then press and hold Shift as you drag.

Shapes

Resize a Shape

1. Select the shape you want to resize.

2. Drag one of the sizing handles.

   ◆ To resize the object in the vertical or horizontal direction, drag a sizing handle on the side of the selection box.

   ◆ To resize the object in both the vertical and horizontal directions, drag a sizing handle on the corner of the selection box.

   ◆ To resize the object with precise measurements, click the **Format** tab under Drawing Tools, and then specify exact height and width settings in the Size group.

   A live layout preview (**New!**) appears for the objects.

Adjust a Shape

1. Select the shape you want to adjust.

2. Click one of the adjustment handles (small yellow diamonds), and then drag the handle to alter the form of the shape.

   A live layout preview (**New!**) appears for the objects.

Did You Know?

You can replace a shape. Replace one shape with another, while retaining the size, color, and orientation of the shape. Click the shape you want to replace, click the Format tab, click the Edit Shape button, point to Change Shape, and then click the new shape you want.

Adding Text to a Shape

You can add text to a shape in the same way you add text to a text box. Simply, select the shape object, and then start typing. Shapes range from rectangles and circles to arrows and stars. When you place text in a shape, the text becomes part of the object. If you rotate or flip the shape, the text rotates or flips too. You can use tools, such as an alignment button or Font Style, on the Mini-toolbar and Home tab to format the text in a shape like the text in a text box.

Add Text to a Shape

1. Select the shape in which you want to add text.

2. Right-click the shape, and then click **Add Text**.

3. Type the text you want.

4. To edit the text in a shape, click the text to place the insertion point, and then edit the text.

Did You Know?

You can copy and move shapes. To copy a shape, select the shape, click the Copy button on the Home tab, and then click the Paste button. To move a shape, position the cursor (which changes to a 4-headed arrow), and then drag it to a new location.

You can align text in a shape. Select the shapes with the text you want to change, click the Format tab under Drawing Tools, click the Align Text button, and then select an alignment option: Top, Middle, or Bottom.

Creating and Editing Freeforms

When you need to create a customized shape, use the freeform tools. Choose a freeform tool from the Lines category in the list of shapes. Freeforms are like the drawings you make with a pen and paper, except that you use a mouse for your pen and a document for your paper. A freeform shape can either be an open curve or a closed curve. You can edit a freeform by using the Edit Points command to alter the vertices that create the shape.

Draw a Freeform Polygon

1. Click the **Insert** tab.

2. Click the **Shapes** button and then click the **Freeform** shape in the Shapes gallery under Lines.

3. Click the document where you want to place the first vertex of the polygon.

4. Move the pointer, and then click to place the second point of the polygon. A line joins the two points.

   ◆ To draw a line with curves, drag a line instead of clicking in steps 3 and 4.

5. Continue moving the mouse pointer and clicking to create additional sides of your polygon.

6. Finish the polygon. For a closed polygon, click near the starting point. For an open polygon, double-click the last point in the polygon.

Did You Know?

You can convert a shape to a freeform. Select the shape, click the Edit Shape button, and then click Convert To Freeform.

You can switch between a closed curve and an open curve. Right-click the freeform drawing, and then click Close Path or Open Path.

Modifying a Freeform

Each vertex indicated by a black dot (a corner in an irregular polygon and a bend in a curve) has two attributes: its position, and the angle at which the curve enters and leaves it. You can move the position of each vertex and control the corner or bend angles. You can also add or delete vertices as you like. When you delete a vertex, Word recalculates the freeform and smooths it among the remaining points. Similarly, if you add a new vertex, Word adds a corner or bend in your freeform. To edit a freeform, click the freeform object, click the Format tab under Drawing Tools, click the Edit Shape button, click Edit Points, modify any of the points (move or delete), and then click outside to set the new shape.

Adding a Quick Style to a Shape

Instead of changing individual attributes of a shape—such as shape fill, shape outline, and shape effects—you can quickly add them all at once with the Shape Quick Style gallery. The Shape Quick Style gallery provides a variety of different formatting combinations. To quickly see if you like a Shape Quick Style, point to a thumbnail in the gallery to display a live preview of it in the selected shape. If you like it, you can apply it.

Add a Quick Style to a Shape

1. Select the shapes you want to modify.

2. Click the **Format** tab under Drawing Tools.

3. Click the scroll up or down arrow, or click the **More** list arrow in the Shapes Styles group to see additional styles.

   The current style appears highlighted in the gallery.

4. Point to a style.

   A live preview of the style appears in the current shape.

5. Click the style you want from the gallery to apply it to the selected shape.

Did You Know?

You can add a Quick Style to a text box. A shape is a text box without a fill and outline (border), so you can apply a Quick Style to a text box using the same steps.

Adding Formatting to Shape Text

You can format text in a shape the same way you format text on a document page. You can change several font attributes—such as bold, italic, underline, font color and gradient, outline, shadow, reflection, glow, 3-D, or highlight—to enhance data to catch the reader's attention. The main formats you apply to text are available on the Home tab in the Font group or in the Font dialog box. However, you can also use the WordArt Styles on the Format tab under Drawing Tools. Some of the additional formats available include strikethrough, subscript, superscript, small caps, all caps, underline style, and hidden.

Add a Style to Shape Text

1. Select the shapes with the text you want to modify.

2. Click the **Home** tab.

3. To change fonts, click the **Font** list arrow or click the **Font Size** list arrow, and then click the style or size you want.

4. To apply formatting, click one or more of the formatting buttons on the Ribbon: **Bold**, **Italic**, **Underline**, **Strikethrough**, **Subscript**, **Superscript**, **Text Effects**, **Text Highlight Color**, or **Font Color**.

   ◆ **Underline Styles.** Click the **Underline** button arrow, and then select a style.

   ◆ **Text Styles.** Click the **Text Effects** button, click a preset style or point to an option (Outline, Shadow, Reflection, or Glow), and then select a style.

   ◆ **Gradient Text.** Click the **Font Color** button, point to **Gradient**, and then select a style. To create a custom gradient, click **More Gradients**.

   ◆ **WordArt Text.** Click the Format tab under Drawing Tools, and then use buttons in the WordArt Styles group.

5. To use the Font dialog box to change font attributes, click the **Font Dialog Box Launcher**, select the options you want, and then click **OK**.

Text Effects button

Applying Color Fills

When you create a closed drawing object such as a square, it applies the Shape Fill color to the inside of the shape, and the Shape Outline color to the edge of the shape. A line drawing object uses the Shape Outline color. You can set the Shape Fill to be a solid, gradient, texture or picture, and the Shape Outline can be a solid or gradient. If you want to make multiple changes to a shape at the same time, the Format Shape pane (**New!**) allows you to do everything in one place. If the solid color appears too dark, you can make the color fill more transparent. If you no longer want to apply a shape fill to an object, you can remove it.

Apply a Color Fill to a Shape

1. Select the shape you want to modify.

2. Click the **Format** tab under Drawing Tools.

3. Click the **Shape Fill** button.

4. Select the fill color option you want.

5. To remove a color fill, click the **Shape Fill** button, and then click **No Fill**.

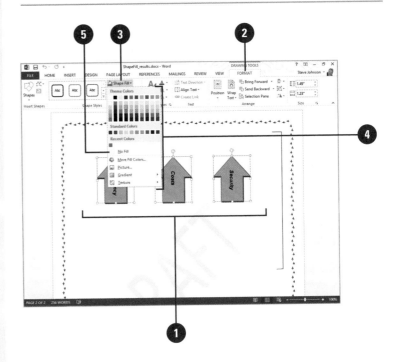

Did You Know?

You can set the color and line style for an object as the default. Right-click the object, and then click Set as Default Shape. Any new objects you create will use the same styles.

You can use the document background as the fill for a shape. Right-click the object, click Format Shape, click Fill in the left pane, click the Background option, and then click Close.

You can undo changes made in the Format Shape pane. Since changes made in the Shape Format pane are instantly applied, it's not possible to Cancel it. To remove changes, click the Undo button on the Quick Access Toolbar.

Formatting a SmartArt Shape

In the same way you can apply shape fills, outlines, and effects to a shape, you can also apply them to shapes in a SmartArt graphic. You can modify all or part of the SmartArt graphic by using the Shape Fill, Shape Outline, and Shape Effects buttons. Shape Fill can be set to be a solid, gradient, texture or picture, or set the Shape Outline to be a solid or gradient. In addition, you can change the look of a SmartArt graphic by applying effects, such as glow and soft edges. If a shape in a SmartArt graphic contains text, you can use WordArt style galleries to modify shape text.

Apply a Shape Color Fill with a Transparency

1. Select the shape you want to modify.

2. Click the **Format** tab under Drawing Tools.

3. Click the **Shape Styles Dialog Box Launcher**.

4. Click the **Fill & Line** button in the Format Shape pane (**New!**).

5. Click the **Solid fill** option.

6. Click the **Color** button, and then select the fill color you want.

7. Drag the **Transparency** slider or enter a number from 0 (fully opaque) to 100 (fully transparent).

   All your changes are instantly applied to the shape.

8. Click the **Close** button in the pane.

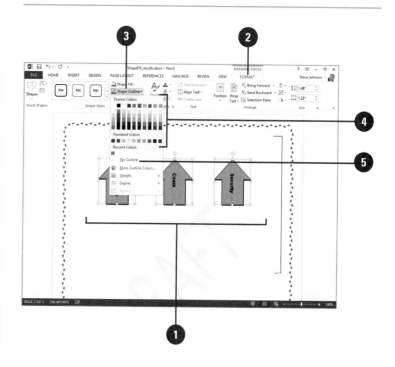

Apply a Color Outline to a Shape

1. Select the shape you want to modify.

2. Click the **Format** tab under Drawing Tools.

3. Click the **Shape Outline** button.

4. Select the outline color you want.

5. To remove an outline color, click the **Shape Outline** button, and then click **No Outline**.

Applying Picture or Texture Fills

Applying a shape fill to a drawing object can add emphasis or create a point of interest in your document. You can insert a picture or texture into a shape. You can insert a picture from a file, clip art on Office .com (**New!**), Bing Image Search (**New!**), SkyDrive (**New!**), or SharePoint **New!**). Stretch a picture or texture to fit across the selected shape or repeatedly tile it horizontally and vertically to fill the shape. When you stretch an image, you can also set offsets, which determine how much to scale an image to fit a shape relative to the edges. A positive offset number moves the image edge toward the center of the shape, while a negative offset number moves the image edge away from the shape. If the image appears too dark, you can make the picture more transparent.

Apply a Picture or Texture Fill to a Shape

1. Select the shape you want to modify.

2. Click the **Format** tab under Drawing Tools.

3. Click the **Shape Fill** button.

   ◆ Click **Picture**, browse and select a picture file, and then click **Insert**.

      ◆ **From a file.** Select a file on your computer or network.

      ◆ **Office.com.** Select an online clip art image (**New!**).

      ◆ **Bing Image Search.** Select an online image (**New!**).

      ◆ **SkyDrive or SharePoint.** Select a file on a SkyDrive or SharePoint (**New!**).

   ◆ Point to **Texture**, and then select a texture.

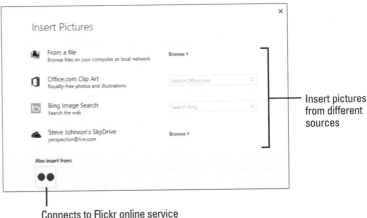

Insert pictures from different sources

Connects to Flickr online service

Did You Know?

You can apply a custom picture or texture fill. Right-click the object you want to modify, click Format Shape, click the Fill & Line button, click the Picture Or Texture Fill option, select a picture or texture, select the related options you want, and then click the Close button in the pane.

Applying Gradient Fills

Gradients are made up of two or more colors that gradually fade into each other. They can be used to give depth to a shape or create realistic shadows. Apply a gradient fill to a shape—now including lines—by using a gallery or presets for quick results, or by using the Format Shape pane (**New!**) for custom results. A gradient is made up of several gradient stops, which are used to create non-linear gradients. If you want to create a gradient that starts blue and goes to green, add two gradient stops, one for each color. Gradient stops consist of a position, a color, and a transparency percentage.

Apply a Gradient Fill to a Shape

1. Select the shape you want to modify.

2. Click the **Format** tab under Drawing Tools.

3. Click the **Shape Fill** button.

4. Point to **Gradient**, and then select a gradient from the gallery.

   Four gradient modes are available: linear (parallel bands), radial (radiate from center), rectangle (radiate from corners), and path (radiate along path).

Apply a Gradient Fill with Presets

1. Right-click the shape you want to modify, and then click **Format Shape** or **Format Object**.

2. Click the **Fill & Lines** button (**New!**), and then expand **Fill**.

3. Click the **Gradient fill** option.

4. Click the **Preset colors** button arrow, and then select the built-in gradient fill you want.

   All your changes are instantly applied to the shape.

5. Click the **Close** button in the pane.

Custom gradient options

Applying Shape Effects

You can change the look of a shape by applying effects, like shadows, reflections, glow, soft edges, bevels, and 3-D rotations. Apply effects to a shape by using the Shape Effects gallery for quick results, or by using the Format Shape pane (**New!**) for custom results. From the Shape Effects gallery you can apply a built-in combination of 3-D effects or individual effects to a shape. To quickly see if you like a shape effect, point to a thumbnail in the Shape Effects gallery to display a live preview of it in the selected shape. If you like it, you can apply it. If you no longer want to apply a shape effect to an object, you can remove it. Simply select the shape, point to the effect type in the Shape Effects gallery, and then select the No effect type option.

Add a Preset Effect to a Shape

1. Select the shape you want to modify.

2. Click the **Format** tab under Drawing Tools.

3. Click the **Shape Effects** button, and then point to **Preset**.

   The current effect appears highlighted in the gallery.

4. Point to an effect.

   A live preview of the style appears in the current shape.

5. Click the effect you want from the gallery to apply it to the selected shape.

   ◆ **3-D Options.** Click to select 3-D and other shape options in the Format Shape pane (**New!**).

6. To remove the preset effect, click the **Shape Effects** button, point to **Preset**, and then click **No Presets**.

Did You Know?

3-D effects take precedence. If you add a 3-D effect, such as a bevel or 3-D rotation, to a shape and then add soft edges, the soft edge effect doesn't appear in the shape until you delete the 3-D effect.

Shape options

Add Individual Effects to a Shape

1. Select the shape you want to modify.

2. Click the **Format** tab under Drawing Tools.

3. Click the **Shape Effects** button, and then point to one of the following:

   ◆ **Shadow** to select No Shadow, one of the shadow types (Outer, Inner, or Perspective), or Shadows Options.

   ◆ **Reflection** to select No Reflection, one of the Reflection Variations, or Reflection Options.

   ◆ **Glow** to select No Glow, one of the Glow Variations, More Glow Colors, or Glow Options.

   ◆ **Soft Edges** to select No Soft Edges, a point size to determine the soft edge amount, or Soft Edges Options.

   ◆ **Bevel** to select No Bevel, one of the bevel variations, or 3-D Options.

   ◆ **3-D Rotation** to select No Rotation, one of the rotation types (Parallel, Perspective, or Oblique), or 3-D Rotation Options.

   When you point to an effect, a live preview of the style appears in the current shape.

4. Click the effect you want from the gallery to apply it to the selected shape.

Aligning and Distributing Objects

In addition to using grids and guides to align objects to a specific point, you can align a group of objects to each other. The Align commands make it easy to align two or more objects relative to each other vertically to the left, center, or right, or horizontally from the top, middle, or bottom. To evenly align several objects to each other across the document, either horizontally or vertically, select them and then choose a distribution option. Before you select an align command, specify how you want Word to align the objects. You can align the objects in relation to the document or to the selected objects.

Distribute Objects

1. Select the objects you want to distribute.

2. Click the **Format** tab under Drawing Tools.

3. Click the **Align** button.

4. On the Align menu, click the alignment method you want:

   ◆ Click **Align to Page** if you want the objects to align relative to the document page.

   ◆ Click **Align to Margin** if you want the objects to align relative to the document margin.

5. On the Align submenu, click the distribution command you want:

   ◆ Click **Distribute Horizontally** to evenly distribute the objects horizontally.

   ◆ Click **Distribute Vertically** to evenly distribute the objects vertically.

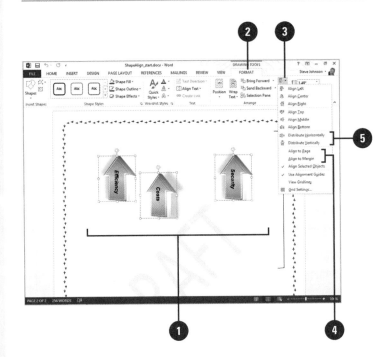

Align Objects with Other Objects

1. Select the objects you want to align.

2. Click the **Format** tab under Drawing Tools.

3. Click the **Align** button.

4. On the Align menu, click the alignment method you want:

   ◆ Click **Align to Page** if you want the objects to align relative to the document page.

   ◆ Click **Align to Margin** if you want the objects to align relative to the document margin.

   ◆ Click **Align Selected Objects** if you want the objects to align relative to the selected objects.

5. On the Align menu, click the alignment command you want:

   ◆ Click **Align Left** to line up the objects with the left edge of the selection or document.

   ◆ Click **Align Center** to line up the objects with the center of the selection or document.

   ◆ Click **Align Right** to line up the objects with the right edge of the selection or document.

   ◆ Click **Align Top** to line up the objects with the top edge of the selection or document.

   ◆ Click **Align Middle** to line up the objects vertically with the middle of the selection or document.

   ◆ Click **Align Bottom** to line up the objects with the bottom of the selection or document.

Aligned objects

Aligning Objects to Grids and Guides

Word uses a grid to align an individual object or a group of objects to a vertical or horizontal line. Turning on the visible grid option makes it easier to create, modify, and align a shape. In addition, you can use alignment guides (**New!**) to align objects. Alignment guides (**New!**) appear when you drag objects close to pages, margins, and paragraphs. Within the Drawing Grid dialog box, you can select from a variety of options, such as displaying alignment guides, snapping objects to the grid or to other objects and displaying drawing guides on-screen.

Set Options for the Grid or Alignment Guides

1. Select the objects you want to arrange.

2. Click the **Format** tab under Drawing Tools.

3. Click the **Align** button, and then click **Grid Settings**.

4. To show or hide alignment guides (**New!**), select or clear the **Display alignment guides** check box, and then select or clear the **Page guides**, **Margin guides**, or **Paragraph guides** check boxes.

5. Select the grid setting you want:

   ◆ **Grid settings.** Specify the grid horizontal and vertical spacing.

   ◆ **Grid origin.** To start the grid, select the **Use margins** check box, and then specify the horizontal and vertical origin.

   ◆ **Show grid.** To show the grid, select the **Display gridlines on screen** check box, select or clear the **Vertical every** check box, and then enter a value for the vertical and horizontal gridlines, if you turn it on.

6. To set objects to snap into place, select the following check boxes:

   ◆ **Snap objects to other objects.**

   ◆ **Snap objects to grid when the gridlines are not displayed.**

7. Click **OK**.

Show or Hide the Gridlines or Alignment Guides

1. Select the objects you want to arrange.

2. Click the **Format** tab under Drawing Tools.

3. Click the **Align** button, and then click **View Gridlines** or **Use Alignment Guides** (**New!**).

   ◆ You can also select or clear the **Gridlines** check box on the View tab to show or hide the gridlines.

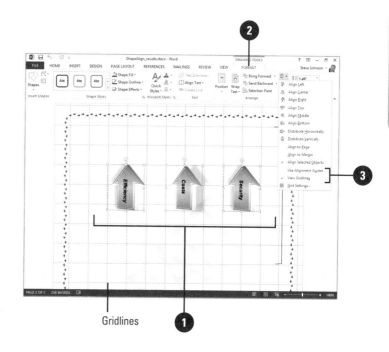

Gridlines

Align an Object to a Grid or Use the Alignment Guides

1. If you want, display gridlines on the screen (horizontal and vertical) or turn on alignment guides (**New!**).

2. Drag the object's center or edge near the guide. Word aligns the center or edge to the grid or alignment guide (**New!**).

Did You Know?

You can use the keyboard to override grid settings. To temporarily override settings for the grids and guides, press and hold the Alt key as you drag an object.

Align to grid

Guide

Align to margin

Changing Stacking Order

Multiple objects on a document appear in a stacking order, like layers of transparencies. Stacking is the placement of objects one on top of another. In other words, the first object that you draw is on the bottom and the last object that you draw is on top. You can change the order of this stack of objects by using the Bring to Front, Send to Back, Bring Forward, and Send Backward commands on the Format tab under Drawing Tools.

Arrange a Stack of Objects

1 Select the objects you want to arrange.

2 Click the **Format** tab under Drawing Tools.

3 Click the stacking option you want.

◆ Click the **Bring to Front** button arrow, and then click **Bring to Front, Bring Forward**, or **Bring in Front of Text** to move a drawing to the top of the stack or up one location in the stack.

◆ Click the **Send to Back** button arrow, and then click **Send to Back, Send Backward**, or **Send Behind Text** to move a drawing to the bottom of the stack or back one location in the stack.

Did You Know?

You can view a hidden object in a stack. Press the Tab key or Shift+Tab to cycle forward or backward through the objects until you select the object you want.

You can connect two shapes. Click the Insert tab, click the Shapes button or list arrow, click a connector (located in the Lines category), position the pointer over an object handle (turns red), drag the connector to the object handle (turns red) on another object. An attached connector point appears as red circles, while an unattached connector point appears as light blue.

Bring to front

Rotating and Flipping Objects

After you create an object, you can change its orientation on the document by rotating or flipping it. Rotating turns an object 90 degrees to the right or left; flipping turns an object 180 degrees horizontally or vertically. For a more freeform rotation, which you cannot achieve in 90 or 180 degree increments, drag the green rotate lever at the top of an object. You can also rotate and flip any type of picture—including bitmaps—in a document. This is useful when you want to change the orientation of an image, such as changing the direction of an arrow.

Rotate an Object to any Angle

1. Select the object you want to rotate.

2. Position the pointer (which changes to the Free Rotate pointer) over the green rotate lever at the top of the object, and then drag to rotate the object.

3. Click outside the object to set the rotation.

Free Rotate pointer

Rotate or Flip an Object Using Preset Increments

1. Select the object you want to rotate or flip.

2. Click the **Format** tab under Drawing Tools.

3. Click the **Rotate** button, and then click the option you want.

   ◆ Rotate. Click **Rotate Right 90°** or **Rotate Left 90°**.

   ◆ Flip. Click **Flip Vertical** or **Flip Horizontal**.

Grouping and Ungrouping Objects

Objects can be grouped, ungrouped, and regrouped to make editing and moving them easier. Rather than moving several objects one at a time, you can group the objects and move them all together. Grouped objects appear as one object, but each object in the group maintains its individual attributes. You can change an individual object within a group without ungrouping. This is useful when you need to make only a small change to a group, such as changing the color of a single shape in the group. You can also format specific shapes, drawings, or pictures within a group without ungrouping. Simply select the object within the group, change the object or edit text within the object, and then deselect the object. However, if you need to move an object in a group, you need to first ungroup the objects, move it, and then group the objects together again.

Group Objects Together

1. Select the shapes you want to group together.

2. Click the **Format** tab under Drawing Tools.

3. Click the **Group** button, and then click **Group**.

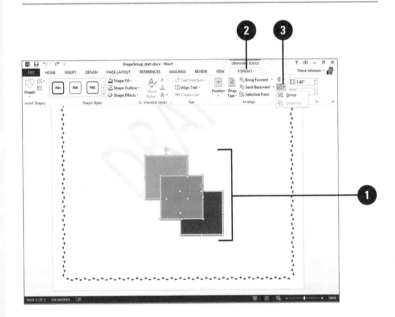

Did You Know?

You can use the Tab key to select objects in order. Move between the drawing objects on your document (even those hidden behind other objects) by pressing the Tab key.

You can use the shortcut menu to select Group related commands. Right-click the objects you want to group, point to Group, and then make your selections.

You can no longer ungroup tables. Due to the increased table size and theme functionality, tables can no longer be ungrouped.

Ungroup Objects

1. Select the grouped object you want to ungroup.

2. Click the **Format** tab under Drawing Tools.

3. Click the **Group** button, and then click **Ungroup**.

Did You Know?

You can troubleshoot the arrangement of objects. If you have trouble selecting an object because another object is in the way, you can use the Selection pane to help you select it.

Selecting Objects Using the Selection Pane

Sometimes it's hard to select an object when it is behind another one. With the Selection pane, you can now select individual objects and change their order and visibility. When you open the Selection pane, Office lists each shape on the current document by name (in terms of object type). You can click a shape title to select a "hard-to-select" object on the document, use the Re-order buttons to change the stacking order on the document, or click the eye icon next to a shape title to show or hide "hard-to-see" individual objects.

Select Objects Using the Selection Pane

1. Open the document with the objects you want to select.

2. Click the **Format** tab under Drawing or Picture Tools.

3. Click the **Selection Pane** button.

   Titles for all the shapes on the current document appear in the pane.

   ◆ **Rename Objects.** Click the object name in the Selection pane, click the name again to edit it, rename the object, and then press Enter.

4. To select an object, click the title in the pane.

   To select more than one object, hold down the Ctrl key while you click object titles.

5. To change the order of the objects, select an object, and then click the Re-order **Move Up** or **Move Down** buttons in the pane.

6. To show or hide individual objects, click the eye icon in the pane.

7. When you're done, click the **Close** button on the pane.

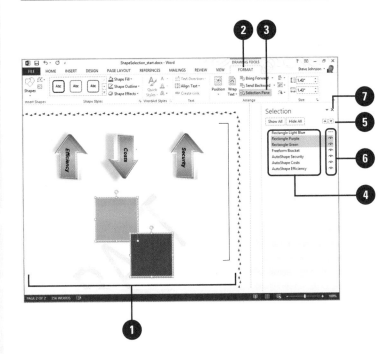

Working with Long Documents

Introduction

When working with long documents, the ability to split up the tasks can be crucial to meeting a deadline. Microsoft Word can do just that. By creating a master document in an Outline format, you can simply select the sections of the master that will be sectioned off as a subdocument. Word creates a number of subdocuments off the master, based on how you decide to group them. Once the subdocuments are created, they become separate files that others can open, develop, save and re-insert into the master.

Using master documents and subdocuments by many individuals could be a formatting nightmare. Word has an automatic formatting tool to help you create an overall format for your long document. In order to help your readers process your document, headers and footers, along with a cross reference, are a great way to keep them focused on the material at hand.

Once your long document is created and will be bound in some fashion, it's important to make sure that you have enough white space around the margins so that text won't get cut off during the binding process. And, as you navigate through the document, be sure to check for any special items that might require your attention. You can use the Go To function or Navigation pane to quickly move from object to object, section to section, or page to page, to name a few. The Select Browse Object button is also a way to navigate through your long document. Browse by comments, graphics, tables or footnotes. The availability for Word to seek out these objects and for you to review them is crucial to your long document being a success.

Other documents items, such as a Table of Contents and an Index can all be done very easily in Word. When you need to know that final word count, you can find it quickly through the References tab.

What You'll Do

Create an Outline

Create a Multiple-Author Document

Create Documents Using Automatic Formatting

Create Headers and Footers

Insert Page Numbers and the Date and Time

Insert Cross References

Prepare for a Bound Document

Find Topics in a Long Document

Insert a Table of Contents

Create an Index

Determine Word Count Statistics

Add a Cover Page

Creating an Outline

Outlines are useful for organizing information, such as topics in an essay. An outline typically consists of main headings and subheadings. You can create an outline from scratch in Outline view or change a bulleted or numbered list into an outline using the bullets and numbering commands on the Home tab. In Outline view, you can use buttons in the Outlining Tools group or drag the mouse pointer to move headings and subheadings to different locations or levels.

Create an Outline in Outline View

1. In a new document, click the **View** tab, and then click the **Outline View** button.

2. Type a heading, and then press Enter.

3. Type another heading or press Tab to add a subheading under the heading.

4. To change a heading or subheading to a different level and apply the corresponding heading style, place the insertion point in the heading, and then click the **Promote** or **Demote** button until the heading is at the level you want, or click the **Promote to Heading** or **Promote to Body** button.

5. To move a heading or subheading to a different location, place the insertion point in the heading, and then click the **Move Up** or **Move Down** button until the heading is moved where you want it to go.

6. When you're done, click the **Close Outline View** button.

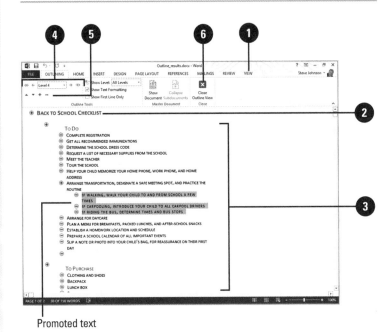

Promoted text

Change the Outline Display in Outline View

1. Open the document with the outline, click the **View** tab, and then click the **Outline View** button.

2. Use the Outlining Tools to change the display in Outline view.

   ◆ **Show Level.** Click the list arrow, and then select the level you want to display.

   ◆ **Show Text Formatting.** Select or clear to show or hide text formatting.

   ◆ **Show First Line Only.** Select to show the first line only.

3. When you're done, click the **Close Outline View** button.

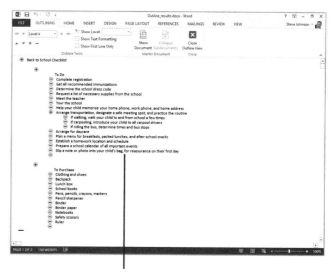

No formatting

Creating a Multiple-Author Document

When several people are going to collaborate on a document by dividing the workload by section or heading, you can create a master document so that everyone can work concurrent with one another instead of passing one file around. The process of creating a master document begins with an outline. When the outline is complete, individual headings or sections can have subdocuments assigned to them. These subdocuments can be distributed to the collaborators and completed separately. When ready, they can then be combined back into the master document so that all the information is contained in a single file. After you have created a master document, those sections that you have designated as subdocuments can be created and saved as separate files. These files can then be reinserted into the master document as they are completed.

Create a Master Document

1. In a new document, click the **View** tab, and then click the **Outline View** button.

2. Enter headings to outline the presentation of topics in the master document, pressing Enter after each entry.

3. Select a heading, and then click one of the buttons in Outline view to assign a heading style (Heading 1 through Heading 9).

   ◆ Click the **Promote** or **Demote** button to increase or decrease the heading level of the headlines and body text.

4. Select the heading that you want to make into a subdocument.

5. Click the **Show Document** button.

6. Click the **Create Subdocument** button.

7. Click the **File** tab, and then click **Save As**.

8. Select the location, type a name, and then click **Save**.

9. When you're done, click the **Close Outline View** button.

Subdocument

Insert a Subdocument

1. Open the master document in which you want to add a subdocument.

2. Click the **View** tab, and then click the **Outline View** button.

3. Click the **Show Document** button.

4. If the subdocuments are collapsed (appear with links), click the **Expand Subdocument** button.

5. Place the insertion point where you want the subdocument.

6. Click the **Insert Subdocument** button.

7. Locate and select the subdocument file you want to insert, and then click **Open**.

8. To open the subdocument, double-click the subdocument or Ctrl+click the subdocument link. Close the subdocument to return to the master document.

9. When you're done, click the **Close Outline View** button.

Double-click to open subdocument   Subdocuments

Did You Know?

You can collapse, or hide, all of your subdocuments. To hide (collapse) the subdocuments in a master document, click the Collapse Subdocuments button in Outline view. All subdocuments are collapsed. To show (expand) the subdocuments, click the Expand Subdocuments button.

You can lock and unlock a master document. Click the Show Documents button in Outline view, select text in the master document, and then click Lock Document. To unlock, click Expand Subdocuments button to remove the lock on the files.

Creating Documents Using Automatic Formatting

Word can automatically perform some formatting functions for you as you type a document. For example, you can change straight quotation marks to smart (curly) quotes, hyphens to en-dashes or em-dashes, an asterisk before and after text to bold text, or an underscore before and after text to italic text. You can also type a number and text or a bullet and text to start a numbered or bulleted list. If you had AutoFormat disabled when you created the document, you still have the option of using the feature to find and correct errors in formatting.

Set Up Automatic Formatting As You Type

1. Click the **File** tab, and then click **Options**.

2. In the left pane, click **Proofing**, and then click **AutoCorrect Options**.

3. Click the **AutoFormat As You Type** tab.

4. Select or clear the AutoFormat check boxes you want to use.

5. Click **OK**.

   Your choices take effect, but they only apply to text you will be entering subsequently. In this case, AutoFormat does not correct errors retroactively.

Change Document Formatting with AutoFormat

1. Click the **AutoFormat** button on the Quick Access Toolbar.

   ◆ The AutoFormat button is not on the Quick Access Toolbar by default. Use the Customize pane in Word Options to add the button.

2. Click **Options**.

3. Click the **AutoFormat** tab to select the formatting options you want.

4. Click the other tabs to make any additional changes to your document.

5. Click **OK**.

6. Click the **AutoFormat now** option to have Word automatically format the document, or click the **AutoFormat and review each change** option to review, and then accept or reject each change.

7. Click **OK**.

   If you chose the AutoFormat and review each change option, then continue.

8. Click **Review Changes** to look at changes individually.

9. Click **Style Gallery** if you want to preview your document, and then click **OK**.

10. Use the Accept and Reject buttons to accept or reject the review changes.

11. Click **Close** or **Cancel**.

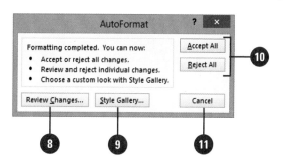

Adding Headers and Footers

Most books, including this one, use headers and footers to help you keep track of where you are. A **header** is text printed in the top margin of every page within a document. **Footer** text is printed in the bottom margin. Commonly used headers and footers contain your name, the document title, the file name, the print date, and page numbers. If you divide your document into sections, you can create different headers and footers for each section.

Create and Edit Headers and Footers

1. Click the **Insert** tab.

2. Click the **Header** or **Footer** button.

3. Click a built-in header or footer, or click **Edit Header** or **Edit Footer** to modify an existing one.

   TIMESAVER *Double-click a header or footer to edit it.*

   The Design tab under Header & Footer Tools appears on the Ribbon.

4. If necessary, click the **Go to Header** or **Go to Footer** button to display the header or footer text area.

5. Click the header or footer box, and then type the text you want. Edit and format header or footer text as usual.

6. To insert common items in a header or footer, click a button: **Date & Time**, **Quick Parts**, **Pictures**, or **Online Pictures**.

7. When you're done, click the **Close Header and Footer** button.

Header field

Did You Know?

You can quickly remove a header or footer. Click the Insert tab, click the Header or Footer button, and then click Remove Header or Remove Footer.

Create Different Headers and Footers for Different Pages

1 Click the **Insert** tab.

2 Click the **Header** or **Footer** button.

3 Click a built-in header or footer, or click **Edit Header** or **Edit Footer** to modify an existing one.

The Design tab under Header & Footer Tools displays on the Ribbon.

4 To create different headers or footers for odd and even pages, click to select the **Different Odd & Even Pages** check box.

To create a unique header or footer for the document's first page, click to select the **Different First Page** check box.

To show document text, select the **Show Document Text** check box.

5 When you're done, click the **Close Header and Footer** button.

Did You Know?

You can change header and footer position. Double-click the header or footer you want to change, and then adjust the Header from Top or Footers from Bottom settings on the Ribbon.

There are default tab stops used to align header and footer text. Typically, headers and footers have two default tab stops. The first, in the middle, centers text. The second, on the far right, aligns text on the right margin. To left align text, don't press Tab. You can add and move the tab stops as needed. In addition, you can use the alignment buttons on the Home tab.

Inserting Page Numbers and the Date and Time

Page numbers help you keep your document in order or find a topic from the table of contents. Number the entire document consecutively or each section independently; pick a numbering scheme, such as roman numerals or letters. When you insert page numbers, you can select the position and alignment of the numbers on the page. The date and time field ensures you know which printout is the latest. Word uses your computer's internal calendar and clock as its source. You can insert the date and time for any installed language. Add page numbers and the date in a footer to conveniently keep track of your work.

Insert and Format Page Numbers

1. Click the **Insert** tab.

2. Click the **Page Number** button.

3. Point to the position you want (**Top of Page**, **Bottom of Page**, **Page Margins**, or **Current Position**), and then select a position.

4. Click the **Page Number** button, and then click **Format Page Numbers**.

5. Click the **Number format** list arrow, and then select a numbering scheme.

6. Select the starting number.

7. Click **OK**.

Did You Know?

You can quickly remove page numbers. Click the Insert tab, click the Page Number button, and then click Remove Page Numbers.

Insert the Date or Time

1. To insert the date or time on a single page, display the page, and then click the **Insert** tab.

    ◆ To place the date or time on every page, display or insert a header or footer.

    The Design tab under Header & Footer Tools displays on the Ribbon.

2. Click to place the insertion point where you want to insert the date or time.

3. Click the **Date & Time** button.

4. If necessary, click the **Language** list arrow, and then select a language.

5. To have the date or time automatically update, select the **Update automatically** check box.

6. Click the date and time format you want.

7. To set the current date and time (based on your computer clock) as the default, click **Set As Default**, and then click **Yes**.

8. Click **OK**.

Inserting Cross References

Cross references direct the reader to related information located elsewhere in the document. Cross references can refer to figures or illustrations, sidebars, section headings, even individually marked paragraphs. Without distracting the reader of the document, cross references can be an easy tool to help navigate through a larger document. You can cross-reference only items in the same document. To cross-reference an item in another document, you need to first combine the documents into a master document.

Create a Cross Reference

1. Select the text that starts the cross reference in the document.

2. Click the **References** tab.

3. Click the **Cross-Reference** button.

4. Click the **Reference type** list arrow, and then select the type of item to which you will refer (heading, footnote, bookmark, etc.).

5. Click the **Insert reference to** list arrow, and then select the type of data (page, paragraph number, etc.) that you will be referencing.

6. Click the specific item, by number, to which you want to refer.

7. To let users move to the referenced item, select the **Insert as hyperlink** check box.

8. To include data regarding the relative position of the referenced item, select the **Include above/below** check box.

9. Click **Insert**.

10. Repeat the steps for each additional cross reference that you want to insert into the document, and then click either **Close** or **Cancel**.

Preparing for a Bound Document

If your finished document will be bound in some fashion, especially if you will use a form of binding such as is found in books, you must allow additional margin space for the binding process; otherwise some of your text can be in the binding fold and therefore unreadable. If you open a book, the crease between the two facing pages is referred to as the gutter. You must take care to ensure that nothing except white space is in the gutter.

Change the Gutter Margin Setting

1. Click the **Page Layout** tab.

2. Click the **Page Setup Dialog Box Launcher**.

3. If necessary, click the **Margins** tab.

4. Enter a value for the gutter margin.

5. Click the **Gutter Position** list arrow, and then click **Left** or **Top** depending on the orientation of your intended binding (Left would be for a normal book, Top would be for a book that flips open from top to bottom).

6. Click **OK**.

Did You Know?

You can set aside a gutter for printing. The size of the gutter you should use varies greatly depending on the binding process that will be used. Check with your printer before finalizing this setting to ensure that you allow the correct amount of space.

You can use a gutter even if you are printing on both sides. Remember that, if you are using double-sided printing, the gutter will be to the left on odd-numbered pages and to the right on even-numbered pages.

Finding Topics in a Long Document

Instead of searching through pages of text in your document for that certain paragraph, bookmark, tables, footnote or endnote, caption, or other object, you can navigate a lengthy document using the Find and Replace dialog box or the Navigation pane. Providing that you have set up your long document with headings, bookmarks, captions, object numbers and the like, you will be able to use those as "clues" in which to locate the specific items you are looking for.

Move to Pages or Document Items Using Go To

1. Click the **Home** tab.

2. Click the **Find** button arrow, and then click **Go To**.

3. Click the type of item to which you want to move to (page, table, etc.).

4. Use one of the following methods:

   ◆ **Specific item.** Type the name or number of the item in the Enter box, and then click **Go To**.

   ◆ **Next or previous item of the same type.** Empty the Enter box, and then click **Next** or **Previous**.

5. Click **Close**.

Go to the next heading

Move to Pages or Document Items Using Navigation Pane

1 Click the **Home** tab.

2 Click the **Find** button.

> **TIMESAVER** *Click the Page number on the Status bar.*

◆ You can also select the **Navigation Pane** check box on the View tab to open the Navigation pane.

The Navigation pane opens.

3 Click the **Headings** or **Pages** tab.

4 To search for text within the document, type the text you want to find in the Search box, press Enter, and then click the **Results** tab to see the matching results.

The results are highlighted in the document.

◆ **View results.** Click the **Next** or **Previous** button below the Search box.

◆ **Cancel search.** Click the **Close** button in the Search box.

5 Click a heading name, thumbnail of a page, or search result to display it.

6 To close the Navigation pane, click the **Close** button on the pane.

5 Headings in the document

Highlighted search results

5 Search results in the document

Inserting a Table of Contents

A **table of contents** provides an outline of main topics and page locations. Word builds a table of contents based on the styles in a document that you choose. By default, Heading 1 is the first-level entry, Heading 2 the second level, and so on. In a printed table of contents, a **leader**, a line whose style you select, connects an entry to its page number. In web documents, entries become hyperlinks. Hide nonprinting characters before creating a table of contents so text doesn't shift to other pages as you print.

Insert a Table of Contents

1. Position the insertion point where you want the table of contents.

2. Click the **References** tab.

3. Click the **Table of Contents** button.

4. Do one of the following:

   ◆ **Add.** Click a Table of Contents style from the gallery.

   ◆ **Remove.** Click **Remove Table of Contents**.

   ◆ **Customize.** Click **Customize Table of Contents**, click the **Table of Contents** tab, select the format, levels, and options you want, and then click **OK**.

Did You Know?

You can update the table of contents. As you continue to add information to a document, you can quickly update the table of contents. Click the References tab, and then click the Update Table button in Table of Contents group.

You can add a specific paragraph to the table of content. Select the paragraph you want to add, click the References tab, and then click the Add Text button in the Table of Contents group.

Use to customize a Table of Contents

Create a Table of Contents Manually

1. Select the text you want to include in your table of contents.

2. Click the **References** tab.

3. Mark entries using heading styles or individual text.

   - **Heading styles.** Click the heading style you want in the Styles group on the Home tab.

   - **Individual text.** Click the **Add Text** button, and then click the table of contents level you want: **Level 1**, **Level 2**, or **Level 3**.

4. To mark additional entries, select the text, use the options in Step 3.

5. Click the place where you want to insert the table of contents.

6. Click the **Table of Contents** button, and then click **Insert Table of Contents**.

7. Click **Options**.

8. Select the **Styles** check box.

9. Specify the TOC levels you want to use.

10. Click **OK**.

11. Select the formatting options you want.

12. Click **OK**.

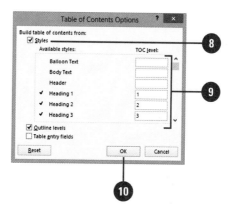

Did You Know?

You can delete a table of contents.
Click the References tab, click Table of Contents, and then click Remove Table of Contents.

Creating an Index

An index appears at the end of a document and alphabetically lists the main topics, names, and items used in a long document. Each index listing is called an entry. You can create an index entry for a word, phrase, or symbol for a topic. In an index, a cross-reference indicates another index entry that is related to the current entry. There are several ways to create an index. Begin by marking index entries. Some index entries will refer to blocks of text that span multiple pages within a document.

Create an Index

1. Click the **References** tab.

2. To use existing text as an index entry, select the text. To enter your text as an index entry, click at the point where you want the index entry inserted.

3. Click the **Mark Entry** button or press Alt+Shift+X.

4. Type or edit the entry. The entry can be customized by creating a sub-entry or a cross-reference to another entry.

5. To format the text for the index, right-click it in the Main Entry or Sub-entry box, click **Font**, select your formatting options, and then click **OK**.

6. To select a format for the page numbers that will appear in the index, select the **Bold** or **Italic** check boxes.

7. To mark the index entry, click **Mark** or **Mark All** for all similar text.

    Repeat steps 2-7 for additional index entries, and then click **Close**.

8. Go to the page where you want to display your Index.

9. Click the **Insert Index** button.

10. Click the **Index** tab, and then select any options you want.

11. Click **OK**.

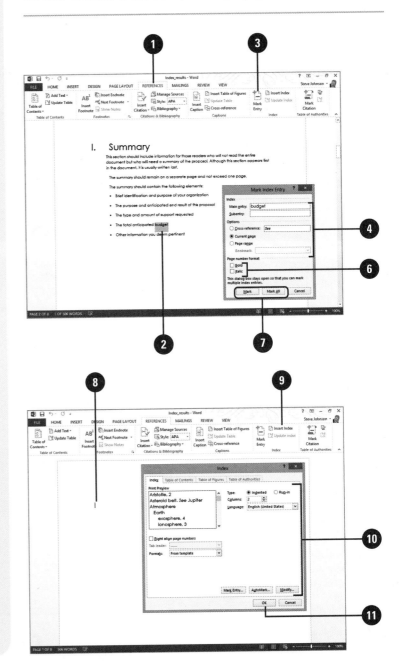

Create Multiple Page Index Entries

1. Click the **Insert** tab.

2. Select the text in which you want the index entry to refer.

3. Click the **Bookmark** button.

4. Enter a name, and then click **Add**.

5. Click after the end of the text in the document that you just marked with a bookmark.

6. Click the **References** tab.

7. Click the **Mark Entry** button or press Alt+Shift+X.

8. Enter the index entry for the marked text.

9. To format the text for the index, right-click the Main Entry or Sub-entry box, click **Font**, select your formatting options, and then click **OK**.

10. To select a format for the page numbers that will appear in the index, select the **Bold** or **Italic** check boxes.

11. Click the **Page Range** option.

12. Select the bookmark name you entered in Step 4.

13. Click **Mark**.

14. Repeat steps 2-13 for additional index entries, and then click **Close** or **Cancel**.

Determining Word Count Statistics

Producing lengthy documents for business, school or as contract work can often be regulated by the word count. Legal briefs may charge by the line or word, or school papers might need to be a certain length in word count. Either way, if you need to determine your word count, there is an easier way than counting each word manually. You can quickly determine the number of words in your document by viewing the Status bar. It appears in the lower-left corner next to the number of pages in your document. You can also use the Word Count button on the Review tab to find out word count statistics, including number of pages, characters, paragraphs, and lines. You have the choice whether to include or exclude text boxes, footnotes, and endnotes in the word count statistics.

Find Out Document Word Count Statistics

1. If you want to find out statistics for only part of a document, select the text you want to count.

2. Click the **Review** tab.

3. Click the **Word Count** button.

   TIMESAVER *Click the Word count on the Status bar.*

4. Select or clear the **Include textboxes, footnotes and endnotes** check box.

5. Click **Close**.

Did You Know?

You can count words in a text box. Select the text in the text box. The Status bar displays the number of words. To count the words in multiple text boxes, press and hold Ctrl while you select the text in each text box.

Word count

Adding a Cover Page

A cover page provides an introduction to a report, or an important memo you want to circulate to others. Word makes it easy to add a cover page to any document. You can quickly select one from a gallery of styles that fit your document. If you can't find the cover page you need, check out Office.com. Each cover page includes text boxes sample text, which you can change, and defined fields, such as a title and author's name, that automatically get filled in with information from document properties.

Insert a Cover Page

1. Click the **Insert** tab.

2. Click the **Cover Page** button to display a gallery of cover pages.

3. Click the cover page you want.

   ◆ **Add from Office.com.** Click **More Cover Pages from Office.com**.

   Word inserts a cover at the beginning of your document.

4. To remove a cover page, click the **Cover Page** button, and then click **Remove Current Cover Page**.

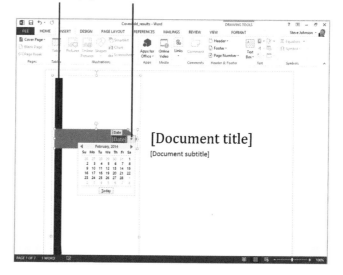

Cover page   Quick Part field; click the list arrow to select a date.

Working with Technical Documents

Introduction

Microsoft Word has many additional features that help you develop a more technical document. Research papers, business proposals and the like, all require more than just a document with some graphics or special text formatting.

You can find research material and incorporate it into your work quickly and easily. You can access informational services and insert the material right into your document without leaving Word. Material such as dictionaries, thesauruses, research sites, language translations, stock quotes, and company information are all at your finger tips.

With all of this research, it might be necessary to create footnotes or endnotes to reference your sources. You can format the notes to be similar in text to your document, or have an entirely different look. When working with a lot of text, you can create a bookmark to help you jump to various topics in your document.

Creating captions for your graphics is easy with Word. Once you've created captions, you can create a Table of Figures—similar to a Table of Contents, but this item keeps track of your graphics. You can format text in your document to have number lines. This is helpful if you need to locate a specific section of text—such as a legal briefing—in a long document. You can also create an outline in Word to help organize your document.

Some more technical features such as summing up the values in your tables and calculating values, are done with the help of Word's Formula feature. You can also document an equation for that scientific or mathematical paper.

What You'll Do

Insert Building Blocks Using Quick Parts

Insert and Create AutoText

Insert Research Material

Create Footnotes or Endnotes

Modify Footnotes or Endnotes

Format Footnotes or Endnotes

Create a Bibliography

Create a Bookmark

Create Captions

Create a Table of Figures

Number Lines

Create an Equation

Insert Symbols

Insert and Use Field Codes

Inserting Building Blocks Using Quick Parts

A **Quick Part** is a defined field or set of fields that contains information you can use throughout a document. Word calls these building blocks. Instead of typing the company name, address and phone number every time you need it in a document, you can insert a text box field with the information. Word provides a variety of defined Quick Parts—including Author, Company, Company Address, Company E-mail, Manager and Status—you can quickly insert in a document. The Quick Part fields insert information you provide in Document Properties or a placeholder, which you can fill in the first time. If a predefined field doesn't meet your needs, you can create your own or get more on Office.com. If you need to modify a Quick Part, you can use the building block organizer, which stores your custom Quick Parts and those provided by Word. Word uses Quick Parts as part of the program to build page covers, headers and footers, pull quotes, and side bar to name a few.

Insert a Quick Part Building Block

1. Click where you want to insert a text box.

2. Click the **Insert** tab.

3. Click the **Quick Parts** button.

4. Point to **Document Property**, and then click the predefined Quick Part you want to insert.

5. Modify the predefined Quick Part; click the list arrow (if available) to define it.

Did You Know?

You can create your own Quick Part. Select the text box you want to use, click the Insert tab, click the Quick Parts button, and then click Save Selection To Quick Parts Gallery.

Create a Quick Part Field

1. Click the **Insert** tab.

2. Click the **Quick Parts** button, and then click **Field**.

3. Click the **Categories** list arrow, and then click a category to narrow down the field names.

4. Click the field name you want to use.

5. Specify field property information.

6. Click the format you want to apply.

7. Click **OK**.

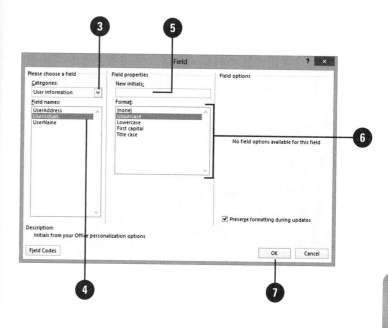

Work with Building Blocks

1. Click the **Insert** tab.

2. Click the **Quick Parts** button, and then click **Building Blocks Organizer**.

3. Select the Quick Part building block you want to modify.

4. Click **Edit Properties**.

5. Specify the properties you want to change, including Name, Gallery, Category, Description, Save in, and Options.

6. Click **OK**.

7. To insert or delete a building block, select it, and then click **Insert** or **Delete**.

8. Click **Close**.

Inserting and Creating AutoText

AutoText stores text and graphics you want to reuse, such as a company logo, boilerplate text, or formatted table. For example, you can use AutoText to quickly insert the text To Whom It May Concern or a graphic of your signature. You can use the AutoText entries that come with Word, or create your own. AutoText is part of Word's building block approach to creating customized documents. Word calls these building blocks. To insert AutoText, you use the Quick Parts button and then AutoText menu.

Insert AutoText from the AutoText Gallery

1. Click where you want to insert AutoText.

2. Click the **Insert** tab.

3. Click the **Quick Parts** button, and then point to **AutoText**.

4. Click the AutoText entry you want from the AutoText gallery.

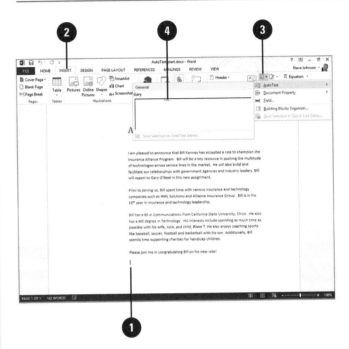

Create AutoText

1. Select the text or graphic in which you want to create an AutoText entry.

2. Click the **Insert** tab.

3. Click the **Quick Parts** button, and then point to **AutoText**.

4. Click **Save Selection to AutoText Gallery**.

5. Type an AutoText name, or use the suggested one.

6. Click **OK**.

Did You Know?

You can delete an AutoText entry. Click the Insert tab, click the Quick Parts button, point to AutoText, right-click the entry you want to delete, click Organize And Delete, click Delete, click Yes, and then click Close.

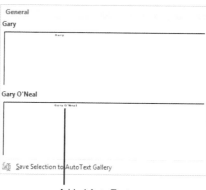

Added Auto Text

Inserting Research Material

With the Research pane, you can access data sources and insert research material right into your text without leaving Word. The Research pane can help you access electronic dictionaries, thesauruses, research sites, and proprietary company information. You can select one reference source, search in all reference books, or search reference sites on the web, such as Bing, Factiva iWorks, and HighBeam Research. This research pane allows you to find information and quickly and easily copy and paste it into your work. If you have a hard time finding research information on a specific topic, you can use the Research Options command to enable and update additional reference books and research web sites from which to search.

Research a Topic

1. Click the **Research** button on the Quick Access Toolbar.

   ◆ The Research button is not on the Quick Access Toolbar by default. Use the Customize pane in Word Options to add the button.

2. Type the topic you would like to research.

3. Click the list arrow, and then select a reference source, or click **All Reference Books**.

4. Click the **Start Searching** button (green arrow).

5. Select the information in the pane that you want to copy.

   To search for more information, click one of the words in the list or click a link to an online site.

6. Select the information you want, and then copy it.

   In the Research pane, you can point to the item you want, click the list arrow, or right-click selected text, and then click **Copy**.

7. Paste the information into your document.

8. When you're done, click the **Close** button on the pane.

Change Research Options

1. Click the **Research** button on the Quick Access Toolbar.

   ◆ The Research button is not on the Quick Access Toolbar by default. Use the Customize pane in Word Options to add the button.

2. In the pane, click **Research Options**.

   ◆ You can also click Research Options in the Privacy Option pane of the Trust Center.

3. Do any of the following:

   ◆ **Services.** To activate or remove research services.

   ◆ **Add Services.** To add research services.

   ◆ **Update/Remove.** To update or remove a service provider.

   ◆ **Parental Control.** To turn on parental controls.

4. Do any of the following:

   ◆ **Properties.** To display properties for the selected service.

   ◆ **Favorite.** To make the selected service your favorite.

5. Click **OK**.

6. When you're done, click the **Close** button on the pane.

Did You Know?

You can open Research Options from the Options dialog box. Click the File tab, click Options, click Trust Center in the left pane, click Trust Center Settings, click Privacy Options, and then click Research Options.

Creating Footnotes or Endnotes

Footnotes are used to provide additional information that is inappropriate for the body of the text, and to document your references for information or quotes presented in the body of the document. Footnotes are appropriate for academic, scientific, and, occasionally, business purposes. Footnotes appear at the bottom of the page on which the information is cited, and Word automatically inserts a reference mark at the insertion point to associate the information presented with the note at the bottom of the page. Creating and manipulating endnotes is identical to performing the same functions for footnotes. Endnotes differ from footnotes in that they appear at the end of the document or section (in the case of longer documents), not the bottom of the page on which the reference mark appears.

Create a Footnote or Endnote

1. Position the insertion point where you want to insert a footnote.

2. Click the **References** tab.

3. To quickly create a footnote or endnote, click the **Insert Footnote** or **Insert Endnote** button, and then enter footnote or endnote text.

4. To create or customize the footnote or endnote, click the **Footnotes Dialog Box Launcher**.

5. Click the **Footnotes** or **Endnotes** option, click the list arrow next to the option, and then select the location where you want to place the footnote or endnote.

6. Verify that the Number Format option of 1,2,3... is selected.

7. Click **Insert** to insert a reference mark in the text. Word moves the insertion point to the bottom of the page corresponding to the number of the reference mark.

8. Type the text of your footnote or endnote.

9. Click the **Show Notes** button and the **Next Footnote** button to show/hide notes and locate them.

10. Click in the document to continue with your work.

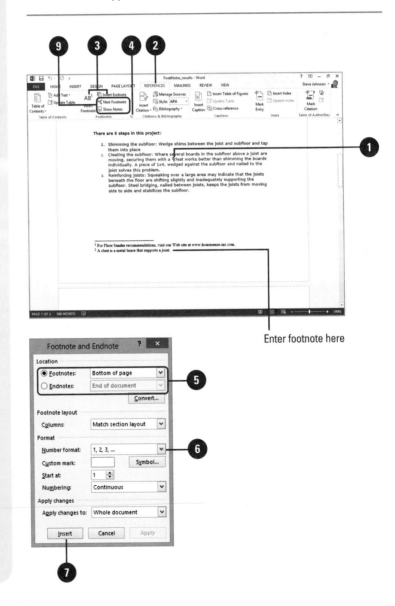

Enter footnote here

Modifying Footnotes or Endnotes

Editing the actual text of a footnote or endnote is just like editing any text, except that you must first access the note. Use the Show Notes button to display all the notes, click to position your insertion point at the bottom of the page or in the Notes pane, and then edit. As you change other text in a document, Word repositions your notes. When your edits affect sentences with notes, or when you move, copy, or delete notes in your document, Word renumbers the other notes for you. When you move, copy, or delete a note, you work with the note reference mark in the document, not the text in the Notes pane. You can move, copy, or delete a note in the same way you would text in a document.

Edit a Footnote or Endnote

1. To quickly view a footnote or endnote, point to the reference mark to display a ScreenTip with the contents of the note.

2. To go to a note, double-click the reference mark in the document.

   ◆ In Draft view, the Notes pane opens.

3. Click to place the insertion point in the Notes pane or at the bottom of the page where you want to edit the note text, and then edit the note text as if you were editing text in the document.

4. If necessary, click the **Close** button on the Notes pane.

5. To move or copy a note, select the reference mark, click the **Cut** or **Copy** button on the Home tab, click to place the insertion point, and then click the **Paste** button.

Did You Know?

You can delete a footnote or endnote. Select the reference mark for the footnote or endnote you want to delete, and then press Delete.

ScreenTip for the footnote

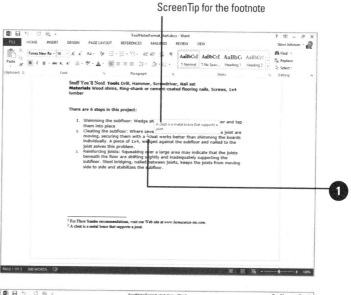

Formatting Footnotes or Endnotes

Footnote or endnote reference marks appear as 1,2,3... by default. Word provides you with various options in order to customize the reference marks the way you wish. If you'd like to change your footnotes or endnotes to be a,b,c or Roman numerals i, ii, iii, you can do that through the Insert menu. You can format the location of the footnote or endnote to be at the bottom of the text, or at the bottom of the page. You can also have Word renumber your footnotes or endnotes after each section of your document, and change the font and other formatting for a reference mark. You format a footnote or endnote reference mark in the same way you format any other text in a document.

Change a Footnote or Endnote Format

1. Click to place the insertion point in the section in which you want to change the footnote or endnote format.

2. Click the **References** tab.

3. Click the **Footnote & Endnote Dialog Box Launcher**.

4. Click the **Number Format** list arrow, and then click the format you want.

5. To change the starting point, click the Start at **Up** or **Down** arrows.

6. If necessary, click the **Apply changes to** list arrow, and then click **Whole Document**.

7. Click **Apply**, and then click **Cancel**.

Format Footnotes or Endnotes in a Document

① In the body text, select the footnote or endnote reference mark.

② Click the **Home** tab.

③ Use the formatting buttons on the **Home** tab or click the **Font Dialog Box Launcher** to format the reference marks the way you want.

Font Dialog Box Launcher

Font dialog box; make font changes

Did You Know?

You can create a footnote or endnote continuation notice when a note is too long. Click the Draft View button on the Status bar, click the References tab, and then click the Show Notes button. If necessary, click the View Footnote Area or View Endnote Area option, and then click OK. In the Notes pane, click the list arrow, click Footnote Continuation Notice or Endnote Continuation Notice, and then type the text you want to use for the notice.

You can convert one or more notes to footnotes or endnotes. Click the Draft View button on the Status bar, and then click the Show Notes button. If necessary, click View Footnote Area or View Endnote Area option, and then click OK. Select the number of the note or notes you want to convert, right-click it, and then click Convert To Footnote or Convert To Endnote. To convert all notes to footnotes or endnotes, click the Footnote & Endnote Dialog Box Launcher, click Convert, click the option you want, click OK, and then click Close.

Creating a Bibliography

A **bibliography** is a list of sources that you cited during the research of a project. A bibliography typically appears at the end of a document and provides information about the source of your research. When you create a bibliography, you can choose a standard style, which is widely accepted by universities and businesses. So, all you need to do is create a citation and enter the source information. If you're not sure what source you want to use, you can insert a placeholder and fill in the source information later. After you finish adding sources to a document, you can use the Manage Source dialog box to choose which ones you want to use before you create the bibliography.

Add a Citation and Source to a Document

1. Click the **References** tab.

2. Click the **Style** list arrow, and then click the style you want.

    If you're not sure, ask your professor or a business associate, or search the Internet.

3. Click to place the insertion point where you want to place the citation.

4. Click the **Insert Citation** button, and then click **Add New Source**.

    ◆ To add new placeholder to fill in the source information later, click **Add new placeholder**, type a placeholder name, and then click **OK**.

5. Click the **Type of Source** list arrow, and then select a source type.

6. Enter the bibliography information for the source.

7. Click **OK**.

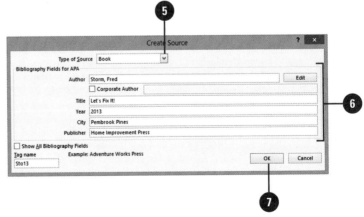

Manage Sources and Placeholders

1. Click the **References** tab.

2. Click the **Manage Sources** button.

   All the sources from previous documents appear in the Master List, and currently cited sources in the Current List.

3. To search for sources, click in the Search box, type search criteria, and then press Enter.

4. To sort source information, click the **Sort** list arrow, and then select a sort type.

5. To edit a placeholder, click the placeholder you want to edit in the Current List, and then click **Edit**.

6. Use the Copy and Delete buttons to move sources around or delete them.

7. Click **Close**.

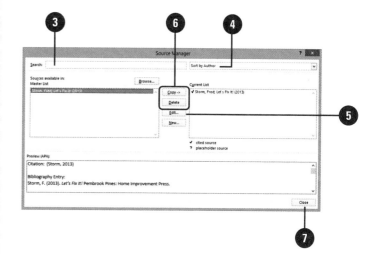

Create a Bibliography

1. Click to place the insertion point where you want to insert a bibliography.

2. Click the **References** tab.

3. Click the **Bibliography** button.

4. Click the bibliography format style you want to insert.

5. To update a bibliography, select the bibliography, click the tab button, and then click **Update Bibliography**.

Creating a Bookmark

Instead of scrolling through a long document to find a specific word, phrase or section you can use bookmarks. **Bookmarks** are used to mark text so that you, or your reader, can quickly return to it. Using bookmarks as a destination make it easy to navigate through a long document. You can also navigate through documents with bookmarks by selecting a bookmark as a destination in the Go To dialog box.

Create a Bookmark

1 Click in your document where you want to insert a Bookmark.

2 Click the **Insert** tab.

3 Click the **Bookmark** button.

4 Type a one word descriptive name for your Bookmark.

5 Click **Add**.

Did You Know?

You can go to different locations in Word. Click the Home tab, click the Find button arrow, click Go To, select the Go To What option you want, specify a location, and then click Next or Previous. When you're done, click Close.

Go to a Bookmark Location

1. Click the **Home** tab.

2. Click the **Find** button arrow, and then click **Go To**.

3. On the Go To tab, click **Bookmark**.

4. Click the **Enter bookmark name** list arrow, and then select the bookmark you want to move to.

5. Click **Go To**.

6. If you want, choose another bookmark.

7. Click **Close**.

Did You Know?

You can go to different locations in Word. Click the Home tab, click the Find button arrow, click Go To, select the Go To What option you want, specify a location, and then click Next or Previous. When you're done, click Close.

Creating Captions

Captions are helpful not only to associate images with the text that refers to them, but also to provide the reader with amplifying information about the figure, table, chart, or other illustration displayed. You can use preset captions provided, such as Figure, or you can create your own custom caption for your document.

Insert a Caption

① Select the image that you want to caption.

② Click the **References** tab.

③ Click the **Insert Caption** button.

④ If you want to use a Label other than the default setting of Figure, which is appropriate for most art, click the **Label** list arrow, and then click **Equation** or **Table**.

⑤ If you want to use a numbering sequence other than the default setting of 1,2,3..., click **Numbering**, make your selections, and then click **OK**.

⑥ Click **OK**.

Did You Know?

You can have Word automatically add a caption field. Whenever you insert a particular type of file, such as a bitmapped image, click AutoCaption. In the Add Caption When Inserting list, click the check boxes to select the instances where you want the feature to apply, select the Label, Positioning and Numbering options you want, and then click OK.

You can add custom labels for captions. Click New Label, type the name of the New Label, and then click OK.

Creating a Table of Figures

If you are creating a document in which there are many illustrations (art, photographs, charts, diagrams etc.), it is often helpful to the reader of your document to provide a Table of Figures. A **Table of Figures** is like a Table of Contents except that it deals only with the graphic content of a document, not the written content. To create the Table of Figures, Word looks for text with the Style code that you specify (Figure, Table, etc). You can also add a **tab leader** to make the table easier to read.

Create a Table of Figures

1. Position the insertion point where you want the Table of Figures to appear.

2. Click the **References** tab.

3. Click the **Insert Table of Figures** button.

4. Click the **Table of Figures** tab.

5. Click the **Tab leader** list arrow, and then select the tab leader you want to use.

6. Click the **Formats** list arrow, and then select the format you want to use for the Table of Figures.

7. If you want to create a Table of Figures from something other than the default Figure style, or the Table style, click **Options**.

8. Click the **Style** list arrow, select the text formatting that you want Word to search for when building the Table of Figures, and then click **Close**. All figure callouts of the selected style are tagged for inclusion in the Table of Figures.

9. Click **OK**.

10. Click **OK**.

Table of Figures

Numbering Lines

Many legal documents use the formatting convention of numbering every line of text to make it easier for multiple parties to refer to very specific text in a longer document in the context of their discussions. Other types of documents that sometimes use this convention are movie and television scripts. You can have Word automatically number each line of text within a document.

Number Each Line in a Document Quickly

1. If you want to show or hide line numbers to only selected text, select the text you want.

2. Click the **Page Layout** tab.

3. Click the **Line Numbers** button, and then click the option you want:

   ◆ **None**. Remove line numbers from the document.

   ◆ **Continuous**. Add line numbers to the document starting from line 1.

   ◆ **Restart Each Page**. Restart line numbers on each page.

   ◆ **Restart Each Section**. Restart line numbers at each section.

   ◆ **Suppress for Current Paragraph**. Remove line numbers from the selected text.

Line numbers

Customize Line Numbering Options

1. If you want to display line numbers to only selected text, select the text you want.

2. Click the **Page Layout** tab.

3. Click the **Line Numbers** button, and then click **Line Numbering Options**.

4. If you're adding line numbers to part of a document, click the **Apply to** list arrow, and then click **Selected text**.

5. Click **Line Numbers**.

6. Click the **Add line numbering** check box.

7. Select the options you want: Start at, From text, Count by, and Numbering.

8. Click **OK**.

9. Click **OK**.

Creating an Equation

If you are creating a scientific or academic paper that involves complex equations, you may need to display them in the text without actually using them in conjunction with a table. The standard keyboard does not have all of the mathematical symbols you might need to create the equation, so you can use the Equations gallery to quickly insert a common equation or the Design tab under Equation Tools to create a custom equation. The Equations gallery is part of Word's building block approach to creating customized documents.

Insert a Common Equation from the Equations Gallery

1. Click where you want to insert an equation.

2. Click the **Insert** tab.

3. Click the **Equation** button arrow.

4. Click a common equation from the Equations gallery.

   The equation appears in the document as a building block.

5. Click to place the insertion point in the equation and then edit it like you would text.

6. To change the equation display, click the **Equations Options** list arrow, and then click the option you want.

   ◆ **Save as New Equation**. Saves the equation as a new building block in the Equations gallery.

   ◆ **Professional**. Displays equation in 2D form.

   ◆ **Linear**. Displays equation in 1D form.

   ◆ **Change to Inline** or **Display.** Changes the equation position to inline with text or display in the middle of the line.

   ◆ **Justification**. Changes alignment: Left, Right, Centered, or Centered as a Group.

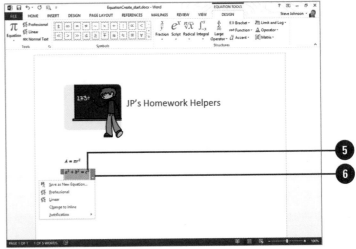

Create an Equation

1. Click where you want to insert an equation.

2. Click the **Insert** tab.

3. Click the **Equation** button arrow, and then click **Insert New Equation**.

   A blank equation building block appears.

4. Click the **Design** tab under Equation Tools.

5. Type any part of the equation, or click any of the buttons in the Structures group you want, and then select the equation segment you want.

6. Select the placeholder you want to insert more of the equation.

7. Click the scroll up or down arrow, or click the **More** list arrow in the Symbols group, and then select the symbol you want to insert.

8. Continue to insert structures and symbols to complete your equation.

Did You Know?

You can display an equation as regular text. Select an equation, click the Design tab under Equation Tools, click the Linear button, and then click the Normal Text button.

You can change default equation options. Select an equation, click the Design tab under Equation Tools, click the Tools Dialog Box Launcher, specify the options you want, and then click OK.

Inserting Symbols

Word comes with a host of symbols for every need. Insert just the right one to keep from compromising a document's professional appearance with a missing accent or mathematical symbol (å). In the Symbol dialog box, you use the Recently used symbols list to quickly insert a symbol that you want to insert again. If you don't see the symbol you want, use the Font list to look at the available symbols for other fonts installed on your computer.

Insert Recently Used Symbols and Special Characters Quickly

1. Click the document where you want to insert a symbol or character.

2. Click the **Insert** tab.

3. Click the **Symbol** button.

4. Click one of the recently used symbols or special characters from the list to insert it into the document.

Trademark symbol

Did You Know?

You can insert a symbol using a character code. When the From box displays ASCII (decimal), you can use the number shown in the Character Code box to insert a character or symbol. Place your insertion point where you want the character on the slide, make sure Num Lock is on, hold down the Alt key, and then use the numeric keypad to type 0 (zero) followed by the character code. Then release the Alt key. The code applies to the current code page only, so some characters may not be available this way.

Insert Symbols and Special Characters

1. Click the document where you want to insert a symbol or character.

2. Click the **Insert** tab.

3. Click the **Symbol** button, and then click **More Symbols**.

4. To see other symbols, click the **Font** list arrow, and then click a new font.

5. Click a symbol or character.

   You can use the Recently used symbols list to use a symbol you've already used.

6. Click **Insert**.

Did You Know?

You can assign a shortcut key to insert a symbol within the document. Click the Insert menu, click Symbol, click a symbol, click Shortcut Key, enter the shortcut key information requested, and then click Close.

Trademark symbol

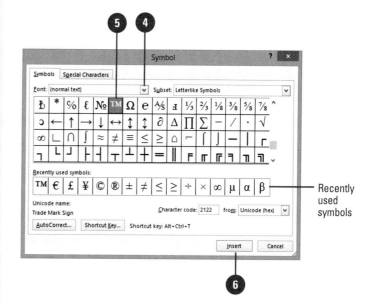

Recently used symbols

Inserting and Using Field Codes

Field codes are placeholders for data that change in a document. This is useful for creating form letters and labels. Word automatically insert fields when you insert a page number or building block, or when you create a table of contents. You can also manually insert fields to automate parts of a document, such as performing calculations (using the = (formula field) or merging data. Field codes appear between curly brackets ({}).

Fields work like formulas in Microsoft Excel, the field code is like the formula, and the field result is like the value that the formula creates. A field codes looks like this: { FIELD NAME Properties *Switches* }. The FIELD NAME is the name that appears in the list of field names in the Field dialog; not all fields have parameters and some parameters are optional. Properties are any instruction or variable that are used in a particular field; not all fields have properties. *Switches* are any optional settings that are available for a field.

Inserting and Using a Field

1. Click where you want to insert a field.

2. Click the **Insert** tab, click the **Quick Parts** button, and then click **Field**.

3. Select a category, and then select a field. If you want to see field codes, click **Field Codes**. To return back, click **Hide Codes**.

   A brief field description appears; for a detailed look, search the field in Help.

4. Select any properties or options. There are three formatting switches: Format (*), Numeric (\#), and Date-Time (\@). These define how to display field results.

5. Click **OK**.

If you know the field code for a field, you can also insert a field using a shortcut; press Ctrl+F9, and then type the field code (not by typing the brace characters). Here are some example fields and their results:

♦ { = SUM(Sales) \# $#,##0.00 * MERGEFORMAT} displays $1,354.54.

♦ { = { Price } *7.7% \# "$#,##0.00 'is sales tax'" } displays $1.35 is sales tax.

♦ { = DATE \@ "dddd, MMMM d, yyyy" } displays Friday, March 12, 2013.

To go to the next or previous field, press F11or Shift+F11. To edit a field, right-click the field, and then click Edit Field. You can apply formatting to a field just like you would text. Simply, select the field, and then apply the formatting using commands on the Home tab. You can also change the shaded background of fields; click the File tab, click Options, click Advanced, click the Field shading list arrow, click Never, Always, or When selected, and then click OK.

Displaying and Updating Fields

To switch the display between field codes and it's results, press Alt+F9; for only a selected field, press Shift+F9. You can manually update one or more fields; select the fields, and then press F9 or right-click a field, and then click Update Field. To lock a field so that the results are not updated, click the field, and then press Ctrl+F11; press Ctrl+Shift+F11 to unlock it.

Creating Mail Merge Documents

Introduction

Whether you are looking to personalize your annual Christmas letter to friends and family, or prepare a direct-mail marketing piece to 10,000 customers of your business, Word's Mail Merge Wizard is up to the task. To perform a mail merge, you need a **form letter** that contains the text you want to send out, plus **merge fields** for the information that you want to use to personalize each letter, such as the recipient's address, first name in the greeting line, and so forth. These fields can be added manually, or as part of the Mail Merge Wizard process.

You must have a **data document** that contains all of this information in either comma or tab delimited format. Most databases, such as Access or Outlook (contacts), can automatically export into this format. Alternately, you can manually create a data document if you do not have an existing database of contact information that you can use for the merge. Equipped with these two sources, the Mail Merge Wizard can quickly and easily create thousands of personalized letters, address labels, and envelopes, in a fraction of the time it would otherwise take you to do these tasks.

If you prefer a more manual approach to creating a mail merge document, you can perform the process using commands on the Mailings tab. The mail merge process follows the same general steps. First, set up the main document. Second, connect the document to a data source. Third, refine the list of recipients or items. Fourth, add mail merge fields, and fifth, preview and complete the merge. If you need to stop working during the mail merge process, you can save the document and resume it again later. Word saves all information regarding the mail merge and returns you to the place in the pane where you left off.

What You'll Do

Start the Mail Merge

Import Data from a Database

Import Data from Outlook

Create a Data Document

Edit the Data Source

Sort and Filter Data

Create a Form Letter

Preview the Mail Merge

Complete the Mail Merge

Merge to E-Mail

Create Merged Mailing Labels

Create Merged Envelopes

Address Envelopes and Labels

Starting the Mail Merge

Did you ever send the same letter to several people and spend a lot of time changing personal information, such as names and addresses? If so, form letters will save you time. **Mail merge** is the process of combining names and addresses stored in a data file with a main document (usually a form letter) to produce customized documents. There are four main steps to merging. First, select the document you want to use. Second, create a data file with the variable information. Third, create the main document with the boilerplate (unchanging information) and merge fields. Finally, merge the main document with the data source to create a new document with all the merged information. When you start the mail merge, you need to open the letter that you want to mail merge or type one. Don't worry about addressing the letter or adding a greeting line, you can accomplish that with the Mail Merge Wizard.

Start the Mail Merge Wizard

1. Click the **Mailings** tab.

2. Click the **Start Mail Merge** button, and then click **Step by Step Mail Merge Wizard**.

   The Mail Merge pane opens, displaying Step 1 of 6.

3. Select the type of document you are working on (in this case the Letters option).

4. Click **Next: Starting document** on the pane to display Step 2 of 6.

5. Click a starting document option (such as Use the current document).

6. Click **Next: Select recipients** on the pane to display Step 3 of 6.

Did You Know?

You can set up the main document manually. Create a new or existing document, click the Mailings tab, click the Start Mail Merge button, select a document type (Letters, E-Mail Messages, etc.), and then select any options, if prompted.

Importing Data from a Database

Now it is time to specify the recipients for your mail merge. To do so, you must identify a **data document** as the source of the recipient information you will use to personalize the mailing. If you have an existing database of information to work with, this is the easiest method. The mail merge works with most standard database and spreadsheet programs including Microsoft Access and Microsoft Excel. Before you can import data into the Mail Merge Wizard from an external database, you must first export it from the database you are using. Follow the instructions for that database to export a file in either comma or tab delimited format, and remember which format you chose. Export the file to the My Data Sources folder.

Import Data from an Existing Database

1. On Step 3 of 6 in the Mail Merge pane, click the **Use an existing list** option.

2. Click **Browse** on the pane.

3. Locate and select the database file from which you want to import the recipient data.

4. Click **Open**.

5. If necessary, select a data source, such as a table in an Excel worksheet or Access database, and then click **OK**.

   The Mail Merge Recipient dialog box opens, displaying the data source for the merge.

6. Edit the recipient data (if necessary), and then click **OK**.

7. Click **Next: write your letter** on the pane to display Step 4 of 6.

Importing Data from Outlook

If you are already using Outlook to manage your contact database, you can import your Outlook contact records into the Mail Merge Wizard quickly and easily. For example, a contact record for a person or company might contain an address, telephone, e-mail address, and so forth. An item record might contain the part number, description, quantity on hand, and so on. The information in each record is organized by fields. The fields of the database correspond to the merge fields you specify in the Form Letter. Additional fields other than the ones to be used by the merge can exist, and will be ignored by the Mail Merge Wizard. For example, a direct mail piece would use the address field in a record as a merge field and ignore the e-mail address field for that record, whereas an e-mail merge would do exactly the opposite.

Import Data from Outlook

1. On Step 3 of 6 in the Mail Merge pane, click **Select from Outlook contacts**.

2. Click **Choose Contacts Folder**.

3. If an Outlook profile dialog box opens, select a profile, and then click **OK**.

   The Select Contact List Folder dialog box opens.

4. Select the contacts list you want to use.

5. Click **OK**.

   The Mail Merge Recipients dialog box opens, displaying the data source for the merge.

6. Edit the recipient data (if necessary), and then click **OK**.

7. Click **Next: Write your letter** on the pane to display Step 4 of 6.

Did You Know?

You can connect the document to a data source manually. In the document, click the Mailings tab, click the Select Recipients button, and then select the data source you want, and any related options, if prompted.

Creating a Data Document

When you are only doing a limited number of pieces in a mail merge, or you cannot input the records into one of the previously mentioned programs for permanent use and then export them to the Mail Merge Wizard to perform the task at hand, you can use the Wizard to create your recipient list. You can also use Word to manually type a data document. The first line of the document should contain the merge field names separated by commas or tabs (choose one format and be consistent throughout the document). For example, FirstName, LastName, Address, City, State, Zip. Note that field names cannot contain spaces. At the end of the field name line, press Enter. Input all of the data for a given record separated by commas on the lines that follow, press Enter after each record entry. When all entries are entered, save the document as a text file and import it as an existing file in Step 3 of 6 in the Mail Merge Wizard.

Create a Data Document

1. On Step 3 of 6 in the Mail Merge pane, click the **Type a new list** option.

2. Click **Create**.

3. Input your information for the first record, and then click **New Entry**.

4. Continue to input additional records; click **New Entry** after each one until all records have been entered, and then click **OK**.

   The Save Address List dialog box opens, displaying the My Data Sources folder.

5. Enter a name, and then click **Save** to save your work.

   The Mail Merge Recipients dialog box opens, displaying the data source for the merge.

6. Edit the recipient data (if necessary), and then click **OK**.

7. Click **Next: Write your letter** on the pane to display Step 4 of 6.

Editing the Data Source

Regardless of the original source of your data, an external database, manually prepared list, Outlook records, or an Address List that you created within the Mail Merge Wizard, periodically you will want to make some changes to the data before completing the merge. The time to do so is in Step 3 of 6 of the Mail Merge Wizard.

Edit a Data Document

1. On Step 3 of 6 in the Mail Merge pane, click **Edit recipient list.**

2. Select the data source.

3. Click **Edit**, and then make the changes you want to the fields.

4. To add records to the merge, select any existing record, and then click **New Entry.**

5. To remove the selected record from the data document permanently, click **Delete Entry.**

6. Click **OK.**

7. If you want to retain the record in the data document, but exclude it from the merge, clear the check mark next to the record.

   All records begin selected by default and must be manually deselected from the merge.

8. When you're done, click **OK.**

9. Click **Next: Write your letter** on the pane to display Step 4 of 6.

Did You Know?

You can refine the data source manually. In the document, click the Mailings tab, click the Edit Recipient List button, and then make the changes you want, and any related options, if prompted.

Sorting and Filtering Data

When you are working with large numbers of records, it is often helpful to organize those records in a particular order. For example, if you are doing a bulk mailing via the USPS, they require that the pieces of the mailing be sorted in zip code order for you to receive the savings associated with the bulk mail rate. Word can easily accomplish this task for you so the records are merged and printed in zip code order. You can sort and filter records by any of the merge fields in the record.

Sort and Filter Records

1. On Step 3 of 6 in the Mail Merge pane, click **Edit recipient list**.

2. To sort the data in a column, click the field column heading (not the list arrow inside of it).

3. To filter out data in a field column by a specific criterion or value, click the list arrow in the column heading, and then select a filter option or value.

   TIMESAVER *Click the Filter link in the Mail Merge Recipients dialog box.*

4. To perform advance sorts, where you compare the values of certain fields, click the list arrow for any field, and then click **Advanced.**

5. If you chose an advanced sort, select or enter filter and sort criteria in the Field, Comparison, and Compare to box, and then click **OK**.

6. When you're done, click **OK**.

7. Click **Next: write your letter** on the pane to display Step 4 of 6.

Did You Know?

You can display all the data in a column. In the Mail Merge Recipient dialog box, click the column heading list arrow used for a filter, and then click All.

Creating a Form Letter

The only difference between a normal letter and a **form letter** is the presence of merge fields in the latter. Merge fields can exist anywhere in the document, and correspond to any field in the data document. For example, you can insert the FirstName field periodically in a document to reaffirm to the reader that you are speaking directly to them, and minimize the negative reactions that many people feel when they receive a form letter. The most commonly used fields in a form letter are the address block and the greeting line. Each merge field corresponds to a piece of information in the data source and appears in the main document with the greater than and less than characters around it. For example, the <<Address Block>> merge field corresponds to name and address information in the data source. Word incorporates insert commands for each of these in the Mail Merge Wizard.

Create a Form Letter

1. On Step 4 of 6 in the Mail Merge pane, position the insertion point in the letter where you want the address block to appear.

2. Click **Address Block** on the pane.

3. Select the Address Block options you want.

4. Click **OK** to insert the block in the document.

5. Position the insertion point where you want the greeting to appear.

6. Click **Greeting Line**.

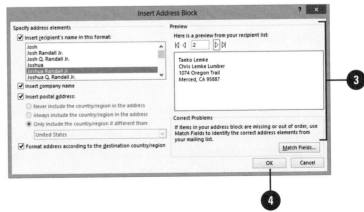

7 Select the format you want for the greeting line.

8 Click **OK** to apply the style to the merge field.

9 If you want to add other merge fields in the body of the form letter, position the insertion point where you want the information, and then click **More Items** on the pane.

10 Select the merge field you want to place, click **Insert**, and then click **Close**.

11 When you're done, click **Next: Preview your letters** on the pane to display Step 5 of 6.

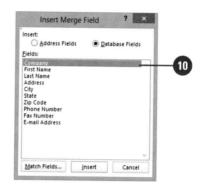

Did You Know?

You can edit the style of a field. Right click on the field to bring up a menu of options, and then click Edit.

You can have common words used as field names. Information in a data file is stored in merge fields, labeled with one-word names, such as FirstName, LastName, City, and so on. You can insert merge field names in the main document as blanks or placeholders, for variable information. When you merge the data file and main document, Word fills in the blanks with the correct information.

You should beware of those extra spaces. Don't press the Spacebar after entering data in a field. Extra spaces will appear in the document between the data and the next word or punctuation, leaving ugly gaps or floating punctuation. Add spaces and punctuation to your main document instead.

Letter with merged fields

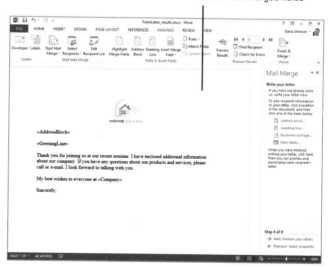

Previewing the Mail Merge

Although Word has automated much of the mail merge process for you, it is always a good idea to review the merged letters before printing them. You might find changes to the body text or even the merge fields that you want to make before the merge is final. The preview process occurs in Step 5 of 6 in the Mail Merge pane.

Preview the Mail Merge

1. On Step 5 of 6 in the Mail Merge pane, click the double arrows on the pane to scroll through the merge letters one at a time.

2. To find a given recipient or group of recipients quickly, click **Find a recipient** on the pane.

3. If you chose Find, enter search criterion, click the **All fields** option, or **This field** option, and then select a field.

4. Click **Find Next** to proceed to the next matching record.

5. When you're done, click **Close**.

6. Click **Next: Complete the merge** on the pane to display Step 6 of 6.

Did You Know?

You can exclude a recipient from the merge. Click the Exclude This Recipient button on the pane on Step 5 of 6.

You can auto check for errors. In the document, click the Mailings tab, click the Auto Check for Errors button, select an option to simulate or complete the merge with error checking and reporting, and then click OK.

You can preview the mail merge results manually. In the document, click the Mailings tab, click the Preview Results button, view the results, and then make the changes you want.

Completing the Mail Merge

After you set up a data document and enter merge fields into the main document, you are ready to merge the document to create a new document with all the merged information. The new document contains individualized copies of the main document for each record in the data source. You can edit the new document to personalize individual copies in the main document, and then print the end result.

Personalize and Print the Mail Merge

1. Proceed to Step 6 of 6 in the Mail Merge pane.

2. If you want to make additional changes to the letters, click **Edit Individual Letters**.

3. Specify the settings you want to use for the merged records and the selected range of the records are saved to a separate file for editing.

4. Click **OK**.

5. When you're ready to print, click **Print** on the pane.

6. Click the **All** option to print the entire merge or click another option to print only a selected portion of the merge.

7. Click **OK**.

Did You Know?

You can complete the mail merge manually. In the document, click the Mailings tab, click the Find & Merge button, and then click Print Documents or Edit Individual Documents. When you're done, save the main document.

Merging to E-mail

Instead of merging data to create a form letter you can print, you can merge data to an e-mail document. The steps to merge an e-mail document rather than a letter are essentially the same, but there are a few small differences.

Mail Merge to E-mail

1. On Step 1 of 6 in the Mail Merge pane, click the **E-mail messages** option.

2. Click **Next: Starting document** on the pane to display Step 2 of 6.

3. Click a starting document option (such as Use The Current Document).

4. Click **Next: Select Recipients** on the pane to display Step 3 of 6.

5. Click a recipient option (such as Use an existing list or Type a new list).

6. Click **Browse**, double-click a data document, and then click **OK** to select the mail recipients.

7. Click **Next: Write your e-mail message** on the pane to display Step 4 of 6.

Did You Know?

You can set up the main document for E-mail messages manually. Create a new or existing document, click the Mailings tab, click the Start Mail Merge button, and then click E-mail Messages.

8 Type your e-mail, click a location in the document, click one of the field items on the pane (such as Address Block or Greeting Line), select the options you want, and then click **OK**.

9 Click **Next: Preview your e-mail message** on the pane to display Step 5 of 6.

10 Preview the data in the letter, and then make any changes.

11 Click **Next: Complete the merge** on the pane to display Step 6 of 6.

12 Click **Electronic Mail**.

13 Select the mail format you want to use, normal text, HTML mail, or sending the document as an attachment.

14 Specify the range of records you want to send, and then click **OK**.

Creating Merged Mailing Labels

You can use a data document to create more than one kind of merge document. For example, you can use a data document to print mailing labels or envelopes to use with your mailing. The process for creating mailing labels is similar to the mail merge process for form letters, except that you insert the merge field into a main document that contains a table with cells in a specific size for labels. During the process for creating mailing labels, you can select brand-name labels in a specific size, such as Avery Standard 1529. After you merge the data into the main document with the labels, you can print the labels on a printer.

Create Labels Using Mail Merge

① Click the **Mailings** tab.

② Click the **Start Mail Merge** button, and then click **Step by Step Mail Merge Wizard**.

The Mail Merge pane opens, displaying Step 1 of 6.

③ Click the **Labels** option.

④ Click **Next: Starting document** on the pane to display Step 2 of 6.

⑤ Click a starting document option button (such as Change Document Layout), and then click **Label Options**.

⑥ Select the label options you want, and then click **OK**.

⑦ Click **Next: Select recipients** on the pane to display Step 3 of 6.

Did You Know?

You can set up the main document for labels manually. Create a new or existing document, click the Mailings tab, click the Start Mail Merge button, click Labels, select the label options you want, and then click OK.

8. Click a recipient option button (such as Use An Existing List or Type A New List), click **Browse**, double-click a data document, select a data source and click **OK**, select the recipients you want, and then click **OK**.

9. Click **Next: Arrange your labels** at the bottom of the pane. Step 4 of 6 appears on the pane.

10. Click in the first label of the document, and then click one of the field items on the pane (such as Address Block or Greeting Line), select the options you want, and then click **OK**.

11. Click **Update all labels**.

12. Click **Next: Preview your labels** at the bottom of the pane. Step 5 of 6 appears on the pane.

13. Preview the data in the letter and make any changes, and then click **Next: Complete the merge** at the bottom of the pane. Step 6 of 6 appears on the pane.

14. Click **Print**.

15. Click a Print Records option, and then click **OK**.

16. When you're done, click the **Close** button on the pane, and then save the form letter.

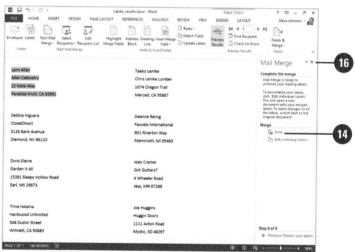

Creating Merged Envelopes

If your printer is set up to accept a batch feed of blank envelopes, you can skip the steps required to create mailing labels, and merge the addresses from the data document directly onto the envelopes. To determine if your printer supports this function, consult the documentation that accompanied your hardware.

Create Envelopes

1. Click the **File** tab, click **New**, click **Blank Document**, and then click **Create**.

2. Click the **Mailings** tab.

3. Click the **Start Mail Merge** button, and then click **Step by Step Mail Merge Wizard**. The Mail Merge pane opens. Step 1 of 6 appears on the pane.

4. Click the **Envelopes** option.

5. Click **Next: Starting document** on the pane to display Step 2 of 6.

6. If necessary, click the **Use the current document** option.

7. Click **Envelope Options**.

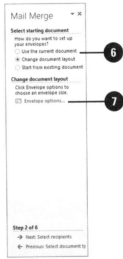

Did You Know?

You can set up the main document for envelopes manually. To create a new or existing document, click the Mailings tab, click the Start Mail Merge button, click Envelopes, select the envelope options you want, and then click OK.

⑧ Click the **Envelope Options** tab.

⑨ Select the appropriate envelope size and layout.

⑩ Click the **Printing Options** tab.

⑪ Select the printer, feed type, and tray to use for printing.

⑫ Click **OK**.

⑬ Click **Next: Select recipients** on the pane to display Step 3 of 6.

⑭ If necessary, click the **Use an existing list** option, and then choose the same list you used mail merge to print the letters.

⑮ Click **Next: Arrange your envelope** on the pane to display Step 4 of 6.

⑯ If you want to include a return address on the mailing, type it now, position the insertion point where you want the recipient's mailing address to appear, click **Address Block** on the pane to insert the merge field, select your options, and then click **OK**.

⑰ Complete the remaining steps just as you would with creating mailing labels.

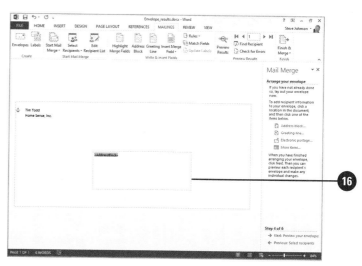

Addressing Envelopes and Labels

When you write a letter, you can use Word to print an address on an envelope or mailing label. Word scans your document to find a delivery address. You can use the one Word finds, enter another one, or select one from your Address Book. You can specify a return address, or you can omit it. Addresses can contain text, graphics, and bar codes. The POSTNET bar code is a machine-readable depiction of a U.S. zip code and delivery address; the FIM-A code identifies the front of a courtesy reply envelope. You can print a single label or multiple labels.

Address and Print Envelopes

1. Click the **Mailings** tab, click the **Envelopes** button, and then click the **Envelopes** tab, if necessary.

2. Type the recipients name and address, or click the **Insert Address** button to search for it.

3. Type your name and address.

4. Click **Options**, select a size, placement, bar code, font, and then click **OK**.

5. Insert an envelope in your printer, and then click **Print**.

Insert Address button

Address and Print Mailing Labels

1. Click the **Mailings** tab, click the **Labels** button, and then click the **Labels** tab.

2. Type the recipients name and address, or the Insert Address button to search for it.

3. Select which labels to print.

4. Click **Options**, select a type or size, and click **OK**.

5. Insert labels in your printer, and then click **Print**.

Proofing and Printing Documents

11

Introduction

After finalizing your document, there are some necessary steps you should do prior to printing. You can check for inconsistent formatting in your document. If you have established a certain style, checking your formatting can ensure that your document is formatted correctly.

You can also look up and use synonyms and antonyms to make your document more interesting. Under the Review tab, you can use a Thesaurus, translate a word or document into another language, or even use multiple languages with the Word program. Of course, no document should be printed without first going through the spell checker to check your spelling and grammar usage. You can add personalized names, terms, company information to your spell checker, so that when you are using the spell checker, it won't make unnecessary stops on words that are spelled and used correctly.

If your document is larger, page numbers might be necessary to help your reader follow along. You can insert page numbers for single or double sided printing, and you can even add chapter numbers. When getting ready to print, you might want to preview your document to make sure that your margins are appropriate for your text and printing. If, after previewing your document, you find that some text should be on a different page, you can insert page breaks to end the page early, so that common text stays together on a page. You can also insert a whole new page in your document.

When it's finally time to print, you can print all or part of a document, change your page orientation to print landscape or portrait, print double-sided or specialized documents, and even print document properties.

Checking for Inconsistent Formatting

By default, Word does not automatically check for inconsistent formatting as you create documents. To instruct Word to mark the document for inconsistent formatting, and also to check documents that you have already prepared for inconsistent formatting, you need to change editing options in the Word Options dialog box. Word will automatically detect any inconsistent format elements and mark them with a blue wavy underline. When you turn on the Keep track of formatting option you can also use the Select Text with Similar formatting command on the shortcut menu that appears if you right-click selected text.

Change Editing Options

1. Click the **File** tab, and then click **Options**.

2. In the left pane, click **Advanced**.

3. Select the **Keep track of formatting** check box.

4. Select the **Mark formatting inconsistencies** check box.

5. Click **OK**.

The formatting inconsistencies are indicated by a blue wavy underline.

Change Inconsistent Formatting

1. In the document, right-click any wavy, blue line to open a list of Formatting commands.

2. Click the appropriate choice based on the error in the text to make the necessary correction.

   ◆ **Make this text consistent with formatting**...

   ◆ **Ignore Once.**

   ◆ **Ignore Rule.**

Did You Know?

You can find similar inconsistent formatting quickly. You can also click the Select button on the Home tab, and then click Select Text With Similar Formatting to facilitate global changes of mistakes that have been repeated throughout the document.

Checking Spelling and Grammar

A document's textual inaccuracies can distract the reader, so it's important that your text be error-free. Word provides a spelling checker so that you can check the spelling in an entire document for words not listed in the dictionary (such as misspellings, names, technical terms, or acronyms) or duplicate words (such as *the the*). As you type, a red wavy line appears under words not listed in Word's dictionary (such as misspellings or names) or duplicated words. A blue wavy underline appears under words or phrases with grammatical errors. You can correct these errors as they arise or after you finish the entire document. You can use the Spelling & Grammar button on the Review tab to check the entire document using the Spelling or Grammar pane (**New!**), or you can avoid spelling errors on a document by enabling the AutoCorrect feature to automatically correct words as you type.

Correct Spelling and Grammar as you Type

1. Right-click a word with a red or green wavy underline.

2. Click a substitution, an option, or click **Ignore** (or **Grammar**) to skip any other instances of the word.

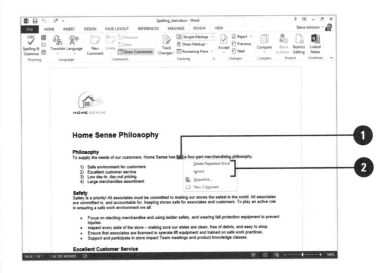

For Your Information

Finding out Document Readability

Word can help you determine the readability of your documents. When you set the readability option and check spelling and grammar, Word displays information and statistics about the reading level of the document, including the Flesch Reading Ease score and the Flesch-Kincaid Grade Level score. The readability scores are based on the average number of syllables per word and words per sentence. To display readability statistics, click the File tab, click Options, click Proofing in the left pane, select the Check Grammar With Spelling check box, select the Show Readability Statistics check box, and then click OK.

Check Spelling All at Once

① Click at the beginning of the document or select the text you want to correct.

② Click the **Review** tab.

③ Click the **Spelling & Grammar** button.

◆ You can also click the **Spelling & Grammar** button on the Status bar to start the process.

As it checks the document, Word provides alternatives for misspelled words or problematic sentences in the Spelling or Grammar pane (**New!**).

④ To change the language, click the **Language** list arrow, and then select a language (**New!**).

⑤ Choose an option:

◆ Click **Ignore** to skip the word, or click **Ignore All** to skip every instance of the word.

◆ Click **Add** to add a word to your dictionary, so it doesn't show up as a misspelled word.

◆ Click a suggestion, and then click **Change** to make a substitution or click **Change All**.

◆ If no suggestion is appropriate, click in the document and edit the text yourself. Click **Resume** to continue.

⑥ Click **OK** to return to the document.

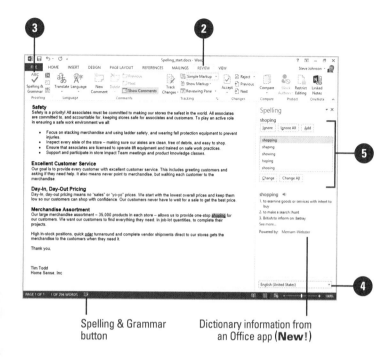

Spelling & Grammar button

Dictionary information from an Office app (**New!**)

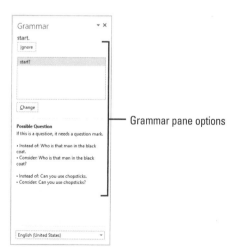

Grammar pane options

Using Custom Dictionaries

Before you can use a custom dictionary, you need to enable it first. You can enable and manage custom dictionaries by using the Custom Dictionaries dialog box. In the dialog box, you can change the language associated with a custom dictionary, create a new custom dictionary, or add or remove an existing custom dictionary. If you need to manage dictionary content, you can also change the default custom dictionary to which the spelling checker adds words, as well as add, delete, or edit words. All the modifications you make to your custom dictionaries are shared with all your Microsoft Office programs, so you only need to make changes once. If you mistakenly type an obscene or embarrassing word, such as *ass* instead of *ask*, the spelling checker will not catch it because both words are spelled correctly. You can avoid this problem by using an exclusion dictionary. When you use a language for the first time, Office automatically creates an exclusion dictionary. This dictionary forces the spelling checker to flag words you don't want to use.

Use a Custom Dictionary

1. Click the **File** tab, and then click **Options**.

2. In the left pane, click **Proofing**.

3. Click **Custom Dictionaries**.

4. Select the check box next to **CUSTOM.DIC (Default)**.

5. Click the **Dictionary language** list arrow, and then select a language for a dictionary.

6. Click the options you want:

   ◆ Click **Edit Word List** to add, delete, or edit words.

   ◆ Click **Change Default** to select a new default dictionary.

   ◆ Click **New** to create a new dictionary.

   ◆ Click **Add** to insert an existing dictionary.

   ◆ Click **Remove** to delete a dictionary.

7. Click **OK** to close the Custom Dictionaries dialog box.

8. Click **OK**.

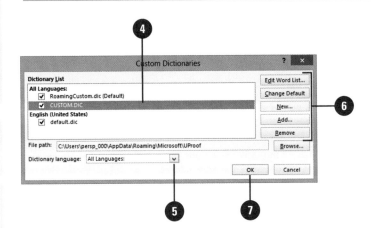

Find and Modify the Exclusion Dictionary

① In Windows Explorer, go to the folder location where the custom dictionaries are stored.

◆ **Windows 8 or 7.** C:\Users*user name*\AppData\Roaming\Microsoft\UProof

TROUBLE? *If you can't find the folder, change folder settings to show hidden files and folders.*

② Locate the exclusion dictionary for the language you want to change.

◆ The file name you want is ExcludeDictionary *Language Code*Language *LCID*.lex.

For example, ExcludeDictionary EN0409.lex, where EN is for English.

Check Word Help for an updated list of LCID (Local Identification Number) numbers for each language.

③ Open the file using Microsoft Notepad or WordPad.

④ Add each word you want the spelling check to flag as misspelled. Type the words in all lowercase and then press Enter after each word.

⑤ Save and close the file.

UProof folder with Office dictionaries

Changing Proofing Options

You can customize the way Microsoft Office spell checks a document by selecting proofing settings in Options. Some spelling options apply to specific Office programs, such as Check spelling as you type, while other options apply to all Microsoft Office programs, such as Ignore Internet and file addresses, and Flag repeated words. If you have ever mistakenly used *their* instead of *there*, you can use contextual spelling to fix it. While you work in a document, you can set options to have the spelling checker search for mistakes in the background.

Change Office Spelling Options

1. Click the **File** tab, and then click **Options**.

2. In the left pane, click **Proofing**.

3. Select or clear the spelling options you want.

   ◆ **Ignore words in UPPERCASE**.

   ◆ **Ignore words that contain numbers**.

   ◆ **Ignore Internet and file addresses**.

   ◆ **Flag repeated words**.

   ◆ **Enforce accented uppercase in French**.

   ◆ **Suggest from main dictionary only**. Select to exclude your custom dictionary.

   ◆ **French modes**. Select an option for working with French.

   ◆ **Spanish modes**. Select an option for working with Spanish.

4. Click **OK**.

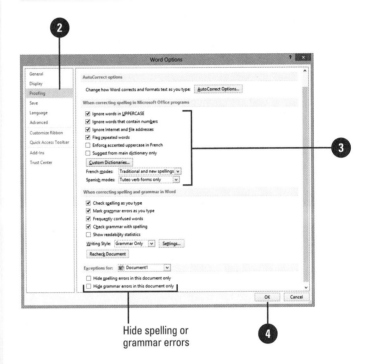

Hide spelling or grammar errors

Did You Know?

You can hide spelling or grammar errors for a specific document. Click the File tab, click Options, click Proofing, click the Exceptions For list arrow, select the file you want, select the check boxes to hide spelling or grammar error for this document only, and then click OK.

Change Word Spelling Options

1. Click the **File** tab, and then click **Options**.

2. In the left pane, click **Proofing**.

3. Select or clear the Word spelling options you want.

   ◆ **Check spelling as you type.**

   ◆ **Use contextual spelling.**

   ◆ **Mark grammar errors as you type.**

   ◆ **Check grammar with spelling.**

   ◆ **Show readability statistics.**

   ◆ **Writing Style.** Select to check grammar only or grammar and style.

4. Click **OK**.

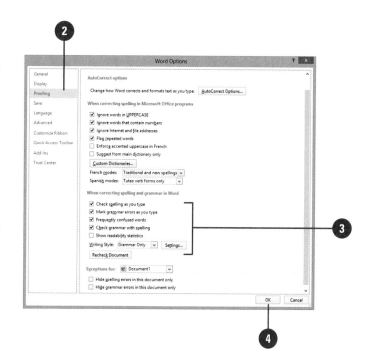

Change Grammar Settings

1. Click the **File** tab, and then click **Options**.

2. In the left pane, click **Proofing**.

3. Click **Settings**.

4. Under Require, click the list arrow, and then select the option you want: **always**, **never**, or **don't check**.

5. Under Grammar, select the check boxes with the grammar and style options you want and clear the ones you don't want.

6. Click **OK**.

7. Click **OK**.

Setting Languages for Proofing

When you're working with more than one language at a time in a document, you can enable a language option to make it easier to switch between languages when typing and editing text. When you select the Detect language automatically option, Word automatically detects the language you are typing and uses the appropriate proofing tool for the language. Along with this option, you can also select the Automatically switch keyboard to match language of surround text option in the Advanced pane of the Word Options dialog box to work more efficiently with multiple languages.

Set a Language for Proofing

1. Click the **Review** tab.

2. Click the **Language** button, and then click **Set Proofing Language**.

3. Review the list of languages above the double line in the Mark selected text as list. Office only detects languages above the double line.

   ◆ **Quickly add a language.** Double-click a language in the Mark selected text as list.

   ◆ **Add/remove a language.** On the Review tab, click the **Language** button, and then click **Language Preferences**.

4. Select or clear the following check boxes:

   ◆ **Do not check spelling or grammar.** Select to not check spelling or grammar for the languages.

   ◆ **Detect language automatically.** Select to automatically detect the language you are typing and enables the proofing tools for the language.

5. To set a language as the default, select the language, and then click **Set As Default.**

6. Click **OK**.

Set an Option to Automatically Switch Keyboard Language

1. Click the **File** tab, and then click **Options**.

2. In the left pane, click **Advanced**.

3. Select the **Automatically switch keyboard to match language of surrounding text** check box.

   ◆ If the option is not available, you need to enable a keyboard layout for a language in the Language pane of the Word Options dialog box.

4. Click **OK**.

See Also

See "Using Multiple Languages" on page 298 for information on enabling a keyboard layout to use with Microsoft Office programs.

Added keyboard layouts

Translating Text to Another Language

If you need to quickly translate a word into another language, you can enable the Mini Translator that translates words when you point to them. The Mini Translator also includes a toolbar, which provides options to copy the translation to the Clipboard or play the word audibly. Before you get started, you need to choose the translation language you want to use. If you don't get the results you want, you can also use the Research pane to translate text. With the Research pane, you can translate single words or short phrases into different languages by using bilingual dictionaries and incorporate it into your work. If you need to translate an entire document for basic subject matter under-standing, Web-based machine translation services are available using the Translate Document command. A machine translation is helpful for general meaning, but may not preserve the full meaning of the content.

Translate Text Using the Mini Translator

1. Click the **Review** tab.

2. Click the **Translate** button, click **Choose Translation Language**, specify a language for the Mini Translator, and then click **OK**.

3. Click the **Translate** button, and then click the Mini Translator language you set for translation to highlight the icon next to the command.

4. Point to the word you want to display the Mini Translator with the translated word. You can also use the toolbar to perform the following options:

   ◆ **Expand.** Opens the Research pane with more options.

   ◆ **Copy.** Copies the translation to the Clipboard.

   ◆ **Play** and **Stop.** Plays or stops the word audibly.

   ◆ **Help.** Opens Help.

5. To turn off the Mini Translator, click the **Translate** button, and then click the Mini Translator language to clear the highlighted icon next to the command.

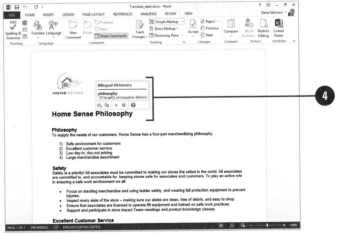

Translate Text Using the Research Pane

① Select the text you want to translate.

② Click the **Review** tab.

③ Click the **Translate** button, and then click **Translate Selected Text**.

If this is the first you have used translation services, click **OK** to install the bilingual dictionaries and enable the service.

④ If necessary, click the list arrow, and then click **Translation**.

⑤ Click the **From** list arrow, and then select the language of the selected text.

⑥ Click the **To** list arrow, and then select the language you want to translate into.

⑦ To customize which resources are used for translation, click **Translation options**, select the look-up options you want, and then click **OK**.

⑧ Right-click the translated text in the Research pane that you want to copy, and then click **Copy**.

⑨ Paste the information into your document.

⑩ When you're done, click the **Close** button on the pane.

Translation options

See Also

See "Using Multiple Languages" on page 298 for information on adding languages to use with Microsoft Office programs.

Using Multiple Languages

International Microsoft Office users can change the language that appears on their screens by changing the default language settings. Users around the world can enter, display, and edit text in all supported languages—including European languages, Japanese, Chinese, Korean, Hebrew, and Arabic—to name a few. You'll probably be able to use Office programs in your native language. If the text in your document is written in more than one language, you can automatically detect languages or designate the language of selected text so the spelling checker uses the right dictionary. You can set preferences for editing, display, ScreenTip, and Help languages. If you don't have the keyboard layout or related software installed, you can click links to add or enable them.

Add a Language to Office Programs

1. Click the **File** tab, click **Options**, and then click **Language**.

   ◆ You can also click **Microsoft Office 2013 Language Preferences** on the All Apps screen (Win 8) or on the Start menu under Microsoft Office and Microsoft Office Tools (Win 7).

2. Click the **Language** list arrow, and then select the language you want to enable.

3. Click **Add**.

4. To enable the correct keyboard layout for the installed language, click the **Not enabled** link to open the Text Services and Input Language dialog box, where you can select a keyboard layout, and then click **OK**.

5. Set the language priority order for the buttons, tabs, and Help for the Display and Help languages.

6. Set your ScreenTip language to Match Display Language or a specific language.

7. Click **OK**, and then click **Yes** (if necessary) to quit and restart Office.

Select Different Languages in a Document

1. Click the **Language** button on the Status bar.

   ◆ You can also click the **Review** tab, click the **Language** button, and then click **Set Proofing Language**.

2. Click the language you want to use from the list of languages above the double line in the Mark selected text as list.

   Office only detects languages above the double line.

3. To automatically detect the language you are typing and enables the proofing tools for the language, select the **Detect language automatically** check box.

4. To set a language as the default, select the language, and then click **Set As Default.**

5. Click **OK**.

6. Type text in the selected language.

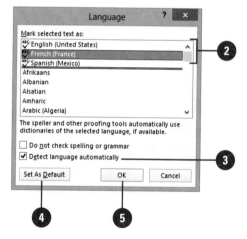

Finding the Right Words

Repeating the same word in a document can reduce a message's effectiveness. Instead, replace some words with synonyms or find antonyms. This feature can save you time and improve the quality and readability of your document. You can also select a Thesaurus for another language. Foreign language thesauruses can be accessed at the bottom of the Thesaurus pane (**New!**). If you have an App for Office dictionary installed—see the next topic for details—from the Office Store, a definition appears in the pane (**New!**). If you want to replace the selected word with a synonym or other available alternative, you can use a shortcut menu to insert it.

Use the Thesaurus

1 Select the text you want to look up.

2 Click the **Review** tab.

3 Click the **Thesaurus** button.

TIMESAVER *Press Shift+F7to open the Research pane.*

4 Click the **Language** list arrow, and then select a language.

5 Point to the word in the pane.

6 Click the list arrow, and then click one of the following:

◆ **Insert** to replace the word you looked up with the new word.

◆ **Copy** to copy the new word and then paste it within the document.

7 To change the text, type a word or click a word in the pane.

8 If a dictionary is installed, a definition for the selected word appears in the pane.

◆ Listen to definition. Click the Audio button next to the word.

◆ More on the web. Click **See more** to open the dictionary web site or **Get a Dictionary** to install other dictionaries.

9 When you're done, click the **Close** button on the pane.

Getting Word Definitions

If you're not sure what a word means, you can use the Define button (**New!**) on the Review tab to quickly look it up in a dictionary, such as Merriam-Webster or Bing Dictionary. If you don't have a dictionary installed on your computer, you can download one from the Office Store directly from within Word. If you select a word from your document to define or enter one in the Dictionary pane. Many definitions include links to other words, which you can click to view. If you want to use a definition in a document, you can select and copy it in the pane.

Get the Definition of a Word

1. Select the text you want to get a definition.

2. Click the **Review** tab.

3. Click the **Define** button (**New!**).

   TIMESAVER *Press Ctrl+F7 to open the Dictionary pane.*

4. If no dictionary is available, a list of dictionary you can download appears. If so, select a dictionary, and then click **Download**.

   The definition for the selected text appears in the pane.

5. To get the definition for another word, enter the work in the Search box, and then press Enter.

6. If a link is available to another word, click the link to view it.

7. To copy the definition, select it in the pane, right-click the selection, and then click **Copy**.

8. When you're done, click the **Close** button on the pane.

Setting Up Page Margins

Margins are the blank space between the edge of a page and the text. The default setting for Word documents is 1.25 inches on the left and right, and 1 inch on the top and bottom. You can use the mouse pointer to adjust margins visually for the entire document, or you can use the Page Setup dialog box to set precise measurements for an entire document or a specific section. When you shift between portrait and landscape page orientation, the margin settings automatically change. If you need additional margin space for binding pages into a book or binder, you can adjust the left or right gutter settings. Gutters allow for additional margin space so that all of the document text remains visible after binding. Unless this is your purpose, leave the default settings in place.

Adjust Margins Visually

1. Click the **View** tab.

2. If necessary, select the **Ruler** check box to display it.

3. Click to place the insertion point in the text where you want to change the margins.

4. Position the pointer over a margin boundary on the horizontal or vertical ruler.

5. Press and hold Alt, and then click a margin boundary to display the measurements of the text and margin areas as you adjust the margins.

6. Drag the left, right, top, or bottom margin boundary to a new position.

Did You Know?

You can preset gutter measurements. To set the gutters for normal binding, display the Margins tab in the Page Setup dialog box, click the Multiple Pages list arrow, and then click Book Fold.

Select Standard Margins Quickly

1 Click the **Print Layout** tab.

2 Click the **Margins** button, and then click the margin setting you want:

◆ **Last Custom Setting.**

◆ **Normal.**

◆ **Narrow.**

◆ **Moderate.**

◆ **Wide.**

◆ **Mirrored.**

◆ **Office 2003 Default.**

Create Custom Margins Using Page Setup

1 Click the **Print Layout** tab.

2 Click the **Margins** button, and then click **Custom Margins**.

The Page Setup dialog box opens, displaying the Margins tab.

3 Type new margin measurements (in inches) in the Top, Bottom, Left, or Right boxes, and Gutter boxes.

4 Click the page orientation you want.

5 Click the **Apply to** list arrow, and then click **Selected Text**, **This Point Forward**, or **Whole Document**.

6 To make the new margin settings the default for all new Word documents, click **Set As Default**, and then click **Yes**.

7 Click **OK**.

Adjusting Paper Settings

Every document you produce and print might need a different page setup. You can achieve the look you want by printing on a standard paper size (such as letter, legal, or envelope), international standard paper sizes, or any custom size that your printer accepts. The default setting is 8.5 x 11 inches, the most common letter and copy size. You can also print several pages on one sheet. If you want to create a custom paper size, you can input custom settings for special print jobs on odd-sized paper.

Set the Paper Size

1. Click the **Page Layout** tab.

2. Click the **Page Setup Dialog Box Launcher**.

3. Click the **Paper** tab.

4. Click the **Paper size** list arrow, and then select the paper size you want, or specify a custom size.

5. Select the paper source for the first page and other pages.

6. Click the **Apply to** list arrow, and then click **This section**, **This point forward**, or **Whole document**.

7. Verify your selections in the Preview box.

8. To make your changes the default settings for all new documents, click **Set As Default**, and then click **Yes**.

9. Click **OK**.

Did You Know?

You can improve printing speed. If printing is slow, you can turn off background printing to speed up the process. In the Page Setup dialog box on the Paper tab, click Print Options, click Advanced in the left pane, clear the Print In Background check box, and then click OK.

Controlling the Way Pages Break

When you're creating a document, sometimes a line of text, known as a widow or orphan, in a paragraph doesn't fit on a page and looks out of place on the next page. A **widow** is the last line of a paragraph printed by itself at the top of a page. An **orphan** is the first line of a paragraph printed by it self at the bottom of a page. You can use the Widow/ Orphan Control option to automatically correct the problem. If a widow or orphan occurs, Word adjusts the paragraph to make sure at least two lines appear together on the next page. When two paragraphs need to remain grouped to maintain their impact, regardless of where the normal page break would have occurred, you can keep paragraphs together on a page or in a column. If you need to start a paragraph at the top of a page, you can automatically generate a page break before a paragraph.

Control Pagination

1. Select the paragraph in which you want to control.

2. Click the **Page Layout** tab.

3. Click the **Paragraph Dialog Box Launcher**.

4. Click the **Line and Page Breaks** tab.

5. Choose an option:

   - Select the **Widow/Orphan control** check box to avoid paragraphs ending with a single word on a line or a single line at the top of a page.

   - Select the **Keep with next** check box to group paragraphs together.

   - Select the **Keep lines together** check box to keep paragraph lines together.

   - Select the **Page break before** check box to precede a paragraph with a page break.

6. Click **OK**.

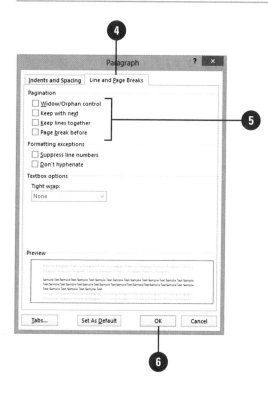

Inserting New Pages and Sections

When you fill a page, Word inserts a page break and starts a new page. As you add or delete text, this **soft page break** moves. A soft page break appears as a dotted gray line in Normal view. To start a new page before the current one is filled, insert a **hard page break** that doesn't shift as you edit text. A hard page break appears as a dotted gray line with the text page break centered in Normal view. A **section** is a mini-document within a document that stores margin settings, page orientation, page numbering, and so on. In any view, you can collapse (**New!**) or expand (**New!**) sections or parts of a document with headings. In Print Layout view, you can show or hide the white space on the top and bottom of each page and the gray space between pages as desired.

Insert and Delete a Hard Page Break

1. Click where you want to insert a hard page break.

2. Use one of the following:

   ◆ **Page Break.** Click the **Insert** tab, and then click the **Page Break** button.

   ◆ **Blank Page.** Click the **Insert** tab, and then click the **Blank Page** button.

   ◆ **Page or Section Break.** Click the **Page Layout** button, click **Page Break**, and then click the page break option you want.

   TIMESAVER *Press Ctrl+Enter to insert a page break.*

3. To delete a page break, click the page break in Print Layout view, and then press the Delete key. To move a page break, drag it to a new location.

Did You Know?

You can opt to start a new line, but not a new paragraph. Insert a text wrapping break to force text to the next line in the same paragraph—the perfect tool to make a phrase fall on one line. Press Shift+Enter where you want to insert a text wrapping break.

Insert and Delete a Section Break

1. Click where you want to insert a section break.

2. Click the **Page Layout** tab.

3. Click the **Page Breaks** button, and then select the type of section break you want.

   ◆ **Next Page**. Starts the section on a new page.

   ◆ **Continuous**. Starts the section wherever the point is located.

   ◆ **Even Page**. Starts the section on the next even-numbered page.

   ◆ **Odd Page**. Starts the section on the next odd-numbered page.

4. To delete a section break, click the section break in Print Layout view, and then press Delete.

Section break commands

Collapse or Expand Sections and Headings

1. Click any view button.

2. Point to a section or part of a document with headings.

   A collapse button appears. The expand button remains displayed.

3. Click the **Collapse** (gray angled arrow) (**New!**) or **Expand** (white arrow) (**New!**) button.

Did You Know?

You can show or hide white space between pages. Click the Print Layout View button, point to the gap between pages (the Hide or Show White Space cursor appears), and then double-click the gap between the pages.

Previewing a Document

Before printing, you should verify that the page looks the way you want. You save time, money, and paper by avoiding duplicate printing. Print Preview shows you the exact placement of your data on each printed page. You can view all or part of your document as it will appear when you print it. Print Preview shows you the pages based on the properties of the selected printer. For example, if the selected printer is setup to print color, Print Preview displays in color. The Print screen on the File tab makes it easy to zoom in and out to view a document more comfortably, switch between pages, preview page breaks, set print options, and print all from the same place.

Preview a Document

① Click the **File** tab, and then click **Print**.

② Click the **Zoom to Page** button to toggle the zoom in and out to the page.

③ To adjust the zoom, drag the **Zoom** slider or click the **Zoom In** or **Zoom Out** buttons.

④ To switch pages, click the **Next Page** or **Previous Page** button, or enter a specific page in the Current Page box.

⑤ If you want to print, click the **Print** button.

Print Preview

Printing a Document

When you're ready to print your document, you can choose several printing options on the Print screen on the File tab, such as choosing a new printer, selecting the number of pages in the document you want printed and the number of copies, specifying the page size, margins, and orientation, and selecting any scaling or pages to fit on a printed page. You can also use the Page Setup dialog box to control the appearance of pages, such as margins, orientation, paper size and source and the layout of sections, headers and footers, and page alignment. You can quickly print a copy of your document without using the Print screen by clicking the Quick Print button on the Quick Access Toolbar.

Print All or Part of a Document

1. Click the **File** tab, and then click **Print**.

   TIMESAVER *To print without the Print screen, press Ctrl+P, or click the Quick Print button on the Quick Access Toolbar.*

2. Click the **Printer** list arrow, and then click the printer you want to use.

3. To change printer properties, click the **Printer Properties** link, select the options you want, and then click **OK**.

4. Select whether you want to print the entire document or only the pages you specify.

5. Select the other print options you want to use, such as sides to print, collated, orientation, size, margins, or pages per sheet.

6. To change page options, click the **Page Setup** link, select the options you want, and then click **OK**.

7. Click **Print**.

Print Preview

Printing Specialized Documents

Two-sided printing is appropriate for bound reports, pamphlets, brochures and many other types of Word documents. Not all printers support automatic two-sided printing. If your printer does not support two-sided printing, you can use the Manually Print on Both Sides option on the Print screen to help you complete the process. In addition to printing two-side documents, you can also print multiple pages on a page, which is useful for creating handouts for a presentation.

Print a Two-Sided Document

1. Click the **File** tab, and then click **Print**.

2. If necessary, click the **Printer** list arrow, and then click the printer you want to use.

3. Select an option for printing on both sides:

   - **Print on Both Sides (Long edge).** Prints on both sides where pages flip on the long edge.

   - **Print on Both Sides (Short edge).** Prints on both sides where pages flip on the short edge.

   - **Manually Print on Both Sides.** The first side of each alternate page will be printed. Then you will be prompted to reinsert the pages into the printer so that the second side can be printed.

4. Select the other print options you want to use.

5. Click **Print**.

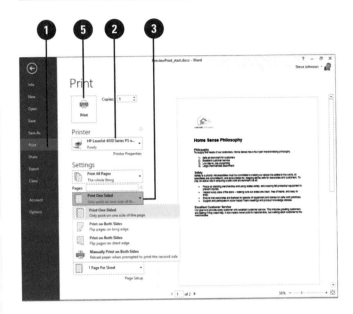

Print Multiple Pages Per Sheet

① Click the **File** tab, and then click **Print**.

② If necessary, click the **Printer** list arrow, and then click the printer you want to use.

③ Select an option for printing multiple pages per sheet:

  ◆ **1 Page Per Sheet.**

  ◆ **2 Page Per Sheet.**

  ◆ **4 Page Per Sheet.**

  ◆ **6 Page Per Sheet.**

  ◆ **8 Page Per Sheet.**

  ◆ **16 Page Per Sheet.**

  ◆ **Scale to Paper Size.** Select a paper size for the scaling of the document pages per sheet.

④ Select the other print options you want to use.

⑤ Click **Print**.

Printing Document Properties

In addition to printing the actual document, you can also print other aspects of a document, such as document properties, document markup, styles, AutoText entries, or shortcut key assignments. If you're working with others who have made a lot of changes to your document, you can use the Print screen on the File tab to select options to print a table of document properties or a list of markup, styles, or AutoText entries. If you want a list of keyboard shortcuts available in Word, you can select the Key assignments options to print out a list.

Print Document Properties

1. Click the **File** tab, and then click **Print**.

2. If necessary, click the **Printer** list arrow, and then click the printer you want to use.

3. Select what you want to print under Document Properties:

   ◆ **Document properties.** Prints a table of properties and values.

   ◆ **List of markup.** Prints a list of markup only from the document.

   ◆ **Styles.** Prints a list of styles used in the document.

   ◆ **AutoText Entries.** Prints a list of AutoText available.

   ◆ **Key assignment.** Prints a list of customized shortcut keys.

   ◆ **Print Markup.** Prints the document with the markup.

4. Select the other print options you want to use.

5. Click **Print**.

Publishing Documents on the Web

Introduction

Web pages are multimedia documents that provide information and contain links to other documents on the Internet, an intranet, a local network, or a hard disk. These links—also called hyperlinks—are highlighted text or graphics that you click to follow a pathway from one web page to another. Incorporating hyperlinks within your documents adds an element of connectivity to your work. Web pages are based on **Hypertext Markup Language (HTML)**—a simple coding system used to format web pages. A browser program, such as Microsoft Internet Explorer, interprets these special codes to determine how a certain web page should be displayed. Different codes mark the size, color, style, and placement of text and graphics as well as which words and graphics should be marked as hyperlinks and to what files they link.

Web technology is available for all your Microsoft Office programs. Word provides you with the tools you need to create and save your documents as a web page and to publish it on the web. Word makes it easy to create a web page without learning HTML. Saving your documents in HTML format means you can use most web browsers to view them. By saving your documents as web pages, you can share your data with others via the Internet. You can also preview how your document will look as a web page in Word or in your browser. Word uses HTML as a companion file format; it recognizes the .html filename extension as accurately as it does those for Word.

What You'll Do

Open a Web Page

Preview a Web Page

Create Hyperlinks

Create a Hyperlink Between Frames

Use and Remove Hyperlinks

Save a Web Page

Change Web Page Options

Transfer Files Over the Web

Create a Blog Posting on the Web

Open an Existing Blog Posting

View a Blog Posting on the Web

Manage Blog Accounts

Opening a Web Page

After saving a document as a web page, you can open the web page, an HTML file. This allows you to quickly and easily switch from HTML to the standard Word format and back again without losing any formatting or functionality. For example, if you create a formatted chart in a Word document, save the document file as a web page, and then reopen the web page in Word, the chart will look the same as the original chart in Word. Word preserves the original formatting and functionality of the document. You can also open a web page from Word in your web browser.

Open a Document as a Web Page

1. Click the **File** tab, and then click **Open**.

2. Click **Computer**.

3. Click **Browse** or a recent folder.

4. Click the **Files of type** list arrow, and then click **All Web Pages**.

5. Navigate to the location where you want to open the web file, and then select the HTML file.

6. Click **Open**.

Recent folder locations

Open a Document as a Web Page in a Browser

1. Click the **File** tab, and then click **Open**.

2. Click **Computer**.

3. Click **Browse** or a recent folder.

4. Click the **Files of type** list arrow, and then click **All Web Pages**.

5. Navigate to the location where you want to open the web file, and then select the HTML file.

6. Click the **Open** button arrow, and then click **Open in Browser**.

7. If prompted, click **Yes** to the warning alert to view the web page.

Did You Know?

You can change the appearance of web pages and Help Viewer window. In the Internet Options dialog box for Windows, click Accessibility on the General tab, select the Ignore Colors Specified On Web Pages check box, and then click OK. In the Internet Properties dialog box, click Colors to select text and background colors or Fonts to change text style.

Document web page in a browser

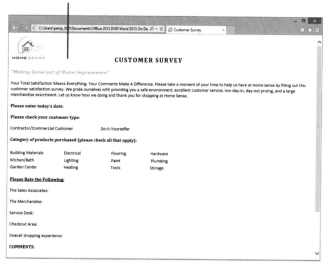

Previewing a Web Page

You can view any document as if it were already on the web by previewing the web page. By previewing a file you want to post to the web, you can see if there are any errors that need to be corrected, formatting that needs to be added, or additions that need to be made. Just as you should always preview a document before you print it, you should preview a web page before you post it. Previewing the web page is similar to using the Print Preview feature before you print a document. This view shows you what the page will look like once it's posted on the Internet. You do not have to be connected to the Internet to preview a document as a web page. Web Layout view shows you how a document will be displayed on the web. If the document includes formatting or layouts that cannot be achieved in HTML, Word switches to an HTML layout that closely matches the original look.

Preview a Web Page in Word

1. Open the document you want to view as a web page.

2. Click the **Web Layout View** button. on the Status bar.

   ◆ You can also click the **Web Layout View** button on the View tab.

View a Web Page from a Browser

1. Open the document you want to view as a web page.

2. Click the **Web Page Preview** button on the Quick Access Toolbar.

   ◆ The Web Page Preview button is not on the Quick Access Toolbar by default. Use the Customize pane in Word Options to add the button.

   Your default web browser starts and displays the web page.

3. Click the **Close** button to quit your web browser, and then return to Word.

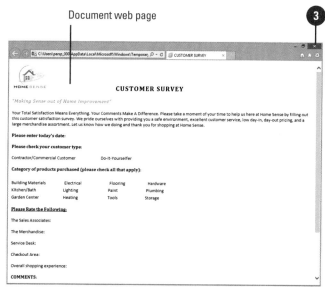

Document web page

Creating Hyperlinks

With instant access to the Internet, your documents can contain links to specific sites so you and anyone else using your documents can access web information. You can create a **hyperlink**—a graphic object or colored, underlined text that you click to move (or jump) to a new location (or destination). The destination can be in the same document, another file on your computer or network, or a web page on your intranet or the Internet. When you point to hyperlinked text or an object, the cursor changes to a pointing hand to indicate it's a hyperlink.

Insert a Hyperlink Within a Document

1. Click where you want to insert the hyperlink, or select the text or object you want to use as the hyperlink.

2. Click the **Insert** tab.

3. Click the **Hyperlink** button.

   TIMESAVER *Press Ctrl+K.*

4. Click **Place in This Document**.

5. Click a destination in the document.

6. Type the text you want to appear as the hyperlink.

7. Click **ScreenTip**.

8. Type the text you want to appear when someone points to the hyperlink.

9. Click **OK**.

10. Click **OK**.

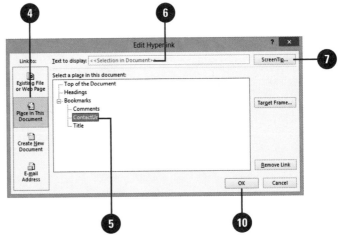

Insert a Hyperlink Between Documents

1. Click where you want to insert the hyperlink, or select the text or object you want to use as the hyperlink.

2. Click the **Insert** tab.

3. Click the **Hyperlink** button.

4. Click **Existing File or Web Page**.

5. Enter the name and path of the destination file or web page.

   ◆ Or click the **Bookmark** button, select the bookmark, and then click **OK**.

6. Type the text you want to appear as the hyperlink.

7. Click **ScreenTip**.

8. Type the text you want to appear when someone points to the hyperlink.

9. Click **OK**.

10. Click **OK**.

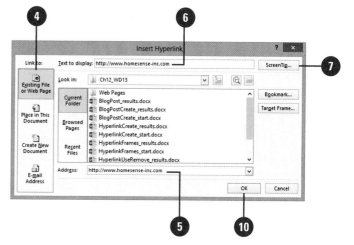

Did You Know?

You can create a hyperlink to send e-mail messages. Click where you want to insert the hyperlink, click the Hyperlink button on the Insert tab, click E-Mail Address, enter the recipient's e-mail address, enter a subject, enter the hyperlink display text, and then click OK.

Creating a Hyperlink Between Frames

If you have a web page document that contains frames, you can create a hyperlink between frames. A **frame** is a named web page that appears in a window region on a web page within a web browser. You can have multiple frames on a web page and each frame can have a border and be scrollable and resizeable. You use the Target Frame button in the Insert Hyperlink dialog box to create a hyperlink between frames. If you continually create hyperlinks to the same target frame, you can set a default to save time in the future.

Set the Default Target Frame for All Hyperlinks

1. Open the frames page you want to set as the default.

2. Click the **Insert** tab.

3. Click the **Hyperlink** button.

4. Click **Target Frame**.

5. Click the frame in the program in the diagram where you want the destination of the hyperlink.

6. Select the **Set as default for all hyperlinks** check box.

7. Click **OK**.

8. Click **OK**.

Create a Hyperlink Between Frames

1. Select the text or picture you want to display as the hyperlink.

2. Click the **Insert** tab.

3. Click the **Hyperlink** button.

4. Click **Existing File or Web Page**.

5. Click the **Look in** list arrow, locate and select the file you want to use, or type the address you want to link to.

   ◆ To link to a specific location in a document, click **Bookmark**, select the bookmark you want, and then click **OK**.

6. Click **Target Frame**.

7. Click the frame in the diagram where you want the destination of the hyperlink to display.

8. Click the list arrow, and then select the frame where you want the document to appear.

9. Click **OK**.

10. Click **OK**.

Using and Removing Hyperlinks

Hyperlinks connect you to information in other documents. Rather than duplicating the important information stored in other documents, you can create hyperlinks to the relevant material. When you click a hyperlink for the first time (during a session), the color of the hyperlink changes, indicating that you have accessed the hyperlink. If a link becomes outdated or unnecessary, you can easily revise or remove it. Word also repairs broken links. Whenever you save a document with hyperlinks, Word checks the links and repairs any that aren't working. For example, if a file was moved, Word updates the location.

Use a Hyperlink

1. Position the mouse pointer over any hyperlink.

2. Press and hold Ctrl (which changes to a hand pointer), and then click the hyperlink.

   Depending on the type of hyperlink, the screen:

   ◆ Jumps to a new location within the same document.

   ◆ Jumps to a location on an intranet or Internet web site.

   ◆ Opens a new file and the program in which it was created.

   ◆ Opens Outlook and displays a new e-mail message.

Did You Know?

You can edit a hyperlink. Right-click the hyperlink, and then click Edit Hyperlink. Make the changes you want, and then click OK.

You can copy or move a hyperlink. Right-click the hyperlink you want to copy or move, click Copy or Cut. Right-click the cell you want to copy or move the hyperlink to, and then click Paste.

Remove a Hyperlink

1. Right-click the cell containing the hyperlink you want to remove.

2. Click **Remove Hyperlink** to remove the hyperlink and keep the text.

Did You Know?

You can select a hyperlink without activating the link. Click the cell that contains the hyperlink, hold down the mouse button until the pointer becomes a cross, and then release the mouse. If the hyperlink is a graphic, hold down Ctrl, and then click the graphic.

You can create a custom ScreenTip for a hyperlink. Select the hyperlink you want to customize, click the Insert tab, click the Hyperlink button, click ScreenTip, type the ScreenTip text you want, and then click OK twice.

Saving a Web Page

You can place an existing Office document on the Internet for others to use. In order for any document to be placed on the web, it must be in HTML (Hypertext Markup Language) format—a simple coding system that specifies the formats a web browser uses to display the document. This format enables you to post, or submit information and data on a web site for others. You don't need any HTML knowledge to save a document as a web page. When you save a document as a web page, you can save it using the Web Page or Single File Web Page format. The Web Page format saves the document as an HTML file and a folder that stores supporting files, such as a file for each graphic, document, and so on. Word selects the appropriate graphic format for you based on the image's content. A single file web page saves all the elements of a web site, including text and graphics, into a single file in the MHTML format, which is supported by Internet Explorer 4.0.1 or later.

Save a Document as a Web Page

1. Click the **File** tab, and then click **Save As**.

2. Click **Computer**, and then click **Browse** or a recent folder.

3. Click the **Save as type** list arrow, and then click **Web Page.**

4. Click the **Save in** list arrow, and then select a location for your web page.

5. Type the name for the web page.

6. To change the title of your web page, click **Change Title**, type the new title in the Set Page Title box, and then click **OK**.

7. To save a thumbnail preview of the web page, select the **Save Thumbnail** check box.

8. Click **Save**.

9. If necessary, click **Yes** to keep formatting.

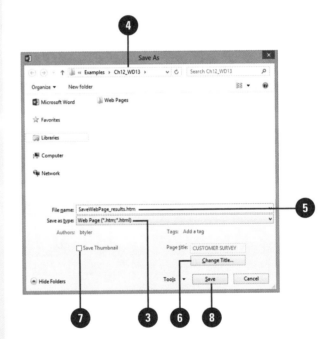

Save a Document as a Single File Web Page

1. Click the **File** tab, and then click **Save As**.

2. Click **Computer**, and then click **Browse** or a recent folder.

3. Click the **Save as type** list arrow, and then click **Single File Web Page.**

4. Click the **Save in** list arrow, and then select a location for your web page.

5. Type the name for the web page.

6. To change the title of your web page, click **Change Title**, type the new title in the Set Page Title box, and then click **OK**.

7. To save a thumbnail preview of the web page, select the **Save Thumbnail** check box.

8. Click **Save**.

9. If necessary, click **Yes** to keep formatting.

   The web page is saved as a single file.

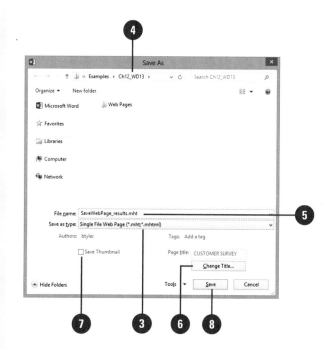

Did You Know?

You can reduce web page size by filtering HTML in Word. You can save web pages in filtered HTML to reduce the file size. In Word, click the Office menu, point to Save As, click Other Formats, click the Save As File Type list arrow, click Web Page, Filtered, and then click Save.

Changing Web Page Options

When you save or publish a document as a web page, you can change the appearance of the web page by changing Office's Web options. You can set Web options to save any additional hidden data necessary to maintain formulas, allow PNG as a graphic format, rely on CSS for font formatting, reply on VML for displaying graphics in browser, and save new web pages as Single File Web Pages. Web pages are saved using the appropriate international text encoding so users on any language system are able to view the correct characters.

Change Web Page Options

1. Click the **File** tab, and then click **Options**.

2. In the left pane, click **Advanced**.

3. Click **Web Options**.

4. Click the **Browsers** tab.

5. Click the **Target Browsers** list arrow, and then select the version you want to support.

6. Select or clear the web page options:

   ◆ **Allow PNG as a graphics format.**

   ◆ **Rely on CSS for font formatting.** Cascading Style Sheets for web page formatting.

   ◆ **Reply on VML for displaying graphics in browsers.** VML is Vector Markup Language, XML based graphics.

   ◆ **Save new Web pages as Single File Web Pages.**

7. Click the **Files** tab, and then select or clear the file related web page options:

   ◆ File names and locations.

   ◆ Default editors.

8. Click **OK**.

9. Click **OK**.

Transferring Files Over the Web

File Transfer Protocol (FTP) is an inexpensive and efficient way to transfer files between your computer and others on the Internet. You can download or receive, from another computer, any kind of file, including text, graphics, sound, and video files. To download a file, you need an ID and password to identify who you are. Anonymous FTP sites are open to anyone; they usually use *anonymous* as an ID and your *e-mail address* as a password. You can also save the FTP site address to revisit the site later.

Add FTP Locations

1. Click the **File** tab, click **Open**, click **Computer**, and then click **Browse**.

2. Click **Computer** in the left pane.

3. Right-click a blank area, and then click **Add a network location**.

4. Follow the Add Network Location wizard to create a link to an FTP site or other network, and then click **Finish** to complete it.

   ◆ To complete the process, you need the complete address for a FTP site, and a user name and password.

Access a FTP Site

1. Click the **File** tab, click **Open**, click **Computer**, and then click **Browse**.

2. Click **Computer** in the left pane.

3. Double-click the FTP site to which you want to log in.

4. Enter a password (your E-mail address or personal password), and then select a log on option.

5. Click **Log On**.

6. Select a folder location, and then select a file.

7. Click **Open**.

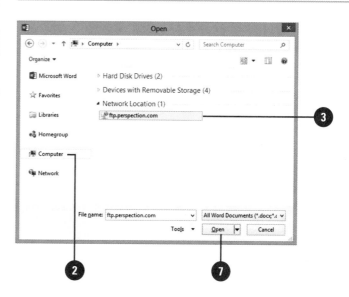

Creating a Blog Posting on the Web

A **blog** is a web site that provides journal style information on a particular subject, such as news or a diary. Blog is short for web log. However, you may have heard of other types: vlog (video) or podcasting (audio). A blog combines text, images, and links to other blogs, web pages, and related topics. In Word, you can create and publish blog postings. Before you can publish a posting, you need to setup an account with a blog service provider and then register it with Word, where you can manage them. Service providers include Windows Live Spaces, Blogger, and Microsoft Windows SharePoint Services with more coming online all the time. Most services are free, so everyone can create an account. Visit Windows Live Space at *http://spaces.live.com* or Blogger at *http://www.blogger.com* and follow the online instructions.

Create a New Blog Posting

1. Click the **File** tab, and then click **New**.

2. In the Search box, type **blog**, and then press Enter.

3. Click **Blog post**.

4. Click **Create**.

5. If you have not registered a blog account with Word, click **Register Now** or click **Register Later**.

6. To create a new blog posting, select the placeholder title, type a new title, and then type the blog message you want below it.

   ◆ To insert a blog category, click the **Insert Category** button, and then select a category.

   ◆ To insert visuals, click the **Insert** tab, and then use the buttons to insert other content.

7. To post the blog, click the **Publish** button arrow, and then click **Publish** or **Publish as Draft**.

8. When you're done, close and save the posting as a Word document.

Blog posting title   Blog posting category

Create a New Blog Posting from an Existing Document

① Open the document you want to use as a blog posting.

② Click the **File** tab, and then click **Share**.

③ Click **Post to Blog**.

④ Click the **Post to Blog** button.

⑤ If you have not registered a blog account with Word, click **Register Now** or click **Register Later**.

⑥ To complete the new blog posting, select the placeholder title, type a new title, and then make any other changes you want.

◆ To insert a blog category, click the **Insert Category** button, and then select a category.

◆ To insert visuals, click the **Insert** tab, and then use the buttons to insert other content.

⑦ To post the blog, click the **Publish** button arrow, and then click **Publish** or **Publish as Draft**.

⑧ When you're done, close and save the posting as a Word document.

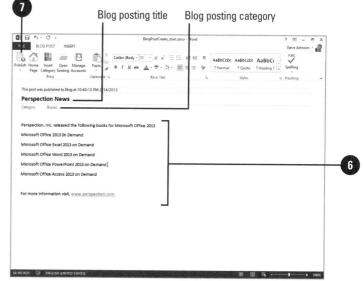

Blog posting title   Blog posting category

Opening an Existing Blog Posting

If you've already published a blog posting and want to make some changes to it, you can open the existing posting, make the changes you want, and then republish it. In addition to editing the text of a blog posting, you can also insert graphical elements—such as pictures, clip art, shapes, SmartArt, charts, screenshots, WordArt and symbols—using the Insert tab. Instead of using plain text, you can also format blog text by using the common formatting tools—typically found on the Word Home tab—on the Blog Post tab. Before you can open and republish a posting, you need to select the blog service provider and sign in to the account.

Open an Existing Blog Posting and Republish

1. Open the document with the saved posting you want to open, and then click the **Blog Post** tab.

2. Click the **Open Existing** button, select the blog, and then click **OK**.

3. Select the account with the blog you want to open.

4. Select the blog posting you want open.

5. Click **OK**.

6. Edit the blog posting text and insert any additional visuals you want.

   ◆ To insert visuals, click the **Insert** tab, and then use the buttons to insert other content.

7. Format the blog posting text using tools on the Blog Post tab.

8. When you're done, click the **Publish** button arrow, and then click **Publish** or **Publish as Draft**.

9. When you're done, close and save the posting as a Word document.

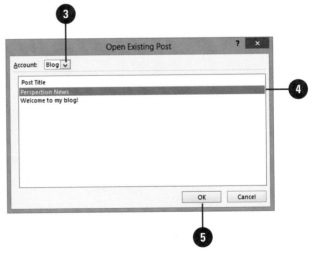

Viewing a Blog Posting on the Web

After you create and publish a blog within Word, you can quickly access and view the blog posting online in your web browser from Word too. After you open the document with the saved posting, you can use the Home Page button on the Blog Post tab to view the blog posting from the blogging site in your web browser. Once you're online, you can view and manage blog postings with the available blogging site tools.

View a Blog Posting on the Web

1. Open a document with a saved posting, and then click the **Blog Post** tab, or create a new blog posting.

2. Click the **Home Page** button.

   The blog web site opens, displaying the blog posting.

3. View the blog posting on the site.

4. Use the online tools to create and manage blog posting. Options vary depending on the blogging site.

5. Click the **Close** button to quit your web browser, and then return to Word.

SharePoint site blog

Managing Blog Accounts

Before you can publish a posting, you need to setup an account with a blog service provider and then register it with Word, where you can manage them. If you have more than one blog account, you can register them all with Word and use the Blog Accounts dialog box to manage the accounts. You can register new accounts, change old accounts, set an account as the default, and remove accounts you no longer need. If you need to open your blog account, you can click the Home page button on the Blog Post tab in Word to view your account in a web browser. Two common sites you can open include WordPress at *www.wordpress.com* or Blogger at *www.blogger.com*.

Manage a Blog Account

1. Open a document with a saved posting, and then click the **Blog Post** tab, or create a new blog posting.

2. Click the **Manage Accounts** button.

3. Use any of the following buttons to manage your blog accounts:

   ◆ **New.** Click to register an established blog account with Word.

   ◆ **Change.** Click to change the registration information for the selected account.

   ◆ **Set As Default.** Click to set the selected account as the default.

   ◆ **Remove.** Click to remove the selected account.

5. Click **Close**.

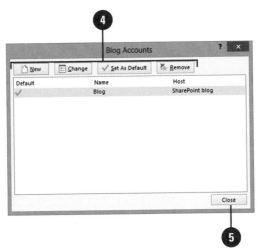

Protecting and Securing Documents

13

Introduction

When you've developed content in your document and want feedback, you can electronically send a document to reviewers so that they can read, revise, and comment on the document without having to print it. Instead of reading handwritten text or sticky notes on your printout, you can get clear and concise feedback.

Adding a password to protect your document is not only a good idea for security purposes, it's an added feature to make sure that changes to your document aren't made by unauthorized people. You can protect all or part of a document. In each case, you'll be asked to supply a password, and then enter it again when you want to work on the file. Not only can you guard who sees your document, you can set rights on who can add changes and comments to your document. If you need to validate the authenticity of a document, you can add an invisible digital signature, an electronic secure stamp of authentication on a document, or a visible signature line. A signature line allows you to create a paperless signature process for documents, such as contracts.

The Trust Center is a place where you set security options and find the latest technology information as it relates to document privacy, safety, and security from Microsoft. The Trust Center allows you to set security and privacy settings and provides links to Microsoft privacy statements, a customer improvement program, and trustworthy computing practices.

What You'll Do

Inspect Documents

Add Security Encryption to a Document

Add Password Protection to a Document

Restrict Formatting and Editing

Add a Digital Signature

Add a Signature Line

Avoid Harmful Attacks

Use the Trust Center

Select Trusted Publishers and Locations

Set Document Related Security Options

Set App Catalog Security Options

Set Add-In, ActiveX, and Macro Security Options

Change Message Bar Security Options

Set Privacy Options

Work with Office Safe Modes

Mark a Document as Read-Only

Inspecting Documents

While you work on your document, Word automatically saves and manages personal information and hidden data to enable you to create and develop a document with other people. The personal information and hidden data includes comments, revision marks, versions, ink annotations, document properties, invisible content, header and footer information, hidden text, document server properties, custom XML data, and Office apps (**New!**). The **Document Inspector** uses inspector modules to find and remove any hidden data and personal information specific to each of these modules that you might not want to share with others. If you remove hidden content from your document, you might not be able to restore it by using the Undo command, so it's important to make a copy of your document before you remove any information.

Inspect a Document

1. Click the **File** tab, click **Save As**, click **Computer**, click **Browse**, save a copy of the original, and then click **Save**.

2. Click the **File** tab, and then click **Info**.

3. Click the **Check for Issues** button, and then click **Inspect Document**.

4. Select the check boxes with the content you want to find and remove:

   - **Comments, Revisions, Versions, and Annotations.** Includes comments, versions, revision marks, and ink annotations.

   - **Document Properties and Personal Information.** Includes metadata document properties (Summary, Statistics, and Custom tabs), the file path for publishing web pages, document server properties, and content type information.

   - **Content Apps.** Includes any content apps (**New!**) saved in the document body.

   - **Task Pane Apps.** Includes any task pane apps (**New!**) saved in the document.

   - **Custom XML Data.** Includes any custom XML data.

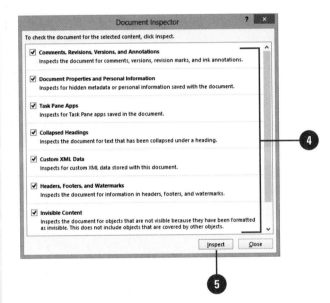

◆ **Headers, Footers, and Watermarks.** Includes information in headers, footers, and watermarks.

◆ **Invisible Content.** Includes objects formatted as invisible. Doesn't include objects covered by other objects.

◆ **Hidden Text.** Includes information formatted as hidden text.

5 Click **Inspect**.

A progress meter appears while Word inspects the document.

6 Review the results of the inspection.

7 Click **Remove All** for each inspector module in which you want to remove hidden data and personal information.

TROUBLE? *Before you click Remove All, be sure you want to remove the information. You might not be able to restore it.*

8 To reinspect the document, click **Reinspect**, and then click **Inspect**.

9 Click **Close**.

Did You Know?

What is metadata? Metadata is data that describes other data. For example, text in a document is data, while the number of documents is metadata.

Inspector progress

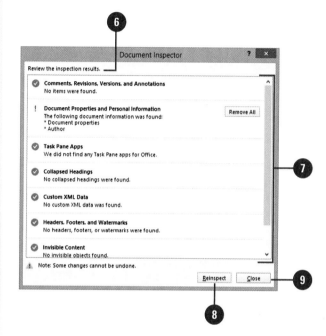

Adding Security Encryption to a Document

File encryption is additional security you can apply to a document. **File encryption** scrambles your password to protect your document from unauthorized people from breaking into the file. You don't have to worry about the encryption, Word handles everything. All you need to do is remember the password. If you forget it, you can't open the file. Password protection takes effect the next time you open the document. To set password protection using file encryption, select the File tab, point to Prepare, select Encrypt Document, enter a password, write it down for safekeeping, and then reenter the password again. Password protection takes effect the next time you open the document.

Apply File Encryption

1. Click the **File** tab, and then click **Info**.

2. Click the **Protect Document** button, and then click **Encrypt with Password**.

3. Type a password.

4. Click **OK**.

5. Retype the password.

6. Click **OK**.

Did You Know?

You can use a strong password. Hackers identify passwords as strong or weak. A strong password is a combination of uppercase and lowercase letters, numbers, and symbols, such as Grea8t!, while a weak one doesn't use different character types, such as Hannah1. Be sure to write down your passwords and place them in a secure location.

Open File with Encryption

1. Click the **File** tab, click **Open**, navigate to a document with the password encryption, and then click **Open**.

2. Type the password.

3. Click **OK**.

Remove File Encryption

1. Click the **File** tab, click **Open**, navigate to a document with the password encryption, and then click **Open**.

2. Type the password, and then click **OK**.

3. Click the **File** tab, and then click **Info**.

4. Click the **Protect Document** button, and then click **Encrypt with Password**.

5. Delete the file encryption password.

6. Click **OK**.

Adding Password Protection to a Document

You can assign a password and other security options so that only those who know the password can open the document, or to protect the integrity of your document as it moves from person to person. At times, you will want the information to be used but not changed; at other times, you will want only specific people to be able to view the document. Setting a document as read-only is useful when you want a document, such as a company-wide bulletin, to be distributed and read, but not changed. Password protection takes effect the next time you open the document.

Add Password Protection to an Office Document

1. Open the document you want to protect.

2. Click the **File** tab, click **Save As**, click **Computer**, and then click **Browse**.

3. Click **Tools**, and then click **General Options**.

4. Type a password in the Password to open box or the Password to modify box.

   IMPORTANT *It's critical that you remember your password. If you forget your password, Microsoft can't retrieve it.*

5. Select or clear the **Read-only recommended** check box to make the document read-only.

6. To set macro security options in the Trust center, click **Macro Security**.

7. Click **OK**.

8. Type your password again.

9. Click **OK**.

10. If you entered passwords for Open and Modify, type your password again, and then click **OK**.

11. Click **Save**, and then click **Yes** to replace existing document.

Open a Document with Password Protection

1. Click the **File** tab, click **Open**, navigate to a document with password protection, and then click **Open**.

2. Click **Read Only** if you do not wish to modify the document, or type the password in the Password dialog box.

3. Click **OK**.

Change or Remove the Password Protection

1. Click the **File** tab, click **Open**, navigate to a document with password protection, and then click **Open**.

2. Type the password in the Password dialog box.

3. Click **OK**.

4. Click the **File** tab, click **Save As**, click **Computer**, click **Browse**, click **Tools**, and then click **General Options**.

5. Select the contents in the Password to modify box or the Password to open box, and then choose the option you want:

   ◆ Change password. Type a new password, click **OK**, and then retype your password.

   ◆ Delete password. Press Delete.

6. Click **OK**.

7. Click **Save**, and then click **Yes** to replace existing document.

Restricting Formatting and Editing

If you want to protect parts of a document, yet grant permission for specific users to change other parts of the document, you can set restriction and protection options in the Restrict Formatting and Editing pane. If you only want to prevent users from formatting a document, you can also restrict users from making any formatting changes or limit formatting to a selection of styles.

Restrict Formatting Changes

1. Open the document you want to protect.

2. Click the **Review** tab.

3. Click the **Restrict Editing** button.

4. Select the **Limit formatting to a selection of styles** check box.

5. Click **Settings**.

6. If necessary, select the **Limit formatting to a selection of styles** check box.

7. Select the check boxes next to the styles you want to allow in the document. To provide a standard minimum amount of restriction, click **Recommended Minimum**.

8. To allow AutoFormat, block theme or color scheme switching, or block Quick Style Set switching, select the check boxes.

9. Click **OK**.

10. If a message alert appears, click **Yes** to remove styles, or click **No** to keep the formatting.

11. Click **Yes, Start Enforcing Protection**.

12. To assign a password, type a password, and then reenter it.

13. Click **OK**.

14. Click the **Close** button on the pane.

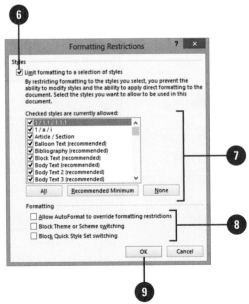

Allow Changes to Part of a Protected Document

1. Open the document you want to protect.

2. Click the **Review** tab.

3. Click the **Restrict Editing** button.

   ◆ Click the **File** tab, click **Info**, click the **Protect Document** button, and then click **Restrict Editing**.

4. If the document is already protected, click **Stop Protection**.

5. If you assigned a password to help protect the document, type the password.

6. Select the **Allow only this type of editing in the document** check box.

7. Click the list arrow, and then select an editing protection option: **Tracked changes**, **Comments**, **Filling in forms**, **No changes (Read only)**.

8. To add specific user, click **More users**, enter names as shown in the example (separated by semicolons), and then click **OK**.

9. Select the parts of the document you want to be unrestricted, and the check box next to the user you want to be able to edit it.

10. Click **Yes, Start Enforcing Protection**.

11. Click the **Password** option, type a password and reenter it, or click the **User authentication** option, which encrypts the document.

12. Click **OK**.

13. Click the **Close** button on the pane.

Add users for editing privileges

Adding a Digital Signature

After you've finished a document, you might consider adding an invisible digital signature—an electronic, secure stamp of authentication on a document. Before you can add a digital signature, you need to get a **digital ID**, or **digital certificate**, which provides an electronic way to prove your identity. A digital certificate checks a public key to validate a private key associated with a digital signature. To assure a digital signature is authentic, it must have a valid (non expired or revoked) certificate issued by a reputable certification authority (CA), and the signing person must be from a trusted publisher. If you need a verified authenticate digital certificate, you can obtain one from a trusted Microsoft partner CA. If you don't need a verified digital certificate, you can create one of your own. If someone modifies the file, the digital signature is removed and revoked. If you're not sure if a document is digitally signed, you can use the Signatures pane to view or remove valid signatures.

Add a Digital Signature to a Document

1. Click the **File** tab, click **Info**, click the **Protect Document** button, and then click **Add a Digital Signature**.

2. Click the **Commitment Type** list arrow, and then select an option: **None**, **Created and approved this document**, **Approved this document**, or **Created this document**.

3. Enter a purpose for signing this document.

4. Click **Details**.

5. Enter your name or role/title and address.

6. Click **OK**.

7. To change the digital signature, click **Change**, select the one you want, and then click **OK**.

8. Click **Sign**.

9. If prompted, click **Yes** to use the certificate, and then click **OK**.

View or Remove Signatures

1. Click the **Signature** icon on the Status bar, or click the **File** tab, click **Info**, and then click the **View Signatures** button.

   The Signatures pane appears, displaying valid signatures in the document. Invalid signatures are no longer automatically removed.

2. Point to a signature, and then click the list arrow.

3. To see signature details, click **Signature Details**, select a signature, click **View**, click **OK** when you're done, and then click **Close**.

4. To remove a signature, point to a signature, click the list arrow, click **Remove Signature**, click **Yes**, and then if necessary click **OK**.

5. Click the **Close** button on the pane.

Signature icon

Signature details

Adding a Signature Line

If you prefer a visible signature line instead of an invisible digital signature, you can insert a visible signature line along with a digital certificate of authenticity. Signature lines allow you to create a paperless signature process for documents, such as contracts. A visible signature line looks like a typical signature line with a name, a date and a line for a signature. When you send a document out with a signature request, the signer sees a signature line and a notification request with instructions. The signer can type—or ink with a Tablet PC—a signature next to the *X*, or select a signature image. To add a signature line and digital signature at the same time, first you insert a signature line into your document, and then you sign it.

Add a Signature Line

1. Click the **Insert** tab.

2. Click to place the insertion point where you want to insert a signature line.

3. Click the **Signature Line** button arrow, and then click **Microsoft Office Signature Line**.

4. If an alert message appears, click **Signature Services from the Office Marketplace** to open an informational web site where you can sign up for a digital certificate, or click **OK** to create your own.

5. Type information about the person who will be signing on this signature line.

6. If you want, type any instructions for the signer.

7. To show the signature date, select the **Allow the signer to add comments in the Sign dialog** check box.

8. To show the signature date, select the **Show sign data in signature line** check box.

9. Click **OK**.

Sign the Signature Line

1. Double-click the signature line that needs a signature.

2. To add a printed version of your signature, type your name.

   If you have a Tablet PC, you can sign your name.

3. To select an image of your written signature, click **Select Image**, navigate to the signature image, and then click **Select**.

4. To specify information, select a **Commitment Type**, and then specify a purpose for signing this document.

5. Click **Sign**.

6. To view the signature, click the **Signature** icon on the Status bar, or click the **File** tab, click **Info**, and then click the **View Signatures** button.

7. To make changes to the signature, point to the signature, click the list arrow, and then select the command you want.

Message bar; click to edit document

Signature line 6

Avoiding Harmful Attacks

Spreading Harmful Viruses

Many viruses and other harmful attacks spread through file downloads, attachments in e-mail messages, and data files that have macros, ActiveX controls, add-ins, or Visual Basic for Applications (VBA) code attached to them. Virus writers capitalize on people's curiosity and willingness to accept files from people they know or work with, in order to transmit malicious files disguised as or attached to benign files. When you start downloading files to your computer, you must be aware of the potential for catching a computer virus, worm, or Trojan Horse. Typically, you can't catch one from just reading a mail message or downloading a file, but you can catch one from installing, opening, or running an infected program or attached code.

Understanding Harmful Attacks

Phishing is a scam that tries to steal your identity by sending deceptive e-mail asking you for bank and credit card information online. Phishers spoof the domain names of banks and other companies in order to deceive consumers into thinking that they are visiting a familiar web site.

Phishers create a web address that looks like a familiar web address but is actually altered. This is known as a **homograph**. The domain name is created using alphabet characters from different languages, not just English. For example, the web site address "www.microsoft.com" looks legitimate, but what you can't see is that the "i" is a Cyrillic character from the Russian alphabet.

Don't be fooled by spoofed web sites that looks like the official site. Never respond to requests for personal information via e-mail;

most companies have policies that do not ask for your personal information through e-mail. If you get a suspicious e-mail, call the institution to investigate and report it.

Spam is unsolicited e-mail, which is often annoying and time-consuming to get rid of. Spammers harvest e-mail addresses from web pages and unsolicited e-mail. To avoid spam, use multiple e-mail addresses (one for web forms and another for private e-mail), opt-out and remove yourself from e-mail lists. See the Microsoft Windows and Microsoft Office Help system for specific details.

Spyware is software that collects personal information without your knowledge or permission. Typically, spyware is downloaded and installed on your computer along with free software, such as freeware, games, or music file-sharing programs. Spyware is often associated with **Adware** software that displays advertisements, such as a pop-up ad. Examples of spyware and unauthorized adware include programs that change your home page or search page without your permission. To avoid spyware and adware, read the fine print in license agreements when you install software, scan your computer for spyware and adware with detection and removal software (such as Ad-aware from Lavasoft), and turn on Pop-up Blocker. See the Microsoft Windows Help system for specific details.

Avoiding Harmful Attacks Using Office

There are a few things you can do within any Office program to keep your system safe from the infiltration of harmful attacks.

1) Make sure you activate macro, ActiveX, add-in, and VBA code detection and notification. You can use the Trust Center to help protect you from attached code attacks. The Trust Center checks for trusted publisher and code locations on your computer and provides security options for add-ins, ActiveX controls, and macros to ensure the best possible protection. The Trust Center displays a security alert in the Message Bar when it detects a potentially harmful attack.

2) Make sure you activate web site spoofing detection and notification. You can use the Trust Center to help protect you from homograph attacks. The *Check Office documents that are from or link to suspicious web sites* check box under Privacy Options in the Trust Center is on by default and continually checks for potentially spoofed domain names. The Trust Center displays a security alert in the Message Bar when you have a document open and click a link to a web site with an address that has a potentially spoofed domain name, or you open a file from a web site with an address that has a potentially spoofed domain name.

3) Be very careful of file attachments in e-mail you open. As you receive e-mail, don't open or run an attached file unless you know who sent it and what it contains. If you're not sure, you should delete it. The Attachment Manager provides security information to help you understand more about the file you're opening. See the Microsoft Office Help system for specific details.

Avoiding Harmful Attacks Using Windows

There are a few things you can do within Microsoft Windows to keep your system safe from the infiltration of harmful attacks.

1) Make sure Windows Firewall is turned on. Windows Firewall helps block viruses and worms from reaching your computer, but it doesn't detect or disable them if they are already on your computer or come through e-mail. Windows Firewall doesn't block unsolicited e-mail or stop you from opening e-mail with harmful attachments.

2) Make sure Automatic Updates is turned on. Windows Automatic Updates regularly checks the Windows Update web site for important updates that your computer needs, such as security updates, critical updates, and service packs. Each file that you download using Automatic Update has a digital signature from Microsoft to ensure its authenticity and security.

3) Make sure you are using the most up-to-date antivirus software. New viruses and more virulent strains of existing viruses are discovered every day. Unless you update your virus-checking software, new viruses can easily bypass outdated virus checking software. Companies such as McAfee and Symantec offer shareware virus checking programs available for download directly from their web sites. These programs monitor your system, checking each time a file is added to your computer to make sure it's not in some way trying to change or damage valuable system files.

4) Be very careful of the sites from which you download files. Major file repository sites, such as FileZ, Download.com, or TuCows, regularly check the files they receive for viruses before posting them to their web sites. Don't download files from web sites unless you are certain that the sites check their files for viruses. Internet Options monitors downloads and warns you about potentially harmful files and gives you the option to block them.

Using the Trust Center

The **Trust Center** is a place where you set security options and find the latest technology information as it relates to document privacy, safety, and security from Microsoft. The Trust Center allows you to set security and privacy settings—Trusted Publishers, Trusted Locations, Trusted Documents, Trusted App Catalogs (**New!**), Add-ins, ActiveX Settings, Macro Settings, Protected view, Message Bar, External Content, File Block Settings, and Privacy Options—and provides links to Microsoft privacy statements, a customer improvement program, and trustworthy computing practices.

View the Trust Center

① Click the **File** tab, and then click **Options**.

② In the left pane, click **Trust Center**.

③ Click the links in which you want online information at the Microsoft Online web site.

◆ **Show the Microsoft Word privacy statement.** Opens a Microsoft web site detailing privacy practices.

◆ **Office.com privacy statement.** Opens a Microsoft Office web site detailing privacy practices.

◆ **Customer Experience Improvement Program.** Opens the Microsoft Customer Experience Improvement Program (CEIP) web site.

◆ **Microsoft Office Feedback "Send a Smile" Privacy Statement.** Opens a Microsoft web site with information about Microsoft's privacy statement (**New!**).

◆ **Microsoft Trustworthy Computing.** Opens a Microsoft web site detailing security and reliability practices.

④ When you're done, close your web browser or dialog box, and return to Word.

⑤ Click **OK**.

Selecting Trusted Publishers and Locations

The Trust Center security system continually checks for external potentially unsafe content in your documents. Hackers can hide web beacons in external content—images, linked media, data connections and templates—to gather information about you or cause problems. When the Trust Center detects potentially harmful external content, the Message Bar appears with a security alert and options to enable or block the content. Trusted publishers are reputable developers who create application extensions, such as a macro, ActiveX control, or add-in. The Trust Center uses a set of criteria—valid and current digital signature, and reputable certificate—to make sure publishers' code and source locations are safe and secure. If you are sure that the external content is trustworthy, you can add the content publisher and location to your trusted lists, which allows it to run without being checked by the Trust Center.

Modify Trusted Publishers and Locations

1. Click the **File** tab, and then click **Options**.

2. In the left pane, click **Trust Center**.

3. Click **Trust Center Settings**.

4. In the left pane, click **Trusted Publishers**.

5. Select a publisher, and then use the **View** and **Remove** buttons to make the changes you want.

6. In the left pane, click **Trusted Locations**.

7. Select a location, and then use the **Add new location**, **Remove**, and **Modify** buttons to make the changes you want.

8. Select or clear the **Allow Trusted Locations on my network (not recommended)** check box.

9. Select or clear the **Disable all Trusted Locations** check box.

10. Click **OK**.

11. Click **OK**.

Setting Document Related Security Options

The Trust Center security system allows you to set file-related options to check for potentially unsafe content in your documents. In Trusted Documents, you can set options to open trusted documents without any security prompts for macros, ActiveX controls and other types of active content in the document. For a trusted document, you won't be prompted the next time you open the document even if new active content was added to the document or changes were made to existing active content. You should only trust documents if you trust the source. Protected view provides a place to open potentially dangerous files, without any security prompts, in a restricted mode to help minimize harm to your computer. If you disable Protected view, you could expose your computer to possible harmful threats. In File Block Settings, you can select the Open and Save check boxes to prevent each file type from opening, or just opening in Protected view, and from saving.

Set Options for Trusted Documents

1. Click the **File** tab, and then click **Options**.

2. In the left pane, click **Trust Center**.

3. Click **Trust Center Settings**.

4. In the left pane, click **Trusted Documents**.

5. Select or clear the check boxes you do or don't want.

    ◆ **Allow documents on a network to be trusted.**

    ◆ **Disable Trusted Documents.**

6. To clear all trusted documents so they are no longer trusted, click **Clear**.

7. Click **OK**.

8. Click **OK**.

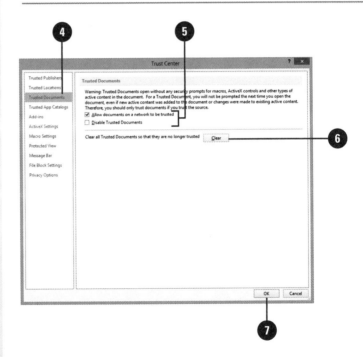

Set Options for Protected View

1. Click the **File** tab, and then click **Options**.

2. In the left pane, click **Trust Center**.

3. Click **Trust Center Settings**.

4. In the left pane, click **Protected View**.

5. Select or clear the check boxes you do or don't want.

   ◆ **Enable Protected View for files originating from the Internet.**

   ◆ **Enable Protected View for files located in potentially unsafe locations.**

   ◆ **Enable Protected View for Outlook attachments.**

6. Click **OK**.

7. Click **OK**.

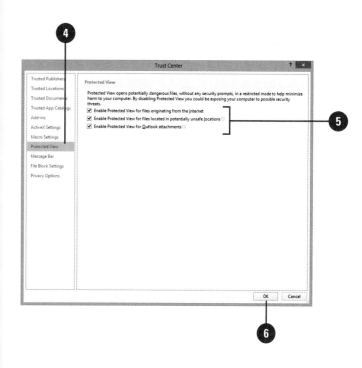

Set Options for File Block Settings

1. Click the **File** tab, and then click **Options**.

2. In the left pane, click **Trust Center**.

3. Click **Trust Center Settings**.

4. In the left pane, click **File Block Settings**.

5. Select the **Open** and **Save** check boxes you want to block for the different file types from opening or saving or clear the ones you don't want.

6. Select the open behavior option you want.

7. Click **OK**.

8. Click **OK**.

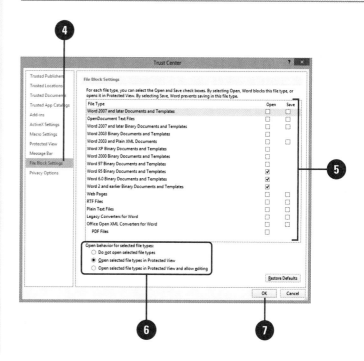

Setting App Catalog Security Options

You can store apps for SharePoint and Office apps for your organization's internal use in an App Catalog site (**New!**). The App Catalog site is a special site collection on a web application. When you create an App Catalog site, you get two libraries for apps: Apps for SharePoint and Apps for Office. App Catalog security options in the Trust Center allow you to set security settings that allow you to specify the trusted app catalogs you want to use.

Set App Catalog Security Options

1. Click the **File** tab, and then click **Options**.

2. In the left pane, click **Trust Center**.

3. Click **Trust Center Settings**.

4. In the left pane, click **Trusted App Catalogs**.

5. Select or clear the check boxes you do or don't want.

   ◆ **Don't allow any apps to start.** Select to not let any apps start.

   ◆ **Don't allow apps from the Office Store to start.** Select to not allow apps from the Office Store to start.

6. Enter a URL for the app catalog, and then click **Add catalog**.

7. To remove or clear a URL, select the URL, and then click **Remove** or **Clear**.

8. Click **OK**, and then click **OK** to save your settings.

   The settings will be applied the next time you start Office.

9. Click **OK**.

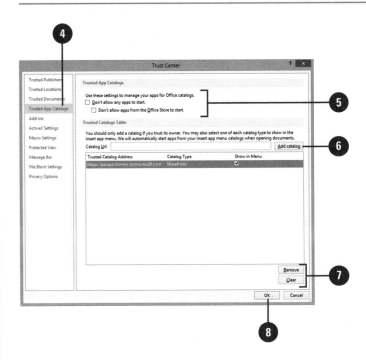

For Your Information

Creating an App Catalog on Office 365

If you have an Office 365 Enterprise team site, you can create an App Catalog site. In your browser, sign-in to your Office 365 Enterprise team site, click Admin, and then click SharePoint. In SharePoint admin center, click App on the left menu, click App Catalog to create a new App Catalog site, and then specify the details you want for your App Catalog site. After you create an App Catalog site, you can add apps to it, such as the ones you create and package from Access 2013.

Setting Add-in Security Options

An add-in, such as smart tags, extends functionality to Microsoft Office programs. An add-in can add buttons and custom commands to the Ribbon. When an add-in is installed, it appears on the Add-Ins tab of an Office program and includes a special ScreenTip that identifies the developer. Since add-ins are software code added to Microsoft Office programs, hackers can use them to do malicious harm, such as spreading a virus. The Trust Center uses a set of criteria—valid and current digital signature, reputable certificate and a trusted publisher—to make sure add-ins are safe and secure. If it discovers a potentially unsafe add-in, it disables the code and notifies you in the Message Bar. If the add-in security options are not set to the level you need, you can change them in the Trust Center.

Set Add-in Security Options

1. Click the **File** tab, and then click **Options**.

2. In the left pane, click **Trust Center**.

3. Click **Trust Center Settings**.

4. In the left pane, click **Add-ins**.

5. Select or clear the check boxes you do or don't want.

   ◆ **Require Application Add-ins to be signed by Trusted Publisher.** Select to check for a digital signature on the .dll file.

   ◆ **Disable notification for unsigned add-ins (code will remain disabled).** Only available if the above check box is selected. Select to disable unsigned add-ins without notification.

   ◆ **Disable all Application Add-ins (may impair functionality).** Select to disable all add-ins without any notifications.

6. Click **OK**.

7. Click **OK**.

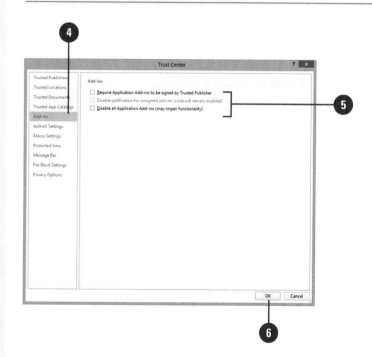

Setting ActiveX Security Options

An ActiveX control provides additional functionality, such as a text box, button, dialog box, or small utility program. ActiveX controls are software code, so hackers can use them to do malicious harm, such as spreading a virus. You can use the Trust Center to prevent ActiveX controls from harming your computer. If the ActiveX security options are not set to the level you want, you can change them in the Trust Center. If you change ActiveX control settings in one Office program, it effects all Microsoft Office programs. The Trust Center uses a set of criteria—checks the kill bit and Safe for Initialization (SFI) settings—to make sure ActiveX controls run safely.

Change ActiveX Security Settings

1. Click the **File** tab, and then click **Options**.

2. In the left pane, click **Trust Center**.

3. Click **Trust Center Settings**.

4. In the left pane, click **ActiveX Settings**.

5. Click the option you want for ActiveX in documents not in a trusted location.

   ◆ Disable all controls without notification.

   ◆ Prompt me before enabling Unsafe for Initialization controls with additional restrictions and Save for Initialization (SFI) controls with minimal restrictions (default).

   ◆ Prompt me before enabling all controls with minimal restrictions.

   ◆ Enable all controls with restrictions and without prompting (not recommended, potentially dangerous controls can run).

6. Click **OK**.

7. Click **OK**.

Setting Macro Security Options

A macro allows you to automate frequently used steps or tasks to save time and work more efficiently. Macros are written using VBA (Visual Basic for Applications) code, which opens the door to hackers to do malicious harm, such as spreading a virus. The Trust Center uses a set of criteria—valid and current digital signature, reputable certificate and a trusted publisher—to make sure macros are safe and secure. If the Trust Center discovers a potentially unsafe macro, it disables the code and notifies you in the Message Bar. You can click Options on the Message Bar to enable it or set other security options. If the macro security options are not set to the level you need, you can change them in the Trust Center.

Change Macro Security Settings

1. Click the **File** tab, and then click **Options**.

2. In the left pane, click **Trust Center**.

3. Click **Trust Center Settings**.

4. In the left pane, click **Macro Settings**.

5. Click the option you want for macros in documents not in a trusted location.

   ◆ Disable all macros without notification.

   ◆ Disable all macros with notification (default).

   ◆ Disable all macros except digitally signed macros.

   ◆ Enable all macros (not recommended, potentially dangerous code can run).

6. If you're a developer, select the **Trust access to the VBA project object model** check box.

7. Click **OK**.

8. Click **OK**.

Changing Message Bar Security Options

The Message Bar displays security alerts when Office detects potentially unsafe content in an open document. The Message Bar appears below the Ribbon when a potential problem arises. The Message Bar provides a security warning and options to enable external content or leave it blocked. If you don't want to receive alerts about security issues, you can disable the Message Bar.

Modify Message Bar Security Options

1. Click the **File** tab, and then click **Options**.

2. In the left pane, click **Trust Center**.

3. Click **Trust Center Settings**.

4. In the left pane, click **Message Bar**.

5. Click the option you want for showing the Message bar.

   ◆ Show the Message Bar in all applications when active content, such as ActiveX controls and macros, has been blocked (default).

   This option is not selected if you selected the Disable all macros without notification check box in the Macros pane of the Trust Center.

   ◆ Never show information about blocked content.

6. Click **OK**.

7. Click **OK**.

Setting Privacy Options

Privacy options in the Trust Center allow you to set security settings that protect your personal privacy online. For example, the *Check Office documents that are from or link to suspicious web sites* option checks for spoofed web sites and protects you from phishing schemes. If your kids are doing research online using the Research pane, you can set Privacy Options to enable parental controls and a password to block sites with offensive content.

Set Privacy Options

1 Click the **File** tab, and then click **Options**.

2 In the left pane, click **Trust Center**.

3 Click **Trust Center Settings**.

4 In the left pane, click **Privacy Options**.

5 Select or clear the privacy check boxes you do or don't want.

The options allow or prevent Office connections to the Internet and suspicious web sites, or install new services for the Research pane.

6 Click **Research Options**.

7 Click **Parental Control**.

8 Select the **Turn on content filtering to make services block offensive results** check box.

9 Select the **Allow users to search only the services that can block offensive results** check box, if necessary.

10 Enter a password, so users cannot change these settings.

11 Click **OK**, retype the password, and then click **OK**.

12 Click **OK**.

13 Click **OK**.

Working with Office Safe Modes

Microsoft Office uses two types of safe modes—Automated and User-Initiated—when it encounters a program problem. When you start an Office program, it automatically checks for problems, such as an extension not properly loading. If the program is not able to start the next time you try, the programs starts in **Automated Safe mode**, which disables extensions—macros, ActiveX controls, and add-ins—and other possible problem areas. If you're having problems and the Office program doesn't start in Automated Safe mode, you can start the program in **User-Initiated Safe mode**. When you start an Office program in Office Safe mode, not all features are available. For instance, templates can't be saved, AutoCorrect list is not loaded, preferences cannot be saved, and all command-line options are ignored (except /a and /n). Before you can use Office Safe mode, you need to enable it in the Trust Center. When you're in safe mode, you can use the Trust Center to find out the disabled items and enable them one at a time to help you pin point the problem.

Enable Safe Mode

1. Click the **File** tab, and then click **Options**.

2. In the left pane, click **Trust Center**.

3. Click **Trust Center Settings**.

4. In the left pane, click **ActiveX Settings**.

5. Select the **Safe Mode (helps limit the control's access to your computer)** check box.

6. Click **OK**.

7. Click **OK**.

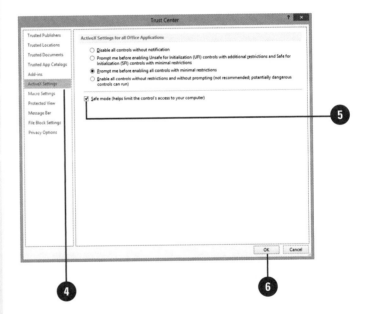

See Also

See "Maintaining and Repairing Office" on page 434 for information on fixing problems with a Microsoft Office program.

View Disabled Items

1 Click the **File** tab, and then click **Options**.

2 In the left pane, click **Add-Ins**.

3 Click the **Manage** list arrow, and then click **Disabled Items**.

4 Click **Go**.

5 In the dialog box, you can select an item, click **Enable** to activate and reload the add-in, and then click **Close**.

6 Click **OK**.

Did You Know?

You can use the Run dialog box to work in Safe mode. At the command prompt, you can use the */safe* parameter at the end of the command-line to start the program.

You can start an Office app in safe mode. In Windows 7, click the Start button on the taskbar, point to All Programs, and then click Microsoft Office. Press and hold Ctrl, and then click Microsoft <Program> 2013.

Marking a Document as Read-Only

As a precaution to prevent readers and reviews from making accidental changes, you can use the Mark as Final command to make a Word document read-only. The Mark as Final command disables or turns off typing, editing commands, and proofing marks, and sets the *Status property* field in the Document Information Panel to Final. The Mark as Final command is not a security option; it only prevents changes to the document while it's turned on and it can be turned off by anyone at any time.

Mark a Document as Final

1. Click the **File** tab, click **Info**, click the **Protect Document** button, and then click **Mark as Final**.

2. Click **OK**, and then click **OK** again, if necessary.

   The document is marked as final and then saved.

3. If necessary, click **OK**.

   The Mark as Final icon appears in the Status bar to indicate the document is currently marked as final.

   IMPORTANT *A Word 2013 document marked as final is not read-only when opened in an earlier version of Microsoft Word.*

Did You Know?

You can enable editing for a document marked as final. Click the Edit Anyway button in the Message Bar or click the File tab, click Info, click the Protect Document button, and then click Mark As Final again to toggle off the Mark As Final feature.

Protect Document button

Marked as final   Click to edit

Mark as Final icon

Reviewing and Sharing Documents

Introduction

If you work in an office environment with Microsoft Word, or are part of some other group that routinely collaborates in document preparation, learning the basics of document sharing is a must. The greater the number of people that interact with a document before it reaches final form, the more critical it becomes for you to keep track of versions, comments, the source of all editing marks, and adequately manage the process of correcting them.

Because working together on a document may be crucial to the success of its completion, there might be various levels of security that need to be set for your readers. Some may have full access to read and make changes, while others are limited to just reading the document, and still others may only be able to read part of the document because it contains hidden text.

After you finish making changes to a document, you can quickly send it to another person for review using e-mail or an instant message. Word allows you to send documents out for review as an attachment, either a document, PDF, or XPS document, using e-mail from within the program so that you do not have to open your e-mail program. If you are a member of an online fax service—such as eFax, InterFAX, MyFax, or Send2Fax—you can use Office to send and receive faxes over the Internet directly from within Word.

What You'll Do

Prepare for Comments and Track Changes

Insert Comments

Read and Edit Comments

Use Track Changes

Compare and Merge Documents

Share Templates

Send a Document Using E-mail

Send a Document by Internet Fax

Send a Document by Instant Message

Preparing for Comments and Track Changes

When you enter a comment or make a change in a document with track changes, Word includes the name and initials of the person who made the comment or change. You can set or change this information in the Word Options dialog box, which you can access from the Track Changes button on the Review tab or when you switch accounts under user accounts (**New!**). When you work with comments or track changes, you can choose to display them in balloons that show off the right-side of the document or in the Reviewing pane that show vertically or horizontally in a separate pane. After you choose how you want to display comments and track changes, you can use the Show Markup button to show or hide different elements—including Comments, Ink, Insertion and Deletions, and Formatting—on the screen during your review. If you have multiple people reviewing a document, you can use the Show Markup button to display the reviewers you want to display. Once you choose the elements you want to show, you can use the Display for Review list arrow on the Review tab to choose how to view the proposed changes to a document. You can show the original or final proposed document with or without showing markup.

Set User Information for Comments and Track Changes

1. Click the **Review** tab.

2. Click the **Track Changes** button, and then click **Change User Name**.

   ◆ You can also click the **File** tab, click **Options**, and then click **General** in the left pane.

3. Type your name.

4. Type your initials.

5. Click **OK**.

Use Balloons or Reviewing Pane

1. Click the **Review** tab.

2. Click the **Show Markup** button, point to **Balloons**, and then select the option you want:

   ◆ **Show Revisions in Balloons.**

   ◆ **Show All Revisions Inline.** Show changes in the document.

   ◆ **Show Only Comments and Formatting in Balloons.** Hide content changes.

3. Click the **Reviewing Pane** button arrow, and then click **Reviewing Pane Vertical** or **Reviewing Pane Horizontal**.

   ◆ To show or hide the Reviewing pane, click the **Reviewing Pane** button.

Reviewing pane

Show or Hide Elements Using Show Markup

1. Click the **Review** tab.

2. Click the **Show Markup** button, and then select the option you want: **Comments, Ink, Insertion and Deletions, Formatting, Balloons**, or **Specific People (New!)**.

   ◆ For the Specific People option, you can show individual or All Reviewer's contributions.

3. Click the **Display for Review** list arrow, and then select a version of reviewing marks: **Simple Markup (New!), All Markup (New!), No Markup**, or **Original**.

Inserting Comments

Comments are useful when someone who is editing the document has questions pertaining to the document. Perhaps a particular passage needs to be clarified. Maybe the formatting of an item is inconsistent. In Word, you can insert a comment or respond to a comment as you review a document and provide feedback. When you insert a comment in Print Layout view, it displays a bubble icon (**New!**), opens a balloon or displays the Reviewing pane where you can enter a comment. Each comment includes the name and initials of the person who made the comment, which you can change in the Options dialog box or when you switch accounts under user accounts (**New!**). After you insert a comment, you can click in the comment balloon and edit it normally. As you review comments, you can quickly reply to them with the Reply button (**New!**) in the comment. When a comment is addressed and no longer needs attention, you can mark it as done (**New!**), which grays it out.

Insert a Comment

1. Select the text or location where you want to insert a comment.

2. Click the **Review** tab.

3. Click the **Show Comments** button to show or hide comment balloons.

   ◆ If the command is grayed out, select **Comments** on the Show Markup list, and **Simple Markup** on the Display for Review list.

   When you hide comment balloons, comment bubble icons appear.

4. Click the **New Comment** button.

5. Type your comment in the balloon, and then click outside the balloon or pane to save it.

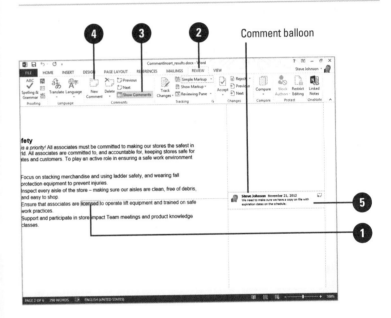

Comment balloon

Did You Know?

You can insert a voice comment. On a Tablet PC, add the Insert Voice button command to the Quick Access Toolbar using the Customize pane in Word Options. Click the Insert Voice button, click the Start button and record the voice comment. When you're done, press the Stop button.

Comment bubble icon

Click to display the comment

Inserted comment

Reply to or Mark a Comment

1. Click the **Review** tab.

2. Click the **Show Markup** button, and then click **Comments**.

3. Click the **Show Comments** button to show or hide comment balloons.

   ◆ If the command is grayed out, select **Simple Markup** on the Display for Review list.

   When you hide comment balloons, comment bubble icons appear.

4. Point to the balloon or bubble icon for the comment in which you want to reply.

5. Click the **Reply** button in the comment.

6. Type your response in the reply comment balloon, and then click outside the balloon or pane to save it.

7. To mark a comment as done, right-click the comment, and then click **Mark Comment Done**.

   The comment grays out, indicating it's complete.

   ◆ **Unmark a comment.** Right-click the comment again, and then click **Mark Comment Done**.

   ◆ **Collapse or expand a marked comment.** Click the parent comment to collapse or the child comment to expand.

Click to collapse the marked comment

Click to expand the marked comment

Comment bubble icon

Marked as done

Did You Know?

You can insert a handwritten comment. On a Tablet PC, click the Review tab, click the New Comment button, and then write in the comment. To show ink, click the Show Markup button, and then click Ink.

Reading and Editing Comments

Before you can view, read and edit comments, you need to show them on the screen. The Show Markup button on the Review tab allows you to show or hide comments and tracking information. You can edit the text in a comment the same way you edit text in a document. If you have dealt with a comment or no longer need it, you can delete it. If you prefer to delete comments all at once, you can use the Delete button on the Review tab to delete all comments shown or all comments in the document.

Display and Read a Comment

1. Click the **Review** tab.

2. Click the **Show Markup** button, and then click **Comments**.

3. Click the **Show Comments** button to show or hide comment balloons.

    ◆ If the command is grayed out, select **Simple Markup** on the Display for Review list.

4. Read the comment.

5. Click the **Previous** or **Next** button to read another comment.

Edit a Comment

1. Click the **Review** tab.

2. Click the **Show Markup** button, and then click **Comments**.

3. Click the **Show Comments** button to show or hide comment balloons.

    ◆ If the command is grayed out, select **Simple Markup** on the Display for Review list.

4. Click the text in the comment, make your changes, and then click outside the balloon to save it.

Delete Comments for a Specific Reviewer

1. Click the **Review** tab.

2. Click the **Show Markup** button arrow, and then point to **Specific People**.

3. Click the name of the reviewer whose comments you want to delete, or click **All Reviewers**.

4. Click the **Delete** button arrow, and then click **Delete All Comments Shown**.

Delete All Comments

1. Click the **Review** tab.

2. Click the **Delete** button arrow, and then click **Delete All Comments in Document**.

Did You Know?

You can quickly delete a comment. Select the comment, and then click the Delete button on the Review tab, or right-click the comment, and then click Delete Comment.

You can also use the Reviewing Pane to work with comments. Click the Review tab, click the Reviewing Pane button arrow, click Reviewing Pane Vertical or Reviewing Pane Horizontal.

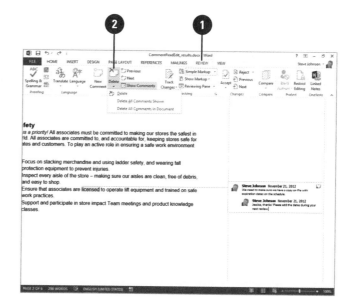

Using Track Changes

Tracking changes in a document allows you to make revisions to a document without losing the original text. Word shows changed text in a different color from the original text and uses revision marks, such as underlines, to distinguish the revised text from the original, and balloon by default off to the side with revision details. You can change the display for the review to show a simple markup (**New!**) with only where markups appear (red bars), all markup changes with details (gray bars), no markup, or original text. You can review changes by using buttons on the Review tab and on the page (**New!**), which allow you to accept and reject changes and comments. If you compare and merge two documents, you can review the changes and accept or reject the results.

Track Changes as You Work

1. Open the document you want to track changes.

2. Click the **Review** tab.

3. Click the **Track Changes** button, and then click **Track Changes**.

   TIMESAVER *Press Ctrl+Shift+E to turn tracking on or off.*

4. Make changes to your document. The changes are reflected using alternate color characters, along with comments in balloons at the side of the screen (in Print Layout or Web Layout view).

5. Click the **Track Changes** button to turn off track changes.

All markup (gray bars)

Simple markup (red bars)

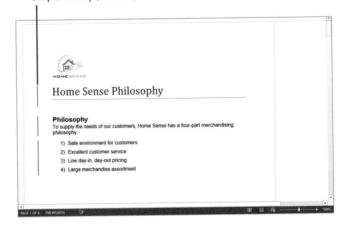

Did You Know?

You can lock track changes on. Click the Review tab, click the Track Changes button arrow, click Lock Tracking (**New!**), set passwords, and then click OK.

You can show or hide balloons. Click the Review tab, click the Show Markup button, point to Balloons, and then select Show Revisions In Balloons, Show All Revisions Inline, or Show Only Comments And Formatting In Balloons.

Review Changes

1. Open the document you want to review.

2. Click the **Review** tab.

3. Click the **Display for Review** list arrow, and then select a version of reviewing marks: **Simple Markup** (**New!**), **All Markup** (**New!**), **No Markup**, or **Original**.

   TIMESAVER *Click a track change line to toggle between Simple Markup (red bars) and All Markup (gray bars).*

4. To show different types of marks, click the **Show Markup** list arrow, and then select to enable or disable: **Comments**, **Ink**, **Insertions and Deletions**, **Formatting**, **Balloons**, or **Specific People**.

5. Use the buttons on the Review tab to review changes:

   ◆ Click the **Next** button or the **Previous** button to view changes one at a time.

   ◆ Click the **Accept** button or the **Reject** button to respond to the revisions.

   ◆ Click the **Accept** button arrow, and then click **Accept All Changes in Document** to accept all changes at once.

   ◆ Click the **Reject** button arrow, and then click **Reject All Changes in Document** to reject all changes at once.

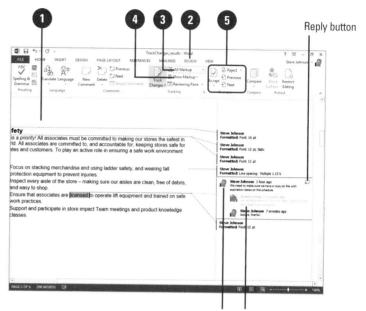

Reply button

Original comment   Reply comment, marked done

Did You Know?

You can show or hide the Reviewing pane. The Reviewing pane shows a list of changes in a pane. Click the Review tab, click the Reviewing Pane button, and then click the option you want.

For Your Information

Printing a Document with Track Changes

If you want to review a print out of document changes, Word provides several options for printing documents with track changes. Before you can print a document with track changes and comment showing, you need to switch to Print Layout view and display the tracked changes and comments you want to print. Click the Review tab, click the Show Markup button, and then select the options or reviewers you want to display. Click the Display For Review list arrow, and then select the option you want to display. Click the File tab, click Print, click the Print What list arrow, click Document Showing Markup or List Of Markup, select other print options you want, and then click OK. To change the print layout for track changes, click the Track Changes button arrow, click Change Tracking Options, click the Paper Orientation In Printing list arrow, select the option you want, and then click OK.

Comparing and Merging Documents

If you want to compare an earlier version of a document with the current version, or if you receive multiple edited versions of the original document back from the recipients, you can compare the documents and merge the changes into one document. The changes can be merged into one document or viewed for comparison. When you compare or merge documents, the text that differs between the two versions will be highlighted in a different color or with track reviewing marks.

Compare Documents

1. Click the **Review** tab.

2. Click the **Compare** button, and then click **Compare**.

3. Click the **Original document** list arrow, and then select the original document you want to use, or click the **Browse** button and double-click it.

4. Click the **Revised document** list arrow, and then select the revised document you want to use, or click the **Browse** button and double-click it.

   If necessary, click **More**.

5. Select and clear the comparison settings you want and don't want.

6. Click the Show changes at option you want (**Character level** or **Word level**).

7. Click the Show changes in option you want (**Original document**, **Revised document**, or **New document**).

8. Click **OK**.

9. If necessary, select a keep formatting option, and then click **OK**.

Compared results   Compared document   Original and revised documents

Merge Documents

① Click the **Review** tab.

② Click the **Compare** button, and then click **Combine**.

③ Click the **Original document** list arrow, and then select the original document you want to use, or click the **Browse** button and double-click it.

④ Click the **Revised document** list arrow, and then select the revised document you want to use, or click the **Browse** button and double-click it.

If necessary, click **More**.

⑤ Select and clear the comparison settings you want and don't want.

⑥ Click the Show changes at option you want (**Character level** or **Word level**).

⑦ Click the Show changes in option you want (**Original document**, **Revised document**, or **New document**).

⑧ Click **OK**.

⑨ If necessary, select a keep formatting option, and then click **Continue with Merge**.

Combined results   Combined document   Original and revised documents

Did You Know?

You can show and hide source documents in results. Click the Compare button on the Review tab, point to Show Source Documents, and then select an option: Hide Source Documents, Show Original , Show Revised, or Show Both.

Sharing Templates

To save time, Word allows you to copy features from one template to another. Once you create a style or macro you never have to create it again. You can simply copy it to another template to use it with a whole new set of documents. You can also replace all the styles in a document with those from a different template by attaching the new template to that document. Word uses two types of templates—global and document. All documents have access to the Normal global template, and many documents have document templates attached that provide formatting instructions. You can load templates as needed to serve as global templates. When you load global templates, you can specify whether they are to be available for the current session only or available whenever you start Word. If you want to change the template used by the current document (typically Normal.dotx) to another one, use the Attach button in the Template and Add-Ins dialog box.

Load, Unload, or Attach Templates

1. Open the document with the template you want to use to attach another template, and then click the **Developer** tab.

2. Click the **Document Template** button.

3. Select or clear the check box next to the global template or add-in you want to load or unload.

4. To add or remove a global template or add-in, do one of the following:

   ◆ Add. Click **Add**, navigate to the folder that contains the add-in, click the **Files of type** list arrow, select **Word Add-Ins**, click the add-in, and then click **OK**.

   ◆ Remove. Select the item you want to remove, and then click Remove.

5. To attach a template to a document (transfer styles), click **Attach**, locate and select the template file, and then click **Open**.

6. Click **OK**.

Use to attach template

Copy Functionality Between Templates

1. With one template open, click the **Developer** tab.

2. Click the **Document Template** button.

3. Click **Organizer** on the Templates tab.

4. Click a tab on the Organizer dialog box with the part of the template that you want to copy.

5. To copy items either to or from a different template, click **Close File**.

6. Click **Open File**, and then open the template (or file) you want.

7. Click the items you want to copy in either list.

8. Click **Copy**.

9. When you're done, click **Close**.

10. Click **OK**.

Did You Know?

Templates can be password protected from unwanted changes. If the Copy button is unavailable in the Organizer dialog box, check to see if the template has been password protected against tracked changes, comments, or forms. If so, these settings must be changed before the elements can be copied to the template.

See Also

See "Setting Developer Options" on page 447 for information on showing the Developer tab.

Sending a Document Using E-mail

After you finish making changes to a document, you can quickly send it to another person for review using e-mail. Word allows you to send documents out for review as an attachment—either a document, PDF, or XPS document—or as a link (document in a shared location) using e-mail from within the program so that you do not have to open your e-mail program. An e-mail program, such as Microsoft Outlook, needs to be installed on your computer before you begin. When you send your document out for review, reviewers can add comments and then send it back to you.

Send a Document for Review Using E-mail

1. Click the **File** tab, click **Share**, and then click **E-mail**.

2. Click the **Send as Attachment** or **Send a Link** button.

3. If the Compatibility Checker appears, click **Continue** or **Cancel** to stop the operation.

   IMPORTANT *To complete the following steps, you need to have an e-mail program installed on your computer and an e-mail account set-up.*

   An e-mail message opens in Microsoft Outlook with your document attached. The subject line contains the file name of the document that you are sending.

4. Enter your recipients and subject line (appears with document name by default).

   ◆ To add recipients from your address book or contacts list, click **To**, click the recipient names, click **To**, **Cc**, or **Bcc** until you're done, and then click **OK**.

5. Enter a message for your reviewer with instructions.

6. Click the **Send** button.

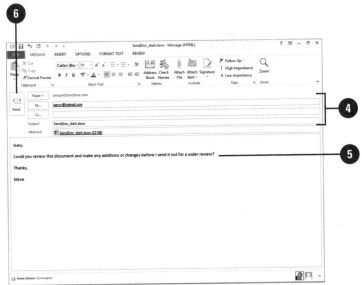

Send a Document as a PDF or XPS Using E-mail

1. Click the **File** tab, click **Share**, and then click **E-mail**.

2. Click the **Send as PDF** or **Send as XPS** button.

3. If the Compatibility Checker appears, click **Continue** or **Cancel** to stop the operation.

   IMPORTANT To complete the following steps, you need to have an e-mail program installed on your computer and an e-mail account set-up.

   An e-mail message opens in Microsoft Outlook with your document attached. The subject line contains the file name of the document that you are sending.

4. Enter your recipients and subject line (appears with document name by default).

   ◆ To add recipients from your address book or contacts list, click **To**, click the recipient names, click **To**, **Cc**, or **Bcc** until you're done, and then click **OK**.

5. Enter a message for your reviewer with instructions.

6. Click the **Send** button.

See Also

See "Creating a PDF Document" on page 404 or "Creating an XPS Document" on page 405 for information on working with PDF and XPS documents.

PDF file as an attachment

Sending a Document by Internet Fax

If you are a member of an online fax service—such as eFax, InterFAX, MyFax, or Send2Fax—you can use Office to send and receive faxes over the Internet directly from within Word. If you're not a member, a web site can help you sign up. You also need to have Microsoft Outlook and Word installed to use the fax service and Outlook must be open to send your fax. If Outlook is not open and you send the fax, it will be stored in your Outbox and not sent until you open Outlook again.

Send a Document by Internet Fax

1. Click the **File** tab, click **Share**, and then click **E-mail**.

2. Click the **Send as Internet Fax** button.

3. If you're not signed up with an Internet Fax service, click **OK** to open a web page and sign up for one. When you're done, return to Word, and then repeat Step 1.

4. If the Compatibility Checker appears, click **Continue** or **Cancel** to stop the operation.

   An e-mail message opens in Microsoft Outlook with your document attached as a .tif (image) file.

5. Enter a Fax Recipient, Fax Number and Subject (appears with document name by default).

   ◆ You can enter a fax number from your address book. Country codes in your address book must begin with a plus sign (+).

   ◆ To send your fax to multiple recipients, click **Add More**, and then enter fax information.

6. In the Fax Service pane, choose the options you want.

7. Complete the cover sheet in the body of the e-mail message.

8. Click the **Send** button.

For Your Information

Using Fax Templates

If you want to use an Office fax template, you can download a template from Office.com (**New!**). Click the File tab, click New, type *fax* in the Search for online templates box, press Enter, click an Office app, click the fax template you want, and then click Create.

Sending a Document by Instant Message

Microsoft Lync is an instant messaging program that allows you to hold online meetings with an audio and video experience. Lync uses a SharePoint or Office 365 site as the host location for the online meeting. With Lync, you can send an Office document to a participant in an instant message. You can use the Send IM button (**New!**) on the Share screen to start an instant message conversation in Lync and transfer the currently opened document. After the files gets transferred, you can carry on with the instant message conversation by using the action buttons to work with messages, dial pad to call, add video, share presentation content, or work with audience.

Send a Document by Instant Message

1. Click the **File** tab, click **Share**, and then click **Send by Instant Message**.

   ◆ If the command is not available on the Share screen, start Microsoft Lync and connect the IM account to your Microsoft account.

2. Enter a contact name or click the Address Book button to select a contact, enter a subject and message for the instant message.

3. Click the **Send IM** button.

   Microsoft Lync opens and then transfers the document in the Conversation window.

4. In the Conversation window, you can continue the session.

5. Use the action buttons to work with messages, dial pad to call, add video, share presentation content, or work with audience.

6. To end the meeting, click the **More Options** button, and then click **End Meeting**.

See Also

See "Communicating Online with Lync" on page 402 for more information on using Microsoft Lync.

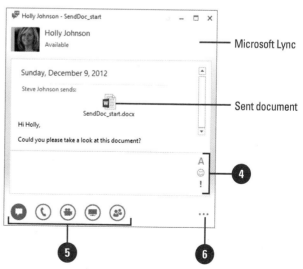

Microsoft Lync

Sent document

Sharing Information Between Programs

15

Introduction

Microsoft Word has the power and flexibility to share information between programs. You can create, store, and manage information in the program that works best for you, and then move that information to another program. You can also import or export data to and from Word to make your documents be the best they can be.

Completing a successful project in Word is not always a solitary venture; sometimes you may need to share data with others or obtain data from other programs. In many offices, your co-workers (and their computers) are located across the country or around the world. You can merge information from different programs into a single document, and you can link data between programs.

You can create one seamless document that includes data from several programs. You can include Excel data, Power-Point slides, or an Access database into your document. The ability to copy data from Excel and create a chart using Excel to embed and display the information in a chart are all features that help make Word a useful tool when creating more technical documents.

In your Word documents, you can create and share notes from OneNote 2013, a digital notebook program, and give a presentation online using Office Presentation Services or Microsoft Lync, an instant messaging and online meeting program using a SharePoint or Office 365 site. Word also allows you to save a document as an XPS or PDF file, which are secure fixed-layout formats you can send to others.

What You'll Do

Share Information Between Programs

Export and Import Data

Link and Embed Files

Work with XML Data

Create a Word Document with Excel Data

Create a Presentation with Word Text

Use an Access Database to Create Word Documents

Create a Word Outline from a Presentation

Create and Open OneNotes

Work with OneNote

Present a Document Online

Present a Document at an Online Meeting

Communicate Online with Lync

Create a PDF Document

Create an XPS Document

Sharing Information Between Programs

Office can convert data or text from one format to another using a technology known as **object linking and embedding** (OLE). OLE allows you to move text or data between programs in much the same way as you move them within a program. The familiar cut and paste or drag and drop methods work between programs and documents just as they do within a document. In addition, all Office programs have special ways to move information from one program to another, including importing, exporting, embedding, linking, and hyperlinking.

Importing and Exporting

Importing and exporting information are two sides of the same coin. **Importing** copies a file created with the same or another program into your open file. The information becomes part of your open file, just as if you created it in that format. Some formatting and program-specific information such as formulas may be lost. **Exporting** converts a copy of your open file into the file type of another program. In other words, importing brings information into your open document, while exporting moves information from your open document into another program file.

Embedding

Embedding inserts a copy of a file created in one program into a file created in another program. Unlike imported files, you can edit the information in embedded files with the same commands and toolbar buttons used to create the original file. The original file is called the **source file**, while the file in which it is embedded is called the **destination file**. Any changes you make to an embedded object appear only in the destination file; the source file remains unchanged.

Linking

Linking displays information from one file (the source file) in a file created in another program (the destination file). You can view and edit the linked object from either the source file or the destination file. The changes are stored in the source file but also appear in the destination file. As you work, Office updates the linked object to ensure you always have the most current information. Office keeps track of all the drive, folder, and file name information for a source file. However, if you move or rename the source file, the link between files will break.

Once the link is broken, the information in the destination file becomes embedded rather than linked. In other words, changes to one copy of the file will no longer affect the other.

Embedding and Linking

Term	Definition
Source program	The program that created the original object
Source file	The file that contains the original object
Destination program	The program that created the document into which you are inserting the object
Destination file	The file into which you are inserting the object

Hyperlinking

The newest way to share information between programs is hyperlinks—a term borrowed from web technology. A **hyperlink** is an object (either colored, underlined text or a graphic) that you click to jump to a different location in the same document or a different document. (See "Creating Hyperlinks" on page 318 and "Using and Removing Hyperlinks" on page 322 for more information about creating and navigating hyperlinks in Microsoft Word documents.)

Deciding Which Method to Use

With all these different methods for sharing information between programs to choose from, sometimes it is hard to decide which method to use. To decide which method is best for your situation, answer the following questions:

1. Do you want the contents of another file displayed in the open document?

   - **No**. Create a hyperlink. See "Creating Hyperlinks" on page 318.

   - **Yes**. Go to question 2.

2. Do you want to edit the content of the file from within the open document?

   - **No**. Embed the file as a picture. See "Linking Linking and Embedding Files" on page 384.

   - **Yes**. Go to question 3.

3. Is the source program (the program used to create the file) available on your computer?

   - **No**. Import the file. See "Exporting and Importing Data" on page 382.

   - **Yes**. Go to question 4.

4. Do you want to use the source program commands to edit the file?

   - **No**. Import the file. See "Exporting and Importing Data" on page 382.

   - **Yes**. Go to question 5.

5. Do you want changes you make to the file to appear in the source file (the original copy of the file)?

   - **No**. Embed the file. See "Linking and Embedding Files" on page 384.

   - **Yes**. Link the file. See "Linking and Embedding Files" on page 384.

Exporting and Importing Data

When you **export** data, you save an open document in a new format so that it can be opened in an entirely different program. When you **import** data, you insert a copy of a file (from the same or another program) into an open document. You can insert into a Word document a bookmarked section of a Word document or a specific range in an Excel worksheet. For example, you might import an Excel worksheet into a Word document to create a one-page report with text and a table. Or you might want to export a document as a web page or export text as XML data or in the standard Rich Text Format to use in another program.

Import or Export Data Using Copy and Paste

1. Select the text or other element that you want to copy.

2. Click the **Home** tab.

3. Click the **Copy** button.

4. Open the destination file, or click the program's taskbar button if the program is already open.

5. Select the location where you want the data to be copied.

6. Click the **Paste** button or click the **Paste** button arrow, and then point to a paste option icon to display a preview of the data.

7. Click the **Paste Options** button, and then click the option you want.

   ◆ You can point to a paste option icon to display a ScreenTip with the function name, and display a preview of the data.

Did You Know?

You can link a file in Word. If you start to import a file into Word, you can link it instead. Click the Insert tab, click the Object button arrow, click Text From File, select the file to link, click the Insert button arrow, and then click Insert As Link.

Export a File to Another Program Format

1. Open the file from which you want to export data.

2. Click the **File** tab, click **Save As**, click **Computer**, and then click **Browse**.

    ◆ You can also click the **File** tab, click **Export**, click **Change File Type**, select a file type, and then click the **Save As** button.

3. Click the **Save in** list arrow, and then select the folder where you want to save the file.

4. Click the **Save as type** list arrow, and then click the format you want.

5. If you want, change the file name.

6. Click **Save**.

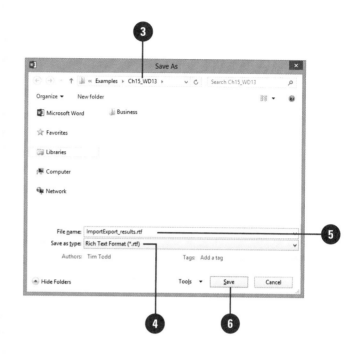

Import a File

1. Click where you want to insert the imported file.

2. Click the **Insert** tab.

3. Click the **Object** button arrow, and then click **Text from File**.

4. Click the **Files of type** list arrow, and then click **Text Files**.

5. Click the **Look in** list arrow, and then select the folder where the text file is located.

6. To import part of a Word document or range from Excel, click **Range**, enter a bookmark name or range, and then click **OK**.

7. Click the text file you want to import.

8. Click **Insert**.

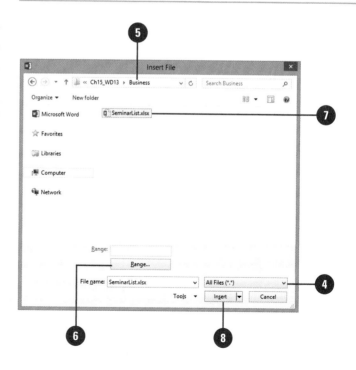

Linking and Embedding Files

Embedding inserts a copy of one document into another. When data is embedded, you can edit it using the menus and toolbars of the program in which it was created (that is, the **source program**). **Linking** displays information stored in one document (the **source file**) into another (the **destination file**). You can edit the linked object from either file, although changes are stored in the source file. For example, you might link an Excel chart or a PowerPoint slide to a Word document so you can update the chart or slide from any of the files. If you break the link between a linked object and its source file, the object becomes embedded. You can use the Object button on the Insert tab to modify a link.

Create a Link to Another File Using Paste Special

1. Open the source file and any files containing information you want to link.

2. Select the information in the source file.

3. Click the **Home** tab.

4. Click the **Copy** button.

5. Click the insertion point in the file containing the link.

6. Click the **Paste** button arrow, and then click **Paste Special**.

7. Click the **Paste Link** option, and then select the object format you want to use.

8. Click **OK**.

Did You Know?

You can edit an embedded object. Edit an embedded object only if the program that created it is installed.

You can manually update or break an object link. Right-click the linked object, and then click Update Link or point to Linked <Item> Object, click Links, click the link you want to update, and then click Manual Update. To break a link, click Break Link.

Paste link option

Embed a New Object

① Click the **Insert** tab.

② Click the **Insert Object** button.

③ Click the **Create New** tab.

④ Click the object type you want to insert.

⑤ Click **OK**.

⑥ Follow the necessary steps to insert the object.

 The steps will vary depending on the object type.

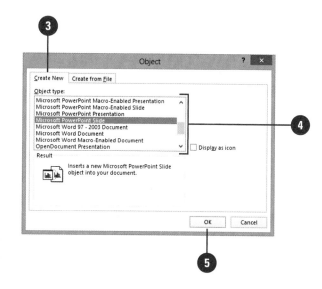

Embed or Link to an Existing Object

① Click the **Insert** tab.

② Click the **Insert Object** button.

③ Click the **Create from File** tab.

④ Click **Browse**, locate and select the file that you want to link, and then click **Open**.

⑤ To create a link to the object, select the **Link to file** check box.

⑥ Click **OK**.

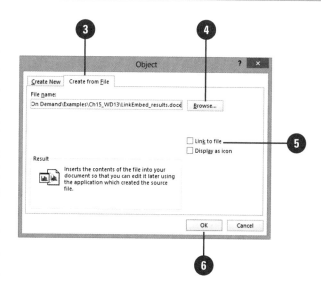

Did You Know?

You can update links each time you open a linked document. When you open a document that contains links, a warning dialog box opens asking you if you want to update all linked information (click Yes) or to keep the existing information (click No).

Working with XML Data

XML (Extensible Markup Language) is a universal language that enables you to create documents in which data is stored independently of the format so you can use the data more seamlessly in other forms. XML is supported in Word. XML allows you to work with the familiar Office interface and create and save documents as XML, without ever knowing the XML language. When you work with XML, you can attach a Word XML Schema or XML Schema (created by a developer)—a set of rules that defines the elements and content used in an XML document—and validate the data against it. Word allows you to open, view, modify, and save XML files and data. An **XML Transformations file (XSLT)** is used to save and transform XML documents into other types of documents, such as HTML or XML, in different views.

Attach or Separate a Schema

1. Click the **Developer** tab.

2. Click the **Document Template** button, and then click the **XML Schema** tab.

3. Click **Add Schema**.

4. Locate and select the XML schema file you want to attach, and then click **Open**.

5. Select or clear a schema to attach or separate it.

6. Click **OK**.

Did You Know?

You can insert XML data. Place the insertion point where you want to insert the data, click the Insert tab, click the Object button arrow, click Text From File, click the Files Of Type list arrow, click XML Files, locate and select the XML file, and then click Insert.

Open, View, and Modify an XML Data File

1. Click the **File** tab, click **Open**, click **Computer**, and then click **Browse**.

2. Click the **Files of type** list arrow, and then click **XML Files**.

3. Locate the XML file you want to open.

4. Select the XML file.

5. Click **Open**.

6. To view the XML mapping, click the **XML Mapping Pane** button on the Developer tab. When you're done, click the Close button on the pane.

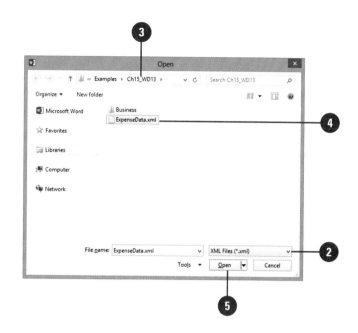

Save an XML Document and Apply a Transformation

1. Open the document you want to save as an XML document.

2. Click the **File** tab, click **Save As**, click **Computer**, and then click **Browse**.

3. Select a location where you want to save the XML data.

4. Click the **Save as type** list arrow, and then click **Word XML Document** or **Word 2003 XML Document**.

5. To apply a transformation for Word 2003 XML Document, select the **Apply transform** check box, click **Transform**, select a transformation file (XSLT), and then click **Open**.

6. Type a name for the XML document.

7. Click **Save**.

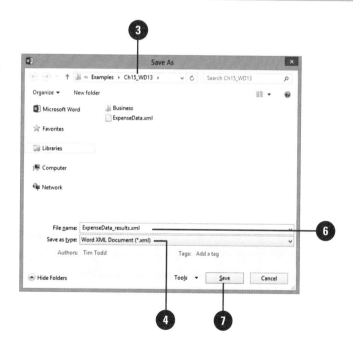

Creating a Word Document with Excel Data

A common pairing of Office programs combines Word and Excel. As you write a sales report, explain a budget, or create a memo showing distribution of sales, you often want to add existing spreadsheet data and charts to your text. Instead of re-creating the Excel data in Word, you can insert all or part of the data or chart into your Word document. You can use the Object button on the Insert tab or copy and paste the information from Excel into Word. The Paste Special command allows you to specify how you want to paste external information into Word. After you insert data or a chart into your word document, you can double-click the embedded Excel object to modify the data or chart.

Insert an Excel Worksheet Range to a Word Document

1. Click in the Word document where you want to copy the Excel range.

2. Click the **Insert** tab.

3. Click the **Object** button arrow, and then click **Text from File**.

4. Click the **Files of type** list arrow, and then click **All Files**.

5. Locate and select the file name of the workbook you want to copy.

6. Click **Range**.

7. Specify the range you want.

8. Click **OK**.

9. Click **Insert**.

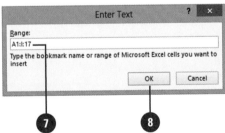

Did You Know?

You can name a range to make it easier to use in Word. If you plan to insert part of an Excel worksheet in a Word document, name the range. This is easier to recall than the specific cell references. Check Help in Microsoft Excel for details.

Copy Data from Excel

① Open both the Word document and the Excel worksheet that contain the data you want to link or embed an object.

② Switch to Excel, and then select the entire worksheet, a range of cells, or the chart you want.

③ Click the **Home** tab, and then click the **Copy** button.

④ Switch to the Word document, and then click where you want the information to appear.

⑤ Click the **Home** tab.

⑥ Use either of the following methods.

◆ **Paste.** Click the **Paste** button, click the **Paste Options** button, point to a paste option icon to display a ScreenTip with the function name and display a preview of the data, and then select an option.

◆ **Paste Special.** Click the **Paste** button arrow, click **Paste Special**, click **Microsoft Excel Worksheet Object**, and then click **OK**.

Did You Know?

You can import Excel data as a picture. Data inserted this way becomes a table that you cannot edit. Select the data you want to import, click the Copy button on the Home tab. Click in the Word document where you want to insert the picture, click the Paste button arrow on the Home tab, and then click Picture. Drag the picture to a new location, or drag its resize handles to enlarge or shrink it.

Excel worksheet

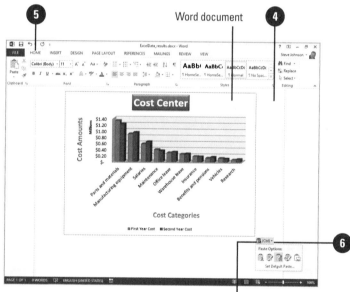

Word document

Paste Options button

Creating a Presentation with Word Text

PowerPoint presentations are based on outlines, which you can create using either PowerPoint, or the more extensive outlining tools in Word. You can import any Word document into PowerPoint, although only paragraphs tagged with heading styles become part of the slides. Each Heading 1 style in a Word document becomes the title of a separate PowerPoint slide. Heading 2 becomes the first level of indented text, and so on. If a document contains no styles, PowerPoint uses the paragraph indents to determine a slide structure. You can edit the slides using the usual PowerPoint commands. You can also copy any table you created in Word to a PowerPoint slide.

Create PowerPoint Slides from a Word Document

1. Open or create a Word document with heading styles.

2. Click the **Send to Microsoft PowerPoint** button on the Quick Access Toolbar.

   ◆ The Send to Microsoft PowerPoint button is not on the Quick Access Toolbar by default. Use the Customize pane in Word Options to add the button.

   PowerPoint opens; each Heading 1 style text becomes the title of a new slide and Heading 2 style text becomes top-level bullets on a slide, and so forth.

3. Save the presentation, and then edit it by adding slides, changing slide layouts, and applying a design template.

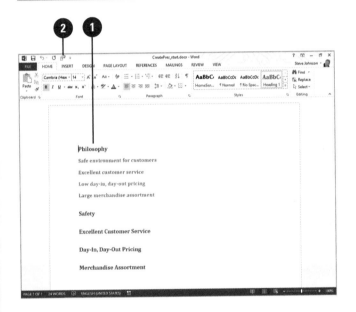

Headings from a Word document

Embed a Word Table in a Slide

1 Click in the Word table you want to use in a slide.

2 Click the table selection box (small black box in the upper-left corner of the table).

3 Click the **Home** tab, and then click the **Copy** button.

4 Click the PowerPoint slide where you want to insert the Word table.

5 Click the **Home** tab, and then click the **Paste** button.

6 Click the **Paste Options** button, and then click the option you want.

◆ You can point to a paste option icon to display a ScreenTip with the function name, and display a preview of the data.

Did You Know?

You can create slides from a Word outline and insert them into an existing PowerPoint presentation. In PowerPoint, display the slide after which you want to insert the new slides. Click the Home tab, click the New Slide button arrow, click Slides From Outline, and then select the Word document you want.

Using an Access Database to Create Word Documents

Access is a great program for storing and categorizing large amounts of information. You can combine, or **merge**, database records with Word documents to create tables or produce form letters and envelopes based on names, addresses, and other Access records. For example, you might create a form letter in Word and personalize it with an Access database of names and addresses. Word uses the Mail Merge pane to step you through the process. Mail merge is the process of combining names and addresses stored in a data file with a main document (usually a form letter) to produce customized documents.

Insert Access Data into a Word Document

1. In Access, click the table or query in the Navigation pane that you want to insert in a Word document.

   IMPORTANT *The database cannot be in exclusive mode.*

2. Click the **External Data** tab.

3. Click the **Word Merge** button.

4. Click the export options you want to use.

5. Click **OK**.

   If you selected the option for linking to an existing Word document, open the document.

6. In Word, follow the step-by-step instructions in the Mail Merge pane to create a letter or mailing list using the data from Access.

See Also

See "Creating a Form Letter" on page 274 for information on using the Mail Merge pane.

Create a Word Document from an Access Database

1. In Access, click the table, query, report, or form in the Navigation pane that you want to save as a Word document.

2. Click the **External Data** tab.

3. Click the **Export to Text File** button (for a .txt file) , or click the **More** button, and then click **Word** (for an .rtf file).

4. Click **Browse**, select a location, enter a name, and then click **Save**.

5. Click the export options you want to use.

6. Click **OK**.

   Word opens and displays the document.

7. Edit the document using Word commands and features.

Did You Know?

You can save in Rich Text Format. A Rich Text Format file (.rtf) retains formatting, such as fonts and styles, and can be opened from Word or other word processing or desktop publishing programs.

Access data in a Word document

Creating a
Word Outline from
a Presentation

You can send both your notes and slides to Word so that you can use a full array of word processing tools. This is especially handy when you are developing more detailed materials, such as training presentations and manuals. By default, PowerPoint pastes the presentation into the Word document. If you change the presentation after sending it to Word, the changes you make to the presentation are not reflected in the Word document. If you click the Paste Link option in the Send To Microsoft Word dialog box, however, you create a link between the Word document and the presentation, so that changes you make in one are reflected in the other.

Create a Word Document from a PowerPoint Presentation

1. In PowerPoint, click the **File** tab, click **Export**, click **Create Handouts**, and then click the **Create Handouts** button.

2. Click the page layout option you want for handouts.

3. To create a link to the presentation, click the **Paste Link** option.

4. Click **OK**.

   Word starts, creates a new document, and inserts your presentation slides with the page layout you selected.

5. Print the document in Word, editing and saving it as necessary.

6. When you're done, click the **Close** button to quit Word.

Creating and Opening OneNotes

Microsoft OneNote is a digital notebook program you can use to gather, manage, and share notes and information. In PowerPoint and Word, you can create and open notes directly from the Review tab by using the Linked Notes button. OneNote auto-links notes to the Office document you're viewing, which you can disable or change in the Advanced section of OneNote Options. You can open a OneNote note by clicking the Linked Notes button. The Linked Notes button is not available on the Review tab until you start the program and create an initial account, which is quick and easy.

Create and Open OneNotes

1. Open a document you want to use to create notes.

2. Click the **Review** tab.

3. Click the **Linked Notes** button.

4. On first document use, select a section or page in which to put the notes, and then click **OK**.

5. In OneNote, enter the notes you want for the page.

6. To work with notes in OneNote, click the **Linked Note** icon, and then click an option:

   ◆ **Linked File(s).** Use to select a linked Office document to view.

   ◆ **Delete Link(s) on This Page.** Use to delete links on the current page.

   ◆ **Linked Notes Options.** Select to open OneNote Options.

7. When you're done, click the **Linked Note** icon in OneNote, and then click **Stop Taking Linked Notes**. To restart it, click **Start Taking Linked Notes** on the File tab.

8. To view linked notes, click the **Linked Notes** button, if available, to open OneNotes, point to a note, and then click the Office program icon.

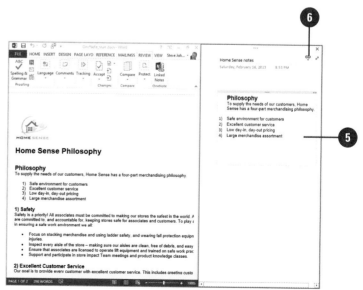

Working with OneNote

Microsoft OneNote can function just like a yellow legal pad. You can take notes, draw pictures, highlight, and scratch out text. However, OneNote is much more. OneNote enables you to flag items within your notes and search for them later. You can create multilevel outlines, gather and paste research information from a variety of sources, insert images or files, move notes around between pages and sections, and create Outlook tasks directly from your notes. With a touch screen, you can draw, erase, and edit using gestures (**New!**). Notes are entered on pages. A page can store pieces of information. Pages are organized into sections. Sections help you organize notes on a particular subject and quickly access them using a section tab. Use folders to group sections together. The notebook is where all your folders, sections, and note pages are stored, which you can save and sync to a SkyDrive (**New!**) for use on other devices. As you work in Office programs, you can use the Send to OneNote tool (**New!**) to take and send notes to OneNote.

Work with OneNote

1. Start **OneNote 2013**.
   - ◆ **Windows 8.** Click the tile on the Start screen.
   - ◆ **Windows 7.** Click **Start** on the taskbar, point to **All Programs**, and then point to **Microsoft Office**.

2. To create a notebook, click the **File** tab, click **New**, click a store location, specify a name and location, and then click **Create Notebook**.

3. To create a section, click the **Create Section** tab, enter a name, and then press Enter.

4. To create a page, click the **Add Page** button, and then enter a title.

5. To enter text, click and then start typing.

6. To insert other content, click the **Insert** tab, and then use the available buttons.

7. To draw on a page, click the **Draw** tab, and then use the available pens, erasers, and tools, or gestures (**New!**) on a touch screen.

Section tabs

Inserted image

Work with Send to OneNote

1. Start Word and open the document you want to send to OneNote.

2. Start **Send to OneNote 2013**.

   ◆ **Windows 8.** Click the tile on the All Apps screen.

   ◆ **Windows 7.** Click **Start** on the taskbar, point to **All Programs**, point to **Microsoft Office**, and then point to **Office 2013 Tools**.

   The program opens as an app on the taskbar.

3. Click any of the following buttons on the Send To OneNote window:

   ◆ **Screen Clipping.** Drag to select a part of the screen to place in OneNote.

   ◆ **Send to OneNote.** Sends the current document to OneNote; Excel and Visio files are editable (**New!**) in OneNote.

   ◆ **New Quick Note.** Creates a new note in OneNote. Type the notes you want in the small OneNote screen.

   Click the **Normal View** button to open OneNote or click the **Close** button. The note appears on the Quick Notes tab in OneNote.

4. Select the location where you want to place the note in OneNote.

5. Click **OK** or **Send to Selected Location**.

6. Select or clear the **Start with OneNote** check box.

7. Click the **Close** button to close the screen or **Exit** link to quit.

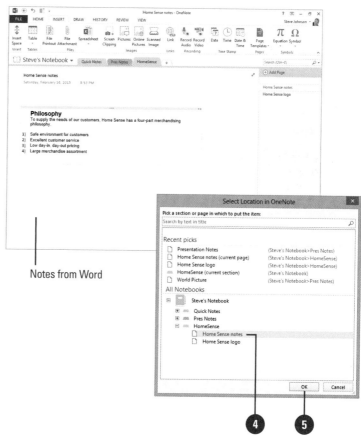

Notes from Word

Presenting a Document Online

If you want to share an Office document (**New!**) with others at different locations, the Office Presentation Service allows you to deliver the document as a presentation over the Internet. The Office Presentation Service is a free service provided by Microsoft for use with your Microsoft account. Before you start the online broadcast, you send a URL link to your remote audience via an e-mail or copied link that they can use to access and watch your show in their browser. If you have notes in OneNote (**New!**), you can show them too. In the browser delivery of your show, some features are changed, including transitions shown as fades, no audio or video, no ink annotations, can't follow a hyperlink, and screensavers and e-mail popup can disrupt the view.

Join in to a Document Broadcast Online

1. Open the email, instant message, or document with the join in link for the presentation.

2. Click the link.

    ◆ You can also open your web browser, and then paste in the copied link.

    Your default web browser opens, displaying the document in the Word Web App.

3. To follow along with the presenter, click **Follow Presenter**.

4. To view shared meeting notes from OneNotes in a new tab, click **Shared Meeting Notes**.

5. To download the broadcast document, if made available by the presenter, click the **File** tab, click **Save As**, click **Download**, specify a name and location, and then click **Save As**.

6. To create a PDF of the broadcast document, click the **File** tab, click **Print**, and then click **Print to PDF**; click a link to view it or click Close.

7. To disconnect from the broadcast, click the **Close** button on your web browser.

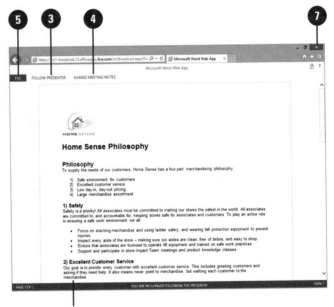

Online broadcast of a document in a web browser

Broadcast a Document Online

1. Click the **File** tab, click **Share**, and then click **Present Online**.

2. Click the **Present Online** list arrow, and then select **Office Presentation Service**.

3. To allow users to download the presented document, select the **Enable remote viewers to download the presentation** check box.

4. Click the **Present Online** button, and then click **Connect**, if prompted.

5. Click the **Copy Link**, **Send in Email** or **Send in IM** link to share the link to access the broadcast.

6. Click **Start Presentation**.

   Your audience can open the link in their browser to follow along with your presentation as you display it.

7. As the presenter in Word, use the buttons on the Present Online tab to do any of the following:

   ◆ **Share Meeting Notes.** Use to share notes from OneNote in the meeting.

   ◆ **Send Invitations.** Use to invite more people to the meeting.

   ◆ **Edit.** Use to pause the meeting and make changes to the document. When you're done, click the **Resume** on the Message bar or **Resume Online Presentation** button on the Present Online tab.

8. To end the broadcast, click the **End Online Presentation** button on the Present Online tab, and then click **End Online Presentation**.

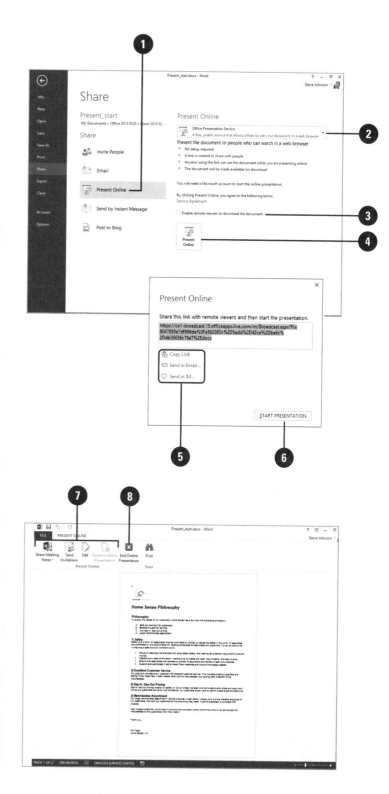

Presenting a Document at an Online Meeting

With Lync, you can present a document to an online meeting. With the Present Online command (**New!**), you can start a Lync meeting with the currently opened document. Microsoft Lync is an instant messaging program that allows you to hold online meetings with an audio and video experience. Lync uses a SharePoint or Office 365 site as the meeting or conversation host. During the meeting, a toolbar appears at the top of the Word window, which appears with a yellow border, where you can control or stop the presentation. Lync opens behind the Word window. You can switch to it in order to invited attendees to participate in the meeting and send instant messages. If not everyone is able to attend, you can also record the meeting (More Options) to play it back later.

Give a Document Presentation at a Lync Meeting

1. Click the **File** tab, click **Share**, and then click **Present Online**.

2. Click the **Present Online** list arrow, and then select **Microsoft Lync**.

3. Click the **Present Online** button.

4. Click **Start a new Lync Meeting**, and then click **OK**. If prompted, sign-in to the meeting with your SharePoint credentials.

5. Specify an audio and video option.

6. Click **OK**.

   A toolbar appears at the top of the Word window, which now appears with a yellow border.

7. To give or take control of the document, click the **Give Control** button on the toolbar, and then click **Give Control Automatically** or **Take Back Control**.

8 To switch to Lync, click the **Lync** icon on the taskbar.

9 Use the action buttons to do any of the following:

- **Dial Pad.** Use to make a phone call.
- **Video.** Use to start or stop a video conversation.
- **Presentable Content.** Use to present content, including presentations, whiteboard drawing, notes (from OneNote) and attachments.
- **People.** Use to invite more participants.

10 When you're done, click **Stop Presenting**.

- You can also click the Stop Presenting button on the toolbar in Word.

11 To end the meeting, click the **More Options** button, click **End Meeting**, and then click **OK**.

Did You Know?

You can record an online meeting in Lync. In the Conversation window in Lync, click the More Options button, and then click Start Recording. When you're done, click the Stop button to edit it.

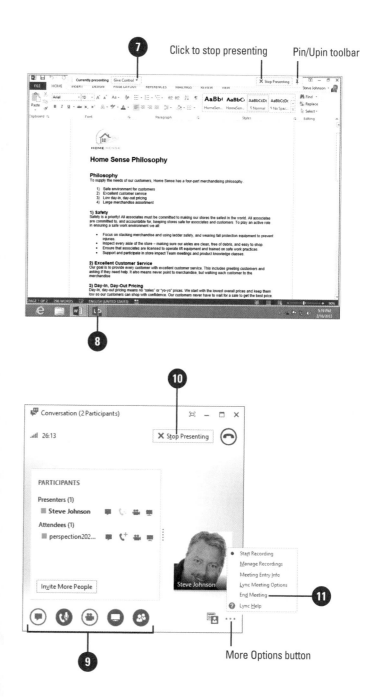

Click to stop presenting

Pin/Upin toolbar

More Options button

Communicating Online with Lync

Microsoft Lync (**New!**) is an instant messaging program that allows you to send and receive instant messages, hold video chats, and share files. Lync uses a SharePoint or Office 365 site as the host location for the online communication. Before you can use Lync, you need to sign-in to the online site. During the conversation, you can send instant messages, make a call, start/stop video, present content, such as your desktop, a program, a PowerPoint presentation, a whiteboard, polls, or notes from OneNote, or invite and work with participants. If not everyone is able to attend, you can also record the session to play it back later. You can manage the recording with the Lync Recording Manager tool (**New!**).

Communicate with Lync

1. Start **Lync 2013**.
   - ◆ **Windows 8.** Click the tile on the Start screen.
   - ◆ **Windows 7.** Click **Start** on the taskbar, point to **All Programs**, and then point to **Microsoft Office**.

2. If prompted, enter a user name and password to sign-in.

3. Double-click a contact.

4. Type text to have a conversation; press Enter to send; press Shift+Enter to start a new line.

5. Use the action buttons to do any of the following:
   - ◆ **Dial Pad.** Use to make a phone call.
   - ◆ **Video.** Use to start or stop a video conversation.
   - ◆ **Presentable Content.** Use to present content, including presentations, whiteboard drawing, notes (from OneNote) and attachments.
   - ◆ **People.** Use to invite more participants.

6. To start a recording, click the **More Options** button, and then click **Start Recording**. Click the **Stop** button to end it.

7. When you're done, click the **Close** button.

My Status/Sign Out · Share a quick message button
Current user signed-in
Settings button
Show Menu button
Search box
Add a Contact button
Lync contacts

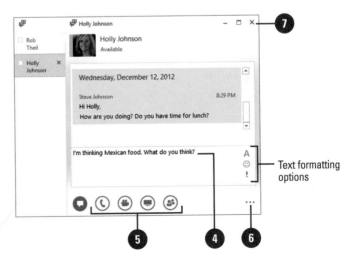

Text formatting options

Add Contacts in Lync

① In Lync, click the **Add a Contact** button.

② Click **Add a Contact in My Organization**, or point to **Add a Contact Not in My Organization**, and then select a contact type.

③ Enter the contact e-mail address.

④ Specify which group to place the contact, and a privacy option.

⑤ Click **OK**.

The contact is added to the contacts list and synced to the SharePoint site.

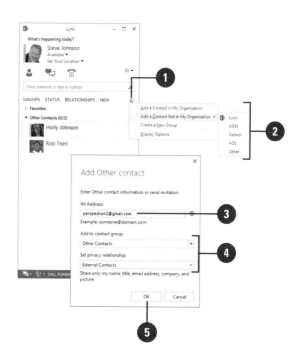

Manage Lync Recordings

① Start **Lync Recording Manager**.

◆ **Windows 8.** Click the tile on the All Apps screen.

◆ **Windows 7.** Click **Start** on the taskbar, point to **All Programs**, point to **Microsoft Office**, and then point to **Office 2013 Tools**.

② Select the recording you want to manage.

③ To play a recording, click **Play**, and then select a player.

④ To rename the title, click **Rename**, and then type a new title.

⑤ To publish the recording as an MP4, click **Publish**, specify a name and location, and then click **OK**.

⑥ To delete a recording, click **Delete**, and then click **Yes** to confirm.

⑦ To exit, click the **Close** button.

Publishing options

Player options

Creating a PDF Document

Portable Document Format (PDF) is a fixed-layout format developed by Adobe Systems that retains the form you intended on a computer monitor or printer. A PDF is useful when you want to create a document primarily intended to be read and printed, not modified. Office allows you to save a document as a PDF file, which you can send to others for review in an e-mail. To view a PDF file, you need to have Acrobat Reader—free downloadable software from Adobe Systems—installed on your computer.

Save a Document as a PDF Document

1. Click the **File** tab, click **Export**, and then click **Create PDF/XPS Document**.

2. Click the **Create PDF/XPS** button.

3. Click the **Save as type** list arrow, and then click **PDF**.

4. Click the **Save in** list arrow, and then click the folder where you want to save the file.

5. Type a PDF file name.

6. To open the file in Adobe Reader after saving, select the **Open file after publishing** check box.

7. Click the **Standard** or **Minimum size** option to specify how you want to optimize the file.

8. Click **Options**.

9. Select the publishing options you want, such as what to publish, range to publish, whether to include non-printing information, or PDF options.

10. Click **OK**.

11. Click **Publish**.

12. If necessary, install Adobe Acrobat Reader and related software as directed.

Creating an XPS Document

XML Paper Specification (XPS) is a secure fixed-layout format developed by Microsoft that retains the form you intended on a monitor or printer. An XPS is useful when you want to create a document primarily intended to be read and printed, not modified. Office allows you to save a document as an XPS file, which you can send to others for review in an e-mail. XPS includes support for digital signatures and is compatible with Windows Rights Management for additional protection. The XPS format also preserves live links with documents, making files fully functional. To view an XPS file, you need to have a viewer—free downloadable software from Microsoft Office Online—installed on your computer.

Save a Document as an XPS Document

1. Click the **File** tab, click **Export**, and then click **Create PDF/XPS Document**.

2. Click the **Create PDF/XPS** button.

3. Click the **Save as type** list arrow, and then click **XPS Document.**

4. Click the **Save in** list arrow, and then click the folder where you want to save the file.

5. Type an XPS file name.

6. To open the file in viewer after saving, select the **Open file after publishing** check box.

7. Click the **Standard** or **Minimum size** option to specify how you want to optimize the file.

8. Click **Options**.

9. Select the publishing options you want, such as what to publish, range to publish, whether to include non-printing information, or XPS options.

10. Click **OK**.

11. Click **Publish**.

Customizing Word

Introduction

Once you've become familiar with Microsoft Word and all its features, you might want to customize the way you work with Word. Each person uses Word in a different way. You can customize the performance of many Word features including its editing, saving, spelling, viewing, printing and security procedures. You can change your view settings so that your Word window looks the way you want it to. Word comes with set defaults—such as showing the vertical ruler, or how many files you've recently opened—which you can change to suit your needs. Taking a few minutes to change Word's default setting saves time in the long run. When you change these options, Word uses them for all subsequent Word sessions until you change them again.

Some of the other Word customization features allow you to set a default font and related attributes to use when you are typing text in text boxes. Other defaults might be the color or line style of a shape object that you create. You can change the location of the Ribbon and the configuration of the Quick Access Toolbar to include commands not available on the Ribbon. To make Word easier to use with touch screens, the program provides Touch/Mouse Mode, which adds or removes more space between commands on the Ribbon.

In addition to Word, Microsoft Office 2013 also comes with other helpful tools including Upload Center, Lync, Lync Recording Manager, SkyDrive Pro, Language Preferences, Spreadsheet or Database Compare, and Telemetry Log or Dashboard.

What You'll Do

Set Start Up Options

Set Office Options

Set General Options

Set Page Display Options

Set Display Options

Set Print Options

Set Editing Options

Change Default Text and Page Settings

Change Default File Locations

Set Advanced Save Options

Set Advanced General Options

Set Compatibility Options

Change Advanced Document Properties

Work with Touch Screens

Access Commands Not in the Ribbon

Customize the Way You Create Objects

Work with Office Tools

Maintain and Repair Office

Setting Start Up Options

You can customize several settings in the Word work environment to suit the way you like to work. You can specify start up options (**New!**) for how you want Word to start including opening files with specified extensions, detecting if Word isn't the default program for word processing, whether to open e-mail attachments and other uneditable files in reading view, and showing the Start screen when Word starts. Taking a few minutes to change Word's default setting saves time in the long run.

Change Start Up Options

1. Click the **File** tab, and then click **Options**.

2. In the left pane, click **General**.

3. Select the Start up options for Word you want:

   ◆ **Default Programs**. Click to select the extensions you wan to open with Word (**New!**).

   ◆ **Tell me if Microsoft Word isn't the default program for viewing and editing spreadsheets**. Select to detect if Word isn't the default word processing program (**New!**).

   ◆ **Open e-mail attachment and other uneditable files in reading view**. Select to to use Read Mode view or clear to use Print Layout view.

   ◆ **Show the Start screen when this application starts**. Select to show it or deselect to show a blank document (**New!**).

4. Click **OK**.

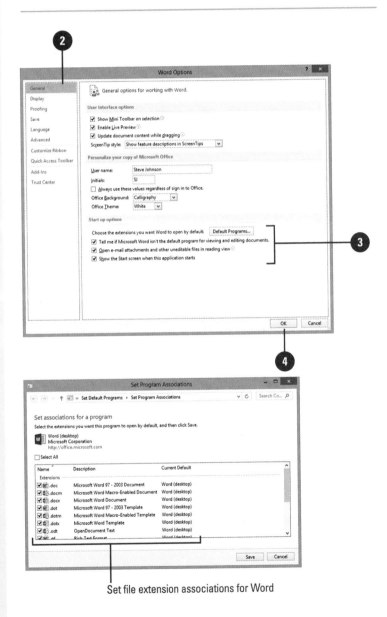

Set file extension associations for Word

Setting Office Options

Word Options includes some common settings for all Office programs that allow you to customize your work environment to your personal preferences. You can change general options to personalize the appearance of the Word window with an Office Background (**New!**) at the top of the program window or Office Theme (**New!**) color scheme. In addition, you can specify if you want to use these settings regardless to whether you are signed in to Office.

Change Office Options

1 Click the **File** tab, and then click **Options**.

2 In the left pane, click **General**.

3 Select Office related options for Word you want:

- **Always use these values regardless of sign in to Office**. Select to always use the Office options (**New!**).

- **Office Background**. Select to apply a background at the top of the program window (**New!**).

- **Office Theme**. Select to apply a color scheme to the program window (**New!**).

4 Click **OK**.

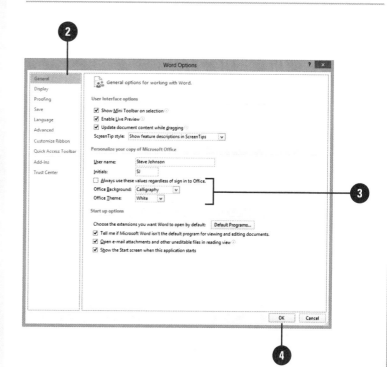

Setting General Options

You can customize the performance of many Word features including its editing, saving, spelling, viewing, printing and security procedures. Each person uses Word in a different way. Word Options allows you to change general options to personalize what appears in the Word window. You can set user interface options to show the Mini Toolbar when working with a selection, enable live preview to show option changes, show content as you move objects instead of a bounding box (**New!**), and specify a ScreenTip style. In addition to signing in to Word with a Microsoft account, you can also personalize Word with your user name and initials, which get used when you track changes in a document.

Change General User Interface Options

① Click the **File** tab, and then click **Options**.

② In the left pane, click **General**.

③ Select the User Interface options for Word you want:

◆ **Show Mini Toolbar on Selection**. Select to show a miniature semi-transparent toolbar that helps you work with selected text.

◆ **Enable Live Preview**. Select to show preview changes in a document.

◆ **Update document content while dragging**. Select to show how content looks as objects are moved (**New!**).

◆ **ScreenTip style**. Click the list arrow to select a screentip option: Show enhanced ScreenTips, Don't show enhanced ScreenTips, or Don't show ScreenTips.

④ Type your name and initials as you want them to appear in Properties, and review comments.

⑤ Click **OK**.

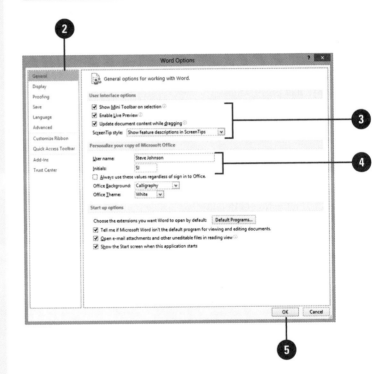

Setting Page Display Options

Sometimes it's hard to determine whether a blank is a tab or space. You can set options on the Display pane in Word Options to show or hide formatting marks. Formatting marks help you see characters that are not visible, such as tabs, spaces, paragraph marks, and hidden text. You can also set page display that show white space between pages in Print Layout view, show highlighted text on the screen and in print, or show tooltip information when you point to a hyperlink or reviewer's comment.

Change Page Display Options

1. Click the **File** tab, and then click **Options**.

2. In the left pane, click **Display**.

3. Select or clear any of the check boxes to change the display options you want.

   ◆ **Show white space between pages in Print Layout view.** Select to display top and bottom margins. (Default on).

   ◆ **Show highlighter marks.** Select to display highlighted text on the screen and in print. (Default on).

   ◆ **Show document tooltips on hover.** Select to display information when you point to a hyperlink or reviewer's comment. (Default on).

4. Select or clear any of the check boxes to display or hide the formatting marks you want.

   ◆ **Tab characters, Spaces, Paragraph marks, Hidden text, Optional hyphens,** or **Object anchors.** (Default off).

   ◆ **Show all formatting marks.** (Default off).

5. Click **OK**.

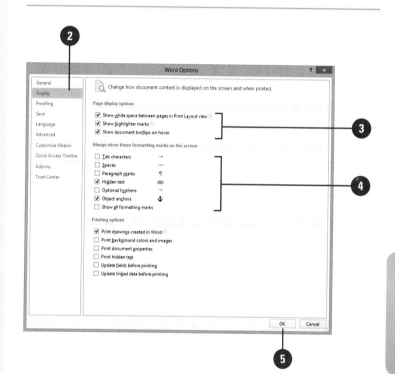

Setting Display Options

Word uses unique characters and formatting to display specialized document elements, such as bookmarks, crop marks, text boundaries and wrapping, and background colors and images. You can set options on the Advanced pane in Word Options to show or hide these elements when you work on a document. In addition, you can also show or hide Word window elements, such as scroll bars, shortcut keys, and the vertical ruler. If you want to change the units of measurement used in a document, which affects the rulers, positioning, and sizing to name a few, you can set the options on the Advanced pane.

Change Display View Options

① Click the **File** tab, and then click **Options**.

② In the left pane, click **Advanced**.

③ Select or clear any of the check boxes to change the display view options you want.

- **Show background colors and images in Print Layout view.** (Default off).

- **Show text wrapped within the document window**. (Default off).

- **Show picture placeholders.** Shows empty boxes; speeds up the display. (Default off).

- **Show drawings and text boxes on screen.** (Default on).

- **Show bookmarks.** (Default on).

- **Show text boundaries.** Shows dotted lines. (Default on).

- **Show crop marks.** Shows corner of margins. (Default off).

- **Show field codes instead of their values.** (Default off).

- **Use draft font in Draft and Outline views.** (Default off).

- **Use fonts that are stored on the printer.** (Default off). (**New!**)

- **Expand all heading s when opening a document.** (Default off). (**New!**)

④ Click **OK**.

Change Display Options

1. Click the **File** tab, and then click **Options**.

2. In the left pane, click **Advanced**.

3. Select or clear any of the check boxes to change the display options you want.

   - **Show measurements in units of**. Set ruler and other measurement units. (Default is Inches).

   - **Style area pane width in Draft and Outline views**. Set the pane width. (Default is 0").

   - **Show pixels for HTML features.** Uses pixels as the unit of measurement for HTML features. (Default on).

   - **Show shortcut keys in ScreenTips.** (Default on).

   - **Show horizontal scroll bar.** (Default on).

   - **Show vertical scroll bar.** (Default on).

   - **Show vertical ruler in Print Layout view.** (Default on).

   - **Optimize character positioning for layout rather than readability.** Select to optimize for printing. (Default off).

   - **Disable hardware graphics acceleration.** Select to disable hardware graphics acceleration. (Default off).

   - **Update document content while dragging.** Shows content as you drag instead of an outline (Default on). (**New!**)

   - **Use subpixel positioning to smooth font on screen.** Uses subpixels to smooth the display of fonts (Default on). (**New!**)

4. Click **OK**.

Setting Recent Document Options

When you display the Start and Open screens in Word, you can use the Recent Documents option to display a list of recently used document for easy access when you want to open them again. In the Advanced pane in Word Options, you can specify the number of recent document that you want to display on the screens. If you want to save yourself even more time accessing recent documents, you can add them to the File tab. In options, you can specify the number of documents that you want to show on the tab. In addition to recent documents, you can also display recent folders, which is also available in the Save As screen. In options, you can specify the number of unpinned folders that you want to show on the screens. A pinned item stays on the screen for availability whenever you need it until you unpin it.

Change Recent Document and Folder Display Options

1. Click the **File** tab, and then click **Options**.

2. In the left pane, click **Advanced**.

3. Select or clear any of the check boxes to change the display view options you want.

   ◆ **Show this number of Recent Documents.** Shows this number of recent documents on the Start and Open screens.

   Set to 0 to turn off the recent documents display.

   ◆ **Quickly access this number of Recent Documents.** Shows this number of recent documents on the File tab. (Default off).

   ◆ **Show this number of unpinned Recent Folders.** Shows this number of unpinned recent folders on the Start, Open, and Save As screens. **(New!)**

   Set to 0 to turn off the recent folders display.

4. Click **OK**.

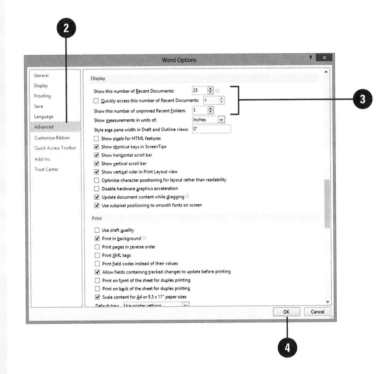

Use Recent Documents or Folders

1. Click the **File** tab, and then click **Open**.

   TIMESAVER *In the Start screen (**New!**), click a recent document.*

2. Click **Recent Documents** or **Computer (New!)**.

3. To pin or unpin a document or folder, point to a document or folder (displays the pin):

   ◆ **Pin a document or folder.** Click the **Pin** icon on the Recent Documents or Recent Folders list.

   ◆ **Unpin a document or folder.** Click the **Unpin** icon to display a pin on the Recent Documents or Recent Folders list.

4. Click the document or folder you want to open.

Did You Know?

You can use recent folders in the Save As screen. Click the File tab, click Save As, and then click Computer. Click a recent folder to quickly open it.

Pinned item

Access local files

Unpinned item

Open recent documents on the Start screen

Click to open a document from the Open dialog box

Setting Print Options

If your document contains a lot of graphics, colors, and drawings, it could slow down the printing process. While you're working on the document, you can turn off options to speed up the printing process. When you're ready to print the final version, you can turn the options back on. If you have marked text in the document as hidden, you can turn on the Print hidden text option to print it. You can also set options to print on both sides of a page (known as duplex printing) and select the default paper tray you like to use.

Change Print Display Options

1. Click the **File** tab, and then click **Options**.

2. In the left pane, click **Display**.

3. Select or clear any of the check boxes to change the print display options you want.

- **Print drawings created in Word.** Clear to speed up the process. (Default on).

- **Print background colors and images.** Clear to speed up the process. (Default off).

- **Print document properties.** Select to print document summary information. (Default off).

- **Print hidden text.** Select to print text marked as hidden without the dotted lines. (Default off).

- **Update fields before printing.** (Default off).

- **Update linked data before printing.** (Default on).

4. Click **OK**.

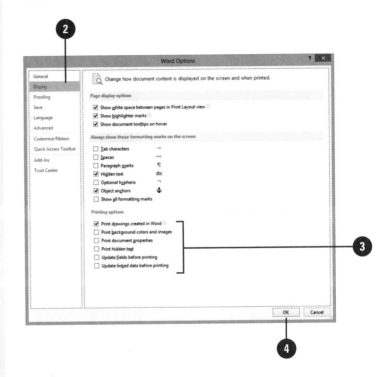

Change Print Options

1. Click the **File** tab, and then click **Options**.

2. In the left pane, click **Advanced**.

3. Select or clear any of the check boxes to change the print options you want.

   ◆ **Use draft quality.** Select for documents with minimal formatting. (Default on).

   ◆ **Print in background.** Set to print while you continue to work. (Default on).

   ◆ **Print pages in reverse order.** (Default off).

   ◆ **Print XML tags.** Select when a Schema is attached to the document. (Default off).

   ◆ **Print field codes instead of their values.** (Default off).

   ◆ **Print on front of the sheet for duplex printing.** Prints in reverse order, so you can flip and print on the back. (Default off).

   ◆ **Print on back of the sheet for duplex printing.** Prints in ascending order so you can print on the front in reverse order. (Default off).

   ◆ **Scale content for A4 or 8.5 x 11" paper sizes.** (Default on).

   ◆ **Default tray.** Select the printer tray you want. (Default is Use printer settings).

4. Click **OK**.

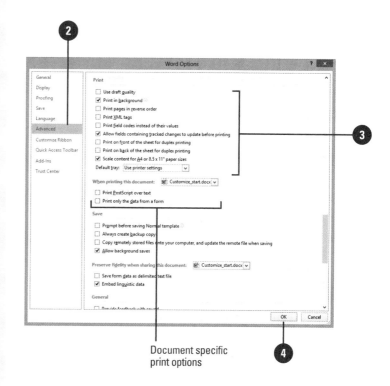

Document specific print options

Setting Editing Options

If you spend a lot of time modifying documents, you can set editing options in Word to customize the way you work. You can set options to automatically select entire words, use smart paragraph selection (includes the paragraph mark), allow text to be dragged and dropped, identify formatting inconsistencies, keep track of formatting, and show AutoComplete suggestions. You can also set cutting, copying, and pasting options to specify preferences when you paste text and graphics.

Change Editing Options

1. Click the **File** tab, and then click **Options**.

2. In the left pane, click **Advanced**.

3. Select or clear any of the check boxes to change the options you want, some options include:

   - **Typing replaces selected text.** (Default on).

   - **When selecting, automatically select entire word.** (Default on).

   - **Allow text to be dragged and dropped.** (Default on).

   - **Use CTRL+ Click to follow hyperlink.** (Default on).

   - **Automatically create drawing canvas when inserting AutoShapes.** (Default off).

   - **Use smart paragraph selection.** (Default on).

   - **Use smart cursoring.** (Default on).

   - **Use the Insert key to control overtype mode.** (Default off).

   - **Prompt to update style.** (Default off).

   - **Use Normal style for bulleted or numbered lists.** (Default off).

   - **Enable click and type.** Select a default paragraph style. (Default on and Normal).

   - **Show AutoComplete suggestions.** (Default on).

   - **Do not automatically hyperlink screenshot.** (Default off). (**New!**)

4. Click **OK**.

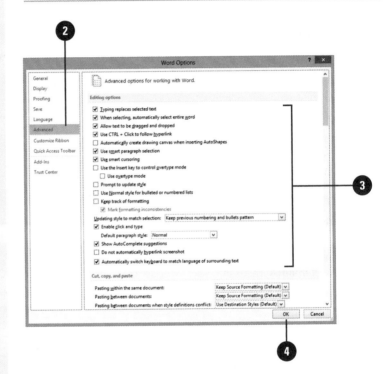

Change Cut, Copy, and Paste Options

1 Click the **File** tab, and then click **Options**.

2 In the left pane, click **Advanced**.

3 Click the list arrow next to any of the following, and then select the option you want:

- ◆ **Pasting within the same document.** (Default: Keep Source Formatting).

- ◆ **Pasting between documents.** (Default: Keep Source Formatting).

- ◆ **Pasting between documents when style definitions conflict.** (Default: Use Destination Styles).

- ◆ **Pasting from other programs.** (Default: Keep Source Formatting).

- ◆ **Insert/paste pictures as.** (Default: In line with text).

4 Select or clear any of the check boxes to change the options you want, some options include:

- ◆ **Keep bullets and numbers when pasting text with Keep Text Only option.** (Default on).

- ◆ **Use the Insert Key for paste.** (Default off).

- ◆ **Show Paste Options button when content is pasted.** (Default on).

- ◆ **Use smart cut and paste.** (Default on).

5 Click **OK**.

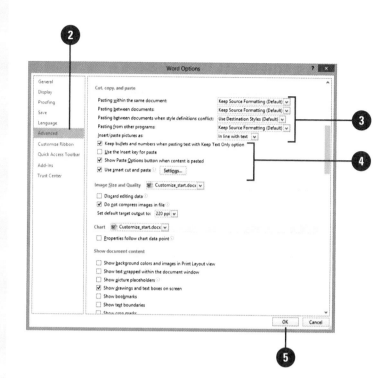

Changing Default Text and Page Settings

When you type text in a document, Word applies a set of default text font and paragraph attributes. Some examples of Word's font default settings include font style, size, and formatting options, such as bold, italic, and underline. You can also include text effects, such as text fill, outline, style, shadow, reflection, glow and soft edges, and 3-D. Some paragraph examples include alignment, indents, and spacing. You might find that having your own personalized font style and color, indent, and spacing settings would really make your documents more custom. In the same way, you can also set default page options—such as margins, paper sizes, and layout—for a new document. To find out the current default settings for your document, you can open a new document, and then type some text.

Change Default Text and Character Spacing

1. Click the **Home** tab.

2. Click the **Font Dialog Box Launcher**.

3. Change the font options to what you want to be the default.

4. Click the **Advanced** tab.

5. Change the character spacing options and OpenType Features to what you want to be the default.

6. To specify text effects, click **Text Effects**, set the options you want, and then click **Close**.

7. Click **Set As Default**.

8. Click the **This document only?** or **All documents based on the Normal.dotm template?** option.

9. Click **OK**.

Change Default Paragraph Text

1 Click the **Home** tab.

2 Click the **Paragraph Dialog Box Launcher**.

3 Click the **Indents and Spacing** or **Line and Page Breaks** tab.

4 Change the paragraph options to what you want to be the default.

5 Click **Set As Default**.

6 Click the **This document only?** or **All documents based on the Normal.dotm template?** option, and then click **OK**.

Change Default Page Setup

1 Click the **Page Layout** tab.

2 Click the **Page Setup Dialog Box Launcher**.

3 Click the **Margins**, **Paper**, or **Layout** tab.

4 Change the margin, paper, and layout options to what you want to be the default.

5 Click **Set As Default**, and then click **Yes**.

Changing Default File Locations

If you always save documents in a specific folder, you can change the default location where documents are saved. You can change the default local folder locations for documents, images, personal templates (that appear on the Start and New screens) (**New!**), AutoRecover files, Word startup, Office tools, and offline documents on file management servers, such as SharePoint. Word specifies default folder locations based typical places where Microsoft stores things. However, if you want to change them to a location better suited for your needs, you can use the Browse button on the Save pane or the File Locations button on the Advanced pane in Word Options to change them. After you make a change, Word uses the new setting for all subsequent Word sessions until you change the setting again.

Change Default File Locations

1. Click the **File** tab, and then click **Options**.

2. In the left pane, click **Save**.

3. Click **Browse**, select a folder location, and then click **OK** or enter a complete folder path location for any of the following:

   ◆ **AutoRecover file location.** Specifies the local folder location where Word creates and stores document files for recovery.

   ◆ **Default location file location.** Specifies the local folder location to open or save documents.

   ◆ **Default personal templates location.** Specifies the local folder location for storing and using custom templates. The templates appear on the Personal tab in the Start and New screens (**New!**).

   ◆ **Server drafts location.** Specifies the local folder for storing draft versions of documents checked out (offline) from SharePoint and other document servers.

4. Click **OK**.

Change Default File Locations All in One Place

1 Click the **File** tab, and then click **Options**.

2 In the left pane, click **Advanced**.

3 Click **File Locations**.

4 Select the file type nd folder location you want to change.

◆ **Documents.** Specifies the local folder location to open or save documents.

◆ **Images.** Specifies the local folder location to insert pictures from file.

◆ **User templates.** Specifies the local folder location for storing and using custom templates.

◆ **Workgroup templates.** Specifies the folder location for custom templates for workgroups.

◆ **AutoRecover files.** Specifies the local folder location where Word creates and stores document files for recovery.

◆ **Tools.** Specifies the local folder location for Office tools.

◆ **Startup.** Specifies the local folder location for document to start when Word starts.

5 Click **Modify**.

6 Select a folder location, and then click **OK**.

7 Click **OK**.

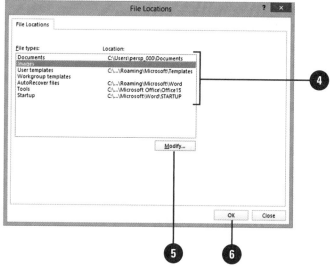

Setting Advanced Save Options

In addition to the standard save options on the Save pane in Word Options, you can also set more advanced save options that allow you to automatically create a backup copy of a document, save form data, and update remotely stored files. If you are using nonstandard fonts to create a document, you can embed the fonts you use so they "travel" (are saved) with your document, Then, if the computer you use to show or print the document does not have all your document fonts installed, the embedded fonts appear in the document and your document quality will not suffer. When you embed fonts, the size of your document increases.

Change Advanced Save Options

1. Click the **File** tab, and then click **Options**.

2. In the left pane, click **Advanced**.

3. Select the save options you want:

   ◆ **Prompt before saving Normal template.** (Default off).

   ◆ **Always create backup copy.** (Default off).

   ◆ **Copy remotely stored files onto your computer, and update the remote file when saving.** (Default off).

   ◆ **Allow background saves.** (Default on).

4. Click the **Preserve fidelity when sharing this document** list arrow, and then select the document you want to specify options.

5. Select the save options you want:

   ◆ **Save form data as delimited text file.** (Default off).

6. Click **OK**.

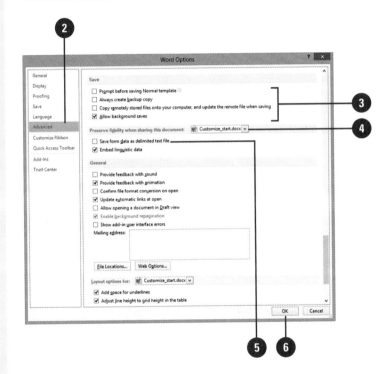

See Also

See "Saving a Document" on page 22 for information on setting save document options.

Change Embedding Options

1. Click the **File** tab, and then click **Options**.

2. In the left pane, click **Save**.

3. Click the **Preserve fidelity when sharing this document** list arrow, and then select the document you want to specify options.

4. Select the document embedding options you want:

   ◆ **Embed fonts in the file.** Select to save fonts in a document file. (Default off).

   ◆ **Embed only the characters used in the document.** Select to save only the fonts you actually use in a document. (Default off).

   ◆ **Do not embed common system fonts.** Select to reduce file size when you use Windows and Office fonts. (Default off).

5. In the left pane, click **Advanced**.

6. Select the document embedding options you want:

   ◆ **Embed linguistic data.** Select to save speech and hand-written text. (Default on).

7. Click **OK**.

Did You Know?

You can set options for saving draft documents to a SharePoint server. Click the File tab, click Options, click Save, select a Save Checked-out Files For option, specify a file path location to the server for document drafts, and then click OK.

Setting Advanced General Options

In addition to display options, the Advanced pane in Word Options also includes options to provide general user feedback. You can set the feedback options to play sound, show simple animation, show add-in user interface error, or display alerts to update links. You can also set options for default file locations and web pages using the File Locations and Web Options buttons.

Change Advanced General Options

1. Click the **File** tab, and then click **Options**.

2. In the left pane, click **Advanced**.

3. Select the general options you want:

   - **Provide feedback with sound.** (Default off).

   - **Provide feedback with animation.** (Default on).

   - **Confirm file format conversion on open.** Select to choose a file converter. (Default off).

   - **Update automatic links at open.** (Default on).

   - **Allow opening a document in Draft view.** (Default off).

   - **Enable background repagination.** Select to repaginate documents as needed. (Default on).

   - **Show add-in user interface errors.** Select to display alerts for custom interface problems. (Default off).

   - **Show customer submitted Office.com content.** Select to show customer content from Office.com. (Default on).

   - **Mailing address.** Enter to use as the default return address for envelopes and letters.

4. Click **OK**.

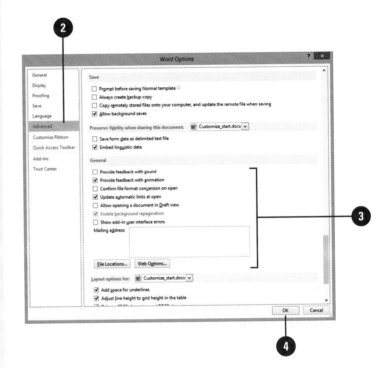

Setting Compatibility Options

If you have an older Word or WordPerfect document that doesn't display very well in Word 2013, you can set compatibility options to simulate the layout of an older format to improve the display. Word 2013 provides compatibility for all previous versions of Word going back to Word for Windows 1.0 and WordPerfect 5.x. Compatibility options are available on the Advanced pane in Word Options. After you select the layout version you want to use, you click the arrow to display the long list of compatibility options.

Set Compatibility Options

1. Open the document with the older format you want to set compatibility options.

2. Click the **File** tab, and then click **Options**.

3. In the left pane, click **Advanced**, and then scroll to the bottom of the dialog box.

4. Click the **Compatibility options for** list arrow, and then select the document in which you want to set options.

5. Click the **Layout this document as if created in** list arrow, and then select the version of Word you want.

6. Select or clear the layout check box options in the list.

7. Click **OK**.

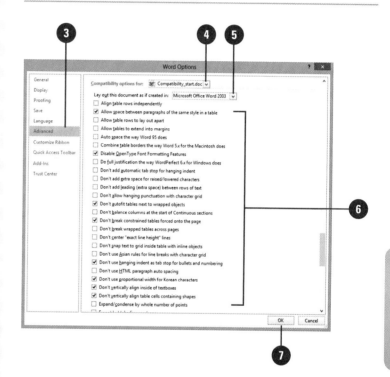

Changing Advanced Document Properties

You can use document properties—also known as metadata—to help you manage and track files. Search tools can use the metadata to find a document based-on your search criteria, such as title, subject, author, category, keywords, or comments. You can create advanced custom properties to associate more specific criteria for search tools to use. If you associate a document property to an item in the document, the document property updates when you change the item.

Customize Advanced Properties

1. Click the **File** tab, and then click **Info**.

2. Click the **Properties** button, and then click **Advanced Properties**.

3. Click the tabs to view and add information:

   ◆ **General**. To find out file location or size.

   ◆ **Summary**. To add title and author information for the document.

   ◆ **Statistics**. To display the number of slides, paragraphs, words and other details about the document.

   ◆ **Contents**. To display document contents.

4. Click the **Custom** tab.

5. Type the name for the custom property or select a name from the list.

6. Select the data type for the property you want to add.

7. Type a value for the property.

8. Click **Add**.

9. Click **OK**.

Working with Touch Screens

If you're working with Word on a touch screen device, all you need is your finger to make gestures (**New!**). A gesture is the movement of one or more fingers on a touch screen or pad. For example, touching the screen is called tapping or dragging your finger with a flicking motion at the end of the movement is called swiping. You can double-tap file or folder in a dialog box or tap and drag to select a range of text in a document to select and edit it. To make Word easier to use with touch screens, the program provides Touch/Mouse Mode (**New!**), which adds or removes more space between commands on the Ribbon.

Use Touch/Mouse Mode

1. Click the **Quick Access Toolbar** list arrow, and then click **Touch/Mouse Mode**.

   This adds the button to the Quick Access Toolbar.

2. Click **Touch/Mouse Mode** button on the Quick Access Toolbar.

3. Click **Mouse** or **Touch**.

Did You Know?

You can use touch commands. In Office, you can use the following touch commands:

Click - Tap in the file.

Double-click - Double-tap in the file.

Drag - Tap and slide.

Zoom - Pinch or stretch two fingers.

Scroll - Touch and slide up or down.

Select - Tap an object. For multiple objects, select one, and then tap and hold the others. For text, tap and drag.

You can make text and objects bigger. In Windows, open the Control Panel, tap Appearance & Personalization, tap Display, and tap Medium - 125% or Larger - 150%, and then tap Apply.

Touch mode

Finger gestures

Swiping gestures

Accessing Commands Not in the Ribbon

If you don't see a command in the Ribbon that was available in an earlier version of Word, you might think Microsoft removed it from the product. To see if a command is available, check out the Quick Access Toolbar or Customize Ribbon section in Word Options. The Quick Access Toolbar or Custom Ribbon give access to commands not in the Ribbon, which you can add to the toolbar or ribbon. For example, you can add the following commands: Create Microsoft Outlook Task, Replace Fonts, AutoFormat, Set AutoShape Defaults, Send to Microsoft PowerPoint, and Web Page Preview.

Add Commands Not in the Ribbon to the Quick Access Toolbar or Ribbon

1. Click the **File** tab, click **Options**, and then click **Quick Access Toolbar** or **Customize Ribbon**.

2. Click the **Choose commands from** list arrow, and then click **Commands Not in the Ribbon**.

3. Click the **Customize Quick Access Toolbar** and then click **For all documents (default)**, or click the **Customize the Ribbon** list arrow, and then click **For All Tabs**.

4. Click the command you want to add (left column).

   TIMESAVER *For the Quick Access Toolbar, click <Separator>, and then click Add to insert a separator line between buttons.*

5. Click **Add**.

6. Click the **Move Up** and **Move Down** arrow buttons to arrange the commands in the order you want them to appear.

7. To reset the Quick Access Toolbar to its original state, click **Reset**, click **Reset only Quick Access Toolbar** or **Reset only selected Ribbon tab**, and then click **Yes**.

8. Click **OK**

Customizing the Way You Create Objects

When you draw an object, Word applies a set of default object attributes. Examples of object default settings include fill color, shadow, and line style. To find out the current default settings for your document, you can draw an object, or create a text object and check the object's attributes. If you change a default setting, Word will use the new setting for all subsequent Word sessions until you change the setting again.

Customize the Way You Create Shape Objects

1. Create a shape.

2. Change the shape attributes, including fill color or effect, text color, outline color and style; and font type, style, and size.

3. Right-click the shape, and then click **Set as Default Shape**.

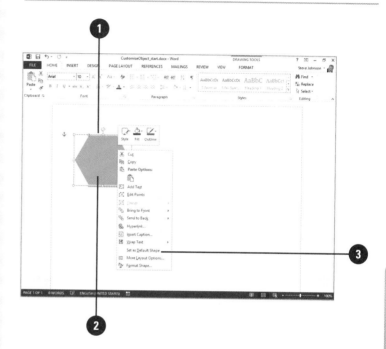

Working with Office Tools

In addition to the main programs, Office 2013 includes some helpful tools including SkyDrive Pro (**New!**), Upload Center, Language Preferences, Spreadsheet or Database Compare (**New!**), and Telemetry Log or Dashboard (**New!**). With SkyDrive Pro, you can connect and synchronize your SkyDrive cloud storage on a SharePoint site with your desktop. As you upload files to a server, like a SharePoint site, you can use the Upload Center to view progress or issues on a transfer. The Upload Center shows you pending uploads, recently uploaded files and all cached files from a server. If you need to compare two Excel spreadsheets, you can use the Spreadsheet Compare tool, a stand-alone app. Telemetry Log records Office events in an Excel spreadsheet to help you troubleshoot problems. Telemetry Dashboard is an Excel spreadsheet that connects to an SQL database to collect client data from other sources in a shared folder.

Compare Spreadsheets

1. Start **Spreadsheet Compare 2013** or **Database Compare 2013**.

   ◆ **Windows 8.** Click the tile on the All Apps screen.

   ◆ **Windows 7.** Click **Start** on the taskbar, point to **All Programs**, point to **Microsoft Office**, and then point to **Office 2013 Tools**.

2. Click the **Browse** folder, and then select the two files you want to compare.

3. Click **OK**.

   The differences appears color coded in the two panes and list.

4. Select or clear option check boxes to show or hide results.

5. Use the Home tab buttons to show results, export results, or copy results to the Clipboard.

6. To exit, click the **Close** button.

See Also

See "Using Multiple Languages" on page 298 for information on using Language Preferences.

Results list   Side by side comparison

Work with the Upload Center

1 Start **Office 2013 Upload Center**.

◆ **Windows 8.** Click the tile on the All Apps screen.

◆ **Windows 7.** Click **Start** on the taskbar, point to **All Programs**, point to **Microsoft Office**, and then point to **Office 2013 Tools**.

◆ **Desktop taskbar.** Click the **Upload Center** icon on the desktop taskbar, and then click **Open Upload Center**.

2 To display pending uploads, click the **View** list arrow, and then click **Pending Uploads**.

3 Use any of the following options:

◆ **Actions.** Use options to open the selected file, open site with the file, save a copy, or discard changes.

◆ **Upload All.** Use to upload all files.

◆ **Pause Uploads.** Use to pause the selected file.

◆ **Settings.** Use to open settings dialog box.

◆ **Refresh.** Use to refresh the files in the Upload Center.

4 To resolve issues or take actions, click **Resolve** or **Actions**, and then select an option.

5 To display recent uploads, click the **View** list arrow, and then click **Recently Uploaded**.

6 To exit Upload Center, click the **Close** button.

Upload Center options

See Also

See "Syncing Documents on SharePoint" on page 476 for information on using SkyDrive Pro.

Maintaining and Repairing Office

At times you may determine that an Office program is not working as efficiently as it once did. This sometimes happens when you install new software or move files into new folders. Office does the work for you with the Repair option, which locates, diagnoses, and fixes any errors in the program itself. Note that this feature does not repair personal files like documents, presentations, or workbooks. If the Repair option does not fix the problem, you might have to reinstall Office. If you need to add or remove features, reinstall Office, or remove it entirely, you can use Office Setup's maintenance feature.

Perform Maintenance on Office Programs

1. Insert the Office disc in your drive or navigate to the folder with the setup program.

2. In File or Windows Explorer, double-click the Setup icon.

3. Click one of the following maintenance buttons.

   ◆ **Add or Remove Features** to change which features are installed or remove specific features.

   ◆ **Remove** to uninstall Microsoft Office 2013 from this computer.

   ◆ **Repair** to repair Microsoft Office 2013 to its original state.

   ◆ **Enter a Product Key** to type the product registration key (located in the product packaging) for Office 2013.

4. Click **Continue**, and then follow the wizard instructions to complete the maintenance.

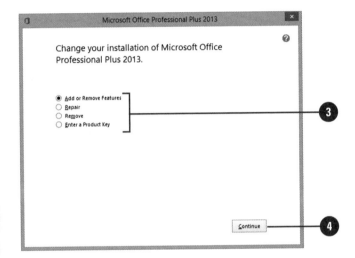

For Your Information

Updating Office 2013 along with Windows 8

Microsoft continually improves Office with updates that include bug fixes and feature improvements. With Windows 8, you can automatically get updates to Office 2013 along with the operating system. To set the update option, open the Desktop app, open the Control Panel, click System and Security, click Windows Update, click Change settings in the left pane, select the Give Me Updates For Other Microsoft Products When I Update Window check box, and then click OK. When Windows 8 scans your system and checks for updates, it also checks for Office 2013 updates as well as other Microsoft products.

Expanding Word Functionality

Introduction

An Office App is a third-party software component that adds functionality or extends features in an Office document. For example, you can add an app called Dictionary - Merriam to use an enhanced dictionary. You can quickly install, insert, and manage apps from the Office Store at Office.com directly from an Office program.

An add-in extends the functionality of Word and other Microsoft Office programs. Word includes a variety of add-ins—programs that are included with Word but not essential to its functionality. Before you can use a Word or a third-party add-in, you need to load it first. When you load an add-in, the feature may add a command to a Ribbon tab.

If you want to customize Microsoft Word and create advanced documents, you'll need to learn how to work with the Microsoft Office programming language, **Microsoft Visual Basic for Applications (VBA)**. VBA is powerful and flexible, and you can use it in all major Office applications. To create a VBA application, you have to learn VBA conventions and syntax. Office makes VBA more user-friendly by providing the Visual Basic Editor, an application that includes several tools to help you write error-free VBA applications. The Visual Basic Editor provides extensive online Help to assist you in this task. A practical way to use VBA is to create macros. Macros can simplify common repetitive tasks that you regularly use in Word.

An ActiveX control is a software component that adds functionality to an existing program. An ActiveX control supports a customizable, programmatic interface for you to create your own functionality, such as a form. Word includes several pre-built ActiveX controls—including a label, text box, command button, and check box—to help you create a user interface.

What You'll Do

Add and Insert Apps for Office

Manage Apps for Office

View and Manage Add-ins

Load and Unload Add-ins

Enhance a Document with VBA

View the Visual Basic Editor

Set Developer Options

Understand How Macros Automate Your Work

Record or Create a Macro

Run and Control a Macro

Add a Digital Signature to a Macro Project

Assign a Macro to a Toolbar or Ribbon

Save and Open a Document with Macros

Use Content Controls to Create Documents

Insert and Use ActiveX Controls

Set ActiveX Control Properties

Add VBA Code to an ActiveX Control

Play a Movie Using an ActiveX Control

Change the Document Information Panel

Adding Apps for Office

With the Office Store at Office.com (**New!**), you can add functionality with a third-party app to an Office program, and then use the app to extend features in a document. For example, you can add an app called Dictionary - Merriam to use an enhanced dictionary or an app called Wikipane to provide an easy way to access Wikipedia. To use Office.com, you need to have a Microsoft account, and be signed in with your Office program. You can insert an app by using the Apps for Office button (**New!**) on the Insert tab. Apps are designed for specific Office programs and only appear for them.

Add an Office App

1. Click the **Insert** tab.

2. Click the **Apps for Office** button (**New!**), and then click **See All**.

    A list of installed or featured apps appears in the dialog box.

3. Click **FEATURED APPS**.

    A list of available apps appears under FEATURED APPS.

4. To add a featured app, click the app title or the **Add** button.

    The app is added to your account at Office.com and inserts an object or opens a pane. Specify the app options you want to apply.

5. To exit, click the **Close** button in the dialog box or pane.

Did You Know?

You can get apps for Office programs. Apps are available for Word, Excel, Outlook, Project, PowerPoint, and SharePoint 2013 from the Office Store at *www.office.com/store*.

See Also

See "Managing Apps for Office" on page 439 for information on showing and hiding installed apps.

MY APPS

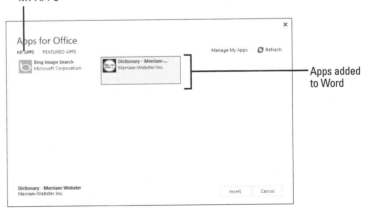

Apps added to Word

Search for Office Apps at Office.com

1 Click the **Insert** tab.

2 Click the **Apps for Office** button (**New!**), and then click **See All**.

A list of installed or featured apps appears in the dialog box.

3 Click **FEATURED APPS**.

A list of available apps appears under FEATURED APPS.

4 Type your search text in the Search box, and then click the **Search** button or press Enter.

The Office Store opens in your web browser.

5 To add an app, click the app, and then click **Add**.

◆ Sign-in to your account, if prompted, or click **Sign in**.

◆ **See All Apps.** Click the **See all products** link.

◆ **Sort Apps.** Click any of the SORT BY options: **Relevance**, **Price**, or **Rating**.

6 To exit, click the **Close** button in your web browser.

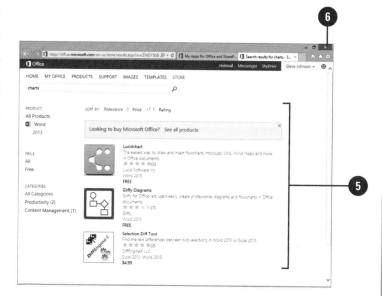

Did You Know?

You can find more apps at the Office Store. Click the Insert tab, click the Apps for Office button, click See All, and then click the Find more apps at the Office Store link. The Office Store web site opens. Sign in, if necessary, and then browse available apps for the Office program you want.

Inserting Apps for Office

After you add an App for Office from the Office Store at Office.com (**New!**), you can use the app in an Office program. Some apps insert an object, while others open a pane. For example, the Dictionary - Merriam app opens in a pane, where you can quickly find a definition. You can insert an app by using the Apps for Office button (**New!**) on the Insert tab. Recently used apps appear on the Apps for Office button menu for easy access. Apps are designed for specific Office programs and only appear for them.

Insert an App for Office

1. Click the **Insert** tab.

2. To insert a recently used app object, click the **Apps for Office** button (**New!**), and then click the recently used app on the menu.

3. To see all apps, click the **Apps for Office** button (**New!**), and then click **See All**.

   A list of installed or featured apps appears in the dialog box.

4. Click **MY APPS**.

   A list of installed apps appears under MY APPS.

5. Click the app tile you want to insert.

6. Click **Insert**.

   The app inserts an object or opens a pane. Specify the app options you want to apply.

See Also

See "Adding Apps for Office" on page 436 for information on finding and adding an Office app to an Office program.

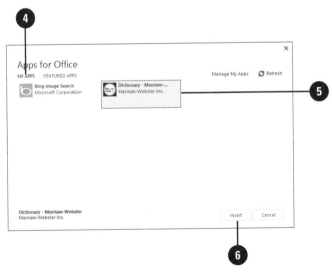

Managing Apps for Office

The apps you add to your Office programs are managed online at Office.com using your web browser. You can access the web site from within your Office program using the Apps for Office button (**New!**) on the Insert tab. To use Office.com, you need to have a Microsoft account, and be signed in with your Office program. At Office.com (**New!**), you can view your Visible and Hidden apps. The Visible list displays the apps available in your Office programs, while the Hidden list displays the apps you've installed and added to your account. In the Visible list, you can hide apps and in the Hidden list, you can retrieve (show) apps. Apps are designed for specific Office programs and only appear for them.

Manage Office Apps

1. Click the **Insert** tab.

2. Click the **Apps for Office** button (**New!**), and then click **See All**.

   A list of installed or featured apps appears in the dialog box.

3. Click **MY APPS**.

   A list of available apps appears under MY APPS.

4. Click **Manage My Apps**, and then wait for your web browser to open.

   ◆ Sign-in to your account, if prompted, or click **Sign in**.

5. To hide an app, click **Visible**, and then click the **Hide** link.

6. To show an app, click **Hidden**, and then click the **Retrieve** link.

7. To exit, click the **Close** button in your web browser.

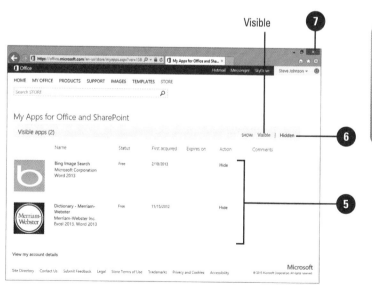

Viewing and Managing Add-ins

An add-in extends functionality to Word and other Microsoft Office programs. An add-in can add buttons and custom commands to the Ribbon or menu items or buttons within the program. You can get add-ins for Word on the Office.com web site in the Downloads area, or on third-party vendor web sites. When you download and install an add-in, it appears on the Add-Ins or other tabs depending on functionality, and includes a special ScreenTip that identifies the developer. You can view and manage add-ins from the Add-Ins pane in Options. In Options from the Customize Ribbon pane, you can also show or hide the Add-ins tab.

View Installed Add-ins

1. Click the **Add-Ins** tab, or click the **File** tab, click **Add-Ins**, point to an add-in menu option, and then select a command.

   Add-ins with buttons and controls appear on the Ribbon. To display a ScreenTip, point to a button or control.

2. Click the **File** tab, and then click **Options**.

3. In the left pane, click **Add-Ins**.

   The installed add-ins appear in the list by category.

   - **Active Application Add-ins.** Lists the registered and running add-ins. A selected check box for a COM add-in appears here.

   - **Inactive Application Add-ins.** Lists the installed add-ins, but not currently loaded. A cleared check box for a COM add-in appears here.

   - **Document Related Add-ins.** Lists template files currently open in a document.

   - **Disabled Application Add-ins.** Lists automatically disabled add-ins causing Office programs to crash.

4. Click an add-in to display information about it.

5. Click **OK**.

Add-in

Information about the selected add-in.

Manage Installed Add-ins

1. Click the **File** tab, and then click **Options**.

2. In the left pane, click **Add-Ins**.

3. Click the **Manage** list arrow, and then click the add-in list you want to display:

   - **COM Add-ins.** Opens the COM Add-Ins dialog box and lists the Component Object Model (COM) add-ins.

   - **Actions.** Opens the AutoCorrect dialog with the Actions tab and list the installed actions.

   - **Word Add-ins.** Opens the Templates and Add-ins dialog box with the Templates tab and lists the currently installed Word add-ins.

   - **Templates.** Opens the Templates and Add-ins dialog box with the Templates tab and lists the currently installed global templates.

   - **XML Schemas.** Opens the Templates and Add-ins dialog box with the XML Schema tab.

   - **XML Expansion Packs.** Opens the Templates and Add-ins dialog box with the XML Expansion Packs tab. XML Expansion Packs provide additional XML functionality.

   - **Disabled Items.** Opens the Disabled Items dialog box and lists the disabled items that prevent Word from working properly. If you want to try and enable an item, select it, click Enable, click Close, and then restart Word.

4. Click **Go**.

5. Click **OK**.

COM Add-Ins dialog box

Templates and Add-ins dialog box

Loading and Unloading Add-ins

Add-ins are additional programs, designed to run seamlessly within Word or Office. There are two main types of add-ins: Word and **Component Object Model (COM)**. Word add-ins are custom controls designed specifically for Word, while COM add-ins are designed to run in one or more Office programs and use the file name extension .dll or .exe. Some add-ins are installed when you run the Setup program, while others can be downloaded from Office.com or purchased from third-party vendors. To load or unload add-ins, Word provides commands you can access from an added button on the Quick Access Toolbar, Developer tab, or the Add-Ins pane in Word Options. When you load an add-in, the feature may add a command to a tab or toolbar. You can load one or more add-ins. If you no longer need an add-in, you should unload it to save memory and reduce the number of commands on a tab. When you unload an add-in, you also may need to restart Word to remove an add-in command from a tab.

Load or Unload a Word Add-in

1. Click the **Developer** tab.

   ◆ To display the Developer tab, use the Customize Ribbon pane in Options.

2. Click the **Add-Ins** or **Document Template** button.

3. Select or clear the check box next to the global template or add-in you want to load or unload.

4. To add or remove a global template or add-in, do one of the following:

   ◆ Add. Click **Add**, navigate to the folder that contains the add-in, click the **Files of type** list arrow, select **Word Add-Ins**, click the add-in, and then click **OK**.

   ◆ Remove. Select the item you want to remove, and then click **Remove**.

5. Click **OK**.

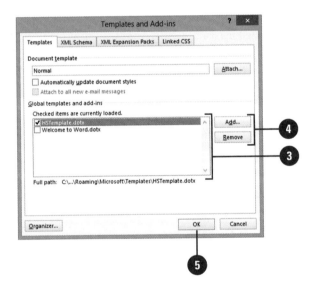

Load or Unload a COM Add-in

1 Click the **Developer** tab.

◆ To display the Developer tab, use the Customize Ribbon pane in Options.

2 Click the **COM Add-Ins** button.

3 Select the check box next to the add-in you want to load, or clear the check box you want to unload.

TROUBLE? *If the add-in is not available in the list, click Add, locate and select the add-in you want, and then click OK.*

4 To remove the selected add-in, click **Remove**.

5 Click **OK**.

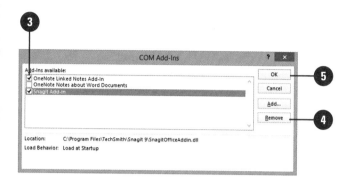

Did You Know?

You can can get more information about COM online. Visit *www.microsoft.com/com.*

You can open an add-in dialog box from Word Options. Click the File tab, click Options, click Add-ins, click the Manage list arrow, click Word Add-ins or COM Add-ins, and then click Go.

See Also

See "Working with the Ribbon and Toolbars" on page 6 for information on adding a button to the Quick Access Toolbar.

See "Setting Developer Options" on page 447 for information on displaying the Developer tab.

For Your Information

Dealing with an Add-in Security Alert

When there is a problem with an add-in, Word disables it to protect the program and your data. When a problem does occur, a security alert dialog box appears, displaying information about the problem and options you can choose to fix or ignore it. You can choose an option to help protect you from unknown content (recommended), enable this add-in for this session only, or enable all code published by this publisher. See "Setting Add-in Security Options" on page 353 for more information about setting options that trigger the Add-in security alert.

Enhancing a Document with VBA

Office applications like Word, Access, Excel, PowerPoint, and Visio share a common programming language: Visual Basic for Applications (VBA). With VBA, you can develop applications that combine tools from these Office products, as well as other programs that support VBA. Because of the language's power and flexibility, programmers often prefer to use VBA to customize their Office applications.

Introducing the Structure of VBA

VBA is an object-oriented programming language because, when you develop a VBA application, you manipulate objects. An object can be anything within your document, such as a shape, text box, picture, or table. Even Word itself is considered an object. Objects can have properties that describe the object's characteristics. Text boxes, for example, have the Font property, which describes the font Word uses to display the text. A text box also has properties that indicate whether the text is bold or italic.

Objects also have methods—actions that can be done to the object. Deleting and inserting are examples of methods available with a record object. Closely related to methods are events. An event is a specific action that occurs on or with an object. Clicking a button initiates the Click event for the button object. VBA also refers to an event associated with an object as an event property. The form button, for example, has the Click event property. You can use VBA to either respond to an event or to initiate an event.

Writing VBA Code

A VBA programmer types the statements, or **code**, that make up the VBA program. Those statements follow a set of rules, called **syntax**, that govern how commands are formulated. For example, to change the property of a particular object, the command follows the general form:

Object.Property = Expression

Where **Object** is the name of a VBA object, **Property** is the name of a property that object has, and **Expression** is a value that will be assigned to the property. The following statement turns on track changes in the active document:

ActiveDocument.TrackRevisions = TRUE

You can use Office and VBA's online Help to learn about specific object and property names. If you want to apply a method to an object, the syntax is:

Object.Method arg1, arg2, ...

Where **Object** is the name of a VBA object, **Method** is the name of method that can be applied to that object, and **arg1**, **arg2**, ... are optional **arguments** that provide additional information for the method operation. For example, to clear the Find and Replace formatting, you could use the following method:

Selection.Find.ClearFormatting
Selection.Find.Replacement.ClearFormatting

Working with Procedures

You don't run VBA commands individually. Instead they are organized into groups of commands called **procedures**. A procedure either performs an action or calculates a value. Procedures that perform actions are called **Sub procedures**. You can run a Sub procedure directly, or Office can run it for you in response to an event, such as clicking a button or opening a form. A Sub procedure initiated by an event is also called an **event procedure**. Office provides event procedure templates to help you easily create procedures for common events. Event procedures are displayed in each object's event properties list.

A procedure that calculates a value is called a **function procedure**. By creating function procedures you can create your own function library, supplementing the Office collection of built-in functions. You can access these functions from within the Expression Builder, making it easy for them to be used over and over again.

Working with Modules

Procedures are collected and organized within **modules**. Modules generally belong to two types: class modules and standard modules. A **class module** is associated with a specific object. In more advanced VBA programs, the class module can be associated with an object created by the user. **Standard modules** are not associated with specific objects, and they can be run from anywhere within a database. This is usually not the case with class modules. Standard modules are listed in the Database window on the Modules Object list.

Building VBA Projects

A collection of modules is further organized into a **project**. Usually a project has the same name as a document. You can create projects that are not tied into any specific document, saving them as Word add-ins that provide extra functionality to Word.

Using the Visual Basic Editor

You create VBA commands, procedures, and modules in Office's **Visual Basic Editor**. This is the same editor used by Word and other Office programs. Thus, you can apply what you learn about creating programs in Word to these other applications.

The Project Explorer

One of the fundamental tools in the Visual Basic Editor is the Project Explorer. The **Project Explorer** presents a hierarchical view of all of the projects and modules currently open in Word, including standard and class modules.

The Modules Window

You write all of your VBA code in the **Modules** window. The Modules window acts as a basic text editor, but it includes several tools to help you write error-free codes. Word also provides hints as you write your code to help you avoid syntax errors.

The Object Browser

There are hundreds of objects available to you. Each object has a myriad of properties, methods, and events. Trying to keep track of all of them is daunting, but the Visual Basic Editor supplies the **Object Browser**, which helps you examine the complete collection of objects, properties, and methods available for a given object.

Viewing the Visual Basic Editor

The Project Explorer displays a hierarchical list of all open projects and modules.

The Modules window allows you to enter VBA commands.

A VBA statement

VBA projects

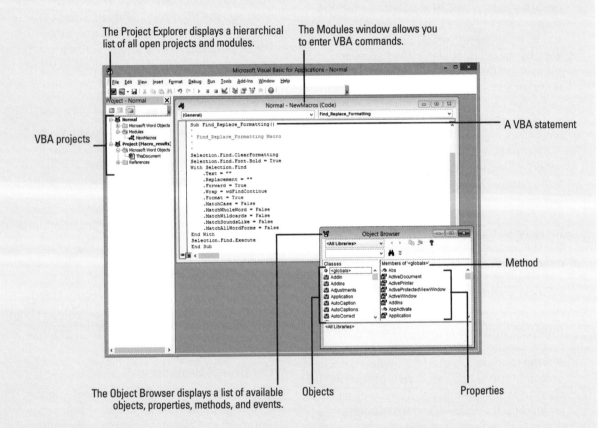

The Object Browser displays a list of available objects, properties, methods, and events.

Objects

Properties

Method

Setting Developer Options

The Developer tab is a specialized Ribbon that you can use to access developer controls, write code, or create macros. You can set an option in the Customize Ribbon pane in Word Options to show or hide the Developer tab. As a developer, you can also set an option to show errors in your user interface customization code.

Set Developer Options

1. Click the **File** tab, and then click **Options**.

2. In the left pane, click **Customize Ribbon**.

3. Select the **Developer** check box to display the Developer tab.

4. In the left pane, click **Advanced**.

5. Select the **Show add-in user interface errors** check box.

6. Click **OK**.

Understanding How Macros Automate Your Work

To complete many tasks in Word, you need to execute a series of commands and actions. To print two copies of a selected text in a document, for example, you need to open the document, select the text, open the Print dialog box, and specify that you want to print two copies. If you often need to complete the same task, you'll find yourself repeatedly taking the same series of steps. It can be tiresome to continually repeat the same commands and actions when you can easily create a mini-program, or macro, that accomplishes all of them with a single command.

Creating a **macro** is easy and requires no programming knowledge on your part. Word simply records the steps you want included in the macro while you use the keyboard and mouse. When you record a macro, Word stores the list of commands with any name

you choose. You can store your macros in the current document or in a new document.

Once a macro is created, you can make modifications to it, add comments so other users will understand its purpose, and test it to make sure it runs correctly.

You can run a macro by choosing the Macro command on the View or Developer tab, or by using a shortcut key or clicking a Quick Access Toolbar button you've assigned to it. From the Macro dialog box, you can run, edit, test, or delete any Word macro on your system, or create a new one.

If you have problems with a macro, you can step through the macro one command at a time, known as **debugging**. Once you identify any errors in the macro, you can edit it.

Indicates the document(s) from which
you can access the selected macro.

When you create a macro, you can add
a description of what the macro does.

Recording a Macro

If you find yourself repeating the same set of steps over and over, you can record a macro. Macros can run several tasks for you at the click of a button. When you turn on the macro recorder, Word records every mouse click and keystroke action you execute until you turn off the recorder. You can even record formatting changes to charts and other objects. Then you can "play," or run, the macro whenever you want to repeat that series of actions—but Word will execute them at a much faster rate. The macro recorder doesn't record in real time, so you can take your time to correctly complete each action.

Record a Macro

1. Click the **Developer** or **View** tab.

2. Click the **Record Macro** button.

   ◆ If you use the View tab, click **View Macros** on the menu.

   TIMESAVER *To quickly start or stop a macro recording, click the Record icon or Stop Record icon on the Status bar (left side).*

3. Type a name for the macro.

4. Assign a shortcut key to use a keystroke combination or assign a button to run the macro.

5. Click the **Store macro in** list arrow, and then select a location.

   ◆ **All Documents**. The macro is available whenever you use Word.

   ◆ **Documents Based On**. The macro is available in documents based on this document.

   ◆ **This Document**. The macro is available only in this document.

6. If you want, type a description.

7. Click **OK**.

8. Execute the commands or actions you want to complete the task.

9. Click the **Stop Recording** button.

Creating a Macro

If you find yourself repeating the same set of steps over and over, or if you need to add new functionality to Word, you could create a macro. If you find it difficult to record a macro, you can create one using a programming language called Microsoft Visual Basic for Applications (VBA). With VBA, you create a macro by writing a script to replay the actions you want. The macros for a particular document are stored in a macro module, which is a collection of Visual Basic codes.

Create a Macro

1. Click the **Developer** or **View** tab.

2. Click the **Macros** button.

   ◆ If you use the View tab, click **View Macros** on the menu.

3. Type a name for the macro.

4. Click the **Macros in** list arrow, and then click **All active templates and documents** or the document to which you want the macro stored.

5. Click **Create**.

   The Microsoft Visual Basic window opens.

6. Click the Module window (if necessary), and then type new Visual Basic commands, or edit existing ones.

   To run the macro, press F5.

7. When you're done, click the **Save** button, click the **File** menu, and then click **Close and Return to Microsoft Word**.

Object Browser helps you insert commands.

Running a Macro

Running a macro is similar to choosing a command in Word. When you record or edit the macro, you have the choice of making it available through a menu command, a keyboard combination, or even a toolbar button. As with other options in Word, your choice depends on your personal preferences—and you can choose to make more than one option available. Where you store a macro when you save it determines its availability later. Macros stored in the Personal Macro document are always available, and macros stored in any other documents are only available when the document is open.

Run a Macro

1. Click the **Developer** or **View** tab.

2. Click the **Macros** button.

   - If you use the View tab, click **View Macros** on the menu.

   TIMESAVER *Click the Macros button on the Status bar.*

3. Click the macro you want to run.

4. Click **Run**.

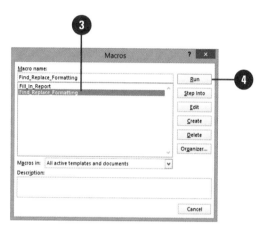

Delete a Macro

1. Click the **Developer** or **View** tab.

2. Click the **Macros** button.

   - If you use the View tab, click **View Macros** on the menu.

3. Click the macro you want to delete.

4. Click **Delete**, and then click **Delete** again to confirm the deletion.

Did You Know?

You can stop a macro. Press Ctrl+Break to stop a macro before it completes its actions.

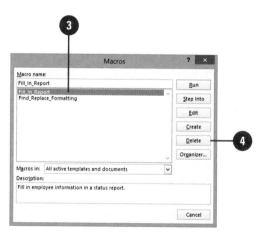

Controlling a Macro

If a macro doesn't work exactly the way you want it to, you can fix the problem using Microsoft Visual Basic for Applications (VBA). VBA allows you to **debug**, or repair, an existing macro so that you change only the actions that aren't working correctly. All macros for a particular document are stored in a macro module, a collection of Visual Basic programming codes that you can copy to other document files. You can view and edit your Visual Basic modules using the Visual Basic editor. By learning Visual Basic you can greatly increase the scope and power of your programs.

Debug a Macro Using Step Mode

1 Click the **Developer** or **View** tab.

2 Click the **Macros** button.

◆ If you use the View tab, click **View Macros** on the menu.

3 Click the macro you want to debug.

4 Click **Step Into**.

The Microsoft Visual Basic window opens.

5 Click the **Debug** menu, and then click **Step Into** (or press F8) to proceed through each action.

◆ You can also use other commands like **Step Over** and **Step Out** to debug the code.

6 When you're done, click the **Save** button, click the **File** menu, and then click **Close and Return to Microsoft Word**.

7 Click **OK** to stop the debugger.

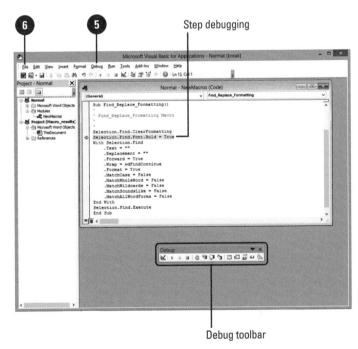

Step debugging

Debug toolbar

Did You Know?

You can display the Debug toolbar. In the Visual Basic editor, click the View menu, point to Toolbars, and then click Debug.

Edit a Macro

1. Click the **Developer** or **View** tab.

2. Click the **Macros** button.

   ◆ If you use the View tab, click **View Macros** on the menu.

3. To open a macro, click the macro you want to change, and then click the **View Code** button.

4. Click the Module window containing the Visual Basic code for your macro.

5. Type new Visual Basic commands, or edit the commands already present.

6. Click the **Save** button, and then click the program **Close** button.

Copy a Macro Module to Another Document

1. Open the document files you want to copy the macro from and to.

2. Click the **Developer** tab.

3. Click the **Visual Basic** button.

4. Click the **View** menu, and then click **Project Explorer**.

5. Drag the module you want to copy from the source document to the destination document.

6. Click the **Save** button, and then click the program **Close** button.

Module VBA code

Properties

Adding a Digital Signature to a Macro Project

If you want to add a digital signature to a document with a macro, you need to add it using the Visual Basic editor. If you open a document that contains a signed macro project with a problem, the macro is disabled by default and the Message Bar appears to notify you of the potential problem. You can click Options or Enable Content in the Message Bar to view or use it. For more details, you can click Show Signature Details to view certificate. If a digital signature has problems—it's expired, not issued by a trusted publisher, or the document has been altered—the certificate information image contains a red X. When there's a problem, contact the signer to have them fix it, or save the document to a trusted location, where you can run the macro without security checks.

Sign a Macro Project

1. Open the document that contains the macro project, and then click the **Developer** tab.

2. Click the **Visual Basic** button to open the Visual Basic window.

3. Click the **Tools** menu, and then click **Digital Signature**.

4. Click **Choose**.

5. Select a certificate in the list.

6. To view a certificate, click **View Certificate** or a link, and then click **OK**.

7. Click **OK**.

8. Click **OK** again.

9. Click the **Save** button, and then click the program **Close** button.

Assigning a Macro to a Toolbar or Ribbon

After you create a macro, you can add the macro to the Ribbon or Quick Access Toolbar for easy access. When you create a macro, the macro name appears in the list of available commands when you customize the Ribbon or Quick Access Toolbar in Word Options. When you point to a macro button on the Ribbon or Quick Access Toolbar, a ScreenTip appears, displaying Macro: *document name!macro name*.

Assign a Macro to a Toolbar or Ribbon

1. Click the **File** tab, click **Options**, and then click **Quick Access Toolbar** or **Customize Ribbon**.

2. Click the **Choose commands from** list arrow, and then click **Macros**.

3. Click the **Customize Quick Access Toolbar** and then click **For all documents (default)**, or click the **Customize the Ribbon** list arrow, and then click **For All Tabs**.

4. Click the macro you want to add (left column).

5. Click **Add**.

6. Click the **Move Up** and **Move Down** arrow buttons to arrange the commands in the order you want them to appear.

7. Click **Modify** or **Rename**.

8. Type a name for the button.

9. Click an icon in the symbol list.

10. Click **OK**.

11. Click **OK**.

See Also

See "Working with the Ribbon and Toolbars" on page 6 and "Accessing Commands Not in the Ribbon" on page 430 for information on using the Quick Access Toolbar.

Macro button

Saving a Document with Macros

Macros are created using Visual Basic for Applications (VBA) code. If you add a macro to a document, you need to save it with a file name extension that ends with an "m", either Word Macro-Enabled Document (.docm), or Word Macro-Enabled Template (.dotm). If you try to save a document containing a macro with a file name extension that ends with an "x" (such as .docx or .dotx), Word displays an alert message, restricting the operation. These Word file types are designated to be VBA code-free.

Save a Document with Macros

1. Click the **File** tab, and then click **Save As**.

2. Click **Computer**, and then click **Browse** or a recent folder.

3. Click the **Save in** list arrow, and then click the drive or folder where you want to save the file.

4. Type a document file name.

5. If necessary, click the **Save as type** list arrow, and then select the macro format you want:

   ◆ **Word Macro-Enabled Document.** A document (.docm) that contains VBA code.

   ◆ **Word Macro-Enabled Template.** A template (.dotm) that includes preapproved macros.

6. Click **Save**.

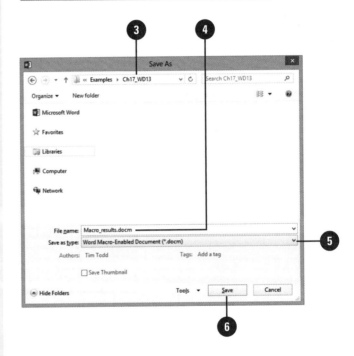

Opening a Document with Macros

When you open a document with a macro, VBA, or other software code, Word displays a security warning to let you know the document might contain potentially harmful code that may harm your computer. If you know and trust the author of the document, you can change security options to enable the macro content and use the document normally. If you don't trust the content, you can continue to block and disable the content and use the document with limited functionality in Protected view. If you don't want a security alert to appear, you can change security settings in the Trust Center in Word Options.

Open a Document with Macros

1. Click the **File** tab, and then click **Open**.

2. Click **Computer**, and then click **Browse** or a recent folder.

3. If necessary, click the **File as type** list arrow, and then the document type that contains a macro.

4. If the file is located in another folder, click the **Look in** list arrow, and then navigate to the file.

5. Click the document with macros you want to open, and then click **Open**.

6. Click the **File** tab, click **Info**, click the **Enable Content** button, and then click **Advanced Options**. To enable all content (make trusted), click **Enable All Content** on the menu.

   ◆ You can also click **Enable Content** in the Message Bar with the Security Warning.

7. If you trust the document content, click the **Enable content for this session** option to use it. If you don't trust it, click the **Help protect me from unknown content (recommended)** option to block and disable the macros.

8. Click **OK**.

6 Enable Content in the Message Bar

Using Content Controls to Create Documents

Forms are an easy way for you to interact with users of your documents, either online or in print, and gain information and feedback from them in the process. Controls—either Content, Form, and ActiveX—are predefined fields or set of fields that contain information you can use throughout a document. Word includes many different types: text boxes for typed entries, date picker, combo boxes, drop-down lists, and check boxes. The fields display information you provided in Document Properties or a placeholder, which you can fill in. After you insert the fields you want, you can change field properties to customize the form. Word uses Content controls and Quick Parts as part of the program to build page covers, headers and footers, pull quotes, and side bar to name a few.

Add Controls to a Document

1. Click the **Developer** tab.

2. Position the insertion point where you want to insert a control.

3. Use the buttons in the Controls group to insert controls.

   - **Rich Text or Text.** Click to insert a text box where you can enter text.

   - **Picture.** Click to insert a placeholder where you can insert a picture.

   - **Combo Box.** Click to insert a combo box control.

   - **Drop Down List.** Click to insert a drop down list control where you can select from a list.

   - **Date Picker.** Click to insert a control to select a date from a pop-up calendar.

   - **Building Block Gallery.** Click to insert a Quick Part control where you can specify the information you want.

   - **Legacy Tools.** Click to select form and ActiveX controls.

   - **Group.** Select contents you want to protect; prevents changes to document.

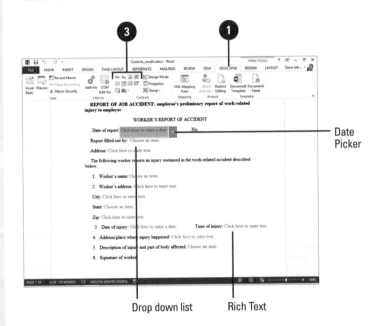

Date Picker

Drop down list   Rich Text

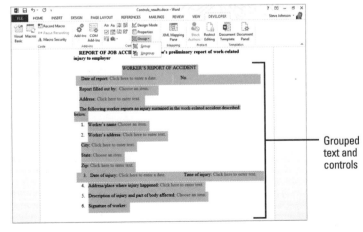

Grouped text and controls

Set or Change Control Properties

① Click the **Developer** tab.

② Select the control you want to set or change properties.

③ Click the **Properties** button.

④ Select the new options you want for the form field.

⑤ Click **OK**.

Did You Know?

You can prevent any changes to a document except content controls. Open the document with content controls, click the Developer tab, select the text you don't want to get changed, click the Group button, and then click Group. You can not change any of the grouped text. However, you can enter text or specify options using the content controls. To remove the protection, click the Group button, and then click Ungroup.

You can protect a form or document. Click the Restrict Editing button on the Developer tab, and then Restrict Formatting and Editing to prevent users of the form from being able to edit its content (not their answers, but the questions and choices themselves).

For Your Information

Mapping Content Controls to XML Data

You can map most content controls to elements in XML data attached to a document. XML data is stored in document parts using the Office XML file formats; for Word the XML file format is .docx. Document parts help define sections of the overall contents of the file. The file format consists of many different types of document parts, including custom XML data part. All document content associated with an XML element maps to data in a custom XML data part. This separation of the XML from the document formatting and layout—known as the Open Packaging Convention—makes it easier to access data. To view the document parts (which is a compressed zip package), add **.zip** to the end of the document name after the .docx, and then double-click the renamed file. The contents of the file appear, displaying a tree structure of individual document parts. You can move the custom.xml document part out of the zip file to open and modify it. You can attach the XML file to other Office documents to reuse data. When you're done changing the XML file, you can move it back into the zip file and use it with the original file.

Inserting ActiveX Controls

An ActiveX control is a software component that adds functionality to an existing program. An ActiveX control is really just another term for an OLE (Object Linking and Embedding) object, known as a Component Object Model (COM) object. An ActiveX control supports a customizable, programmatic interface. Word includes several pre-built ActiveX controls on the Developer tab, including a label, text box, command button, image, scroll bar, check box, option button, combo box, list box, and toggle button. To create an ActiveX control, click the Insert button on the Developer tab, click the ActiveX control you want, and then drag to insert it with the size you want. If there is a problem with an ActiveX control, Word disables it to protect the program and your data. When a problem does occur, a security alert dialog box appears, displaying information about the problem and options you can choose to leave it disabled in Protected view or enable it.

Insert ActiveX Controls

1. Display the document where you want to place the ActiveX control.

2. Click the **Developer** tab.

3. Click the **Design Mode** button (highlighted).

4. Click the **Legacy Tools** button arrow, and then click the button with the ActiveX control you want to use.

   See the next page for a list and description of each ActiveX control.

5. Drag (pointer changes to a plus sign) to draw the ActiveX control the size you want.

6. To resize the control, drag a resize handle (circles) to the size you want.

7. To add Visual Basic code to the ActiveX control, right-click the control, click **View Code**, or to change display properties, click the **Properties** button. To exit, click the **Save** and **Close** buttons.

8. Click the **Design Mode** button (not highlighted) to exit.

For Your Information

Using Form Controls

Form controls are objects that users can interact with to enter or manipulate data. For example, you can add a Check box control to your document so that users can turn an option on and off. You can select a control from the Developer tab and drag to create the control directly on your document just like an ActiveX control. For an example on using form controls, see project downloads for Office 2013 On Demand available on the web at *www.perspection.com*.

Deal with an ActiveX Control Security Alert

1. Click the **File** tab, and then click **Open**.

2. Click **Computer**, and then click **Browse** or a recent folder.

3. Click the **File as type** list arrow, and then click the document type that contains the ActiveX control.

4. If the file is located in another folder, click the **Look in** list arrow, and then navigate to the file.

5. Click the document with the ActiveX control you want to open, and then click **Open**.

6. Click the **File** tab, click **Info**, click the **Enable Content** button, and then click **Advanced Options**. To enable all content (make trusted), click **Enable All Content** on the menu.

   ◆ You can also click **Enable Content** in the Message Bar with the Security Warning.

7. If you trust the document content, click the **Enable content for this session** option to use it. If you don't trust it, click the **Help protect me from unknown content (recommended)** option to block and disable the macros.

8. Click **OK**.

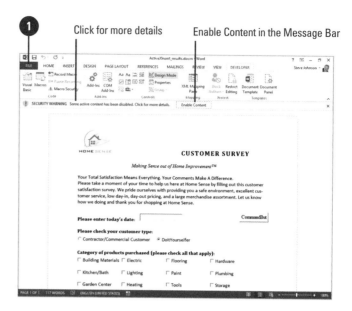

Click for more details   Enable Content in the Message Bar

See Also

See "Setting ActiveX Security Options" on page 354 for more information about setting options that trigger the ActiveX security alert.

See "Setting ActiveX Control Properties" on page 463 for more information about setting ActiveX display properties.

Using ActiveX Controls

ActiveX Controls

Button	Name	Description
A	Label	This button creates a text label. Because the other controls already include a corresponding label, use this button to create labels that are independent of other controls.
abl	Text Box	This button creates a text box in which the user can enter text (or numbers). Use this control for objects assigned to a text or number data type.
⬍	Spin Button	This button creates a box in which the user can click arrows to increase or decrease numbers in a box. Use this control assigned to a number data type.
▭	Command Button	This button creates a button that runs a macro or Microsoft Visual Basic function when the user clicks the button in the form.
🖼	Image	This button inserts a frame, in which you can insert a graphic in your form. Use this control when you want to insert a graphic, such as clip art or a logo.
▲▼	Scroll Bar	This button creates a scroll bar pane in which the user can enter text (or numbers) in a scrollable text box. Use this control or objects assigned to a text or number data type.
☑	Check Box	This button creates a check box that allows a user to make multiple yes or no selections. Use this control for fields assigned to the yes/no data type.
◉	Option Button	This button creates an option button (also known as a radio button) that allows the user to make a single selection from at least two choices. Use this control for fields assigned to the yes/no data type.
▦	Combo Box	This button creates a combo box in which the user has the option to enter text or select from a list of options. You can enter your own options in the list, or you can display options stored in another table.
▤	List Box	This button creates a list box that allows a user to select from a list of options. You can enter your own options in the list, or can have another table provide a list of options.
▣	Toggle Button	This button creates a button that allows the user to make a yes or no selection by clicking the toggle button. Use this control for fields assigned to the yes/no data type.
🛠	More Controls	Click to display other controls, such as Adobe Acrobat Control for ActiveX, Microsoft Forms 2.0, Microsoft InfoPath controls, and Microsoft web Browser.

Setting ActiveX Control Properties

Every ActiveX control has properties, or settings, that determine its appearance and function. You can open a property sheet that displays all the settings for that control in alphabetic or category order directly from Word. The ActiveX controls appear in the Properties window in two columns: the left column displays the name of the control, and the right column displays the current value or setting for the control. When you select either column, a list arrow appears in the right column, allowing you to select the setting you want. After you set properties, you can add VBA code to a module to make it perform.

Set ActiveX Control Properties

1. Click the **Developer** tab.

2. Click the **Design Mode** button (highlighted).

3. Select the control whose properties you want to modify.

4. Click the **Properties** button.

5. To switch controls, click the **Controls** list arrow (at the top), and then select the one you want.

6. Click the **Alphabetic** or **Categorized** tab to display the control properties so you can find the ones you want.

7. Click the property box for the property you want to modify, and then do one of the following:

   ◆ Type the value or information you want to use, such as the control name.

   ◆ If the property box contains a list arrow, click the arrow and then click a value in the list.

   ◆ If a property box contains a dialog button (...), click it to open a dialog box to select options or insert an object, such as a picture.

8. When you're done, click the **Close** button on the Properties window.

9. Click the **Design Mode** button (not highlighted) to exit.

Adding VBA Code to an ActiveX Control

After you add controls and set properties, you can add VBA code to a module to determine how the controls respond to user actions. All controls have a predefined set of events. For example, a command button has a Click event that occurs when the user clicks the button. When you select a control in Design Mode and then click the View Code button, the Visual Basic Editor opens with a Code window, displaying the start of a procedure that runs when the event occurs. The top of the Code window displays the active object and event procedure. The Object list displays the ActiveX control, such as *CommandButton1*, and the Procedure list displays the trigger event, such as *Click*.

Add VBA Code to an ActiveX Control

1. Click the **Developer** tab.

2. Click the **Design Mode** button (highlighted).

3. Select the control to which you want to add VBA code.

4. Right-click the control, and then click **View Code**.

   The Visual Basic Editor window opens.

5. To show the Properties window, click the **Properties window** button.

6. To help with scripting commands, click the **Object Browser** button on the toolbar.

7. Click in the Code window between the beginning and ending line of the procedure, and then type VBA code to perform the task you want.

   The Object list is set to *CommandButton1*, and the Procedure list is set to *Click*.

8. When you're done, click the **Save** button on the toolbar.

9. Click the program **Close** button.

10. Click the **Design Mode** button (not highlighted) to exit.

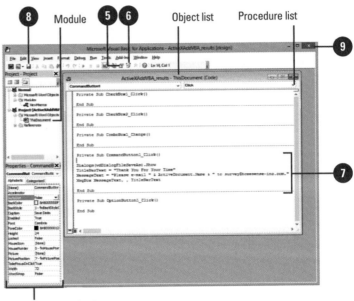

Properties for the ActiveX Control

Playing a Movie Using an ActiveX Control

Although you cannot insert a Flash movie into a Word document, you can play one using an ActiveX control and the Flash player. Before you can use the control, the ActiveX control and Flash player need to be installed on your computer. You can get the ActiveX control at *http://activex.microsoft.com/activex/activex/*. To play the Flash (.swf) movie, you add the Shockwave Flash Object ActiveX control to the document and create a link to the file. If a movie doesn't play, check ActiveX security options in the Trust Center in Word Options.

Play a Flash Movie

1 Save the Flash file to a Flash movie file (.swf) using the Flash software.

2 Click the **Developer** tab.

3 Click the **Design Mode** button (highlighted).

4 Click the **Legacy Tools** button, and then click the **More Controls** button.

5 Click **Shockwave Flash Object**.

6 Click **OK**.

7 Drag to draw the movie control.

8 Right-click the Shockwave Flash Object, and then click **Properties**.

9 Click the **Alphabetic** tab.

10 Click the **Movie** property, click in the value column next to Movie, type full path and file name (c:\MyFolder\Movie.swf), or the URL to the Flash movie you want.

11 To set specific options, choose any of the following:

◆ To play the file automatically when the document appears, set the Playing property to True.

◆ To embed the Flash file, set the EmbedMovie property to True.

12 When you're done, click the **Close** button.

13 Click the **Design Mode** button (not highlighted) to exit.

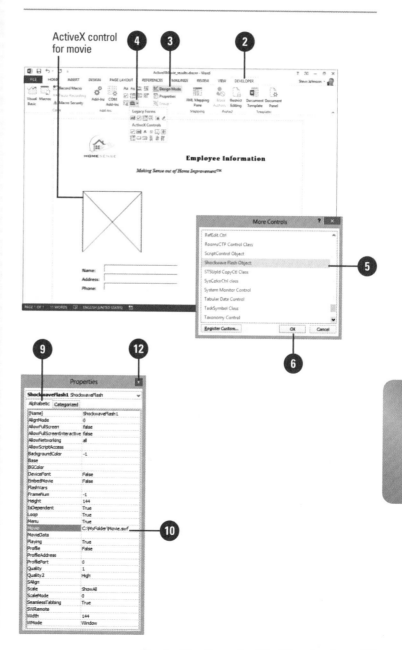

ActiveX control for movie

Changing the Document Information Panel

The Document Information Panel helps you manage and track document property information—also known as metadata—such as title, author, subject, keywords, category, and status. The Document Information Panel displays an XML-based mini-form using an InfoPath Form Template (.xsn) file developed in Microsoft InfoPath. By using an XML InfoPath form, you can create your own form templates to edit the document property data and perform data validation.

Select a Document Information Panel Template

1. Click the **Developer** tab.

2. Click the **Document Panel** button.

3. Click **Browse**, locate and select the custom template you want, and then click **Open**.

   ◆ **URL.** Short for Uniform Resource Locator. The address of resources on the web.

   http://www.perspection.com/ index.htm

   ◆ **UNC.** Short for Uniform or Universal Naming Convention. A format for specifying the location of resources on a local-area network (LAN).

   \\server-name\shared-resource-pathname

   ◆ **URN.** Short for Uniform Resource Name.

4. Click the **Display by default** list arrow, and then select the default properties you want.

5. Select the **Always show Document Information Panel on document open and initial save** check box.

6. Click **OK**.

Working Online with Office Documents

Introduction

Instead of storing and working on Office documents on your desktop, you can store them on the web and work on them with an Office Web App. An Office Web App allows you to work with an Office document in a web browser. The process of using the web instead of a desktop as a base of operation is known as **cloud computing**. SkyDrive and SharePoint are two types of cloud computing sites, where you can store and share information. SkyDrive is a free service provided by Microsoft, which is available at *www.skydrive.com* with a Microsoft account, while SharePoint is web server software created by Microsoft.

When you store an Office document on SkyDrive or on a Microsoft SharePoint server configured with Office Web Apps, such as Office 365 SharePoint, a subscription-based service provided by Microsoft, you can view or edit the document in a web browser using the same look and feel as an Office 2013 program. To make storing files on SkyDrive or SharePoint quick and easy, Office 2013 programs provide command on the Save As screen on the File tab for you to save Office documents directly to a SkyDrive or SharePoint folder.

If you have a Windows Phone, Apple iOS (iPhone and iPad), BlackBerry, or Android, you can use your web browser or Office Web Apps to work with your Office documents from anywhere. You can view and edit Office documents stored on your phone, sent to you as e-mail attachments, or stored on a SkyDrive or SharePoint site. Since the files are synced online, the changes you make on your mobile device are available on your desktop too.

What You'll Do

Work Online with SharePoint and SkyDrive

Sign in to SharePoint or SkyDrive

Save and Open on SharePoint or SkyDrive

Access Documents on SharePoint

Sync Documents on SharePoint

Share Documents on SkyDrive

Access Documents on SkyDrive

Manage Documents on SkyDrive

Download or Upload Documents on SkyDrive

Create Office Documents on SkyDrive

Send Links to Documents on SkyDrive

Compare the Office Desktop App to the Web App

Work with Office Web Apps

Save or Print Documents in Office Web Apps

Co-author Documents with Office Web Apps

Block Co-authoring Documents

Working Online with SharePoint and SkyDrive

Office 2013 is integrated to work with online services (**New!**) to make it easier for you to save and open Office documents on other devices and share Office documents with others. Office provides two main online services: SkyDrive and SharePoint. **SkyDrive** is a personal cloud storage and sharing system on the web provided as a free service by Microsoft at *www.skydrive.com* with a Microsoft account. You can store and share information, such as contacts, e-mail (using hotmail), photos, and files. Microsoft **SharePoint** server is an organizational cloud storage, sharing, and tracking system with customizable apps hosted on the web by an organization. Instead of setting up your own SharePoint site, you can use **Office 365**, a subscription-based Microsoft web site with SharePoint services that allows you to take advantage of expanded cloud capabilities.

Connecting to a SkyDrive or SharePoint Site

You can access and connect to a SkyDrive and SharePoint site by using your web browser or any Office 2013 program. For SkyDrive, you can also use a stand-alone app, such as SkyDrive (Win 8) or SkyDrive for Windows (Win 7 or 8)—an app downloaded from the SkyDrive site that allows you to access files from Windows Explorer.

In order to connect to SkyDrive or SharePoint from Office, you need to sign in and connect with your account. When you set up Office 2013, it requests a Microsoft account to work with SkyDrive and other online services. However, you can add other accounts for Office 365 SharePoint and other online services, such as Facebook, Twitter, Linkedin, and Flickr. To access account settings in Office, click the user name (upper-right corner of any Office program), and then click an account option, or click the File tab, and then click Accounts. You can add, switch, or modify accounts or sign out entirely.

SkyDrive or SkyDrive Pro?

When you install Office 2013, you also get a helpful tool called SkyDrive Pro (**New!**). The name is similar to SkyDrive, however it works with SharePoint, not SkyDrive personal. A SharePoint site includes its own SkyDrive as well as other Document Libraries. With SkyDrive Pro, you can connect to and synchronize the contents of a SkyDrive or Document Library on a SharePoint or Office 365 site with a folder on your desktop. SkyDrive Pro performs the same function for SharePoint sites as the stand-alone SkyDrive apps—SkyDrive (Win 8) or SkyDrive for Windows (Win 7 or 8)—do for a personal SkyDrive.

Using a SkyDrive or SharePoint Site from Office

In Office 2013, you can save and open documents directly to a SkyDrive or SharePoint site. With your Office documents on a SkyDrive or SharePoint site, you can do a lot of things. You can sync the files from the SkyDrive or SharePoint site to your desktop or other devices, such as a tablet or mobile phone for easy access from anywhere. You can view or edit Office documents online from an Office program or Office Web App, and get access to files even when you're offline. You can share a document with other people using e-mail or social networks (**New!**) and even work on the same Office document at the same time with more than one person (**New!**).

Using Office 365

Office 365 is a subscription-based Microsoft web site with SharePoint services that provides cloud-based storage and sync capabilities to keep your Office content up-to-date everywhere. Office 365 provides web-based collaboration and sharing that allows you to work with Outlook mail, calendar, people, newsfeed, SkyDrive, and SharePoint Team sites and public web sites. Newsfeed lets you follow documents, sites and people to track what they are doing. You can also collaborate with instant messaging, video/audio conferencing and online meetings with Lync. In Outlook, you can access Site Mailboxes (**New!**) with e-mail and documents in the same place. You can access Office 365 at *www.office365.com*, where you can sign up for a subscription or trial.

Using Office Web Apps

An Office Web App allows you to work with an Office document in a web browser. When you store an Office document on a SkyDrive or SharePoint site, you can view or edit the document in a web browser using the same look and feel as an Office 2013 program, although some what limited in functionality. Office Web Apps provide a web-based version of Word, Excel, PowerPoint, and OneNote (**New!**). For a SharePoint site, Access and Lync are also available. You can view Office documents in a web browser using a Web App or edit the document in the desktop Office program.

Using Office on Mobile Devices

If you have a Windows Phone, Apple iOS (iPhone and iPad), BlackBerry, or Android, you can use your web browser or Office Web Apps to work with your Office documents from any-

where. You can view and edit Office documents stored on your phone, sent to you as e-mail attachments, or stored on a SkyDrive or SharePoint site. Since the files are synced online, the changes you make on your mobile device are available on your desktop too.

Using Office Co-authoring

If you're working on a SharePoint site, you can have multiple authors work on the same Office document from a Document Library at the same time without intruding on one another's work or locking out other users. When multiple authors are working on the same document, you can see who is editing the document and where they are working in the Status bar or on the File tab Info screen. Any changes made by other authors get merged into the main document where you can review and modify them. You can co-author Office documents using Word, Excel, PowerPoint, and Visio Professional (**New!**) as well as Word Web App (**New!**) and PowerPoint App (**New!**), which include support for comments and revision marks (**New!**).

Word Web App in a web browser

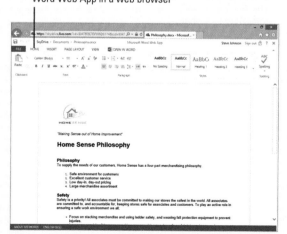

Signing in to SharePoint or SkyDrive

Office provides access to two main online services: SkyDrive and SharePoint. SkyDrive personal is a free storage and sharing service provided by Microsoft. SharePoint is a web-hosted server for storage, sharing, and tracking documents. Instead of setting up your own SharePoint site, you can use Office 365 SharePoint, a subscription-based service provided by Microsoft. Before you can work with Office documents on SkyDrive or SharePoint, you need to create a Microsoft account for SkyDrive or a site account for SharePoint. When you set up Office 2013, it requests a Microsoft account to work with online services, such as SkyDrive. If you already have a Hotmail, Messenger, Windows Live, or Xbox Live account, you can use it as your Microsoft account. To get a SharePoint account, you need to contact your site administrator or sign up for Office 365. After you establish accounts, you need to add them to Office in order to work seamlessly with the online services (**New!**).

Sign in to Office 365 SharePoint

1. Open your web browser, and go to *www.office365.com*.

2. If you don't have an account, click the link to get a free trial. Follow the online instructions to create the account.

3. Click the **Sign in** link.

4. Enter your User ID and Password for your Office 365 account.

5. Select the **Remember me** and/or **Keep me signed in** check boxes to speed up sign in process in the future. However, it allows others who have access to your computer to sign in.

6. Click **Sign in**.

   Your Office 365 SharePoint site appears in your web browser.

7. To sign out, click the Account Name on the toolbar, and then click **Sign out**.

Sign in to SkyDrive

1. Open your web browser, and go to *www.skydrive.com*.

2. If you don't have a Microsoft account, click the link to get a free account. Follow the online instructions to create the account.

3. Enter you Microsoft account user name and password.

4. Select the **Keep me signed in** check box to speed up sign in process in the future. However, it allows others who have access to your computer to sign in.

5. Click **Sign in**.

   Your SkyDrive site appears in your web browser.

6. To sign out, click the Account Name on the toolbar, and then click **Sign out**.

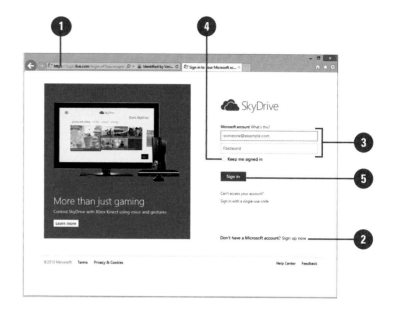

Add Online Storage Services

1. Click the **File** tab, and then click **Account (New!)**.

2. Click **Add a service (New!)**, and then point to **Storage**.

3. Click **Office 365 SharePoint** or **SkyDrive**, and then follow the on-screen connection instructions to sign in and add the service.

4. Click the **Back** button to exit the File tab.

Saving and Opening on SharePoint or SkyDrive

Office is integrated to work with online services (**New!**) to make it easier for you to save and open Office documents on other devices and share Office documents with others. With your Microsoft or SharePoint account, you can save Office documents directly to a SkyDrive (**New!**), a cloud-based online storage system, or Office 365, a Microsoft web site with SharePoint services. When you save documents online, you can have multiple authors work on the same Office document from the server at the same time (**New!**). Before you can use these online services, you need to add (connect) them to Office 2013. During the process, you'll need to provide a user name and password to establish a connection.

Save an Office Document to SharePoint or SkyDrive

1. Create or open an Office document.

2. Click the **File** tab, and then click **Save As**.

3. Click the SkyDrive or SharePoint name.

   ◆ **Sign in.** If prompted, sign-in to your account.

4. Click **Browse** or a recent folder.

5. Navigate to the location where you want to save the file.

6. Type a document file name.

7. Click the **Save as type** list arrow, and then click **<Program> <Document>**, such as PowerPoint Presentation, Word Document, or Excel Workbook.

8. Click **Save**.

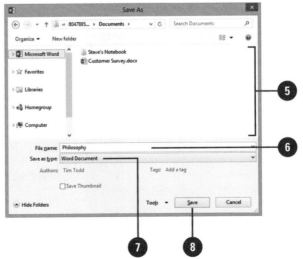

Open an Office Document from SharePoint or SkyDrive

1. Click the **File** tab, and then click **Open**.

2. Click the SkyDrive or SharePoint name.

3. Click **Browse** or a recent folder.

4. Navigate to the location where you want to open the file, and then select the Office file.

5. Click **Open**.

Did You Know?

You can add a place for easy access later. In the Open or Save As screen, click Add a Place, click Office 365 SharePoint or SkyDrive, and then follow the on-screen connection instructions.

Office 365 SharePoint

Accessing Documents on SharePoint

Any Office document that resides on SharePoint (**New!**) can be accessed from any computer or device that has an Internet connection. You can access Office documents on SharePoint using your web browser or File Explorer on your desktop. In your web browser, you can navigate to a document and then open it in an Office Web App. An Office Web App provides a subset of the features in the desktop version. In your desktop, you can open File Explorer, navigate to a document in a SharePoint Document Library or SkyDrive Pro (**New!**), and then open it in the Office Desktop App. SkyDrive Pro is SkyDrive on SharePoint, which is separate and different from SkyDrive personal.

Access SharePoint in a Web Browser

1. Open your web browser, go to SharePoint Team Site web address or *www.office365.com*, and then sign in.

2. Navigate to the SharePoint or SkyDrive folders:

   ◆ **SharePoint.** Click **Sites**, click **Team Site**, and then click a library.

   ◆ **SkyDrive.** Click **SkyDrive**.

3. Click a folder icon to navigate to the folder with the Office document.

4. To navigate back to a previous location, click a navigation or Home link, or click the Back button.

5. To manage files, select the files or folders you want to work with, click the **Files** tab, and then use the toolbar buttons, such as Create Folder, Delete, Upload Document, Download Copy, or Share.

6. To open an Office document in the Office Web App, click the document name link.

   ◆ To edit the document, click the **Edit <document>** menu, and then click **Edit in <program>** or **Edit in <program> Web App**.

   ◆ To exit and return, click the **File** tab, and then click **Exit**.

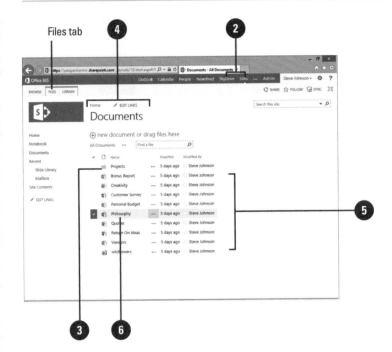

Files tab

Access SharePoint from a Desktop

1. In the Start screen, click the Desktop tile (Win 8).

2. Click the **File Explorer** icon on the taskbar.

3. In the Navigate pane under Favorites, click either of the following:

   ◆ **SharePoint.** Opens the Document Library folders on the SharePoint Team Site.

   ◆ **SkyDrive Pro.** Opens the Documents folder on the SharePoint SkyDrive.

4. Click a folder icon to navigate to the folder with the Office document.

5. To add or remove files, use the following:

   ◆ Add. Copy and paste or drag files to the folder.

   ◆ Remove. Select the files, and then click the **Delete** button on the Home tab.

   The folders are synchronized for both locations, desktop and site.

6. To open an Office document in the Office Desktop App, double-click the document icon.

   ◆ To exit, click the **Close** button.

See Also

See "Syncing Documents on SharePoint" on page 476 for information on setting up to use SkyDrive Pro for SharePoint.

File Explorer in Windows 8

Office 365 SharePoint Document Library

Syncing Documents on SharePoint

With SkyDrive Pro (**New!**), you can connect to and sync the contents of a SkyDrive or Document Library on a SharePoint (Team Site) or Office 365 site with a folder on your desktop. You can set up the sync by entering a site address to the SkyDrive or Document Library or using the SYNC button on the SharePoint or Office 365 site for the open SkyDrive or Document Library. After creating a connection, you'll notice a SkyDrive Pro cloud icon on the notification tray in the taskbar, which you can use to access the desktop folder or modify syncing options. SkyDrive Pro syncs to your user folder by default, though you can change the location. In the Open and Save As dialog boxes in Office programs or in an Explorer window in Windows, you can select the site —SharePoint or SkyDrive Pro—from the Favorites list to access your files.

Set Up or Change SkyDrive Pro for SharePoint

1. Start **SkyDrive Pro 2013**.

   ◆ **Windows 8.** Click the tile on the Start screen.

   ◆ **Windows 7.** Click **Start** on the taskbar, point to **All Programs**, and then point to **Microsoft Office**.

   ◆ **Office 365 Site.** Click **SkyDrive** or **Sites**, display the library to sync, and then click **SYNC** on the toolbar.

   The site is connected to your system or a dialog box opens.

2. Enter the URL address to the SkyDrive or Document library on the SharePoint or Office 365 site.

3. To change the desktop folder, click the **Change** link.

4. Click **Sync Now**.

   After you setup SkyDrive Pro, starting the program opens the folder on your desktop.

Office 365 SharePoint SkyDrive

Click to select a SkyDrive or SharePoint site (Libraries)

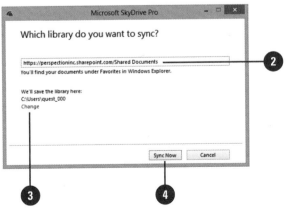

Work with SkyDrive Pro on SharePoint

1. In the desktop, click the **SkyDrive Pro** icon on the desktop taskbar, and then click **Open your SkyDrive Pro folder**.

2. Click **SkyDrive Pro** or **SharePoint** in the Navigate pane under Favorites, and then navigate to the folder you want to use.

3. To add or remove files, use the following:

   ◆ **Add.** Copy and paste or drag files to the folder.

   ◆ **Remove.** Select the files, and then click the **Delete** button on the Home tab.

   The folders are synchronized for both locations, desktop and site.

4. To change syncing options, click the **SkyDrive Pro** icon on the desktop taskbar, and then click any of the following:

   ◆ **Sync a new library.** Use to add a new SharePoint site library.

   ◆ **Sync now.** Use to manually sync files.

   ◆ **Pause syncing.** Use to pause syncing.

   ◆ **View sync programs.** Use to open Office Upload Center.

   ◆ **Stop syncing a folder.** Use to select a folder to stop syncing.

5. To exit SkyDrive Pro, click the **SkyDrive Pro** icon on the desktop taskbar, and then click **Exit**.

See Also

See "Working with Office Tools" on page 432 for information on using Office 2013 Upload Center.

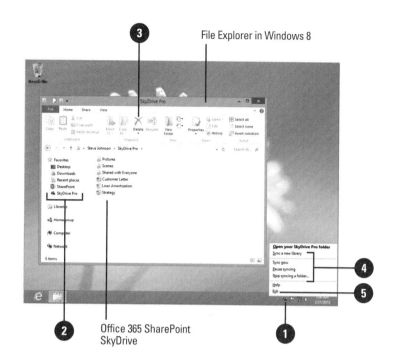

File Explorer in Windows 8

Office 365 SharePoint SkyDrive

Sharing Documents on SkyDrive

After you save an Office document to a SkyDrive (**New!**), you can share it with others. On the Share screen under the File tab, you can use three related options—Invite People (**New!**), Get a Sharing Link (**New!**), and Post to Social Networks (**New!**)—to allow others to access to a SkyDrive document. The Invite People option allows you to send an invitation for other to access the SkyDrive document. The Get a Sharing Link option lets you create links to the document you can share with others. And finally, the Post to Social Networks option lets you make blog posts on your connected social networks, such as Facebook, Linkedin, Twitter, Flickr, or Google.

Invite People to Share a SkyDrive Document

1. Open the Office document you want to share.

2. Click the **File** tab, click **Share**, and then click **Invite People**.

3. If the document is not saved to a SkyDrive, click the **Save To Cloud** button, and then save it to your SkyDrive. If prompted, sign-in to your account.

4. Enter a contact name or click the Address Book button to select a contact.

5. Click the **Access** list arrow, and then click **Can edit** or **Can view**.

6. Enter a message for the invitation.

7. Select or clear the **Require user to sign in before accessing document** check box.

8. Click **Share**.

   An email is sent to the contact with a link to access the SkyDrive document, and contact status appears at the bottom of the Share screen.

   You can click the contacts to send mail or instant messages.

Get a Sharing Link to a SkyDrive Document

1. Open the Office document you want to share.

2. Click the **File** tab, click **Share**, and then click **Get a Sharing Link**.

3. Click the **Create Link** button for View Link or Edit Link.

   A link to the SkyDrive document appears and a status icon appears at the bottom of the Share screen.

4. Select and copy (Ctrl+C) the link, where you can paste it in a place, such as a network, where others can access it.

Post a SkyDrive Document Link to a Social Network

1. In Word and Excel, open the Office document you want to share.

2. Click the **File** tab, click **Share**, and then click **Post to Social Networks**.

   If you're not connected to your social networks, click the **Click here to connect social networks** link to make the connections you want, and then click **Refresh** button.

3. Select the check boxes for the connected social networks you want to post.

4. Click the **Access** list arrow, and then click **Can edit** or **Can view**.

5. Enter a message for the post.

6. Click the **Post** button.

Accessing Documents on SkyDrive

Any Office document that resides on SkyDrive (**New!**) can be accessed from any computer or device that has an Internet connection. You can access Office documents on SkyDrive using your web browser or a SkyDrive app on your desktop or device, including smartphones and tablets. In your web browser, you can navigate to a document and then open it in an Office Web App. An Office Web App provides a subset of the features in the desktop version. In your desktop or device, you can open the SkyDrive app, navigate to a document, and then open it in the Office Desktop App or Office Web App. If you don't have the app on your desktop or device, you can download it at *http://apps.live.com/skydrive*.

Access a SkyDrive in a Web Browser

1. Open your web browser, go to *www.skydrive.com*, and then sign in.

   ◆ You can also go to Windows Live, *www.live.com*, and then click the **SkyDrive** link.

2. Click a folder icon to navigate to the folder with the Office document.

3. To navigate back to a previous location, click a navigation link.

4. To change the view in the current folder, click a view button: **List** or **Tiles**.

5. To sort the documents in the current folder, click the **Sort by:** link, and then click **Name**, **Date modified**, **Date created**, or **Size**.

6. To open an Office document in the Office Web App, click the document icon.

   ◆ To open an Office document in the Office Desktop App, right-click the document, and then click **Open in <program>**.

   ◆ To exit and return, click the **File** tab, and then click **Exit**.

Access a SkyDrive from a Desktop or Device

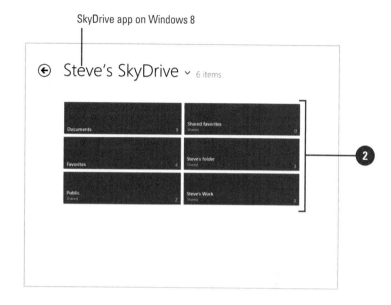

SkyDrive app on Windows 8

1. In the Start screen, click the **SkyDrive** tile.

   ◆ **Download.** You can download the SkyDrive app for devices at *http://apps.live.com/skydrive*.

2. Click a folder icon to navigate to the folder with the Office document.

3. To navigate back to a previous location, click the **Back** button.

4. To change the view in the current folder, click the **Thumbnails** or **Details** button on the App bar.

5. To open an Office document in the Office Desktop App (desktop) or Web App (device), click the document icon.

   ◆ To exit, click the **Close** button (Desktop App or click the **File** tab, and then click **Exit** (Web App).

Did You Know?

You can manage storage space on a SkyDrive. SkyDrive comes with 7 GB of free space that you can use with your Microsoft account. You can view your storage usage and purchase more space if you want under options. In the SkyDrive app (Win 8), click Settings on the Charm bar, and then click Options. In your web browser, click the Settings button, and then click Options.

App bar

Managing Documents on SkyDrive

SkyDrive comes with four default folders: Documents, Favorites, Shared Favorites, and Public. The Documents and Favorites folders are private for your eyes only, while the Shared Favorites and Public folders are viewable by everyone in your SkyDrive (Windows Live) network. If you want to share your documents with others, then you need to add, move, or copy them to the Public folder. Instead of using the default folders, you can create and use your own. If you no longer need a file or folder, you can delete it. You cannot rename a default folder, however, you can rename the ones you create.

Work with SkyDrive Files or Folders in a Web browser

1. Open your web browser, go to *www.skydrive.com*, and then sign in.

2. Navigate to the folder where you want to manage files or folders.

3. To create a folder, click the **Create** list arrow, click **Folder**, type a name for the folder, and then press Enter or click outside the box.

4. Point to a file or folder to display a check box, and then click the check box to select it.

   ◆ You can select multiple files or folders to delete, move, or copy them.

5. To manage the selected file(s) or folder(s), click the **Manage** list arrow, and then click any of the following commands:

   ◆ **Rename.** Type a new name for the folder, and then press Enter or click outside the box.

   ◆ **Delete.** Click **Undo** to cancel it or click the **Close** button.

   ◆ **Move to.** Select the destination folder, and then click **Move**.

   ◆ **Copy to.** Select the destination folder, and then click **Copy**.

New folder

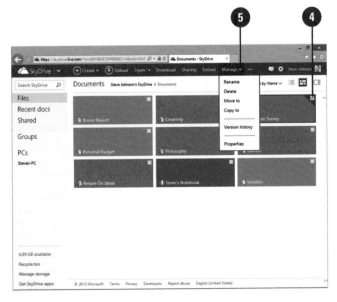

Work with SkyDrive Files or Folders from a Desktop

1. In the Start screen, click the **SkyDrive** tile.

   ◆ **Download.** You can download the SkyDrive app for devices at *http://apps.live.com/skydrive*.

2. Navigate to the folder where you want to manage files or folders.

3. To create a folder, click the **New Folder** on the App bar, type a name for the folder, and then click **Create folder**.

4. Right-click a file or folder to select it.

   ◆ You can select multiple files or folders to delete or move them.

5. To manage the selected file(s) or folder(s), click the **Manage** button on the App bar, and then click any of the following commands:

   ◆ **Rename.** Type a new name for the folder, and then click **Rename**.

   ◆ **Delete.** Click **Delete** to confirm the deletion.

   ◆ **Move.** Select the destination folder, and then click **Move here** on the Apps bar.

SkyDrive app on Windows 8

App bar

Downloading or Uploading Documents on SkyDrive

When you no longer want a document or folder of documents on SkyDrive or you want to share them with others, you can download them to your local drive on your computer. You can download individual files one at a time in their native Office file format, such as .docx, or a multiple selection of documents or an entire folder of documents as a zipped file. The .zip file format compresses all the files in the folder into a single file. You can open a zipped file on Microsoft Windows by double-clicking it and then using an Extract button or by using the Winzip.exe software, which you can download for free from the web at one of many download sites, such as *www.download.com*. If you have one or more documents or entire folder of documents on a local drive, and want to include on your SkyDrive, you can upload them to the cloud site, so you can access them from other computers and devices.

Download or Upload a File or Folder on SkyDrive

1. Open your web browser, go to *www.skydrive.com*, and then sign in.

2. Navigate to the folder where you want to download or upload files or folders.

3. To upload files or folders to the SkyDrive, click the **Upload** button, select the files or folders you want, and then click **Open**.

4. Point to a file or folder to display a check box, and then click the check box to select it. You can select multiple files or folders.

5. To download the selected file(s) or folder(s), click the **Download** button.

6. Click **Save**, navigate to the location where you want to download the file, and then click **Save**.

   The document is downloaded to the specified folder.

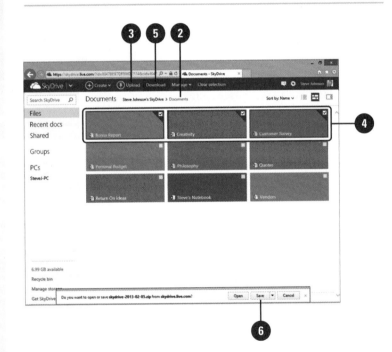

Creating Office Documents on SkyDrive

When you're working on SkyDrive, you create a new Office document. You can create an Excel workbook, a PowerPoint presentation, a Word document, or an OneNote notebook. This option allows you to create a new Office document on a computer that doesn't have the Microsoft Office software. So, if you're working on a different computer while you're on the road that doesn't have the Office programs installed and you need to create a new document to get some work done, you can do it online on SkyDrive.

Create Office Documents on SkyDrive

1. Open your web browser, go to *www.skydrive.com*, and then sign in.

2. Navigate to the folder where you want to create a new Office document.

3. Click the **Create** list arrow, and then click a document option:

   - **Word document.**
   - **Excel workbook.**
   - **PowerPoint presentation.**
   - **OneNote notebook.**

4. Type a name for the document.

5. Click **Create**.

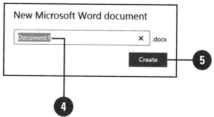

Sending Links to Documents on SkyDrive

After you upload your Office documents to a folder on SkyDrive, you can share access to them with others for review with Office Web Apps. You can share access to individual Office documents or an entire folder on SkyDrive by sending a link in e-mail, posting a link in Twitter, Facebook, LinkedIn or other online services (**New!**), or creating a link (**New!**) and sending it to those you want to access it. In addition, you can also embed a link in a blog or web page, so others can access the folder. The recipients of the link can click it to access the documents on SkyDrive.

Send a Link to a File or Folder

1. Open your web browser, go to *www.skydrive.com*, and then sign in.

2. Navigate to the folder with the documents you want to share.

3. Point to a file or folder to display a check box, and then click the check box to select it. You can select multiple files or folders.

4. Click the **Sharing** button.

5. For a folder, click **Share this folder**. To cancel, click **Don't share this folder**.

6. Click **Send email, Post to <service>** (**New!**), or **Get a link** (**New!**) to select a send method.

7. Specify the following for the selected method:

   ◆ **Send email.** Specify recipients, select or clear options to edit or require sign in, and then click **Share**.

   ◆ **Post to <service>.** Select the check boxes for the services you want, enter a message, select or clear the option to edit, and then click **Post**.

   ◆ **Get a Link.** Click **Create** for View only or View and edit, or click **Make public** for everyone to access. Press Ctrl+C to copy the link, and then click **Done**. You can paste the link for others to use.

Post to   Twitter   Add more services

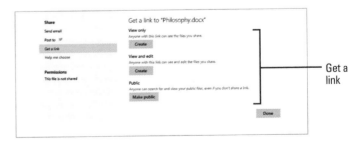
Get a link

Embed a Link to a File or Folder in a Blog or Web Page

1. Open your web browser, go to *www.skydrive.com*, and then sign in.

2. Navigate to the folder with the documents you want to share.

3. Point to a file or folder to display a check box, and then click the check box to select it. You can select multiple files or folders.

4. Click the **Embed** button (**New!**).

5. Click **Generate**.

6. Click the **Copy** link to copy the embed code to the Clipboard.

7. Click **Done**.

8. Paste the code into a blog post or web page.

   ◆ **Blog.** Create a blog post in a blogger, such as Windows Live Writer, and then paste the code.

   ◆ **Web Page.** Open a web page in an HTML editor, and then paste the code.

9. Open your web browser, display the blog post or web page, and then click the link to the shared folder or document on SkyDrive.

Comparing the Office Desktop App to the Web App

An Office Web App provides a subset of the features in the desktop version. Each Office Web App comes with a scaled-down version of the desktop Ribbon and Quick Access Toolbar. The Web Apps Ribbon typically comes with a File tab, Home tab, Insert tab, and View tab. Within each tab, you get a sub-set of commands on the desktop Ribbon. There are no contextual tabs in the Office Web Apps. The Quick Access Toolbar appears above the Ribbon and contains just the Undo and Redo buttons. The content area for each of the Office Web Apps is similar to the desktop version.

Desktop App

File tab
Click to access file commands.

Quick Access Toolbar
Click to access commands on this customizable toolbar.

Tabs
Click to access tools and commands.

Dialog Box Launcher
Click to open dialog boxes or task panes.

Program window
Enter text and data here.

Ribbon
Click to access commands and tools grouped by category onto different tabs.

Lists and Galleries
Click the down arrow to access lists and galleries.

Zoom controls
Use to zoom in or out using the slide, or the buttons.

Status bar
Displays information about the active document.

View buttons
Use to switch between views.

Web App (Edit in Browser)

Quick Access Toolbar
Click to access commands
on a toolbar.

Tabs
Click to access tools
and commands.

File tab
Click to access
file commands.

Ribbon
Click to access
commands and tools
grouped by category
onto different tabs.

**Program
window**
Enter text and data
here.

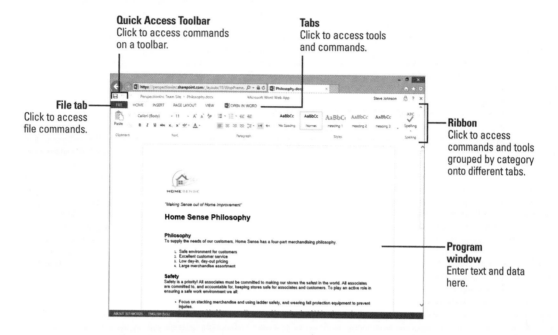

Web App (View in Browser)

File tab
Click to access
file commands.

Menus
Click to access menus
and commands.

**Program
window**
View text and data
here.

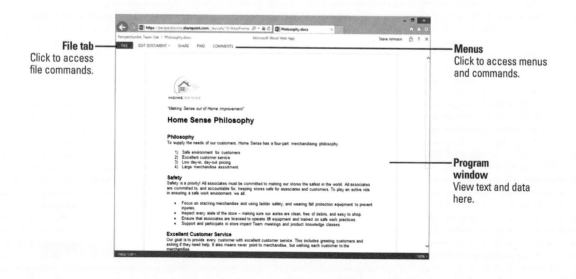

Working with Office Web Apps

An Office Web App allows you to work with an Office document stored on a SkyDrive (**New!**) or SharePoint site in a web browser and on different mobile devices—such as Windows Phones, Apple iOS (iPhones, and iPads), BlackBerry, and Android. Office Web Apps provide a web-based version of Word, Excel, PowerPoint, and OneNote (**New!**). For a SharePoint site, Access and Lync are also available. You can view or edit Office documents in a web browser using a Web App or in the Desktop App. An Office Web App provides a subset of the features in the desktop version.

View an Office Document Using Office Web Apps

1. Open your web browser, and then go to *www.skydrive.com* or SharePoint Team Site web address.

   ◆ **From E-mail or Posts.** If you received an e-mail or a post with a sharing link, click the link to access the document.

2. Navigate to the folder with the document you want to open.

3. Click the Office document you want to view.

   The Web App opens, displaying the document.

4. Use the menus and tools to navigate and view the document.

   ◆ **File management.** You can use the File tab to edit, save as, print, or share the document.

   ◆ **Edit document.** Click the **Edit <document>** menu, and then click **Edit in <program>** or **Edit in <program> Web App.**

5. To exit, click the **File** tab, and then click **Exit** (Web App) or click the **Close** button (desktop program).

SkyDrive

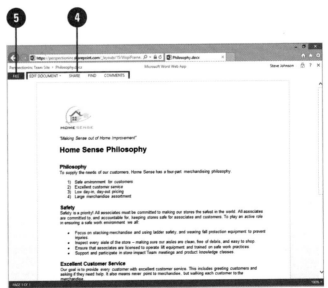

Edit an Office Document Using Office Web Apps

1. Open your web browser, and then go to *www.skydrive.com* or SharePoint Team Site web address.

   ◆ **From E-mail or Posts.** If you received an e-mail or a post with a sharing link, click the link to access the document.

2. Navigate to the folder with the document you want to open.

3. Click the Office document you want to edit.

   The Web App opens, displaying the document.

4. Click the **Edit <document>** menu, and then click **Edit in <program> Web App.**

   ◆ **Edit in Desktop App.** Click the **Edit <document>** menu, and then click **Edit in <program>.**

5. Use the Ribbon tabs to make changes to the Office document; any changes in a Web App are automatically saved.

6. To close the document and switch to work local in the Desktop App, click the **Open in <program>** button.

7. To exit, click the **File** tab, and then click **Exit** (Web App) or click the **Close** button (desktop program).

SkyDrive

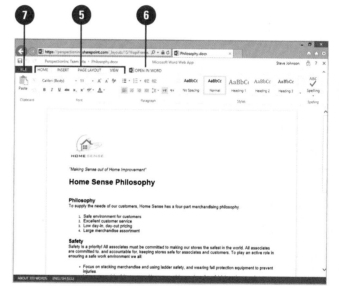

Saving or Printing Documents in Office Web Apps

As you work in an Office document in a web browser, an Office Web App automatically saves your work, so you don't have to do it. However, you might want to download a version to your local computer or network location as a backup or save a copy (in the Excel Web App) of a document in the original location with a different name. Besides saving an Office document, you can also print it to a printer (in the Excel Web App) or create a printable PDF (in the Word Web App and PowerPoint Web App).

Save or Download an Office Document in an Office Web App

1. Open your web browser, and then go to *www.skydrive.com* or SharePoint Team Site web address.

2. Navigate to the folder with the document you want to open.

3. Click the Office document you want to edit.

   The Web App opens, displaying the document.

4. Click the **Edit <document>** menu, and then click **Edit in <program> Web App.**

5. Click the **File** tab, click **Save As**, and then click an option (options vary depending on the Office Web App):

   - **Download.** Downloads the entire document to your computer.

   - **Save a Copy.** In Excel, saves a copy of the workbook in the same online folder as the original.

6. Click **Save**.

7. Navigate to the location where you want to download the file, and then click **Save**.

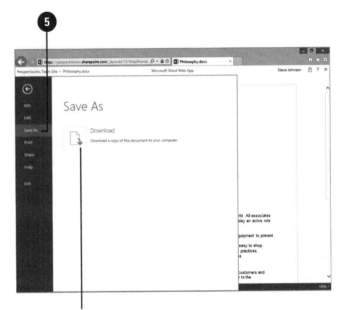

Download button

Print or PDF an Office Document in an Office Web App

1. Open your web browser, and then go to *www.skydrive.com* or SharePoint Team Site web address.

2. Navigate to the folder with the document you want to open.

3. Click the Office document you want to edit.

   The Web App opens, displaying the document.

4. Click the **Edit <document>** menu, and then click **Edit in <program> Web App.**

5. Click the **File** tab, click **Print**, and then click an option (options vary depending on the Office Web App):

   - **Print to PDF.** In Word and PowerPoint, creates saves a copy of the document in the same online folder as the original. Click a link to view the PDF or click **Close**.

   - **Print.** In Excel, select an option to print the current selection or entire sheet, click **Print**, and then click **Print** again in the web browser window.

Print to PDF

Print to a printer in Excel

Co-authoring Documents with Office Web Apps

If you're working with an Office document stored on a SharePoint site, multiple authors can collaborate on the same document at the same time (**New!**), known as co-authoring. Co-authoring allows you to see who is editing the document and where they are working in the Status bar or on the File tab Info screen. With Office Web Apps you can simultaneously edit documents, known as co-authoring. Co-authoring allows two or more people to work on a document at the same time in real-time without the need to save and reject or accept changes. If two people edit the same thing, each Office Web App deals with differently. Before you can co-author a document, you need to send a link in e-mail, online service post, such as Twitter, Facebook, or LinkedIn, to those you want to share the Office document or embed a link in a blog or web page, so others can access it.

Co-author an Office Document on SharePoint

1. Have each author open the Office document from the library on the SharePoint site.

   ◆ **From Office.** Click the **File** tab, click **Open**, click the SharePoint site, click **Browse**, and then open the document.

   ◆ **From Web browser.** Start your web browser, go to the SharePoint site address, and then open the document.

   ◆ **From E-mail or Posts.** If you received an e-mail or a post with a sharing link, click the link to access the document.

2. If prompted, sign in to the SharePoint site.

   The Web App opens, displaying the document.

3. For a Web App, click the **Edit <document>** menu, and then click **Edit in <program>** or **Edit in <program> Web App**.

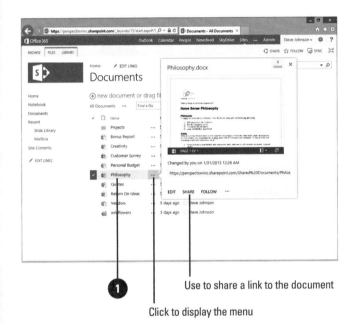

Use to share a link to the document

Click to display the menu

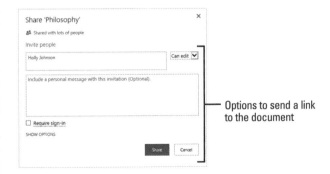

Options to send a link to the document

④ To view who is editing the documents, click the **Authors** button on the Status bar or click the **File** tab, and then click **Info**.

◆ On the Share screen, you can use the **Share with People** button to send a message.

⑤ Each author can edit the document using the program tools.

◆ **Comments and Track Changes.** In Word, PowerPoint, and Excel (desktop), each author can insert and show comments and enable track changes during editing so all the authors can see the changes being made.

⑥ To exit, click the **File** tab, and then click **Exit** (Web App) or click the **Close** button (desktop program).

See Also

See "Working with Office Web Apps" on page 490 for more information on using Office Web Apps.

For Your Information

Roundtripping with Office Web Apps

When you edit or view an Office document with an Office Web App, the file format doesn't change or affect the content of the file. In other words, you can upload an Office file to the web, make changes using an Office Web App, download the file back to your desktop, and then make changes to it using your desktop Office App without any problems. This is called **roundtripping**. Any unsupported features in the Office Web App doesn't affect the Office file during a roundtrip.

Blocking Co-authoring Documents

Co-authoring allows multiple people to edit an Office document stored on a SharePoint site. When multiple people open the same Office document from a SharePoint site, the number of authors editing it appears in the Status bar, which you can click to find out who is currently editing it. If the item is not on the Status bar, you can right-click the Status bar to display it. If you don't want to let multiple authors edit all or part of a Word document, all you need to do is select the content in the document and then use the Block Authors button on the Review tab to prevent others from making changes. At any time, you can release all the blocked areas, so others can edit it.

Block Co-authoring of a Document on SharePoint

1. In Word, open the document from the SharePoint site.

   ◆ You can also open a local Word document, and then save it to the SharePoint site.

2. Select the text you want to prevent others from changing.

3. Click the **Review** tab.

4. Click the **Block Authors** button, and then click **Block Authors**.

   The selected area is marked with an icon and dashed outline to let others know the area is blocked.

5. To unlock all blocked areas, click the **Block Authors** button, and then click **Release All of My Blocked Areas**.

6. Click the **File** tab, and then click **Save** to apply the changes.

See Also

See "Co-authoring Document with Office Web Apps" on page 494 for more information on co-authoring documents on SharePoint.

Blocked content indicator

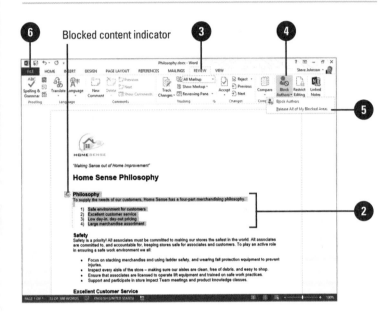

New! Features

Microsoft Word 2013

Microsoft Word 2013 is a powerful word-processing program that enables you to easily compose and edit documents for print or online use. Word 2013 contains many new tools specifically designed to improve the way you interact with the program, and the way you collaborate with one another in preparing documents. With enhancements to the user interface, and the addition of advanced tools, live view page layout, edit PDFs, insert videos, alignment guides, and track changes, you can accomplish a variety of business or personal tasks more easily in Word 2013.

Only New Features

If you're already familiar with Microsoft Word 2010, you can access and download all the tasks in this book with Microsoft Word 2013 New Features to help make your transition to the new version simple and smooth. The Microsoft Word 2013 New Features as well as other 2010 to 2013 transition helpers are available on the web at *www.perspection.com.*

What's New

If you're searching for what's new in Word 2013, just look for the icon: **New!**. The new icon appears in the table of contents and throughout this book so you can quickly and easily identify a new or improved feature in Word 2013. The following is a brief description of each new feature and it's location in this book.

Office 2013

- **Start Screen (p. 2, 12-13, 36-39, 111-114)**   Office programs open to a Start Screen where you have options to open an existing document or create a new blank document or one from a template.

- **Ribbon Display Options (p. 4)** Office includes a Ribbon Display Options button that lets you change the way the Ribbon works. The options include Auto-hide Ribbon, Show Tabs, or Show Tabs and Commands.

- **Enhanced Mini-Toolbar (p. 5, 66, 90-91, 160-161)**   You can use a Mini-Toolbar to apply styles, fills, outlines, and other options. For example, select text or right-click the object you want to modify, click the Style, Fill, or Outline button, and then select an option.

- **Back Button (p. 5)** The File tab provides a Back button that lets you return back to the main screen for the Office program.

- **Options Pane (p. 10, 29, 127, 131, 141, 178-180, 206, 209)** Office changes many dialog boxes—including Format Shape, Format Picture, Format Text, and Format Background—to task panes that appear on the right side of the screen.

- **Strict Open XML (p. 12, 22-25)** You can open documents in the Strict Open XML format to resolve leap year issues with 1900.

- **Pin Recent Files or Folders (p. 12-13, 37, 414-415)** If you frequently open a specific file or folder, you can pin the recently used file or folder to the Start, Open, or Save As screens. If you frequently use a template, you can pin the template to the Start or New screens.

- **SkyDrive (p. 12-13, 22-23, 26, 118-120, 208, 468-473, 478-487)** SkyDrive is a cloud-based online storage system that requires a Microsoft account to access. You can open and save files from a SkyDrive directly from Office, and share them with others. In addition, you can use related options—Invite People, Get a Sharing Link, and Post to Social Networks—to allow others to share documents.

- **SharePoint and Office 365 (p. 12-13, 22-23, 26, 118-120, 208, 468-477)** SharePoint server is an organizational cloud storage, sharing, and tracking system with customizable apps on the web. Office 365 is a subscription-based Microsoft web site with SharePoint services that allows you to take advantage of expanded cloud and sharing capabilities.

- **Windows Help (p. 20-21)** The web browser-like Help Viewer allows you to browse a catalog of topics to locate information, use popular searches, or enter your own phrases to search for information.

- **Save Options (p. 22-23, 422-423)** Office adds new save options, which include Don't Show the Backstage when opening or saving files, Show additional places for saving, even if sign-in may be required, and Save to Computer by default.

- **User Account (p. 27, 118)** Office integrates a user account that lets you connect to online services, such as SkyDrive, Office 365 SharePoint, YouTube, Facebook, Linkedin, Twitter, and Flickr. Within any Office 2013 program, you can add, modify or switch accounts or sign out entirely.

- **Online Services (p. 26, 27, 118-120, 208)** You can connect to and integrate online services into Office programs. The online services include SkyDrive and Office 365 SharePoint for storage, Flickr and YouTube for images and video, and Facebook, Linkedin, and Twitter for sharing and messaging.

- **Document Windows (p. 34, 44-45)** Office documents open in their own program window instead of one program window and a collection of individual windows to make it easier to display several windows at once.

- **New Screen (p. 36-39, 111-114)** The New command on the File tab opens to the New screen where you have options to create a new blank document or one from a template.

- **Personal Templates (p. 38, 111-114, 422-423)** You can specify a default folder, such as My Templates, in Save Options for your own custom personal templates, which you can access from the Start and New screens.

- ◆ **Online Pictures (p. 116-119, 208)** If you need a picture to insert into a document and don't have one, you can search for and insert clip art from Office.com, a picture from the web using Bing Image Search, a picture from your SkyDrive, or a picture from an online service, such as Flickr.

- ◆ **Apps for Office (p. 334, 436-439)** With Office.com, you can add functionality with a third-party app to an Office program, and then use the app to extend features in a document.

- ◆ **Trusted Apps Catalog (p. 348, 352)** An App Catalog site is a special site collection on a web application. You can store apps for SharePoint and Office apps for your organization's internal use in an App Catalog site.

- ◆ **Send Documents by Instant Message (p. 377)** With Lync, you can send an Office document to a participant in an instant message.

- ◆ **Office Presentation Service (p. 398-399)** The Office Presentation Service (OPS) allows you to deliver an Office document as a presentation over the Internet. OPS is a free public service provided by Microsoft for use with your Microsoft account ID.

- ◆ **Office Background and Theme (p. 409)** You can select an Office program background and theme in General Options.

- ◆ **Touch/Mouse Mode (p. 429)** To make Office easier to use with a touch screen, each program provides Touch/Mouse Mode, which adds or removes more space between commands on the Ribbon.

- ◆ **Office Web Apps (p. 469, 488-495)** An Office Web App allows you to work with an Office document stored on a SkyDrive or SharePoint site in a web browser or on different mobile devices. Office Web Apps provide a web-based version of Word, Excel, PowerPoint, and OneNote. If you're working with an Office document stored on a SharePoint site, multiple authors can collaborate on the same document at the same time.

Office Tools

- ◆ **OneNote (p. 396-399)** In an Office program, you can use Send To Notes to send a screen clip, document, or note to OneNote. With Microsoft Lync, you can participate in an online meeting and share OneNotes. With Office Presentation Service, you can give an online document presentation and share OneNotes.

- ◆ **Lync (p. 400-403)** Microsoft Lync is an instant messaging program that allows you to send and receive instant messages, hold video chats, meetings, and share files.

- ◆ **Lync Recording Manager (p. 402-403)** If not everyone is able to attend an online Lync meeting, you can record the session to play it back later. You can manage the recording with the Lync Recording Manager tool.

- ◆ **Spreadsheet or Database Compare (p. 432)** If you need to compare two Excel spreadsheets or Access databases, you can use the Spreadsheet Compare or Database Compare tools.

- ◆ **Upload Center (p. 432-433)**   The Upload Center shows you pending uploads, recently uploaded files and all cached files from a server in one location, which includes working with SkyDrive and SharePoint sites.

- ◆ **Telemetry Log or Dashboard (p. 432-433)**   Telemetry Log records Office events in an Excel spreadsheet to help you troubleshoot problems. Telemetry Database is an Excel spreadsheet that connects to an SQL database to collect client data from other sources in a shared folder.

- ◆ **SkyDrive Pro (p. 432-433, 468-469, 476-477)**   With SkyDrive Pro, you can connect and synchronize your SkyDrive cloud storage on a SharePoint site with your desktop.

- ◆ **Update Office (p. 434)**   With Windows 8, you can automatically get updates to Office 2013 along with the operating system.

Word 2013

- ◆ **Updated File Format (p. 12-13, 15)**   Word 2013 documents are saved in an updated .docx file format. Prior versions of Word documents open in Compatibility mode, which you can convert to the Word 2013 file format.

- ◆ **Read Mode View (p. 16-19)**   Read Mode view displays the full screen and removes distracting screen elements to provide a more comfortable view to read your documents.

- ◆ **Open Editable PDFs (p. 40-41)**   If you have a PDF document, you can open it in Word. The resulting document is optimized using PDF Reflow to allow you to edit the text.

- ◆ **Formatting (p. 68-69, 78-79)**   Word includes enhanced formatting with Number Styles, and Ligatures (letter spacing), and Stylistic Sets.

- ◆ **Quick Style (p. 90-91)**   You can access styles from the Mini-Toolbar when you select text.

- ◆ **Reset Style Set (p. 90)**   You can reset a style back to the default style set when you use the Reset To The Default Style Set command on the More list arrow on the Design tab.

- ◆ **Document Formatting (p. 98-99)**   Each style set consists of a variety of different formatting style combinations, which you can view using the Document Formatting gallery on the Design tab.

- ◆ **Layout Options Button (p. 128-129, 196-197)**   You can set text wrapping options by using the Layout Options button directly on the page or opening the Layout dialog box.

- ◆ **Live Layout Preview (p. 128, 150, 200-201, 410, 413)**   When resizing and moving pictures, shapes, charts, tables, or other objects in your document, you can preview your layout changes on the page with live layout preview.

- ◆ **Insert or Embed Videos (p. 154)**   You can search for and insert or embed an online video from the web using Bing Video Search or a connected online service, such as YouTube.

- ◆ **Insert Table Columns and Rows (p. 160-161)** You can insert rows or columns by using buttons on the Layout tab under Table Tools or on the Mini-Toolbar, or by using an Add button (+) on the table.

- ◆ **Border Styles (p. 168-169)** You can quickly apply Border Styles just like you apply Table or Document Formatting Quick Styles.

- ◆ **Border Painter (p. 168-169)** You can use the Border Painter to copy the format to other cells in your table, just like the Format Painter on the Home tab.

- ◆ **Charting with Excel (p. 173-175)** When you insert and create a chart, it's an embedded object from Excel 2013 with a worksheet window containing sample data. You can edit data in the client program or Excel 2013.

- ◆ **Recently Used Charts (p. 173, 175)** You can quickly select recently used charts in the Chart Type dialog box.

- ◆ **Show or Hide Data Series (p. 174-175)** When you select a data source, you can show or hide individual data series instead of reselecting the range.

- ◆ **Chart Buttons (p. 177, 179, 182, 184)** When you create or select a chart, buttons—Chart Styles, Chart Elements, and Chart Filters—appear on the document for easy access to format the chart, modify chart elements, and filter chart data.

- ◆ **Combo Charts (p. 177)** You can use the Combo chart type to create and modify a chart with multiple data series.

- ◆ **Chart Labels (p. 181)** You can have data labels appears as callouts or just about any shape, and even add leader lines to them.

- ◆ **Alignment Guides (p. 214-215)** When resizing and moving pictures, shapes, charts, tables, or other objects in your document, alignment guides automatically appear to help you align the object on the page.

- ◆ **Spelling or Grammar Pane (p. 288-289)** When you spell or grammar check a document, the Spelling or Grammar pane opens instead of a dialog box, where you can correct errors. If you have an App for Office dictionary installed from the Office Store, a definition appears in the pane.

- ◆ **Thesaurus Pane (p. 300)** If you have an App for Office dictionary installed from the Office Store, a definition appears in the Thesaurus pane. You can also access Foreign languages at the bottom of the Thesaurus pane.

- ◆ **Dictionary Pane (p. 301)** If you're not sure what a word means, you can use the Define button on the Review tab to quickly look it up in a dictionary, such as Merriam-Webster or Bing Dictionary.

- ◆ **Collapse and Expand Sections (p. 306-307)** In any view, you can collapse or expand sections or parts of a document with headings.

- ◆ **Track Changes and Comments (p. 362-365, 368-369)** You can change the display for the review to show a simple markup with only where markups appear (red bars), all markup changes with details (gray bars), no markup, or original text. You can review changes by using buttons on the Review tab and on the page, which allow you to quickly accept and reject changes and comments. You can also lock track changes with password protection.

- **Start Up Options (p. 408)**   You can specify start up options for how you want Word to start including opening files with specified extensions, detecting if Word isn't the default program for word processing, whether to open e-mail attachments and other uneditable files in reading view, and showing the Start screen when Word starts.

- **Improved Word Options (p. 412-418)**   Word includes some new options that include the following: Use fonts that are stored on the printer, Expand all heading s when opening a document, Use subpixel positioning to smooth font on screen, and Do not automatically hyperlink.

What Happened To . . .

- **Exit Command (p. 34)**   The command has been removed from the File tab. Since each document opens in its own program window, it's not needed. To exit, you click the Close button on the program window.

- **Fax Templates (p. 376)**   Fax templates are not included in the Office 2013 installation to reduce the size of the installation. However, you can still download them. Click the File tab, click New, and then type fax in the Search for online templates.

- **Microsoft Office Picture Manager**   Picture Manager has been replaced by Windows Photo Gallery.

- **Microsoft Clip Organizer**   Clip Organizer has been replaced by Online Pictures, which allows you to insert content from the Office.com Clip Art collection and other resources, such as Bing Image/Video search, Flickr, and your SkyDrive or Facebook page.

Microsoft Office Specialist

About the MOS Program

The Microsoft Office Specialist (MOS) certification is the globally recognized standard for validating expertise with the Microsoft Office suite of business productivity programs. Earning an MOS certificate acknowledges you have the expertise to work with Microsoft Office programs. To earn the MOS certification, you must pass a certification exam for the Microsoft Office desktop applications of Microsoft Word, Excel, PowerPoint, Outlook, Access, OneNote, SharePoint, or Office 365. (The availability of Microsoft Office Specialist certification exams varies by program, program version, and language. Visit *www.microsoft.com* and search on *MOS* or *Microsoft Office Specialist* for exam availability and more information about the program.) The Microsoft Office Specialist program is the only Microsoft-approved program in the world for certifying proficiency with Microsoft Office programs.

What Does This Logo Mean?

It means this book has been approved by the Microsoft Office Specialist program to be certified courseware for learning Microsoft Word 2013 and preparing for the certification exam. This book will prepare you for the Microsoft Office Specialist exam for Microsoft Word 2013. Each certification level, either Core or Expert, has a set of objectives, which are organized into broader skill sets. Content that pertains to a Microsoft Office Specialist objective is identified with the following objective number and the specific pages throughout this book:

 WD13C-1.1
WD13C-2.2

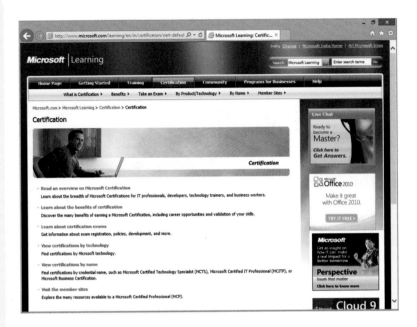

Preparing for a MOS Exam

Every Microsoft Office Specialist certification exam is developed from a list of objectives based on how Microsoft Office programs are actually used in the workplace. The list of objectives determine the scope of each exam, so they provide you with the information you need to prepare for MOS certification. Microsoft Office Specialist Approved Courseware, including the On Demand series, is reviewed and approved on the basis of its coverage of the objectives. To prepare for the certification exam, you should review and perform each task identified with a MOS objective to confirm that you can meet the requirements for the exam.

Taking a MOS Exam

The Microsoft Office Specialist certification exams are not written exams. Instead, the exams are performance-based examinations that allow you to interact with a "live"

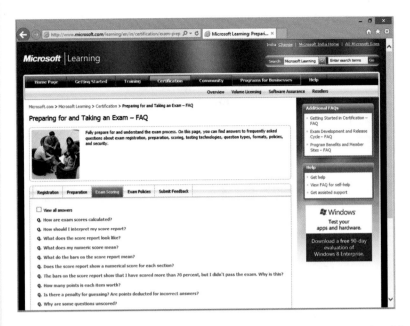

Office program as you complete a series of objective-based tasks. All the standard ribbons, tabs, toolbars, and keyboard shortcuts are available during the exam. Microsoft Office Specialist exams for Office 2013 programs consist of 25 to 35 questions, each of which requires you to complete one or more tasks using the Office program for which you are seeking certification. A typical exam takes from 45 to 60 minutes. Passing percentages range from 70 to 80 percent correct.

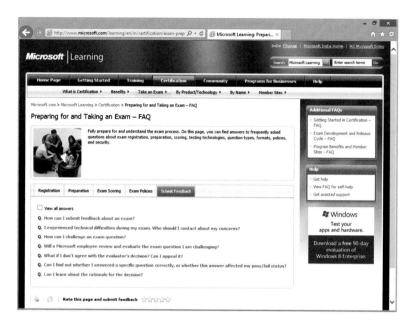

The Exam Experience

After you fill out a series of information screens, the testing software starts the exam and the Office program. The test questions appear in the exam dialog box in the lower right corner of the screen.

◆ The timer starts when the first question appears and displays the remaining exam time at the top of the exam dialog box. If the timer and the counter are distracting, you can click the timer to remove the display.

◆ The counter at the top of the exam dialog box tracks how many questions you have completed and how many remain.

◆ If you think you have made a mistake, you can click the Reset button to restart the question. The Reset button does not restart the entire exam or extend the exam time limit.

◆ When you complete a question, click the Next button to move to the next question. It is not possible to move back to a previous question on the exam.

◆ If the exam dialog box gets in your way, you can click the Minimize button in the upper right corner of the exam dialog box to hide it, or you can drag the title bar to another part of the screen to move it.

Tips for Taking an Exam

◆ Carefully read and follow all instructions provided in each question.

◆ Make sure all steps in a task are completed before proceeding to the next exam question.

◆ Enter requested information as it appears in the instructions without formatting unless you are explicitly requested otherwise.

◆ Close all dialog boxes before proceeding to the next exam question unless you are specifically instructed otherwise.

◆ Do not leave tables, boxes, or cells "active" unless instructed otherwise.

◆ Do not cut and paste information from the exam interface into the program.

◆ When you print a document from an Office program during the exam, nothing actually gets printed.

◆ Errant keystrokes or mouse clicks do not count against your score as long as you achieve the correct end result. You are scored based on the end result, not the method you use to achieve it. However, if a specific method is explicitly requested, you need to use it to get credit for the results.

◆ The overall exam is timed, so taking too long on individual questions may leave you without enough time to complete the entire exam.

◆ If you experience computer problems during the exam, immediately notify a testing center administrator to restart your exam where you were interrupted.

Exam Results

At the end of the exam, a score report appears indicating whether you passed or failed the exam. An official certificate is mailed to successful candidates in approximately two to three weeks.

Getting More Information

To learn more about the Microsoft Office Specialist program, read a list of frequently asked questions, and locate the nearest testing center, visit:

www.microsoft.com

For a more detailed list of Microsoft Office Specialist program objectives, visit:

www.perspection.com

Index